Samuel Foote

The works of Samuel Foote

Vol. I

Samuel Foote

The works of Samuel Foote
Vol. I

ISBN/EAN: 9783742826985

Manufactured in Europe, USA, Canada, Australia, Japa

Cover: Foto ©Andreas Hilbeck / pixelio.de

Manufactured and distributed by brebook publishing software (www.brebook.com)

Samuel Foote

The works of Samuel Foote

THE WORKS OF SAMUEL FOOTE, ESQ.

IN TWO VOLUMES.

VOLUME I.

CONTAINING

TASTE,
THE ENGLISHMAN IN PARIS,
THE KNIGHTS,
THE ENGLISHMAN RETURNED FROM PARIS,
THE AUTHOR,

THE MAYOR OF GARRAT,
THE ORATORS,
THE MINOR,
THE LYAR,
AND
THE PATRON.

LONDON:
PRINTED FOR AND SOLD BY JOHN MURDOCH, BOOKSELLER AND
STATIONER, GLASGOW;
GEO. ROBINSON & CO. AND VERNOR & HOOD, LONDON.

1799.

TASTE:
A COMEDY,
OF TWO ACTS.

Our Gifts in modern days, that rise to put,
Avail from the Vulgar, that like rough the Field;
[illegible] [illegible] [illegible] [illegible] [illegible] [illegible];
[illegible] [illegible] [illegible] [illegible] [illegible] [illegible],
[illegible] [illegible] [illegible] [illegible] [illegible] [illegible],
But [illegible] the [illegible], all the [illegible] of [illegible].

Dean Swift's [illegible].

TO FRANCIS DELAVAL, ESQ.

SIR,

WHEN I consider the long intimacy that has subsisted betwixt us, the obligations I owe to your generous, disinterested friendship, and the protection and encouragement I received both from you and your brother, when necessity filled me in the service of the public; there is no man to whom with equal propriety and pleasure I can address the following work. It would be paying a bad compliment to the town, were I to trouble you with an apology for the inconsiderableness of the present. I thought it worthy their attention, and consequently not beneath the acceptance of my friend. With the aid of a love-plot I could have spun out the piece to the extent of five acts; but besides that I wanted to confine the eye to the single object of my satire, I declare myself a rebel to this universal tyrant, who, not contented with exciting all that is pitiful or terrible in human nature, has claimed the privilege of occasioning every thing that is ridiculous or contemptible in it; and thus, from the abject submission of our dramatic poets, is both Tragedy and Comedy subjected to the power of Love. It may be thought presumptuous in me to have dignified so short a performance with the name of a *Comedy*; but when my reasons why it cannot be called a *Farce* are considered, the critics must indulge me with the use of that title, at least till they can furnish me with a better. As the follies and absurdities of men are the sole objects of Comedy, so the powers of the imagination (plot and incident excepted) are in this kind of writing greatly restrained. No unnatural assemblages, no creatures of the fancy, can procure the protection of the *Comic* Muse; men and things must appear as they are. It is employed either in debasing lofty subjects, or in raising humble ones. Of the two kinds we have examples in the Tom Thumb of Mr F——, and a travestie of the Ulysses, where Penelope keeps an ale-house, Telemachus is a tapster, and the Hero a recruiting serjeant. In both these instances you see nature is reversed; but as I flatter myself in the following sheets her steps have been trode with an undeviating simplicity, give me leave to hope, that, though I have not attained the *Togata*, yet I have reached the *Tabernaria* of the Romans. I once intended to have thrown into this address the contents of many of our conversations on the subject of Comedy; for, in whatever dissipations the world may suppose our days to have been consumed, many, many hours have been consecrated to other subjects than generally employ the gay and the giddy. I hope the present occasion will demonstrate, that pleasure has not been always my pursuit; and, unless I am greatly mistaken, it will soon be discovered, that, joined to the acknowledged best

heart

DEDICATION.

heart in the world. Mr Delaval has a head capable of directing it. As I am now above the reach of common obligations, an acknowledgment of these qualities, in the person of a man who has honoured me with his friendship, is the sole cause of the trouble you now receive. Long has been our union; may it never be divided till the fatal stroke, that demolishes all sublunary connections, shall reach one of us, which one will, I hope, be

Your obliged and affectionate servant,

SAMUEL FOOTE.

PREFACE.

I WAS always apprehensive that the subject of the following piece was too abstracted and singular for the comprehension of a mix'd assembly. *Juno Lucina, Jupiter Tonans, Phidias, Praxiteles*, with the other gentlemen and ladies of antiquity, were, I dare say, utterly unknown to my very good friends of the gallery; nor, to speak the truth, do I believe they had many acquaintances in the other parts of the house. But though I despair of gratifying the *Populum Tributim* of the THEATRE, yet I flatter myself the *Primores Populi* will find me no disagreeable companion in the closet, *et satis magnum Theatrum mihi estis*.

I was neither prompted by a lucrative nor an ambitious motive in this undertaking. My design was to serve a man, who had ever great merit with his friends, and to whom, on the score of some late translations, I think the public vastly indebted. That my good intentions for Mr *Wygstals* have proved successful, is entirely owing to the generosity and humanity of the Managers of Drury-Lane Theatre; they have given him a benefit, and are jointly entitled to my thanks; but as to Mr *Garrick*, I have more personal obligations. I take this opportunity of assuring him, that I shall ever retain the most grateful remembrance of his assistance, assiduity, and kind concern, at the birth, progress, and untimely end of this my last and favourite offspring.

The objects of my satire were such as I thought, whether they were considered in a moral, a political, or a ridiculous light, deserved the notice of the Comic Muse. I was determined to brand those Goths in silence, who had prostituted the useful study of antiquity to trifling superficial purposes; who had blasted the progress of the elegant arts amongst us, by unpardonable frauds and absurd prejudices; and who had corrupted the minds and morals of our youth, by persuading them, that what only serves to illustrate literature was true learning, and active idleness real business. How far this end has been obtained, is now, in the following sheets, more generally submitted to the public.

PROLOGUE.

PROLOGUE.

Written by Mr Garrick, and spoken by him in the character of an Auctioneer.

BEFORE this Court, I *Peter Puff* appear,
A Briton born, and bred an Auctioneer;
Who for myself, and eke a hundred others,
My useful, honest, learned bawling brothers,
With much humility and fear implore ye,
To lay our present desp'rate case before ye.—
 'Tis said this night a certain wag intends
To laugh at us, our calling, and our friends:
If Lords and Ladies, and such dainty folks,
Are cur'd of auction-hunting by his jokes!
Should this odd doctrine spread throughout the land,
Before you buy, be sure to understand;
Oh! think on us what various ills will flow,
When great ones only purchase—what they know.
Why laugh at *Taste?* It is a harmless fashion,
And quite subdues each detrimental passion:
The fair ones hearts will ne'er incline to man,
While thus they rage for—China and Japan.
The Virtuoso, too, and Connoisseur,
Are ever decent, delicate, and pure;
The smallest hair their looser thoughts might hold,
Just warm when single, and when married, cold:
Their blood at sight of beauty gently flows;
Their Venus must be old, and want a nose!
No am'rous passion with deep knowledge thrives;
'Tis the compleatst, indeed, of all our wives!
'Tis said Virtù to such a height is grown,
All artists are encourag'd——but our own.
Be not deceiv'd, I here declare on oath,
I never yet sold goods of *foreign* growth:
Ne'er sent commissions out to Greece or Rome;
My best antiquities are made at home.
I've Romans, Greeks, Italians near at hand,
True Britons all—and living in the Strand.
I ne'er for trinkets rack my pericranium,
They furnish out my room from Herculaneum.
But hush——
Should it be known that English are employ'd,
Our manufacture is at once destroy'd;
No matter what our countrymen deserve,
They'll thrive as ancients, but as moderns starve—
If we should fall—to you it will be owing;
Farewell to *Arts*—they're going, going, going;
The fatal hammer's in your hand, oh Town!
Then set *Us* up—and knock the *Foes* down.

DRAMATIS

DRAMATIS PERSONÆ, 1758.

(DRURY-LANE).

Cantiles,	Mr Palmer.
Puff,	Mr Yates.
Sealy,	Mr Cross.
Novice,	Mr Blakes.
Lord Dupe,	Mr Havard.
Alderman Pentweazel,	Mr Yaswell.
Caleb,	Mr Costollo.
Boy,	Master Cross.
Lady Pentweazel,	Mr Woodward.

ACT I.

SCENE I. A *Painting Room*.

Enter Carmine, followed by the Boy.

Carm. LAY these colours in the window, by the pallet. Any visitors or messages?

Boy. 'Squire Felltree has been here, and insists upon Miss Racket's pictures being immediately finish'd, and carry'd home——As to his wife and children, he says, you may take your own time.

Carm. Well——

Boy. Here has been a message too, from my Lady Pen——I can't remember her name, but 'tis upon the slate. She desires to know if you will be at home about noon.

Carm. Fetch it. (*Exit Boy.*)
Was the whole of our profession confined to the mere business of it, the employment would be pleasing as well as profitable; but as matters are now managed, the art is the last thing to be regarded. Family connections, private recommendations, and an easy, genteel method of flattering, is to supply the delicacy of a Guido, the colouring of a Rubens, and the design of a Raphael——all their qualities centering in one man, without the first requisites, would be useless; and with these, one of them is necessary.

Enter Boy with the Slate.

Carm. Let's see——Oh! Lady Pentweazel from Blowbladder-street——Admit her by all means; and if Puff or Varnish should come, I am at home. (*Exit Boy.*) Lady Pentweazel! ha! ha! Now here's a proof that avarice is not the only, or last passion old age is subject to.——this superannuated beldame gapes for flattery, like a nest of unfledg'd crows for food; and with them, too, gulps down every thing that's offer'd her——no matter how coarse;—well, she shall be fed; I'll make her my introductory key to the whole Bench of Aldermen.

Enter Boy with Puff.

Boy. Mr Puff, Sir.

Carm.

Carm. Let us be private. What have you there?

Puff. Two of Rembrandt's etching by Scrape, in May's Buildings; a paltry affair, a poor tea-guinea job; however, a small game —— you know the proverb —— What became of you yesterday?

Carm. I was detained by Sir Positive Bubble. How went the pictures? The Guido, what did that fetch?

Puff. One hundred and thirty.

Carm. Hum! Four guineas the frame, three the painting, then we divide just one hundred and twenty-three.

Puff. Hold —— not altogether so fast —— Varnish had two pieces for bidding against Squander; and Brush five, for bringing Sir Tawdry Trifle.

Carm. Mighty well; look ye, Mr Puff, if these people are eternally quarter'd upon us, I declare off, Sir; they eat up the profit. There's that damn'd Brush —— but you'll find him out. I have upon his old plan given him copies of all the work I executed upon his recommendation; and what was the consequence? He clandestinely sold the copies, and I have all the originals in my lumber-room.

Puff. Come, come, Carmine, you are no great loser by that. Ah! that lumber-room! that lumber-room out of repair, is the best conditioned estate in the county of Middlesex. Why, now, there's your Sufannah; it could not have produced you above twenty at most, and by the addition of your lumber-room dirt, and the salutary application of the spaltham pot, it became a Guido, worth a hundred and thirty pounds; besides, in all traffic of this kind, there must be combinations.—Varnish and Brush are our jackalls, and it is but fair they should partake of the prey. Courage, my boy! never fear! Praise be to folly and fashion, there are in this town dupes enough to gratify the avarice of us all.

Carm. Mr Puff, you are ignorant and scurrilous, and very impertinent, Mr Puff; and, Mr Puff, I have a strange mind to leave you to yourselves, and then see what a hand you would make of it.——Sir, if I do now and then add some tints of antiquity to my pictures, I do it in condescension to the foible of the world; for, Sir, age, age, Sir, is all my pictures want to render 'em as good pieces as the masters from whom they are taken; and let me tell you,

you, Sir, he that took my Susannah for a Guido, gave no mighty proofs of his ignorance, Mr Puff.

Puff. Why, thou post-painter, thou dauber, thou execrable white-washer, thou——Sirrah, have you so soon forgot the wretched state from which I dragg'd you? The first time I set eyes on you, rascal! what was your occupation then? Scribbling, in scarce legible letters, coffee, tea, and chocolate on a bawdy-house window in Goodman's Fields.

Carm. The meanness of my original demonstrates the greatness of my genius.

Puff. Genius! Here's a dog. Pray, how high did your genius soar? To the daubing diabolical angels for ale-houses, dogs with chains for tanners yards, rounds of beef and roasted pigs for Porridge Island.

Carm. Hannibal Scratchi did the same.

Puff. From that contemptible state did not I raise you to the Cat and Fiddle in Petticoat-lane; the Goose and Gridiron in Paul's Church-yard; the first live things you ever drew, dog.

Carm. Pox take your memory. Well, but, Mr Puff—you are so—

Puff. Nor did I quit you then: Who, Sirrah, recommended you to Prim Stiff, the mercer upon Ludgate-hill; how came you to draw the Queen there?

(*Loud knocks at the door.*)

Carm. Mr Puff, for Heaven's sake! dear Sir, you are so warm, we shall be blown——

Enter Boy.

Boy. Sir, my Lady Pen——

Carm. Send her to the——Show her up stairs. Dear Puff——

Puff. Oh! Sir, I can be calm; I only wanted to let you see I had not forgot, though perhaps you may.

Carm. Sir, you are very obliging. Well, but now, as all is over, if you will retreat a small time——Lady Pentweazel sits for her picture, and she's——

Puff. I have some business at next door; I suppose in half an hour's time——

Carm. I shall be at leisure. Dear Puff——

Puff. Dear Carmine—— (*Exit* Puff.)

Carm. Son of a whore——Boy, shew the lady up stairs.

Enter

Enter Lady Pentweazel.

Lady. Fine pieces!—very likely pieces! and, indeed, all alike. Hum! Lady Fuffock—and, ha! ha! ha! Lady Glumltead, by all that's ugly—Pray now, Mr Carmine, how do you limners contrive to overlook the uglinefs, and yet preſerve the likenefs.

Carm. The art, Madam, may be convey'd in two words; where nature has been ſevere, we ſoften; where ſhe has been kind, we aggravate.

Lady. Very ingeaee, and very kind, truly. Well, good Sir, I bring you a ſubject that will demand the whole of the firſt part of your ſkill; and, if you are at leiſure, you may begin directly.

Carm. Your Ladyſhip is born a little ungrateful to nature, and cruel to yourſelf; even Lady Pantweazel's enemies (if ſuch there be) muſt allow ſhe is a fine woman.

Lady. Oh! your ſervant, good Sir. Why, I have had my day, Mr Carmine; I have had my day.

Carm. And have ſtill, Madam. The only difference I ſhall make between what you were, and what you are, will be no more than what Rubens has diſtinguiſhed between Mary de Medicis, a Virgin and a Regent.

Lady. Mr Carmine, I vow you are a very judicious perſon. I was always ſaid to be like that family. When my piece was firſt done, the limner did me after Venus de Medicis, which I ſuppoſe might be one of Mary's ſiſters; but things muſt change; to be ſitting for my picture at this time of day; ha! ha! ha!—but my daughter Sukey, you muſt know, is juſt married to Mr Deputy Dripping of Candlewick Ward, and would not be ſaid nay; ſo it is not ſo much for the beauty, as the ſimilitude. Ha! ha!

Carm. True, Madam; ha! ha! but if I hit the likeneſs, I muſt preſerve the beauty.—Will your Ladyſhip be ſeated? (*She ſits.*)

Lady. I have heard, good Sir, that every body has a more betterer and more worſerer ſide of the face than the other—now which will you chuſe?

Carm. The right ſide, Madam——the left——now, if you pleaſe, the full——Your Ladyſhip's countenance is ſo exactly proportion'd, that I muſt have it all; no feature can be ſpared.

Lady.

Lady. When you come to the eyes, Mr Carmine, let me know, that I may call up a look.

Carm. Mighty well, Madam——Your face a little nearer to the left, nearer me——your head more up——shoulders back——and chest forward.

Lady. Bless me, Mr Carmine, don't mind my shape this bout; for I'm only in jumps.——Shall I send for my tabbys?

Carm. No, Madam, we'll supply that for the present—Your Ladyship was just now mentioning a daughter—Is she—your face a little more towards me—Is she the sole inheritor of her mother's beauty? Or——have you——

Lady. That! ha! ha! ha!——why that's my youngest of all, except Caleb. I have had, Mr Carmine, live born, and christen'd—stay—don't let me lie now—One—Two—Three——Four——Five——Then I lay fallow——but the year after I had twins——they came in Mr Pentweazel's Sheriffalty; then Roger, then Robin, then Reuben—in short, I have had twenty as fine babes as ever trod in shoe of leather.

Carm. Upon my word, Madam, your Ladyship is an admirable member of the commonwealth; 'tis a thousand pities that, like the Romans, we have not some honours to reward such distinguish'd merit.

Lady. Ay, ay, Mr Carmine, if breeding amongst Christians was as much encouraged as amongst dogs and horses, we need not be making laws to let in a parcel of outlandish locusts to eat us all up.

Carm. I am told, Madam, that a bill for some such purpose is about to pass, and that we begin now to have almost as much regard for the propagation of the species, as the preservation of the game in these kingdoms:—Now, Madam, I am come to the eyes—Oh! that look, that, that, I must despair of imitating.

Lady. Oh! oh! good Sir, have you found out that? Why all my family by the mother's side were famous for their eyes: I have a great aunt among the beauties at Windsor; she has a sister at Hampton Court, a *perdigious* fine woman ——she had but one eye, indeed, but that was a piercer; that one eye got her three husbands——we were called the gimlet-ey'd family. Oh! Mr Carmine, you need not mind these heats in my face; they always discharge themselves about Christmas—my true carnation is not seen in my countenance.

countenance. That's carnation! Here's your flesh and
blood! *(Bruising her arm.*
 Carm. Delicate, indeed! finely turn'd, and of a charming
colour!
 Lady. And yet it has been employ'd enough to spoil the
best hand and arm in the world.——Even before marriage
never idle; none of your gallopping, gossipping, Ranelagh
romps, like the forward minxes of the present age. I
was always employed either in painting your *lamp-lips*,
playing upon the *bassviols*, making paste, or something or
other——All our family had a *geus*; and then I sung!
Every body said I had a monstrous fine voice for music.
 Carm. That may be discerned by your Ladyship's tones
in conversation.
 Lady. Tones——you are right, Mr Carmine; that was
Mr Purcel's word. Miss Molly Griskin, says he (my
maiden name), you have tones.
 Carm. As your Ladyship has preserved every thing else
so well, I dare swear you have not lost your voice. Will
you favour me with an air?
 Lady. Oh! Sir, you are so polite, that it's impossible
——But I have none of your new Playhouse songs——I
can give you one that was made on myself by Laurence
Latestring, a neighbour's son.
 Carm. What you please, Madam.
 Lady.
As I was walking by the side of a river,
I met a young damsel so charming and clever;
Her voice to please it could not fail,
She sung like any nightingale.
  Fal de rol; lugh, lugh, &c.
Bless me! I have such a cough; but there are tones.
 Carm. Inimitable ones.
 Lady. But, Mr Carmine, you limners are all ingenous
men——you sing.
 Carm. A ballad, or so, Madam; music is a sister art;
and it would be a little unnatural not to cultivate an ac-
quaintance there.
 Lady. Why truly we ought not to be ashamed of our re-
lations, unless they are poor; and then, you know——

Enter Boy.

 Boy. Alderman Pentweezel and Mr Puff.
  Lady.

Lady. Oh! he was to call upon me; we go to ſes‑ tion. Defire him to walk up—Mr Pentweazel, you ſi ...t know, went this morning to meet Caleb, my youngeſt boy, at the Bull and Gate. The child has been two years and three quarters at ſchool with Dr Jerk, near Doncaſter, and comes to-day by the York waggon; for it has always been my maxim, Mr Carmine, to give my children learning enough; for, as the old ſaying is,

When houſe and land are gone and ſpent,
Then learning is moſt excellent.

Carm. Your Ladyſhip is quite right. Too much money cannot be employed in ſo material an article.

Lady. Nay, the coſt is but ſmall; but poor ten pounds a year for head, back, books, bed, and belly; and they ſay the children are all wonderful latiners, and come up, lack‑ a-day, they come up as fat as pigs.———Oh! here they are; odds me! he's a thumper. You ſee, Mr Carmine, I breed no ſtarvelings. Come hither, child. Mind your haviours. Where's your beſt bow? Turn out your toes. One would think he had learnt to dance of his father. I'm ſure my family were none ſo aukward. There was my bro‑ ther George, a perfect picture of a man; he danc'd, Lud! But come, all in good time———Hold up thy head, Caleb.

Ald. Prythee, ſweet honey, let the child alone. His Maſter ſays he comes on wonderful in his learning; and as to your bows and your congees, never fear, he'll learn them full enough at home.

Lady. Lack-a-day! well ſaid—We now—If he does, I know who muſt teach him. Well, child, and doſt remem‑ ber me? Hey? Who am I?

Caleb. Anon!

Lady. Doſt know me?

Caleb. Yes; you be mother.

Lady. Nay, the boy had always a good memory. And what haſt learnt, Caleb, hey?

Caleb. I be got into Æſop's Fables, and can ſay all *As in praeſenti* by heart.

Lady. Upon my word—that's more than ever thy father could.

Ald. Nay, nay, no time has been loſt; I queſtioned the lad as we came along; I aſk'd him himſelf———

Lady. Well, well, ſpeak when you are ſpoken to, Mr Alderman.

Alderman. How often muſt I———Well, Caleb, and hadſt a good deal of company in the waggon, boy?

Caleb. O law! Powers of company, Mother. There was Lord Gorman's fat cook, a blackamoor drumming man, two actor people, a recruiting ſerjeant, a monkey, and I.

Lady. Upon my word, a pretty parcel.

Caleb. Yes, indeed; but the——— the fat cook got drunk at Coventry, and ſo fell out at the tail of the waggon; ſo we left him behind. The next day the ſerjeant ran away with the ſhowman's wife; the t'other two went after; ſo only the monkey and I came to town together.

Carm. Upon my word, the young gentleman gives a good account of his travels.

Lady. Ay, ay, Mr Carmine, he's all over the blood of the Griſkins. I warrant the child will make his way. Go, Caleb, go and look at them pretty paintings—Now, Mr Carmine, let us ſee if my good man can find me out.

Ald. Lack-a-day; well, I profeſs they are all ſo handſome, that I am puzzled to know which is thine, chuck.

Puff. I am ſurprized at your want of diſcernment, Mr Alderman; but the poſſeſſion of a jewel deſtroys its value with the wearer; now to me it ſeems impoſſible to err; and though Mr Carmine is generally ſucceſsful, in this inſtance he is particularly happy. Where can you meet with that mixture of fire and ſoftneſs, but in the eyes of Lady Pentweazel?

Lady. Oh, Sir!

Puff. That clearneſs and delicacy of complexion, with that flow of ruddineſs and health.

Lady. Sir! Sir! Sir!

Puff. That fall of ſhoulders, turn of neck, ſet on head, full cheſt, taper waiſt, plump———

Lady. Spare me, ſweet Sir!———You ſee, Mr Pentweazel, other people can find out my charms, tho' you overlook them———Well, I profeſs, Sir, you are a gentleman of great diſcernment; and if buſineſs ſhould bring you into the city; for alas! what pleaſure can bring a man of your refined taſte there?———

Puff. Oh! Ma'am!

Lady. I ſay, Sir, if ſuch an accident ſhould happen, and Blowbladder-ſtreet has any charms———

Puff. Oh! Ma'am! Ma'am! Ma'am! Ma'am!———

Lady.

Lady. It is not impossible but we may receive you, tho' not equal to your merits——
Puff. Ma'am!
Lady. Yet in such a manner as to shew our sense of them. Sir, I'm your very obedient.
Puff. Your Ladyship's most———
Lady. Not a step.
Puff. Ma'am!
Lady. Sir——— Mr Alderman, your bow to the gentleman. The very fittest.
Puff. Ma'am.
Lady. Sir——Your most obedient.
Puff. Your devoted. (*Exeunt* Ald. *and* Wife.
Carm. Ha! ha! Well said, Puff. What a calamity hast thou drawn upon the Knight! Thou hast so tickled the vanity of the harradan, that the poor help-mate will experience a double portion of her contempt.
Puff. Rot them.
Carm. Come, Puff, a matrimonial assistant to a rich Alderman is no contemptible employment.
Puff. Ay, if it were a *sine-cure*.
Carm. No, that you must not expect; but unless I am greatly mistaken in the language of the eyes, her Ladyship's were address'd to you with most persuasive tenderness.
Puff. Well, of that hereafter———But to our business. The auction is about beginning; and I have promised to meet Mr David Dusodorpe, Sir Positive Bubble, and Lord Dupe, to examine the pictures, and fix on those for which they are to bid———But since we have settled the German plan; so Varnish or Brush must attend them.
Carm. Oh! by all means pursue that. You have no conception how dear the foreign accent is to your true virtuoso; it announces taste, knowledge, veracity, and in short, every thing—But can you enough disguise the turn of your face, and tone of your voice? a discovery of Mr Puff in Mynheer Groningen blasts us at once.
Puff. Never fear me. I wish you may have equal success in the part of Canto.
Carm. Pho! mine's a trifle. A man must have very slender abilities indeed, who can't for ten minutes imitate a language and deportment that he has been a witness to for ten years.
Puff. But you must get their tones, their tones; 'tis easy

easy enough. Come, hand up here that there Corregio; an inimitable piece, gentlemen and ladies: The very best work of the best master, subject agreeable, highly finished, and well preserved;—a feast for the ladies; hand it to Sir Positive; a going for fifty; speak, or its gone for fifty: Joy to your Ladyship. Come, the next; but remember, let your bob be bushy, and your bow low.

Carm. Enough, enough; we are strangers to each other, you know.

Puff. Absolute. Oh! but what pictures of yours are in the sale?

Carm. There's my Holy Family by Raphael; the marriage in Cana by Reuben Rouge; Tom Jackson's Teniers; and for busts, Taylor's head without a nose from Herculaneum.

Puff. Are the antique seals come home?

Carm. No; but they will be finish'd by next week.

Puff. You must take care of Novice's collection of medals—he'll want them by the end of the month.

Carm. The coins of the first Emperors are now steeping in copperas; and I have an Otho, a Galba, Nero, and two Domitians reeking from the dunghill.—The rest we can have from Doctor Mummy; a never failing chap, you know.

Puff. Adieu.

Carm. Yours, Sir——a troublesome fellow, this—confounded memory——useful, tho'——Rounds of beef and roasted pigs!—must get ride of him———Ay, but when? ——Why when?—when I have gained my point. But how, how then?——Oh, then it does not signify two pence.

ACT

TASTE. 17

ACT II.

Enter Puff, *as* Monsieur Baron de Groningen, Carmine *as* Canto, *and* Brush.

Canto. COME, bustle, bustle. Brush, you introduce Puff. Puff, how are you in your German?
Puff. I cannot speak for Englandt, but I can mak onder-stand very mightily. Will that do?
Brush. To a hair. Remember you are come hither to purchase pictures for the Elector of Bavaria. Carmine, you must clap Lord Dupe's coat of arms on that half length of Erasmus; I have sold it him, as his great grandfather's third brother, for fifty guineas.
Canto. It shall be done—Be it my province to establish the Baron's reputation as a connoisseur.—*Brush* has seen you abroad at the Court of the reigning Prince of Blantin.
Puff. Yes; I was do bufiness mightily for Prince Blantin.
Brush. Your portraits go first, Carmine. Novice, Sir Positive Bubble, Jack Squander, Lord Dupe, and Mordecai Lazarus, the Jew broker, have appointed me to examine with them the history pieces—Which are most likely to stick?
Canto. Here's a list.
Brush. Hush, hide the Erasmus, I hear the company on the stairs. (*Exit* Carmine, *and re-enters anon.*

Enter Lord Dupe, Bubble, Squander, &c.

Lord. Mr Brush, I am your devoted servant. You have procured my ancestor.
Brush. It is in my possession, my Lord; and I have the honour to assure your Lordship, that the family features are very discernible; and allowing for the difference of dress, there's a strong likeness between you and your predecessor.
Lord. Sir, you have oblig'd me. All those you have mark'd in the catalogue are originals?
Brush. Undoubted. But, my Lord, you need not depend solely on my judgment; here's Mynheer Baron de Groningen, who is come hither to survey, and purchase for the Elector of Bavaria; an indisputable connoisseur; his bidding will be a direction for your Lordship. 'Tis a thousand pities

VOL. I. C that

that any of these masters should quit England. They were conducted hither at an immense expence; and if they now leave us, what will it be but a public declaration, that all taste and liberal knowledge is vanish'd from amongst us?

Lord. Sir—leave the support of the national credit to my care. Could you introduce me to Mynheer?—does he speak English?

Bruſh. Not fluently, but so as to be underſtood. Mynheer, Lord Dupe—the patron of arts, the Petronius for rule, and for well-timed generoſity, the Leo——and the Mecænas——of the preſent age, deſires to know you.

Puff. Sir, you honour me very mightily. I was here of Lord Dupes in Holſtadt. I was tell he was one delatant, one curieufe, one precienſo of his conoſſry.

Lord. The Dutch are an obliging, civilized, well-bred, pretty kind of people. But, pray Sir, what occaſions us the honour of a viſit from you?

Puff. I was come to bid for paints for de Elector of Bavaria.

Lord. Are there any here that deſerve your attention?

Puff. O! dare are good pieces; but dare is one I likes mightily; the off ſky, and home track is fine, and the maiſter is in it.

Lord. What is the ſubject?

Puff. Dat I know not; vat I minds, vat you call the draws and the colors.

Lord. Mr Canto, what is the ſubject?

Canto. It is, my Lord St Anthony of Padua exorciſing the devil out of a ram-cat; it has a companion ſomewhere—Oh! here, which is the ſame ſaint in a wilderneſs, reading his breviary by the light of a glow-worm.

Bruſh. Invaluable pictures, both! and will match your Lordſhip's Corregio in the ſalcon.

Lord. I'll have them. What pictures are thoſe, Mr Canto?

Canto. They are not in the ſale; but I fancy I could procure them for your Lordſhip.

Lord. This, I preſume, might have been a landſkip; but the water, and the men, and the trees, and the dogs, and the ducks, and the pigs, they are all obliterated, all gone.

Bruſh. An indiſputable mark of its antiquity; its very merit; beſides a little varniſh will fetch the figures again.

Lord. Set it down for me—the next.

Canto. That is a Moſes in the bulruſhes. The blended

joy and grief in the figure of the sister in the corner, the distress and anxiety of the mother here, and the beauty and benevolence of Pharaoh's daughter, are circumstances happily imagined, and boldly express'd.

Brush. Lack-a-day, 'tis but a modern performance; the master is alive, and an Englishman—

Lord. Oh! then I would not give it house-room.

Puff. Here is a pretty piece I find stick up here in de corner: I was see in Hollandt, at Loo, a piece mighty like; there was little mices, that was nibble, nibble, nibble, upon vat you call fromage, and little shurels all with broth tails run up the trees; and there was great things, vat you call —Phaw, that have long beards, and cry Ba.

Brush. What, goats?

Puff. Ay, dat was de name.

Lord. I should think, by the cheese and the goats, Mynheer, yours was a Welch piece, instead of a Dutch.

Puff. Ah, 'twas good piece. I wish to my heart Lord Dupes was have that piece.

Enter Novice.

Novice. Where's Mr Brush? My dear Brush, am I too late?

Brush. In pretty good time.

Nov. May I lose my Otho, or be tumbled from my phaeton the first time I jehup my sorrels, if I have not made more haste than a young surgeon to his first labour. But the lots, the lots, my dear Brush, what are they? I'm upon the rack of impatience till I see them, and in a fever of desire till I possess them.

Brush. Mr Canto, the gentleman would be glad to see the busts, medals, and precious reliques of Greece and ancient Rome.

Canto. Perhaps, Sir, we may show him something of greater antiquity—Bring them forward—The first lot consists of a hand without an arm, the first joint of the fore-finger gone, supposed to be a limb of the Apollo Delphos —The second, half a foot, with the toes entire, of the Juno Lucina—The third, the Caduceus of the Mercurius Infernalis—The fourth, the half of the leg of the infant Hercules—all indisputable antiques, and of the Memphian marble.

Puff. Let me see Juno's half foot. All the toes entire?

Canto. All.

Puff.

Puff. Here is a little fwelt by this toe, that looks bad proportion.

All. Hey, hey.

Puff. What's dat?

Canto. That! Pfhaw! dat! Why that's only a corn.

All. Oh!

Puff. Corn! dat was extreme natural; dat is fine, the maifter is in it.

All. Very fine! Invaluable!

Puff. Where is de Hercules' calf? Upon my word 'tis a very large calf; big, big, big, all de way up, all de way down.

Lord. I believe this Hercules was an Irifhman.

Nov. But where are your bufts? Here, here, gentlemen; here's a curiofity; a medal of Oriuna; got for me by Doctor Mummy; the only one in the vifible world; there may be fome under ground.

Lord. Fine, indeed! Will you permit me to tafte it? It has the relifh. (*All tafte.*)

Nov. The relifh! 'Zooks it coft me a hundred guineas.

Puff. By gar, it is a dear bit tho'.

Nov. So you may think; but three times the money fhould not purchafe it.

Lord. Pray, Sir, whofe buft is it that dignifies this coin?

Nov. The Emprefs Oriuna, my Lord.

Lord. And who, Sir, might fhe be? I don't recollect to have heard of the Lady before.

Nov. She, my Lord? Oh! fhe was a kind of a what-d'ye-call'em—a fort of a Queen, or wife, or something or other to fomebody, that liv'd a damn'd while ago—Mummy told me the whole ftory; but before God I've forgot it. But come, the bufts.

Canto. Bring forward the head from Herculaneum. Now, gentlemen, here is a jewel.

All. Ay, ay, let's fee.

Canto. 'Tis not entire, tho'.

Nov. So much the better.

Canto. Right, Sir—the very mutilations of this piece are worth all the moft perfect performances of modern artifts.—Now, gentlemen, here's a touchftone for your tafte!

All. Great! great, indeed!

Nov.

Nov. Great! Amazing! Divine! Oh, let me embrace the dear dismember'd bust! a little farther off. I'm raviſh'd! I'm tranſported! What an attitude! But then the locks! How I adore the ſimplicity of the antients! How unlike the preſent, priggiſh, prick ear'd puppets! How gracefully they fall all adown the cheek! So decent, and ſo grave, and—Who the devil do you think it is, Bruſh? Is it a man or a woman?

Caeſo. The Connoiſſeurs differ. Some will have it to be the Jupiter Tonans of Phidias, and others the Venus of Paphos from Praxiteles; but I don't think it fierce enough for the firſt, nor handſome enough for the laſt.

Nov. Yes, handſome enough.

All. Very handſome; handſome enough.

Caeſo. Not quite—therefore I am inclined to join with Signor Julio de Pampedillo, who, in a treatiſe dedicated to the King of the Two Sicilies, calls it the Serapis of the Ægyptians, and ſuppoſes it to have been fabricated about eleven hundred and three years before the Moſaic account of the creation.

Nov. Prodigious! and I dare ſwear, true.

All. Oh! true, very true.

Puff. Upon my honour, 'tis a very fine buſt; but where is de noſe?

Nov. The noſe; what care I for the noſe? Where is de noſe? Why, Sir, if it had a noſe, I would not give ſixpence for it—How the devil ſhould we diſtinguiſh the works of the antients, if they were perfect?——The noſe, indeed! Why I don't ſuppoſe, now, but, barring the noſe, Roubiliac could cut as good a head every whit ——Bruſh, who is this man with his noſe? The fellow ſhould know ſomething of ſomething too, for he ſpeaks broken Engliſh.

Bruſh. It is Mynheer Groningen, a great Connoiſſeur in painting.

Nov. That may be; but as to ſculpture, I am his very humble ſervant. A man muſt know damn'd little of ſtatuary, that diſlikes a buſt for want of a noſe.

Caeſo. Right, Sir—The noſe itſelf without the head, nay, in another's poſſeſſion, would be an eſtate——But here are behind, gentlemen and ladies, an equeſtrian ſtatue of Marcus Aurelius without the horſe; and a complete ſtatue of the Emperor Trajan, with only the head and legs miſſing;

missing; both from Herculaneum.——This way, gentlemen and ladies.

Enter Lady Pentweazel, Alderman, and Caleb.

Lady. Now, Mr Pentweazel, let us have none of your
blowbladder breeding. Remember you are at the court
end of the town. This is a quality auction.—
Ald. Where of course nothing is sold that is useful.—
I am tutor'd, sweet honey.
Lady. Caleb, keep behind, and don't be meddling.—
Sir————— (*To Brush.*
Brush. Your pleasure, Ma'am.
Lady. I should be glad you would inform me if there
are any lots of very fine old China. I find the quality are
grown infinitely fond of it; and I am willing to shew the
world, that we in the city have taste.
Brush. 'Tis a laudable resolution, Ma'am, and, I dare
say, Mr Canto can support———Bless me, what's that?
(*Caleb throws down a China dish.*
Lady. That boy, I suppose! Well, if the mischievous
brat has not broke a——and look how he stands——Sirrah,
Sirrah, did I not bid you not meddle?———Leave
sucking your thumbs. What, I suppose you learnt that
trick of your friend the monkey in the waggon?
Caleb. Indeed I did not go to do it, mother.
Ald. Pr'ythee, sweet honey, don't be so passionate.—
What's done can't be undone. The loss is not great; come,
come.
Brush. Mr Alderman is in the right. The affair is a
trifle; but a twenty guinea job.
Lady. Twenty guineas! You should have twenty of my
teeth as—————
Canto. You mean if you had them.—Your Ladyship
does not know the value of that piece of China. It is the
right old Japan of the pea-green kind. Lady Mandarin of-
fer'd me, if I could match it, fourscore guineas for the
pair.
Lady. A fine piece, indeed!
Puff. 'Tis ver fine!
Caleb. Indeed, father, I did not break it. 'Twas crack'd
in the middle, and so it fell a two in my hand.
Lady. What, was it crack'd?
Caleb. Yes indeed, mother.

Lady.

Lady. There, gentlemen!

Lord. Ma'am, I would willingly set you right in this affair; you don't seem acquainted with these kinds of things; therefore I have the honour to tell you, that the crack in the middle is a mark of it's antiquity, and enhances it's value; and these gentlemen are, I dare say, of the same opinion.

All. Oh, entirely.

Lady. You are all of a gang, I think. A broken piece of China better than a whole one!

Lord. Ma'am, I never dispute with a Lady; but this gentleman has taste; he is a foreigner, and so can't be thought prejudiced; refer it to him. Our day grows late, and I want the auction to begin.

Ald. Sweet honey, leave it to the gentleman.

Lady. Well, Sir.

Puff. Ma'am, I love to serve de Lady. 'Tis a ver fine piece of China. I was see such another piece fell at Amsterdam for a hundred ducats. 'Tis ver well worth twenty guinea.

Caleb. Mother!—Father! Never stir if that gentleman ben't the same that we see'd at the painting man's, that was so civil to mother, only he has got a black wig on, and speaks outlandish. I'll be far enough if it en't a May-game.

Lady. Hey! let me die but the boy's in the right. My dear, as I'm alive, Mr Puff, that we saw at the limner's. I told you he was a more cleverer man than I ever saw. Caleb is right; some matter of merriment, I warrant.

Puff. I wish it was. (*Afide.*) I no understand.

Canto. So, Maister Puff, you are caught. (*Afide.*)

Lord. This is a most unfortunate old Lady.—Ma'am, you are here under another mistake. This is Mynheer Baron de ⸺

Lady. Mynheer Figs-end. Can't I believe my own eyes? What, do you think, because we live in the city, we can't see?

Nov. Fire me, my Lord, there may be more in this than we can guess. It's worth examining into. Come, Sir, if you are Mynheer, who the devil knows you?

Puff. I was know Maister Canto mightily.

Nov. Mr Canto, do you know this Baron?

Canto. I see the dog will be detected, and now is my time

time to be even with him for his rounds of beef and roasted pigs. (*Aside.*) I can't say I ever saw the gentleman before.

Nov. Oh, oh!

Lord. The fellow is an impostor; a palpable cheat. Sir, I think you came from the Rhine; pray, how should you like walking into the Thames?

Nov. Or what think you, my Lord? The rascal complain'd but now that the bust wanted a nose; suppose we were to supply the deficiency with his?

Lord. But justice, Mr Novice.

Canto. Great rascal, indeed, gentlemen. If rogues of this stamp get once a footing in these assemblies, adieu to all moral honesty. I think an example should be made of him. But, were I to advise, he is a properer subject for the rabble to handle than the present company.

All. Away with him——

Puff. Hands off. If I must suffer, it shall not be singly. Here is the obsequious Mr Brush, and the very courtly Mr Canto, shall be the partners of my distress. Know, then, we all are rogues, if the taking advantage of the absurdities and follies of mankind can be call'd roguery. I own I have been a cheat, and I glory in it. But what point will you virtuosi, you connoisseurs, gain by the detection? Will not the publishing of our crimes trumpet forth your folly?

Lord. Matchless impudence!

Puff. My noble Lord here, the Delatanti, the Curieu, the Precieu of this nation, what infinite glory will he acquire from this story, that the Leo, the Mecænas, the Petronius, notwithstanding his exquisite taste, has been drawn in to purchase, at an immense expence, a cart-load of——rubbish!

Lord. Gentlemen and ladies——I have the honour to take my leave.

Puff. Your Lordship's most obedient——When shall I send you your Correggio, your St Anthony of Padua, your ram cat, my good Lord?

Lord. Rascal! (*Exit.*

Nov. This won't do, Sir.——Tho' my Lord has not spirit enough, damn me if I quit you.

Puff. What, my sprightly Squire! Pray favour me with a sight of your Otho.——It has the relish; an indisputable antique; being a Bristol farthing, coin'd by a soap-boiler

to

to pay his journeymen in the scarcity of cash, and purchased for two pence of a travelling tinker by, Sir, your humble servant, Timothy Puff. Ha, ha, ha!

Nov. My Orinna a Bristol farthing!

Puff. Most assuredly.

Nov. I'll be revenged. (*Going.*

Puff. Stay, stay, and take your bust, my sweet Squire; your Serapis. Two heads, they say, are better than one; lay them together. But the locks! how gracefully they fall all a down! so decent, and so—ha, ha, ha!

Nov. Confound you!

Puff. Why, Sir, if it had a nose, I would not give a six-pence for it—Pray, how many years before the creation was it fabricated, Squire?

Nov. I shall live to see you hang'd, you dog. (*Exit.*

Puff. Nay, but, Squire; ha, ha, ha!——Now, Madam, to your Ladyship I come; to whose discernment, aided by the sagacity of your son Caleb, I owe my discovery.

Ald. Look you, don't think to abuse my Lady. I am one of the——

Puff. Quorum—I know it, Mr Alderman; but I mean to serve your worship by humbling a little the vanity of your wife.

Lady. Come along, chuck. I'll not stay to hear the rascality of the fellow.

Puff. Oh, my Lady Pentweazel, correct the severity of that frown, lest you should have more of the Medusa than the Medicis in your face.

Lady. Saucy jackanapes!

Puff. What, then, I have quite lost my city acquaintance; why, I've promised all my friends tickets for my Lord Mayor's ball, through your Ladyship's interest.

Lady. My interest, indeed, for such a——

Puff. If Blowbladder-street has any charms——Sir—— Ma'am—Not a step—The finest gentleman! ha, ha, ha! ——And what can you say for yourself, you cowardly ill-looking rascal? (*to Canto.*) Desert your friend at the first pinch——your ally——your partner—No apology, Sir—I have done with you. From poverty and shame I took you; to that I restore you. Your crime be your punishment. (*Turning to the Audience.*) Could I be as secure from the censure of this Assembly as I am safe from the re-

sentment of Dupe, Novice, Squander; from the alluring
baits of my amorous city lady; and the dangerous combination of my false friend, I should be happy.

*'Tis from your favour I expect my fate;
Your will alone my triumph can complete.*

THE
Englishman in Paris;

A COMEDY,

OF TWO ACTS.

PROLOGUE.

Between Mr MACKLIN and his WIFE.

She. TO contradict me!—Blockhead! Ideot! fool! sot!
He. But amidst these hard names, our dispute is forgot.
To contradict you, I know, is high treason;
For this will of a wife is always her reason.
She. No, Sir, for once, I'll give up my pretension,
And submit to the Pit our cause of difsention.
He. I agree; for the Pit is our natural Lord.
Ladies, ———— ————
She. —Hey! How come you to claim the first word?
Gentlemen, my husband and I have had a dispute,
Where the difference lies 'twixt a man and a brute;
Which we beg, whilst the folks for the farce are preparing,
You would please to decide, and give us the hearing.
—Hem! Hem!—
After Plutarch of Rome! and Virgil of Greece!
And Iliads, and Eneids, and authors like these,
I boldly affirm, deny it who can,
That in laughter consists the true essence of man:
Whilst my husband—
He. ———— Nay, pray let me state my own case.
And I'll make it as clear as the nose on your face,
That hissing in man preserves the first place.
To begin then with Critics:—'Tis their capital bliss,
Than to laugh—don't you find it more pleasing to hiss?
In this all agree;—Jews, Infidels, Turks!
She. I grant it, sweet Sir,———if you mean at your works.
Yet even 'gainst that I've a potent objection;
For every rule still has its exception:
Tho' they hiss'd at your farces, your Pasquin, and stuff,
At your tragedy sure they laugh'd hearty enough.
And again, Mr Wifeman, regard the world round,
'Tis in mankind alone that laughter is found.
Whilst your favourite hissing, sage Sir, if you please,
You enjoy but in common with serpents and geese,
And ar'n't you ashamed—('tis no time to dissemble).
O Critics! thase creatures in this to resemble?
He. Not a jot; in this place 'tis of singular use,
Of bad poets and players to reform the abuse.
In the practice, kind Sirs! were I fit to advise,
The hissing like geese I would have you despise,
And copy the serpent——be subtle and wise,

But

PROLOGUE.

But fine from his raison.———Well, Sirs, what d'ye say?
To your judgment——
 Sbr.————— Let us wait till the end of the play:
In the progress of that we shall easily find,
Whether laughing or hissing is most to their mind.
 Sbr. I'm sure they will laugh.
 Mr. And I hope they'll be kind.

EPILOGUE

EPILOGUE.

Spoken by Miss Mackliss.

ESCAP'D from my guardian's tyrannical sway,
 By a fortunate voyage on a prosperous day,
I am landed in England, and now must endeavour,
By some means or other, to curry your favour.
 Of what use to be freed from a Gallic subjection,
Unless I'm secure of a British protection?
Without cash,—but one friend—and he too just made,
Egad I've a mind to set up some trade.
Of what sort! in the papers I'll publish a puff,
Which won't fail to procure me customs enough:
" That a Lady from Paris is lately arriv'd,
Who with exquisite art has nicely contriv'd
The best paint for the face,—the best paste for the hands,
A water for freckles, for flushings, and tann.
She can teach you, the neatest coeffure for the head,
To lisp—amble—and simper—and put on the red;
To rival, to rally, to backbite, and sneer,
Um—ap; that they already know pretty well here.
 " The beaux she instructs to bow with a grace,
The happiest shrug—the newest grimace;
To parler François,—So, flatter, and dance,
Which is very near all that they teach ye in France.
 " Not a Buck, nor a Blood, through the whole English nation,
But his roughness she'll soften, his figure she'll fashion.
The merest John Trot in a week you shall see
Bien poli, bien frisé, tout à fait un Marquis."
 What d'ye think of my plan, is it form'd to your goût?
May I hope for disciples in any of you?
Shall I tell you my thoughts, without guile, without art,
Though abroad, I've been bred, I have Britain at heart.
Then take this advice, which I give for her sake,
You'll gain nothing by any exchange you can make;
In a country of commerce, too great the expense,
For their baubles and bows, to give your good sense.

DRAMATIS

DRAMATIS PERSONÆ.

(FIRST PIECE).

Buck,	Mr Palmer.
Sir John Buck,	Mr Waldron.
Sotlde,	Mr Waldron,
Clinks,	Mr Packer.
Margole,	Mr Lamash.
Dancing Master,	Mr R. Palmer.
Roger,	Mr Gravener.
Mrs Subtle,	Mrs Love.
Lucinda,	Miss Collet.

Servants, &c.

ACT I. SCENE I.

Enter Mr Subtle and Mr Claffic.

Mr Sub. WELL, well, that may be; but still I say that a Frenchman—

Claffic. Is a fop; it is their national diseafe; not one of the qualities for which you celebrate them, but owes its origin to a foible; their taste is trifling, their gaiety grimace, and their politeness pride.

Mr Sub. Hey-dey! Why what the duce brings you to Paris then?

Claff. A debt to friendship; not but I think a short refidence here a very neceffary part in every man of fashion's education.

Mr Sub. Where's the ufe?

Claff. In giving them a true relifh for their own domestic happiness, a proper veneration for their national liberties; a contempt for adulation; and an honour for the extended, generous commerce of their country.

Mr Sub. Why there, indeed, you have the preference, Master Claffic; the traders here are a sharp set; cozening people; foreigners are their food; civilities with a—— Aye! aye! a congee for a crown, and a shrug for a shilling; devilish dear, Master Claffic, devilish dear.

Claff. To avoid their exactions, we are, Mr Subtle, recommended to your protection.

Mr Sub. Aye! and wifely they did who recommended you: Buy nothing but on mine or my Lady's recommendation, and you are safe. But where was your charge? where was Mr Buck last night? My Lady made a party at cards on purpofe for him, and my ward Lucinda is mightily taken with him; she longs to see him again.

Claff. I am afraid with the fame fet his father fent him hither to avoid; but we muft endeavour to infpire him with a tafte for the gallantries of this Court, and his paffion for the lower amufements of ours will diminifh of courfe.

Mr Sub. All the fraternity of men-makers are for that purpofe without; taylors, peruquiers, hatters, hofiers—— Is not that Mr Buck's English servant?

Enter Roger.

Claff. Oh! aye, honeſt Roger. So, the old doings, Roger; what time did your maſter come home?

Rog. Between five and ſix, pummell'd to a jelly: Here been two of his old comrades follow'd un already; I count we ſhall ha' the whole gang in a ſe'ennight.

Claff. Comrades, who?

Rog. Dick Daylight and Bob Breadbaſket the bruiſers: They all went to the ſhew together, where they had the devil to pay; belike they had been ſent to Bridewell, hadn't a great gentleman in a blue ſtring come by and releas'd them.——I hear Maſter's bell; do, Maſter Claſſic, ſtep up and talk to'un; he's now ſober, and may hearken to reaſon.

Claff. I attend him. Mr Subtle, you won't be out of the way.

Mr Sub. I ſhall talk a little with the tradeſmen. A ſmoaky fellow this Claſſic; but if Lucinda plays her cards well, we have not much to fear from that quarter: contradiction ſeems to be the life and ſoul of young Buck.—— A tolerable expedition this, if it ſucceeds——Fleece the younker!——Pſhaw, that's a thing of courſe!—but by his means to get rid of Lucinda, and ſecurely pocket her patrimony;—aye! that indeed—

Enter Mrs Subtle.

Oh! Wife! Have you open'd the plot? Does the girl come into it greedily, hey?

Mrs Sub. A little ſqueamiſh at firſt; but I have opened her eyes. Never fear, my dear, ſooner or later women will attend to their intereſt.

Mr Sub. Their intereſt! aye, that's true; but conſider, my dear, how deeply our own intereſt is concern'd, and let that quicken your zeal.

Mrs Sub. D'ye think I am blind? But the girl has got ſuch whimſical notions of honour, and is withal ſo decent and modeſt: I wonder where the duce ſhe got it; I am ſure it was not in my houſe.

Mr Sub. How does ſhe like Buck's perſon?

Mrs Sub. Well enough! But prythee, huſband, leave her to my management, and conſider we have more irons in the fire than one. Here is the Marquis de Soleil to meet

Madam

Madam de Farde to night,—and where to put 'em, unless we can have Buck's apartment—Oh! by the bye, has Count Cog sent you your share out of Mr Puntwell's lodgings a Thursday?

Mr Sub. I intend calling on him this morning.

Mrs Sub. Don't fail! He's a flippery chap, you know.

Mr Sub. There's no fear. Well, but our pretty countrywoman lays about her handsomely! Ha!——Hearts by hundreds! Hum!

Mrs Sub. Aye! that's a noble prize, if we could but manage her; but she's so indiscreet, that she'll be blown before we have made half our market. I am this morning to give audience on her score, to two Counts and a foreign Minister.

Mr Sub. Then strike whilst the iron's hot: But they'll be here before I can talk to my people; send 'em in prythee.

Enter Tradesmen.

Mr Sub. So, gentlemen; Oh! hush! we are interrupted: If they ask for your bills, you have left them at home.

Enter Buck, Classic, *and* Roger.

Buck. Ecod, I don't know how it ended, but I remember how it began. Oh! Master Subtle, how do'st, old Buck, hey? Give's thy paw! And little Lucy, how fares it with she? Hum!

Mr Sub. What has been the matter, Squire? Your face seems a little in dishabille.

Buck. A touch of the times, old boy! a small skirmish; after I was down tho', a set of cowardly sons of——; there's George and I will box any five for their sin.

Mr Sub. But how happened it? The French are generally civil to strangers.

Buck. Oh! damn'd civil! to fall seven or eight upon three: Seven or eight! Ecod we had the whole house upon us at last.

Mr Sub. But what had you done?

Buck. Done! Why, nothing at all! But wounds! how the powder flew about, and the Monsieurs scour'd.

Mr Sub. But what offence had either they or you committed?

Buck. Why, I was telling Domine, last night, Dick Daylight,

light, Bob Breadbasket, and I, were walking through one of their Rues I think they call them here, they are streets in London; but they have such devilish out-of-the-way names for things, that there is no remembering them: so we see crowds of people going into a house, and comedy pasted over the door; in we troop'd with the rest, pay'd our cash, and sat down on the stage: presently they had a dance; and one of the young women with long hair trailing behind her, stood with her back to a rail just by me: Ecod what does me! for nothing in the world but a joke, as I hope for mercy, but ties her locks to the rail; so when 'twas her turn to figure out, souse she slapp'd on her back; 'twas devilish comical, but they set up such an uproar, one whey-fac'd son of a bitch, that came to loose the woman, turn'd up his nose, and call'd me Bête; ecod, I lent him a lick in his leathorn jaws, that will make him remember the spawn of old Marlborough, I warrant him. Another came up to second him, but I let drive at the mark, made the soup-maigre rumble in his bread-basket, and laid him sprawling. Then in pour'd a million of them; I was knock'd down in a trice; and what happen'd after I know no more than you. But where's Lucy? I'll go see her.

Cliff. Oh fie! Ladies are treated here with a little more ceremony: Mr Subtle too has collected these people, who are to equip you for the conversation of the ladies.

Buck. Wounds! all these! What, Mr Subtle, these are Mounseeres too, I suppose?

Mr Sub. No! Squire, they are Englishmen. Fashion has ordain'd, that as you employ none but foreigners at home, you must take up with your own countrymen here.

Cliff. It is not in this instance alone we are particular, Mr Subtle; I have observ'd many of our pretty gentlemen, who condescend to use entirely their native language here, sputter nothing but bad French in the side-boxes at home.

Buck. Look you, Sir, as to you, and your wife, and Miss Lucy, I like you all well enough; but the devil a good thing else have I seen since I lost sight of Dover; the men are all puppies, mincing and dancing, and chattering, and grinning; the women a parcel of painted dolls: their food's fit for hogs; and as for their language, let them learn it that like it, I'll none on't; no nor their frippery neither: So here you may all march to the place from whence you——Harkee! What, are you an Englishman?

Barker.

THE ENGLISHMAN IN PARIS.

Barber. Yes, Sir.

Buck. Domine! look here, what a monster the monkey has made of himself! Sirrah, if your string was long enough, I'd do your business myself, you dog, to sink a bold Briton into such a sneaking, snivelling——the rascal looks as if he had not had a piece of beef and pudding in his paunch these twenty years; I'll be hang'd if the rogue ha'nt been feed upon frogs ever since he came over. Away with your trumpery!

Classic. Mr Buck, a compliance with the customs of the country in which we live, where neither our religion or morals are concern'd, is a duty we owe ourselves.

Mr Sub. Besides, Squire, Lucinda expects that you should usher her to public places, which it would be impossible to do in that dress.

Buck. Why not?

Mr Sub. You'd be mobb'd.

Buck. Mobb'd! I should be glad to see that.——No! no! they ha'nt spirit enough to mob here; but come, since these fellows here are English, and it is the fashion, try on your fooleries.

Mr Sub. Mr Dauphine, come produce—Upon my word, in an elegant taste, Sir: this gentleman has had the honour——

Dauph. To work for all the beaux esprits of the court. My good fortune commenc'd by a small alteration in a cut of the corner of a sleeve for Count Crib; but the addition of a ninth plait in the skirt of Marshal Tonerre, was applauded by Madam la Duchess Rambouillet, and totally establish'd the reputation of your humble servant.

Buck. Hold your jaw and dispatch.

Mr Sub. A word with you.——I don't think it impossible to get you acquainted with Madam de Rambouillet.

Buck. An't she a Papist?

Mr Sub. Undoubtedly.

Buck. Then I'll ha' nothing to say to her.

Mr Sub. Oh fie! Who minds the religion of a pretty woman? Besides, all this country are of the same.

Buck. For that reason I don't care how soon I get out of it: Come, let's get rid of you all as soon as we can.—— And what are you, hey?

Barb. Je suis peruquier, Monsieur.

Buck. Speak English, you son of a whore.

Barb.

Barb. I am a periwig-maker, Sir.

Buck. Then why could not you say so at first? What, are you asham'd of your mother tongue? I knew this fellow was a puppy by his pig-tail. Come, let's see your handy work.

Barb. As I found you were in a hurry, I have brought you, Sir, something that will do for the present: But a peruque is a different *ouvrage*, another sort of a thing here, from what it is *en Angleterre*; we must consult the colour of the complexion, and the *tour de visage*, the form of the face; for which end, it will be necessary to regard your countenance in different lights:———A little to the right, if you please.

Buck. Why, you dog, dy'e think I'll submit to be exercised by you?

Barb. Oh mon Dieu! Monsieur, if you don't, it will be impossible to make your wig *comme il faut*.

Buck. Sirrah, speak another French word, and I'll kick you down stairs.

Barb. Gad's curse! Would you resemble some of your countrymen, who, at their first importation with nine hairs of a side to a brawny pair of cheeks, look like a Saracen's head! Or else their water-gruel jaws, sunk in a thicket of curls, appear, for all the world, like a lark in a soup-dish!

Mr Sub. Come, Squire, submit; 'tis but for once.

Buck. Well, what must I do? [*Places him in a chair.*

Barb. To the right, Sir;—now to the left;—now your full;—and now, Sir, I'll do your business.

Mr Sub. Look at yourself a little; see what a revolution this has occasion'd in your whole figure.

Buck. Yes! a bloody pretty figure indeed! But 'tis a figure I am damnably asham'd of: I would not be seen by Jack Wildfire or Dick Riot for fifty pounds, in this trim, for all that.

Mr Sub. Upon my honour, dress greatly improves you. Your opinion, Mr Classic.

Class. They do mighty well, Sir; and in a little time Mr Buck will be easy in them.

Buck. Shall I! I am glad on't, for I am damnably uneasy at present. Mr Subtle, what must I do now?

Mr Sub. Now, Sir, if you'll call upon my wife, you'll find Lucinda with her, and I'll wait on you presently.

Buck.

Buck. Come along, Domine! but harkee, Mr Subtle, I'll out of my trammels, when I hunt with the King.

Mr Sub. Well! well!

Buck. I'll on with my Jemmys; none of your black bags and jack boots for me.

Mr Sub. No! no!

Buck. I'll thew them the odds on't! Old Silver-tail! I will! Hey!

Mr Sub. Ay! ay!

Buck. Hedge, ſtake, or ſtile! over we go!

Mr Sub. Ay! but Mr Claſſic waits.

Buck. But d'ye think they'll follow?

Mr Sub. Oh no! Impoſſible!

Buck. Did I tell you what a chace ſhe carried me laſt Chriſtmas eve? We unkennel'd at ———

Mr Sub. I am buſy now; at any other time.

Buck. You'll follow us. I have ſent for my hounds and horſes.

Mr Sub. Have you?

Buck. They ſhall make the tour of Europe with me: And then there's Tom Atkins the huntſman, the two whippers-in, and little Joey the groom comes with them. Damny, what a ſtrange place they'll think this? But no matter for that; then we ſhall be company enough of ourſelves. But you'll follow us in?

Mr Sub. In ten minutes!—An impertinent jackanapes! but I ſhall ſoon ha' done with him. So, Gentlemen; well, you ſee we have a good ſubject to work upon. Harkee, Dauphine, I muſt have more than 20 per cent. out of that ſuit.

Dauph. Upon my ſoul, Mr Subtle, I can't.

Mr Sub. Why I have always that upon new.

Dauph. New! Sir! Why as I hope to be———

Mr Sub. Come, don't lie; dont damn yourſelf, Dauphine; don't be a rogue; did not I ſee at Madame Friponst that waiſtcoat and ſleeves upon Colonel Crambo?

Dauph. As to the waiſtcoat and ſleeves, I own——but for the body and lining——may I never ſee———

Mr Sub. Come, don't be a ſcoundrel; five and thirty, or I've done.

Dauph. Well, if I muſt, I muſt.

Mr Sub. Oh! Solitaire! I can't pay that draught of Mr —— theſe ſix weeks; I want money.

Soli.

Sub. Je fuis dans le meme cas——Je——
Mr Sub. What, d'ye mutiny, rascal? About your bufinefs, or———   [*Exeunt.*
I muſt keep thefe fellows under, or I ſhall have a fine time
on't; they know they can't do without me.

Enter Mrs Subtle.

Mrs Sub. The Calais letters! my dear.
Mr Sub. (*reads*) Ah! oh! Calais——the Dover packet
arrived laſt night, loading as follows: Six tailors, ditto
barbers, five milliners, bound for Paris to ſtudy faſhions;
four citizens come to ſettle here for a month by way of
ſeeing the country; ditto their wives; ten French valets,
with nine cooks, all from Newgate, where they had been
ſent for robbing their maſters; nine figure-dancers, exported in September ragged and lean, imported well clad
and in good caſe; twelve dogs, ditto bitches, with two
monkies, and a litter of puppies, from mother Midnight's
in the Haymarket: A precious cargo!—*Poſtſcript.* One
of the coaſters is juſt put in, with his Grace the Duke of
———, my Lord ———, and an old gentleman, whoſe name I
can't learn. Godſo! well, my dear, I muſt run, and try
to ſecure theſe cuſtomers; there's no time to be loſt:
Mean while——

Enter Claffic.

So, Maſter Claffic, what have you left the young couple
together?
Claff. They want your Ladyſhip's prefence, Madam,
for a ſhort tour to the *Tuilleries.* I have received ſome
letters which I muſt anſwer immediately.
Mr Sub. Oh! Well! well! no ceremony; we are all
of a family, you know. Servant.   [*Exit.*
Claff. Roger!

Enter Roger.

Rog. Anon!
Claff. I have juſt received a letter from your old maſter; he was landed at Calais, and will be this evening at
Paris. It is abſolutely neceſſary that this circumſtance
ſhould be conceal'd from his ſon; for which purpoſe you
muſt wait at the Piccardy gate, and deliver a letter I ſhall
give you into his own hand.

Rog.

THE ENGLISHMAN IN PARIS. 41

Rog. I'll warrant you.
Claff. But, Roger, be fecret.
Rog. Oh! lud! Never you fear!
Claff. So, Mr Subtle, I fee your aim. A pretty lodging we have hit upon; the miftrefs a commode, and the mafter a——But who can this ward be? Poffibly the neglected punk of fome riotous men of quality. 'Tis lucky Mr Buck's father is arriv'd, or my authority would prove but an infufficient match for my pupil's obftinacy. This mad boy! how difficult, how difagreeable a tafk have I undertaken? And how general, yet how dangerous an experiment is it to expofe our youth, in the very fire and fury of their blood, to all the follies and extravagance of this fantaftic Court? Far different was the prudent practice of our forefathers:

They fcorn'd to truck, for bafe, unmanly arts,
Their native plainnefs, and their honeft hearts;
Whene'er they deign'd to vifit haughty France,
'Twas arm'd with bearded dart, and pointed lance.
No pompous pageants lur'd their curious eye,
No charms for them had fops or flattery;
Paris they knew, their ftreamers wav'd around,
There Britons faw a Britifh Harry crown'd.
Far other views attract our modern race,
Trulls, tempeft, trinkets, bags, brocades, and lace; }
A fimering form, and a fictitious face.
Roufe! re-affume! refufe a Gallic reign,
Nor let their art win that their arms could never gain.

Vol. I.   F   ACT

ACT II.

Enter Mr Classic *and* Roger.

Roger. OLD maister's at a coffee-house next street, and will tarry till you send for 'un.

Class. Bye and bye, in the dusk, bring him up the back stairs. You must be careful that nobody sees him.

Rog. I warrant you.

Class. Let Sir John know, that I would wait on him myself, but I don't think it safe to quit the house an instant.

Rog. Ay, ay.   (*Exit* Roger.

Class. I suppose, by this time, matters are pretty well settled within, and my absence only wanted to accomplish the scene; but I shall take care to————Oh! Mr Subtle and his Lady.

Enter Mr and Mrs Subtle.

Mrs Sub. Oh! delightfully! Now, my dearest, I hope you will no longer dispute my abilities for forming a female.

Mr Sub. Never, never: How the baggage learn'd!

Mrs Sub. And the booby gap'd!

Mr Sub. So kind, and yet so coy; so free, but then so reserv'd: Oh! she has him!

Mrs Sub. Ay! ay! the fish is hook'd; but then safely to land him.—Is Classic suspicious?

Mr Sub. Not that I observe; but the secret must soon be blaz'd.

Mrs Sub. Therefore dispatch: I have laid a trap to enflame his affection.

Mr Sub. How?

Mrs Sub. He shall be treated with a display of Lucy's talents; her singing, dancing.

Mr Sub. Pshaw! her singing and dancing!

Mrs Sub. Ah! you don't know, husband, half the force of these accomplishments in a fashionable figure.

Mr Sub. I doubt her execution.

Mrs Sub. You have no reason; she does both well enough

enough to flatter a fool; especially with love for her second: besides, I have a coup de maitre, a sure card.

Mr Sub. What's that?

Mrs Sub. A rival.

Mr Sub. Who?

Mrs Sub. The language master: he may be easily equipt for the expedition; a second-hand tawdry suit of cloaths will pass him on our countryman for a Marquis; and then, to excuse his speaking our language so well, he may have been educated early in England. But hush! the Squire approaches; don't seem to observe him.

Enter Buck.

For my part, I never saw any thing so alter'd since I was born: in my conscience, I believe she's in love with him.

Buck. Hush! (*Aside.*

Mr Sub. D'ye think so?

Mrs Sub. Why, where's the wonder? He's a pretty, good-humour'd, sprightly fellow; and, for the time, such an improvement! Why he wears his cloaths as easily, and moves as genteelly, as if he had been at Paris these twenty years.

Mr Sub. Indeed! how does he dance?

Mrs Sub. Why he has had but three lessons from Marfull, and he moves already like Dupré. Oh! three months stay here will render him a perfect model for the English Court.

Mr Sub. Godso! No wonder then, with these qualities, that he has caught the heart of my ward; but we must take care that the girl does nothing imprudent.

Mrs Sub. Oh! dismiss your fears; her family, good sense, and, more than all, her being educated under my eye, render them unnecessary: besides, Mr Buck is too much a man of honour to——— (*He interrupts them.*

Buck. Damn me, if I an't.

Mrs Sub. Bless me! Sir! you here! I did not expect——

Buck. I beg pardon; but all that I heard was, that Mr Buck was a man of honour. I wanted to have some chat with you, Madam, in private.

Mr Sub. Then I'll withdraw. You see I dare trust you alone with my wife.

Buck.

Buck. So you may safely; I have other game in view. Servant, Mr Subtle.

Mrs Sub. Now for a puzzling scene; I long to know how he'll begin. Well, Mr Buck, your commands with me, Sir.

Buck. Why, Madam,—I sh—I sh——but let's shut the door: I was, Madam,——ah! ah! Can't you guess what I want to talk about?

Mrs Sub. Not I, indeed, Sir.

Buck. Well, but try; upon my soul I'll tell you if you're right.

Mrs Sub. It will be impossible for me to divine: but come, open a little.

Buck. Why, have you observ'd nothing?

Mrs Sub. About who?

Buck. Why, about me!

Mrs Sub. Yes; you are new-dress'd, and your cloaths become you.

Buck. Yes! pretty well; but it an't that.

Mrs Sub. What is it?

Buck. Why, ah! ah!—Upon my soul, I can't bring it out.

Mrs Sub. Nay, then it's to no purpose to wait: write your mind.

Buck. No! no! Stop a moment, and I will tell.

Mrs Sub. Be expeditious, then.

Buck. Why, I wanted to talk about Miss Lucinda.

Mrs Sub. What of her?

Buck. She's a bloody fine girl; and I should be glad to——

Mrs Sub. To—— Bless me! What! Mr Buck! And in my house! Oh! Mr Buck, you have deceived me! Little did I think, that, under the appearance of so much honesty, you could go to—ruin the poor girl.

Buck. Upon my soul you're mistaken.

Mrs Sub. A poor orphan too! depriv'd in her earliest infancy of a father's prudence, and a mother's care.

Buck. Why I tell you———

Mrs Sub. So sweet, so lovely in innocence; her mind as spotless as her person.

Buck. Hey-day!

Mrs Sub. And me, Sir! Where had you your thoughts

of

of me? How dar'd you suppose that I would connive at such a——

Buck. The woman's bewitch'd!

Mrs Sub. I! whose untainted reputation the blistering tongue of slander never blasted. Full fifteen years, in wedlock's sacred bands, have I liv'd unreproach'd; and now to——

Buck. Odds fury! she's in heroics!

Mrs Sub. And this from you too, whose fair outside and bewitching tongue had so far lull'd my fears, I dar'd have trusted all my daughters, nay, myself too, singly, with you.

Buck. Upon my soul! and so you might safely.

Mrs Sub. Well, Sir, and what have you to urge in your defence?

Buck. Oh! oh! What, you are got pretty well to the end of your line, are you? And now, if you'll be quiet a bit, we may make a shift to understand one another a little.

Mrs Sub. Be quick, and ease me of my fears.

Buck. Ease you of your fears! I don't know how the devil you got them. All that I wanted to say was, that Miss Lucy was a fine wench; and if she was as willing as me——

Mrs Sub. Willing! Sir! What damon——

Buck. If you are in your airs again, I may as well decamp.

Mrs Sub. I am calm; go on.

Buck. Why, that if she lik'd me, as well as I lik'd her, we might, perhaps, if you lik'd it too, be married together.

Mrs Sub. Oh! Sir! if that was indeed your drift, I am satisfy'd. But don't indulge your wish too much; there are numerous obstacles; your father's consent, the law of the land——

Buck. What laws?

Mrs Sub. All clandestine marriages are void in this country.

Buck. Damn the country: In London now, a footman may drive to May-Fair, and in five minutes be tack'd to a Countess; but there's no liberty here.

Mrs Sub. Some inconsiderate couples have indeed gone off

off poll to Proteſtant States; but I hope my ward will have more prudence.

Buck. Well, well, leave that to me. D'ye think ſhe likes me?

Mrs Sub. Why, to deal candidly with you, ſhe does.

Buck. Does ſhe, by ——

Mrs Sub. Calm your tranſports.

Buck. Well! But how? She did not, did ſhe! Hey! Come now, tell ——

Mrs Sub. I hear her coming; this is her hour for muſic and dancing.

Buck. Could I not have a peep?

Mrs Sub. Withdraw to this corner.

Enter Lucinda, with Singing and Dancing-Maſters.

Luc. The news, the news, Monſieur Gamut, I die, if I have not the firſt intelligence! What's doing at Verſailles? When goes the Court to Marli? Does Rameau write the next opera? What ſay the critics of Voltaire's *Duc de Faix*? Anſwer me all in a breath!

Buck. A brave-ſpirited girl! ſhe'll take a five-barr'd gate in a fortnight.

Gam. The converſation of the Court your Ladyſhip has engroſs'd, ever ſince you left honour'd it with your appearance.

Luc. Oh! you flatterer! have I! Well, and what freſh victims? But 'tis impoſſible; the ſunſhine of a northern beauty is too feeble to thaw the icy heart of a French courtier.

Gam. What injuſtice to your own charms and our diſcernment!

Luc. Indeed! nay, I care not; if I have fire enough to warm one Britiſh boſom, rule! rule! ye Paris belles! I envy not your conqueſts.

Mrs Sub. Meaning you.

Buck? Indeed!

Mrs Sub. Certain!

Buck. Huſh!

Luc. But come, a truce to gallantry, Gamut, and to the buſineſs of the day: Oh! I am quite enchanted with this new inſtrument; 'tis ſo languiſhing and ſo portable, and ſo ſoft and ſo ſilly: But come, for your laſt leſſon.

Gam. D'ye like the words?

Luc.

Luc. Oh! charming! They are so melting, and easy, and elegant. Now for a *coup d'essai*.

Gam. Take care of your expression; let your eyes and address accompany the sound and sentiment.

Luc. But, dear Gamut, if I am out, don't interrupt me; correct me afterwards.

Gam. Allons, commencés.

SONG.

I.
PAR un matin Lisette se leva,
Et dans un bois seulette s'en alla.
                   Ta, la, la, &c.

II.
Elle cherchoit des nids de ça de là,
Dans un buisson le Rossignol chanta.
                   Ta, la, la, &c.

III.
Tout doucement elle s'en approcha,
Savez vous bien, ce qu'elle déniche.
                   Ta, la, la, &c.

IV.
C'étoit l'Amour, l'Amour l'attendoit là,
Le bel Oiseau dit elle que voilà.
                   Ta, la, la, &c.

V.
La pauvre enfant le prit, le caressa,
Sous son mou' hoir en riant le plaça.
                   Ta, la, la, &c.

VI.
Son petit cœur souffrit d'enflames,
Elle gemit, et ne sçait ce qu'elle a.
                   Ta, la, la, &c.

VII.
Elle s'en va se plaindre à son Papa,
En lui parlant la belle soupira.
                   Ta, la, la, &c.

VIII.
Le bon Papa qui s'en doutoit déja,
Lui dit je sçais un remede à cela.
                   Ta, la, la, &c.

IX.

Il prit l'Amour, les ailes lui coupa,
D'un double nœud fortement le lia.
                    Ta, la, la, &c.

X.

Dans la volière auffitôt l'enferma,
Chantez Fripon autant qu'il vous plaira.
                    Ta, la, la, &c.

XI.

Heureufement la belle s'en tira,
Mais on n'a pas toujours ce fecret la.
                    Ta, la, la, &c.

XII.

Jeune beauté que l'Amour guettera,
Craignez le tour qu' à Lifette il joua.
                    Ta, la, la, &c.

Gam. Bravo! bravo!
Buck. Bravo! braviffimo! My Lady, what was the fong about?   [*Afide to my Lady.*
Mrs Sub. Love: 'Tis her own compofing.
Buck. What, does fhe make verfes then?
Mrs Sub. Finely. I take you to be the fubject of thefe.
Buck. Ah! D'ye think fo? Gad! I thought by her ogling 'twas the mufic-man himfelf.
Luc. Well, Mr Gamut; tolerably well, for fo young a fcholar.
Gam. Inimitably, Madam! Your Ladyfhip's progrefs will undoubtedly fix my fortune.

Enter Servant.

Luc. Your Servant, Sir.
Ser. Madam, your dancing-mafter, Monfieur Kitteau.
Luc. Admit him.

Enter Kitteau.

Monfieur Kitteau, I can't poffibly take leffon this morning, I am fo bufy; but if you pleafe, I'll juft hobble over a minuet by way of exercife.

Enter a Servant.   [*After the Dance.*

Serv. Monfieur le Marquis de ———
Luc. Admit him this inftant.

                                        Mrs

Mrs Sub. A lover of Lucinda, a Frenchman of fashion, and vast fortune.

Buck. Never heed; I'll foon do his bufinefs, I'll warrant you.

Enter Marquis.

Luc. My dear Marquis!

Marq. Ma chere adorable! 'Tis an age fince I faw you.

Luc. Oh! An eternity! But 'tis your own fault, tho'.

Marq. My misfortune, *ma Princeffe!* But now I'll redeem my error, and root for ever here.

Buck. I fhall make a fhift to tranfplant you, I believe.

Luc. You can't conceive how your abfence has diftrefs'd me. Demand of thefe gentlemen the melancholy mood of my mind.

Marq. But now that I am arriv'd, we'll dance and fing, and drive care to the——Ha! Monfieur Kitteau! have you practis'd this morning?

Luc. I had juft given my hand to Kitteau before you came.

Marq. I was in hopes that honour would have been referved for me. May I flatter myfelf that your Ladyfhip will do me the honour of venturing upon the fatigue of another minuet this morning with me?

Enter Buck brifkly. Takes her hand.

Buck. Not that you know of, Monfieur.

Marq. Hey! *Diable! quelle bête!*

Buck. Harkee, Monfieur Ragout, if you repeat that word *bête*, I fhall make you fwallow it again, as I did laft night one of your countrymen.

Marq. Quel fauvage!

Buck. And another word; as I know you can fpeak very good Euglifh, if you will. When you don't, I fhall take it for granted you're abufing me, and treat you accordingly.

Marq. Cavalier enough! But you are protected here. Madamoifelle, who is this officious gentleman? How comes he interefted? Some relation, I fuppofe!

Buck. No; I'm a lover.

Marq. Oh! oh! a rival! Eh *morbleu!* a dangerous one too. Ha! ha! Well, Monfieur, what and I fuppofe you prefume to give laws to this Lady; and are determin'd,

Vol. I.   G

min'd, out of your very great and singular affection, to knock down every mortal she likes, *A-la-mode d'Angleterre*; Hey! Monsieur Roast-beef!

Buck. No; but I intend that Lady for my wife; consider her as such, and don't chuse to have her soil'd by the impertinent addresses of every French fop, *A-la-mode de Paris*, Monsieur Friendly!

Marq. Friendly!

Buck. We.

Luc. A truce; a truce, I beseech you, gentlemen: it seems I am the golden prize for which you plead; produce your pretensions; you are the representatives of your respective countries: begin, Marquis, for the honour of France; let me hear what advantages I am to derive from a conjugal union with you.

Marq. Abstracted from those which I think are pretty visible; a perpetual residence in this paradise of pleasures; to be the object of universal adoration; to say what you please, go where you will, do what you like, form fashions, hate your husband, and let him see it; indulge your gallant, and let t'other know it; run in debt, and oblige the poor devil to pay it. He! *ma chère!* there are pleasures for you!

Luc. Bravo! Marquis! These are allurements for a woman of spirit. But don't let us conclude too hastily; hear the other side: What have you to offer, Mr Buck, in favour of England?

Buck. Why, Madam, for a woman of spirit, they give you the same advantages in London as at Paris, with a privilege forgot by the Marquis, an indisputable right to cheat at cards in spite of detection.

Marq. Pardon me, Sir, we have the same; but I thought this privilege so known and universal, that 'twas needless to mention it.

Buck. You'll give up nothing, I find; but to tell you my bluet thoughts, in a word, if any woman can be so abandon'd, as to rank amongst the comforts of matrimony, the privilege of hating her husband, and the liberty of committing every folly and every vice contained in your catalogue, she may stay single for me; for damn me, if I'm a husband fit for her humour; that's all.

Marq. I told you, Mademoiselle!

Luc.

Luc. But say, what have you to offer us counterbalance for these pleasures?

Buck. Why, I have, Madam, courage to protect you, good-nature to indulge your love, and health enough to make gallants useless, and too good a fortune to render running in debt necessary. Find that here if you can.

Marq. Bagatelle!

Luc. Spoke with the sincerity of a Briton; and as I don't perceive that I shall have any use for the fashionable liberties you propose, you'll pardon, Marquis, my national prejudice; here's my hand, Mr Buck.

Buck. Servant, Monsieur!

Marq. Serviteur!

Buck. No offence!

Marq. Not in the least; I am only afraid the reputation of that Lady's taste will suffer a little; and to shew her at once the difference of her choice, the preference, which, if bestowed on me, would not fail to exasperate you, I support without murmuring; so that favour, which would probably have provok'd my fate, is now your protection. *Voilà la politesse Françoise*, Madam; I have the honour to be——*Bon jour, Monsieur.* Tol de rol.
[*Exit.* Marq.

Buck. The fellow bears it well. Now, if you'll give me your hand, we'll in, and settle matters with Mr Subtle.

Luc. 'Tis now my duty to obey.
[*Exeunt.*

Enter Roger, *peeping about.*

Rog. The coast is clear; Sir, Sir, you may come in now, Mr Classic.

Enter Mr Classic *and the Father.*

Claff. Roger, watch at the door. I wish, Sir John, I could give you a more cheerful welcome, but we have no time to lose in ceremony; you are arrived in the critical minute; two hours more would have plac'd the inconsiderate couple out of the reach of pursuit.

Father. How can I acknowledge your kindness? You have preserv'd my son; you have sav'd——

Claff. I have done my duty; but of that——

Rog. Master and the young woman's coming.

Claff.

Class. Sir John, place yourself here, and be a witness how near a crisis is the fate of your family.

Enter Buck and Lucinda.

Buck. Pshaw! What signifies her? 'Tis odds whether she'd consent, from the fear of my father. Besides, she told me, we could never be married here; and so pack up a few things, and we'll off in a post-chaise directly.

Luc. Stay, Mr Buck, let me have a moment's reflection.—What am I about? contriving in concert with the most profligate couple that ever disgrac'd human nature, to impose an indigent orphan on the sole representative of a wealthy and honourable family! Is this a character becoming my birth and education? What must be the consequence? Sure detection and contempt, contempt even from him, when his passions cool.—I have resolv'd, Sir.

Buck. Madam.

Luc. As the expedition we are upon the point of taking is to be a lasting one, we ought not to be over-hasty in our resolution.

Buck. Pshaw! stuff! When a thing's resolv'd, the sooner 'tis over the better.

Luc. But before it is absolutely resolv'd, give me leave to beg an answer to two questions.

Buck. Make haste then.

Luc. What are your thoughts of me?

Buck. Thoughts! Nay, I don't know; why, that you are a sensible, civil, handsome, handy girl, and will make a devilish good wife. That's all I think.

Luc. But of my rank and fortune?

Buck. Mr Subtle says they are both great; but that's no business of mine, I was always determin'd to marry for love.

Luc. Generously said! My birth, I believe, won't disgrace you; but for my fortune, your friend, Mr Subtle, I fear, has anticipated you there.

Buck. Much good may it do him; I have enough for both. But we lose time, and may be prevented.

Luc. By whom?

Buck. By Domine; or perhaps father may come.

Luc. Your father!—You think he would prevent you then.

Buck. Perhaps he would.

Luc.

Luc. And why?

Buck. Nay, I don't know; but pshaw! 'zooks! this is like saying one's catechife.

Luc. But don't you think your father's confent neceffary?

Buck. No! Why 'tis I am to be married, and not he. But come along, old fellows love to be obftinate; but ecod I am as mulifh as he; and to tell you the truth, if he had propos'd me a wife, that would have been reafon enough to make me diflike her; and I don't think I fhould be half fo hot about marrying you, only I thought 'twould plague the old fellow damnably. So, my pretty partner, come along; let's have no more——

Enter Father and Claffic.

Fath. Sir, I am oblig'd to you for this declaration, as to it I owe the entire fubjection of that paternal weaknefs which has hitherto fufpended the correction your abandon'd libertinifm has long provok'd. You have forgot the duty you owe a father, difclaim'd my protection, cancell'd the natural covenant between us; 'tis time I now fhould give you up to the guidance of your own guilty paffions, and treat you as a ftranger to my blood for ever.

Buck. I told you what would happen, if he fhould come; but you may thank yourfelf.

Fath. Equally weak as wicked, the dupe of a raw, giddy girl. But proceed, Sir; you have nothing farther to fear from me; complete your project, and add her ruin to your own.

Buck. Sir, as to me, you may fay what you pleafe; but for the young woman, fhe does not deferve it; but now fhe wanted me to get your confent, and told me that fhe had never a penny of portion into the bargain.

Fath. A ftale, obvious artifice! She knew the difcovery of the fraud muft follow clofe on your inconfiderate marriage, and would then plead the merits of her prior candid difcovery. The Lady, doubtlefs, Sir, has other fecrets to difclofe; but, as her cunning reveal'd the firft, her policy will preferve the reft.

Luc. What fecrets?

Buck. Be quiet, I tell you; let him alone, and he'll cool of himfelf by and by.

Luc. Sir, I am yet the protectrefs of my own honour;

in

in justice to that, I will demand an explanation. What secrets, Sir!

Frib. Oh! perhaps a thousand! But I am to blame to call them secrets; the customs of this gay country give sanction, and stamp merit upon vice; and vanity will here proclaim what modesty would elsewhere blush to whisper.

Luc. Modesty!—You suspect my virtue then!

Fath. You are a Lady; but the fears of a father may be permitted to neglect a little your plan of politeness: therefore to be plain; from your residence in this house, from your connection with these people, and from the scheme which my presence has interrupted, I have suspicions——of what nature, ask yourself.

Luc. Sir, you have reason; appearances are against me, I confess, but when you have heard my melancholy story, you'll own you have wrong'd me, and learn to pity her whom now you hate.

Fath. Madam, you misemploy your time; there tell your story, there it will be believ'd; I am too knowing in the wiles of women, to be soften'd by a Syren tear, or impos'd on by an artful tale.

Luc. But hear me, Sir; on my knee I beg it, nay I demand it; you have wrong'd me, and must do me justice.

Chiff. I am sure, Madam, Sir John will be glad to find his fears are false, but you can't blame him.

Luc. I don't, Sir, and I shall but little trespass on his patience. When you know, Sir, that I am the orphan of an honourable and once wealthy family, whom her father, misguided by pernicious politics, brought with him, in her earliest infancy, to France, that dying here, he bequeath'd me, with the poor remnant of our shattered fortune, to the direction of this rapacious pair; I am sure you'll tremble for me.

Fath. Go on!

Luc. But when you know that, plunder'd of the little fortune left me, I was reluctantly compell'd to aid this plot; forced to comply under the penalty of deepest want; without one hospitable roof to shelter me, without one friend to comfort or relieve me; you must, you can't but pity me.

Fath. Proceed!

Luc. To this when you are told, that, previous to your coming, I had determined never to wed your son, at least without

without your knowledge and consent, I hope your justice then will credit and acquit me.

Fath. Madam, your tale is plausible and moving; I hope 'tis true; here come the explainers of this riddle.

Enter Mr and Mrs Subtle.

Mr Sub. Buck's father!

Fath. I'll take some other time, Sir, to thank you for the last proofs of your friendship to my family; in the mean time, be so candid as to instruct us in the knowledge of this lady, whom, it seems, you have chosen for the partner of my son.

Mr Sub. Mr Buck's partner——I chose——I——I——

Fath. No equivocation or reserve; your plot's reveal'd, known to the bottom; who is the Lady?

Mr Sub. Lady, Sir,—the Lady's a gentlewoman, Sir.

Fath. By what means?

Mr Sub. By her father and mother.

Fath. Who were they, Sir?

Mr Sub. Her mother was of——I forget her maiden name.

Fath. You han't forgot her father's?

Mr Sub. No! no! no!

Fath. Tell it then.

Mr Sub. She has told it you, I suppose.

Fath. No matter, I must have it, Sir, from you; here's some mystery.

Mr Sub. 'Twas Worthy.

Fath. Not the daughter of Sir Gilbert.

Mr Sub. You have it.

Fath. My poor girl! I indeed have wrong'd, but will redress you; and pray, Sir, after the many pressing letters you received from me, how came this truth conceal'd? but I guess your motive. Dry up your tears, Lucinda; at last you have found a father. Hence ye degenerate, ye abandon'd wretches, who, abusing the confidence of your country, unite to plunder those ye promise to protect.

Luc. Am I then justified?

Fath. You are; your father was my first and firmest friend; I mourn'd his loss; and long have sought for thee in vain, Lucinda.

Buck. Pray han't I some merit in finding her? She's mine by the custom of the manor.

Fath.

Forth. Yours—First study to deserve her; she's mine, Sir, I have just redeemed this valuable treasure; and shall not trust it in a spendthrift's hands.

Birk. What would you have me do, Sir?

Faith. Disclaim the partners of your riot, polish your manners, reform your pleasures, and, before you think of governing others, learn to direct yourself. And now, my beauteous ward, we'll for the land where first you saw the light, and there endeavour to forget the long, long bondage you have suffer'd here. I suppose, Sir, we shall have no difficulty in persuading you to accompany us; it is not in France I am to hope for your reformation. I have now learn'd, that he who transports a prodigate son to Paris, by way of mending his manners, only adds the vices and follies of that country to those of his own.

THE
KNIGHTS;
A COMEDY,
IN TWO ACTS.

PREFACE.

AS this is the last opportunity I shall have of addressing the public this year, I think it my duty to return them my warmest acknowledgements for their favourable reception of the following little piece.

The three principal characters I met with in a summer's expedition; they are neither vamped from antiquated plays, pilfered from French farces, nor the baseless beings of the poet's brain. I have given them in their plain natural habit; they wanted no dramatic sussing; nor can I claim any other merit than grouping them together, and throwing them into action. The justice done them then, by the performers has been too strongly distinguished by the town to render any thing from me necessary; I could only wish that the managers of the theatres would employ Mr Costollo, whose peculiar naïveté and strict propriety would greatly become many characters on our stage.

S. FOOTE.

PROLOGUE.

PROLOGUE.

Written and spoken by Mr FOOTE.

HAPPY my Muse, had she first turn'd her art,
From humour's dangerous path, to touch the heart.
They, who in all the blusters of blank verse,
The mournful tales of love and war rehearse,
Are sure the critics censure to escape;
You hiss not heroes now, you only——gape!
Nor (strangers quite to heroes, kings, and queens)
Dare you intrude your judgment on their scenes.
A different lot the Comic Muse attends,
She is obliged to treat you with your friends;
Must search the court, the forum, and the city,
Mark out the dull, the gallant, and the witty,
Youth's wild profusion, th' avarice of age,
Nay, bring the pit itself upon the stage.
First to the bar she turns her various face;
Here! my Lord, I am counsel in this case,
And if so be your Lordship should think fit,
Why, to be sure, my client must submit;
For why? becaufe——Then off she trips again,
And to the sons of commerce shifts her scene;
There, whilst the griping sire, with moping care,
Defrauds the world himself t' enrich his heir,
The prim boy, his father's toil rewarding,
For thousands throws a main at Covent-Garden!
These are the portraits we're oblig'd to shew;
You are all judges if they're like or no:
Here should we fail, some other shape we'll try,
And grace our future scenes with novelty.
I have a plan to treat you with bourlette,
That cannot miss your taste, mia spiletta:
But, should the following piece your mirth excite,
From Nature's volume we'll persist to write;
Your partial favour bade us first proceed,
Then spare th' offender, since you urg'd the deed.

DRAMATIS

DRAMATIS PERSONÆ.

Harrop	Mr Foote.
Sir Gregory Gazette	Mr Yates.
Jenkins	Mr Baker.
Timothy	Mr Castello.
Robin	Mr Crown.
Jenny	Miss Nivess.
Miss Penelope Trifle	Mr Cross.
Miss Sukey Trifle	Miss Myers.

ACT I.

SCENE, *a room.*

Hartop *and* Jenkins *discovered.*

Jenk. I Should not chuse to marry into such a family.

Hart. Choice, dear Dick, is very little concerned in the matter; and, to convince you that love is not the minister of my counsels, know that I never saw but once the object of my present purpose, and that too, at a time, and in a circumstance, not very likely to stamp a favourable impression. What think you of a raw boarding-school girl at Lincoln-Minster, with a mind unpolished, a figure uninformed, and a set of features tainted with the colours of her unwholesome food?

Jenk. No very engaging object indeed, Hartop.

Hart. Your thoughts now were mine then; but some connections I have since had with her father have given birth to my present design upon her. You are no stranger to the situation of my circumstances: my neighbourhood to Sir Penurious Trifle was a sufficient motive for his advancing what money I wanted by way of mortgage; the hard terms he imposed upon me, and the little regard I have paid to œconomy, has made it necessary for me to attempt by some scheme the re-establishment of my fortune: this young lady's simplicity, not to call it ignorance, presented her at once as a proper subject for my purpose.

Jenk. Success to you, Jack, with all my soul! a fellow of your spirit and vivacity mankind ought to support for the sake of themselves; for, whatever Seneca and the other moral writers may have suggested in contempt of riches, it is plain their maxims were not calculated for the world, as it now stands; in days of yore indeed, when virtue was called wisdom, and vice folly, such principles might have been encouraged; but, as the present subjects of our inquiry are, not what a man is, but what he has, as to be rich is to be wise and virtuous, and to be poor ignorant and vicious, I heartily applaud your plan!

Hart. Your observation is but too just! and is it not, Dick, a little unaccountable, that we, who condescend so
servilely

servilely to copy the follies and fopperies of our polite neighbours, should be so totally averse to an imitation of their virtues? In France, Has he wealth? is an interrogation never put till they are disappointed in their inquiries after the birth and wisdom of a fashionable fellow: but here, How much a year?—Two thousand.—The devil! In what country?—Berkshire.—Indeed! God bless us! a happy dog!—How the deuce come I to be interested in a man's fortune, unless I am his steward or his tailor! Indeed knowledge and genius are worth examining into; by those my understanding may be improved, or my imagination gratified; but why such a man's being able to eat ortolans, and drink French wine, is to recommend him to my esteem, is what I cannot readily conceive.

Jest. This complaint may with justice be made of all imitations; the ridiculous side is ever the object imitated. But a truce to moralising, and to our business. Prithee, in the first place, how can you gain admittance to your mistress? and, in the second, is the girl independent of her father? his consent, I suppose, you have no thoughts of obtaining.

Hart. Some farther proposals concerning my estate, such as an increase of the mortgage or an absolute sale, is a sufficient pretence for a visit; and, as to cash, twenty to my knowledge! independent too, you rogue! and, besides, an only child, you know! and then, when things are done they can't be undone, and 'tis well it's no worse, and a hundred such pretty proverbs, will, its great odds, reconcile the old fellow at last. Besides, my papa in posse has a foible, which, if I condescend to humour, I have his soul, my dear.

Jest. Prithee, now you are in spirits, give me a portrait of Sir Penurious; though he is my neighbour, yet he is so domestic an animal that I know no more of him than the common country conversation, that he is a thrifty, wary, man.

Hart. The very abstract of penury! Sir John Cutler, with his transmigrated stockings, was but a type of him. For instance, the barber has the growth of his and his daughters's head once a year for shaving the knight once a fortnight; his shoes are made with the leather of a coach of his grandfather's, built in the year 1; his male servant is footman, groom, carter, coachman, and tailor; his maid employs her leisure hours in plain-work for the neighbours,

bours, which Sir Penurious takes care, as her labour is for his emolument, shall be as many as possible, by joining with his daughter in scouring the rooms, making the beds, &c. thus much for his moral character. Then, as to his intellectual, he is a mere carte blanche; the last man he is with must afford him matter for the next he goes to; but a story is his idol, throw him in that and he swallows it; no matter what, raw or roasted, savoury or insipid, down it goes, and up again to the first person he meets: it is upon this basis I found my favour with the knight, having acquired patience enough to hear his stories, and equipped myself with a quantity sufficient to furnish him; his manner is indeed peculiar, and for once or twice entertaining enough. I'll give you a specimen: —— Is not that an equipage?

Jenk. Hey! yes, faith! and the owner an acquaintance of mine; Sir Gregory Gazette, by Jupiter! and his son Tim with him. Now I can match your knight. He must come this way to the parlour. We'll have a scene; but take your cue, he is a country politician.

Sir Gregory entering, and Waiter.

Sir Greg. What, neither the Gloucester Journal, nor the Worcester Courant, nor the Northampton Mercury, nor the Chester ——? Mr Jenkins, I am your humble servant; a strange town this, Mr Jenkins, no news stirring, no papers taken in! Is that gentleman a stranger, Mr Jenkins? Pray, Sir, not to be too bold, don't you come from London?

Hart. But last night.

Sir Greg. Lack-a-day! that's wonderful! —— Mr Jenkins, introduce me.

Jenk. Mr Hartop, Sir Gregory Gazette.

Sir Greg. Sir, I am proud to —— Well, Sir, and what news? You come from —— Pray, Sir, are you a parliament-man?

Hart. Not I indeed, Sir.

Sir Greg. Good lack! may be belong to the law?

Hart. Nor that.

Sir Greg. Oh, then in some of the offices; the Treasury or the Exchequer?

Hart. Neither, Sir.

Sir Greg. Lack-a-day! that's wonderful! Well, but,
Mr

Mr ———. Pray what name did Mr Jenkins, Ha——Ha——.
Hart. Hartop.
Sir Greg. Ay, true! what, not of the Hartops of Boston?
Hart. No.
Sir Greg. May be not. There is, Mr Hartop, one thing that I envy you Londoners in much;—quires of newspapers!—Now I reckon you read a matter of eight sheets every day?
Hart. Not one.
Sir Greg. Wonderful! then, may be, you are about court; and so, being at the fountain-head, know what is in the papers before they are printed.
Hart. I never trouble my head about them.——An old fool! [*Aside.*
Sir Greg. Good Lord! Your friend, Mr Jenkins, is very close.
Jenk. Why, Sir Gregory, Mr Hartop is much in the secrets above; and it becomes a man so trusted to be wary, you know.
Sir Greg. May be so, may be so. Wonderful! ay, ay, a great man no doubt.
Jenk. But I'll give him a better insight into your character, and that will induce him to throw off his reserve.
Sir Greg. May be so; do, do; ay, ey!
Jenk. Prithee, Jack, don't be so cruel, indulge the knight's humour a little; besides, if I guess right, it may be necessary for the conduct of your design to contract a pretty strict intimacy here. [*Aside.*
Hart. Well, do as you will. [*Aside.*
Jenk. Sir Gregory, Mr Hartop's ignorance of your character made him a little shy in his replies, but you will now find him more communicative; and, in your ear, he is a treasure; he is in all the mysteries of government; at the bottom of every thing.
Sir Greg. Wonderful! a treasure! ay, ay, may be so.
Jenk. And, that you may have him to yourself, I'll go in search of your son.
Sir Greg. Do so, do so; Tim is without, just come from his uncle Tregeagle's at Mavagzzy in Cornwall; Tim is an honest lad: do so, do so. [*Exit Jenk.*] Well, Mr Hartop, and so we have a peace; lack-a-day! long looked for come at last. But pray, Mr Hartop, how many newspapers may you have printed in a week?
Hart.

THE KNIGHTS.

Hart. About a hundred and fifty, Sir Gregory.

Sir Greg. Good now, good now! and all full, I reckon; full as an egg; nothing but news! well, well, I shall go to London one of these days. A hundred and fifty, wonderful! and, pray now, which do you reckon the best?

Hart. Oh, Sir Gregory, they are as various in their excellencies as their uses; if you are inclined to blacken, by a couple of lines, the reputation of a neighbour, whose character neither your nor his whole life can possibly restore, you may do it for two shillings in one paper; if you are displaced, or disappointed of a place, a triplet against the ministry will be always well received at the head of another; and then, as a paper of morning amusement, you have the Fool.

Sir Greg. The Fool! good lack! and pray who and what may that same Fool be?

Hart. Why, Sir Gregory, the author has artfully assumed that habit, like the royal jesters of old, to level his satire with more security to himself and severity to others.

Sir Greg. May be so, may be so! the Fool! ha, ha, ha! well enough! a queer dog, and no fool, I warrant you! Killigrew, ah, I have heard my grandfather talk much of that same Killigrew, and no fool! But what is all this to news, Mr Hartop? Who gives us the best account of the King of Spain, and the Queen of Hungary, and those great folks? Come now, you could give us a little news if you would; come now!—snug!—nobody by!—good now do; come, ever so little!

Hart. Why, as you so largely contribute to the support of the government, it is but fair you should know what they are about.—We are at present in a treaty with the Pope!

Sir Greg. With the Pope! Wonderful! Good now, good now! how, how?

Hart. We are to yield him up a large tract of the Terra Incognita, together with both the Needles, Scilly-rocks, and the Lizard-point, on condition that the Pretender has the government of Laputa, and the Bishop of Greenland succeeds to St Peter's chair; he being, you know, a Protestant, when possessed of the pontificals, issues out a bull, commanding all catholics to be of his religion; they, deeming the Pope infallible, follow his directions, and then, Sir Gregory, we are all of one mind.

VOL. I.   I   *Sir*

Sir Greg. Good lack, good lack! rare news, rare news, rare news! ten millions of thanks, Mr Hartop! But might not I just hint this to Mr Soakum, our vicar? 'twould rejoice his heart.

Hart. O fie, by no means.

Sir Greg. Only a line!—a little hint!—do now.

Hart. Well, Sir, it is difficult for me to refuse you any thing.

Sir Greg. Ten thousand thanks! Now! the Pope! Wonderful! I'll minute it down;——both the Needles?

Hart. Ay, both.

Sir Greg. Good now, I'll minute it;——the Lizard-point,——both the Needles,——Scilly rocks,——Bishop of Greenland,——St Peter's chair.——Why then, when this is finished, we may chance to attack the great Turk, and have holy wars again, Mr Hartop?

Hart. That's part of the scheme.

Sir Greg. Ah! good now! you see I have a head! politics have been my study many a day. Ah, if I had been in London to improve by the newspapers!——They tell me Doctor Drybones is to succeed to the bishopric of——
[*Whispers.*

Hart. No; Doctor—— [*Whispers.*

Sir Greg. Indeed! I was told by my landlord at Ross, that it was between him and the Dean of—— [*Whispers.*

Hart. To my knowledge——

Sir Greg. Nay, you know best, to be sure. If it should ——Hush! here's Mr Jenkins and son Tim. Mum!—Mr Jenkins does not know any thing about the treaty with the Pope?

Hart. Not a word.

Sir Greg. Mum!

Enter Timothy *and* Jenkins.

Jenk. Master Timothy is almost grown out of knowledge, Sir Gregory.

Sir Greg. Good now, good now! ay, ay, ill weeds grow apace. Son Tim, Mr Hartop: a great man, child! Mr Hartop, son Tim.

Hart. Sir, I shall be always glad to know every branch that springs from so valuable a trunk as Sir Gregory Gazette.

Sir Greg. May be so! Wonderful! Ay, ay!

Hart.

Hart. Sir, I am glad to see you in Herefordshire: have you been long from Cornwall?

Tim. Ay, Sir; a matter of four weeks or a month, more or less.

Sir Greg. Well said, Tim! ay, ay, ask Tim any questions, he can answer for himself. Tim, tell Mr Hartop all the news about the elections, and the dinners, and the tides, and the roads, and the pilchers: I want a few words with my master Jenkins.

Hart. You have been so long absent from your native country, that you have almost forgot it.

Tim. Yes sure; I ha' been at uncle Tregeagle's a matter of twelve or a dozen year, more or less.

Hart. Then I reckon you were quite impatient to see your papa and mamma?

Tim. No sure, not I. Father sent for me to uncle; sure Mavagesy is a choice place! and I could a'stay'd there all my born days, more or less.

Hart. Pray, Sir, what were your amusements.

Tim. Nan? what do you say?

Hart. How did you divert yourself?

Tim. Oh, we ha' pastimes enow there: we ha' bull-baiting, and cock-fighting, and fishing, and hunting, and hurling, and wrestling.

Hart. The two last are sports for which that country is very remarkable: in those, I presume, you are very expert.

Tim. Nan? what?

Hart. I say you are a good wrestler?

Tim. Oh! yes sure, I can wrestle well enow: but we don't wrestle after your fashion; we ha' no tripping; faith and foul! we all go upon close hugs or the flying mare. Will you try a fall, master? I wan't hurt you, faith and foul.

Hart. We had as good not venture though.——But have you left in Cornwall nothing that you regret the loss of more 'han hurling and wrestling?

Tim. Nan? what?

Hart. No favourite she?

Tim. Arra, I coupled Favourite and Jowler together, and sure they tugg'd it all the way up. Part with Favourite! no, I thank you for nothing: you must know I nursed Favourite myself; uncle's huntsman was going to millpond to drown all Music's puppies; so I saved she: but, faith, fath, I'll tell you a comical ſtory; at Laſton they both broke looſe and eat a whole loin-a'-veal and a leg of beef: Criſt! how landlord ſwear'd! fath, the poor fellow was almoſt mazed; it made me die wi' laughing: but how came you to know about our Favourite?

Hart. A circumſtance, ſo material to his ſon, could not eſcape the knowledge of Sir Gregory Gazette's friends.— But here you miſtook me a little, 'Squire Tim; I meant whether your affections were not ſettled upon ſome pretty girl; has not ſome Corniſh laſs caught your heart?

Tim. Huſh! 'god, the old man will hear; jog a tiny bit this way—won't a' tell father?

Hart. Upon my honour!

Tim. Why then I'll tell you the whole ſtory, more or leſs. Do you know Mally Pengrouſe?

Hart. I am not ſo happy.

Tim. She's uncle's milkmaid; ſhe's as handſome, lord! her face all red and white, like the inſide of a ſhoulder of mutton: ſo I made love to our Mally, and juſt, fath, as I had got her good will to run away to Exeter and be married, uncle found it out and ſent word to father, and father ſent for me home; but I don't love her a bit the worſer for that: but, 'icod, if you tell father he'll knock my brains out, for he ſays I'll diſparage the family, and mother's as mad as a March hare about it; ſo father and mother ha' brought me to be married to ſome young body in theſe parts.

Hart. What, is my lady here?

Tim. No ſure, Dame Winifred, as father calls her, could not come along.

Hart. I am ſorry for that; I have the honour to be a diſtant relation of her ladyſhip.

Tim. Like enough, fath! ſhe's a-kin to half the world, I think. But don't you ſay a word to father about Mally Pengrouſe. Huſh!

Frank. Mr Hartop, Sir Gregory will be amongſt us ſome time; he is going with his ſon to Sir Penurious Trifle's; there is a kind of a treaty of marriage on foot between Miſs Sukey Trifle and Mr Timothy.

Hart. The devil! I ſhall be glad of every circumſtance that can make me better acquainted with Sir Gregory.

Sir Greg. Good now, good now! may be ſo, may be ſo.

Tim.

THE KNIGHTS.

Tim. Father, sure the gentleman says as how mother and he are a-kin.

Sir Greg. Wonderful! lack-a-day! lack-a-day! how, how? I am proud to——But how, Mr Hartop, how?

Hart. Why, Sir, a cousin-german of my aunt's first husband intermarried with a distant relation of a collateral branch by the mother's side, the Apprices of Lantrindon; and we have ever since quarrered in an escutcheon of pretence the three goats tails rampant, divided by the chevron, field argent, with a leek pendant in the dexter point, to distinguish the second house.

Sir Greg. Wonderful! wonderful! nearly, nearly, related! good now, good now! if Dame Winifred were here she'd make them all out with a wet finger; but they are above me. Prithee, Tim, good now! see after the horses;—and, d'ye hear! try if you can get any news-papers.

Tim. Yes, father. But, cousin What-d'ye-call-um, not a word about Mally Pengronse!

Hart. Mum! [*Exit Timothy.*

Sir Greg. Good now, that boy will make some mistake about the horses now! I'll go myself. Good now, no farther cousin! if you please, no ceremony!——A hundred and fifty a week! the Fool! ha, ha, ha! wonderful! an odd dog. [*Exit Sir Gregory.*

Jenk. So, Jack, here's a fresh spoke in your wheel.

Hart. This is a cursed cross incident!

Jenk. Well, but something must be done to frustrate the scheme of your new cousin. Can you think of nothing?

Hart. I have been hammering:—pray, are the two knights intimate? are they well acquainted with each other's person?

Jenk. Faith, I can't tell; but we may soon know.

Hart. Could you recommend me a good spirited girl, who has humour and compliance to follow a few directions, and understanding enough to barter a little inclination for 3000l. a year and a fool?

Jenk. In part I guess your design: the man's daughter of the house is a good lively lass, has a fortune to make, and no reputation to lose. I'll call her.—Jenny!—But the enemy is at hand;—I'll withdraw and prepare Jenny.—When the worshipful family are retired, I'll introduce the wench. [*Exit Jenkins.*

Enter

THE KNIGHTS.

Enter Sir Gregory *and* Timothy.

Sir Greg. Pray now, cousin, are you in friendship with Sir Penurious Trifle?

Hart. I have the honour, Sir, of that gentleman's acquaintance.

Sir Greg. May be so, may be so! but, lack-a-day, cousin, is he such a miser as folks say? Good now, they tell me we shall hardly have necessaries for ourselves and horses at Gripe-Hall: but, as you are a relation, you should, good now, know the affairs of the family. Here is Sir Penurious's letter; here, cousin.

Hart. "Your overture I receive with pleasure, and should be glad to meet you in Shropshire."—I fancy, from a thorough knowledge of Sir Penurious's disposition, and by what I can collect from the contents of that letter, he would be much better pleased to meet you here than at his own house.

Sir Greg. Lack-a-day! may be so! a strange man! wonderful! But, good now, cousin, what must we do?

Hart. I will this morning pay Sir Penurious a visit; and, if you will honour me with your commands, I'll—

Sir Greg. Wonderful! to-day! good now, that's lucky! cousin, you are very kind: good now! I'll send a letter, Tim, by cousin Hartop.

Hart. A letter from so old an acquaintance, and upon so happy an occasion, will secure me a favourable reception.

Sir Greg. Good lack! good lack! an old acquaintance indeed, cousin Hartop! we were at Herefordshire 'size together.——let's see, wonderful! how long ago? 'twas while I was courting Dame Winny; the year before I married; good now, how long? let's see,—that year the hackney-stable was built, and Peter Ugly, the blind pad, fell into a saw-pit.

Tim. Mother says, father and she was married the 1st of April, in the year 10; and I knows 'tis thereabout, for I am two-and-thirty; and brother Jeremy, and Roger, and Gregory, and sister Nelly, were born'd before I.

Sir Greg. Good now, good now! how time wears away! wonderful! thirty-eight years ago, Tim; I could not have thought it. But come in, let's set about the letter. But pray,

THE KNIGHTS. 71

pray, cousin, what diversions, good now! are going forward in London.

Hart. Oh, Sir, we are in no distress for amusement; we have plays, balls, puppet-shows, masquerades, bull-baitings, boxings, burlettas, routs, drums, and a thousand others. But I am in haste for your epistle, Sir Gregory.

Sir Greg. Cousin, your servant.

[*Exit Sir Greg. and Tim.*]

Hart. I am your most obedient.——Thus far our scheme succeeds; and, if Jenkins's girl can assume the aukward pertness of the daughter with as much success as I can imitate the spirited folly of Sir Penurious, the father, I don't despair of a happy catastrophe.

Enter Jenny.

Jenny. Sir, Mr Jenkins——

Hart. Oh, child, your instructions shall be administered within.

Jenny. Mr Jenkins has opened your design, and I am ready and able to execute my part.

Hart. My dear, I have not the least doubt of either your inclination or ability.—But, pox take this old fellow! what in the devil's name can bring him back?—Scour, Jenny. [*Exit Jenny.*]

Enter Sir Gregory.

Sir Greg. Cousin, I beg pardon, but I have a favour to beg;—good now, could not you make interest at some coffee-house in London to buy, for a small matter, the old books of news-papers, and send them into the country to me? They would pass away the time rarely in a rainy day!

Hart. Sir, I'll send you a cart-load.

Sir Greg. Good now, good now! ten thousand thanks! you are a cousin indeed! But pray, cousin, let us, good now! see some of the works of that same Fool.

Hart. I'll send them you all; but——

Sir Greg. What all? lack-a-day, that's kind, cousin? The Terra Incognita,—both the Noodles,—a great deal of that!—But what Bishop is to be Pope?

Hart. Zounds, Sir, I am in haste for your letter; when I return ask as many questions——

Sir

Sir Greg. Good now, good now! that's true!—I'll in, and about it.—But, cousin, the Pope is not to have Gibraltar?

Hart. No, no; damn it, no! as none but the Fool could say it, so none but idiots would believe him! Pray, Sir Gregory,——

Sir Greg. Well, well, cousin! Lack-a-day, you are so ——But, pray——

Hart. Damn your praying! if you don't finish your letter immediately, you may carry it yourself!

Sir Greg. Well, well, cousin! Lack-a-day, you are such ———— Good now, I go, I go!

Hart. But, if the truth should be discovered, I shall be inavitably disappointed.

Sir Greg. But, cousin, are Scilly-rocks——

Hart. I wish they were in your guts with all my heart! I must quit the field, I find. [*Exit.*

Sir Greg. Wonderful! good now, good now! a passionate man! Lack-a-day! I am glad the Pope is not to have Gibraltar though! [*Exit.*

ACT II.

Sir Gregory, and Timothy reading a Newspaper to him.

Tim. COnstantinople, N. S. Nov. 15. The Grand Seignour ————

Sir Greg. Lack-a-day! good now, Tim, the politics, child; and read the stars, and the dashes, and the blanks, as I taught you, Tim.

Tim. Yes, father. ———— We can assure our readers that the D—— dash is to go to F blank; and that a certain noble L—— is to resign his p——e in the T——y, in order to make r——m for the two three-stars.

Sir Greg. Wonderful! good now, good now! great news, Tim! ah, I knew the two three-stars would come in play one time or other! this London Evening knows more than any of them. Well, child, well!

Tim. From the D. J.

Sir Greg. Ay, that's the Dublin Journal. Go on, Tim.

Tim. Last Saturday a gang of highwaymen broke into

an

an empty houfe on Ormond-Quay, and ftripped it of all the furniture.

Sir Greg. Lack-a-day! wonderful! to what a height thefe rogues are grown!

Tim. The way to Mr Keith's chapel is, turn of your——

Sir Greg. Pfhaw! fkip that Tim; I know that road as well as the Doctor! 'tis in every time.

Tim. I. Word, at the Cat and Gridiron, Petticoat-lane, makes tabby all over for people inclined to be crooked; and, if he was to have the univerfal world for making a pair of ftays, he could not put better ftuff in them.

Sir Greg. Good now! where's that, Tim?

Tim. At the Cat and Gridiron, father.

Sir Greg. I'll minute that: All my Lady Izard's children, good now! are inclined to be crooked.

Enter a Waiter.

Wait. Sir, Mr Jenkins begs to fpeak with you.

Sir Greg. Good now! defire him to walk in.
(*Exit Waiter.*

Enter Jenkins.

Jenk. I thought it might not be improper to prepare you for a vifit from Sir Penurious Trifle: I faw him and his daughter alight at the apothecary's above.

Sir Greg. What, they are come? Wonderful! Very kind, very kind, very kind, indeed! Mr —— Come, Tim, fettle my cravat; good now! let's be a little decent:—remember your beft bow to your miftrefs, Tim.

Tim. Yes, father: but muft not I kifs Mifs Suck?

Sir Greg. Lack-a-day! ay, ay! pray, is coufin Hortop come along?

Jenk. I have not feen him:—but I fancy I had better introduce my neighbours.

Sir Greg. Good now! would you be fo kind! (*Exit Jenkins.*) Stand behind me, Tim! Pull down your ruffles, child!

Tim. But, father, won't Mifs Suck think me bold if I kifs her chaps the firft time?

Sir Greg. Lack-a-day! no, Tim, no! faint heart never won fair lady! ha! Tim, had you but feen me attack Dame Winny!—but times ar'n't as they were; good now! we were another kind of folks in thofe days; ftout hearty

Vol. I.   K   fmack,

fmacks that would have made your mouth water again, and the mark ſtood upon the pouting lip like the print upon a pound of butter: but the maſter-miſſes of the preſent age go, lack-a-day! ſo gingerly about it, as if they were afraid to fill their mouths with the paint upon their miſtreſs's cheeks. Ah, the days I have ſeen!

Tim. Nay, father, I warrant, if that's all, I kiſs her hearty enow, faith and ſoul!

Sir Greg. Huſh! Tim, huſh! ſtand behind me, child.

Enter Hartop *as* Sir Penurious Trifle, *and* Jenny *as* Miſs Sukey, *and* Jenkins.

Sir Greg. Sir Penurious, I am overjoyed!—Good now!

Hart. Sir Gregory, I kiſs your hand! My daughter Suck.

Sir Greg. Wonderful! Miſs, I am proud to —— ſon Tim, Sir Penurious; beſt bow, child! —— Miſs Suck ——

Tim. An't that right, father? (*Kiſſes her.*)

Sir Greg. Good now, good now! I am glad to ſee you look ſo well! you keep your own, Sir Penurious.

Hart. Ay, ay! ſtout enough, Sir Gregory, ſtout enough, brother knight! hearty as an oak! hey, Dick? God, now I talk of an oak; I'll tell you a ſtory of an oak; it will make you die with laughing! hey, you Dick, you have heard it, ſhall I tell it Sir Gregory?

Jenk. Though I have heard it ſo often, yet there is ſomething ſo engaging in your manner of telling a ſtory that it always appears new.

Sir Greg. Wonderful! good now, good now! I love a comical ſtory. Pray, Sir Penurious, let's have it; mind, Tim, mind, child.

Tim. Yes, father; faith and ſoul, I love a choice ſtory to my heart's blood!.

Hart. You knight, I was at Bath laſt ſummer;—a water that people drink when they are ill: you have heard of the Bath, Dick? Hey, you?

Tim. Yes, faith, I know Bath; I was there in way up.

Sir Greg. Huſh, Tim! good now, huſh!

Hart. There's a coffee-houſe, you;—a place where people drink coffee and tea, and read the news.

Sir Greg. Pray, Sir Penurious, how many papers may they take in?

Hart. Pſhaw! damn the news! mind the ſtory.

Sir Greg.

Sir Gryp. Good now, good now! a hasty man, Tim!

Hart. Pox take you both! I have lost the story!—where did I leave off, hey, you Dick?

Tim. About coffee and tea.

Hart. Right, you, right! true, true!—so, God, you knight, I used to breakfast at this coffee-house every morning; it cost me eight-pence though, and I had always a breakfast at home——no matter for that, though there I breakfasted, you Dick, God, at the same table with Lord Tom Truewit:——you have heard of Truewit, you knight; a droll dog! you Dick, he told us the story and made us die with laughing:—you have heard of Charles the Second, you knight; he was son of Charles the First, king here in England, that was beheaded by Oliver Cromwell: so what does Charles the Second, you knight, do; but he fights Noll at Worcester; a town you have heard of, not far off; but all would not do, you; God, Noll made him scamper, made him run, take to his heels, you knight;—Truewit told us the story, made us die with laughing:—I always breakfasted at the coffee-house; it cost me eight-pence, though I had a breakfast at home——so what does Charles do, but hid himself in an oak-tree, you, in a wood called Boscobel, from two Italian words, bosco bello, a fine wood, you, and off he marches; but old Noll would not let him come home; no, says he, you don't come here!—Lord Tom told us the story; made us die with laughing; it cost me eight-pence, though I had a breakfast at home——so, you knight, when Noll died, Monk there, you, afterwards Albemarle, in the North, brought him back; so, you, the cavaliers; you have heard of them? they were friends to the Stuarts; what did they do, God, you Dick, but they put up Charles in a sign, the royal oak; you have seen such signs at country ale-houses; so, God, you, what does a puritan do—the puritans were friends to Noll—but he puts up the sign of an owl in an ivy-bush, and underneath he writes " This is not the royal oak!" you have seen writings under signs, you knight; upon this, say the royalists, God, this must not be; so, you, what do they do, but, God, they prosecuted the poor puritan; but they made him change his sign though; and, you Dick, how d'ye think they changed? God, he puts up the royal oak, and underneath he writes " This is not the owl in the ivy-bush!"—It made us all

die

die with laughing! Lord Tim told the story; I always breakfasted at the coffee-houfe, though it coft me eight-pence, and I had a breakfaft at home————hey, you knight! what, Dick, hey!

Sir Greg. Good now, good now! wonderful!

Tim. A choice tale, 'faith!

Jenk. Oh, Sir Penurious is a moft entertaining companion, that muft be allowed.

Sir Greg. Good now! ay, ay, a merry man! but, lack-a-day, would not the young lady chafe a little refreshment after her ride? fome tea, or fome————

Hart. Hey, you knight! no, no! we intend to dine with thee, man. Well, you Tim, what doft think of thy father-in-law that is to be, hey? a jolly cock, you Tim; hey, Dick! But prithee, boy, what doft do with all this tawdry tinfel on? that hat and waiftcoat? trafh, knight, trafh! more in thy pocket and lefs in thy clothes; hey, you Dick! Cod, you knight, I'll make you laugh: I went to London, you Dick, laft year to call in a mortgage; and what does me I, Dick, but take a trip to a coffee-houfe in St Martin's Lane; in comes a French fellow forty times as fine as Tim, with his muff and perle-vous, and his Frances, and his head, you knight, as white with powder, God, you, as a twelfth cake; and who the devil d'ye think, Dick, this might be? hey, you knight?

Sir Greg. Good now! an amboffador to be fure!

Hart. God, you knight, nor better nor worfer than Mynheer Vancaper, a Dutch figure-dancer at the opera-houfe in the Haymarket.

Sir Greg. Wonderful! good now, good now!

Hart. Pfhaw! pox! prithee, Tim, nobody dreffes now; all plain; look at me, knight, I am in the tip of the mode; now am I in full drefs; hey, Dick!

Jenk. You, Sir, don't want the aids of drefs; but, in Mr Gazette, a little regard to that particular is but a neceffary compliment to his miftrefs.

Hart. Stuff, Dick, ftuff; my daughter, knight, has had other guifu breeding; hey, you! Suck, come forward. Plain as a pike-ftaff, knight; all as nature made her; hey, Tim, no fians! prithee, Tim, off with thy lace and burn it; 'twill help to buy the licence; fhe'll not like thee a bit the better for that; hey, Suck! But, you knight, God

Dick

Dick, a toaſt and tankard would not be amiſs after our walk; hey, you?

Sir Greg. Good now, good now! what you will, Sir Penurious.

Hart. God, that's hearty, you! but we won't part the young couple, hey! I'll ſend Suck ſome bread and cheeſe in; hey, knight! At her, Tim! Come Dick; come, you knight. Did I ever tell you my courtſhip; hey, Dick? 'twill make you laugh.

Yeah. Not as I remember.

Sir Greg. Lack-a-day! let's have it.

Hart. You know my wife was blind, you knight?

Sir Greg. Good now! wonderful! not I.

Hart. Blind as a beetle when I married her, knight; hey, Dick! ſhe was drowned in our orchard; maid Beſs, knight, went to market, you Dick, and wife rambled into the orchard, and, ſouſe, dropped into the fiſh-pond; we found her out next day, but ſhe was dead as a herring; no help for that, Dick; buried her though; hey, you! ſhe was only daughter to Sir Triſtram Muckworm, you; rich enough, you, hey! God, you, what does ſhe do, you, but ſhe falls in love with young Sleek, her father's chaplain; hey, you! upon that what does me I, but ſlips on domine's robes, you; paſſed myſelf upon her for him, and we were tacked together, you knight, hey! God, though I believe ſhe never liked me; but what ſignifies that? hey, Dick! ſhe was rich, you! But, come, let's leave the children together.

Sir Greg. Sir, I wait on you.

Hart. Nay, pray ——

Sir Greg. Good now, good now! 'tis impoſſible!——

Hart. Pox of ceremony, you Dick! hey! God, knight, I'll tell you a ſtory: one of our ambaſſadors in France, you, a deviliſh polite fellow reckoned, Dick; God, you, what does the King of France do, but, ſays he, I'll try the manners of this fine gentleman: ſo, knight, going into a coach together, the king would have my lord go firſt: oh! an't pleaſe your majeſty, I can't indeed; you, hey, Dick! upon which, what does me the king, but he takes his arm thus, you Dick: am I the king of France or you? is it my coach or yours; and ſo puſhes him in thus. Hey, Dick!

Sir Greg. Good now, good now! he, he, he!

Hart.

Hart. God, Dick, I believe I have made a mistake here; I should have gone in first; hey, Dick! knight, God, you, beg pardon. Yes, your coach, not mine; your house, not mine; hey, knight!

Sir Greg. Wonderful! a merry man, Mr Jenkins.
[*Exeunt* the two Knights *and* Jenk.

Tim. Father and cousin are gone, fath and foul!

Jenny. I fancy my lover is a little puzzled how to begin. [*Aside.*

Tim. How —— Fath and foul I don't know what to say! [*Aside.*] How d'ye do, Miss Suck?

Jenny. Pretty well, thank you.

Tim. You have had a choice walk.—'Tis a rare day, fath and foul!

Jenny. Yes, the day's well enough.

Tim. Is your house a good way off here?

Jenny. Dree or four mile.

Tim. That's a long walk, fath!

Jenny. I make nothing of it, and back again.

Tim. Like enow. [*Whistles.*

Jenny. [*Sings.*

Tim. You have a rare pipe of your own, Miss.

Jenny. I can sing loud enough if I have a mind: but father don't love singing.

Tim. Like enow. [*Whistles.*

Jenny. And I an't over fond of whistling.

Tim. Hey, ay! like enow: and I am a bitter bad singer.

Jenny. Hey! ay, like enough.

Tim. Pray, Miss Suck, did ever any body make love to you before?

Jenny. Before when?

Tim. Before now.

Jenny. What if I won't tell you?

Tim. Why then you must let it alone, fath and foul!

Jenny. Like enough!

Tim. Pray, Miss Suck, did your father tell you any thing?

Jenny. About what?

Tim. About I.

Jenny. What should 'a tell?

Tim. Tell! why, as how I and father was come a wooing.

Jenny. Who?

Tim.

Tim. Why you! Could you like me for a sweet-heart, Miss Suck?

Jenny. I don't know.

Tim. Mayhap somebody may ha' got your good-will already?

Jenny. And what then?

Tim. Then! hey! I don't know: but, if you could fancy me ———

Jenny. For what?

Tim. For your true lover.

Jenny. Well, what then?

Tim. Then! hey! why, fath, we may chance to be married if the old folks agree together.

Jenny. And suppose I won't be married to you?

Tim. Nay, Miss Suck, I can't help it, fath and foul! But father and mother bid me come a-courting; and, if you won't ha' me, I'll tell father so.

Jenny. You are in a woundy hurry, methinks.

Tim. Not I, fath! you may stay as long as ———

Enter a Waiter.

Wait. There is a woman without wants to speak with Mr Timothy Gazette. [*Exit.*

Tim. That's I.—I am glad on't! [*Aside.*] Well, Miss Suck, your servant. You'll think about it, and let's know your mind when I come back!—God, I don't care whether she likes me or no; I dont like her half so well as Molly Pengrouse!—[*Aside*]. Well, your servant, Miss Suck! [*Exit.*

Jenny. Was there ever such an unlicked cub?—I don' think his fortune a sufficient reward for sacrificing my person to such a booby: but, as he has money enough, it shall go hard but I please myself! I fear I was a little too backward with my gentleman; but, however, a favourable answer to his last question will soon settle matters.

Enter Jenkins.

Jenk. Now, Jenny! what news child? are things fixed? are you ready for the nuptial knot?

Jenny. We are in a fair way: I thought to have quickened my swain's advances by a little affected coyness; but the trap would not take: I expect him back in a minute, and then leave it to my management.

Jenk.

Jenk. Where is he gone?
Jenny. The waiter called him to some woman.
Jenk. Woman! he neither knows or is known by any body here. What can this mean? no counter-plot! but, pox, that's impossible! you have not blabbed, Jenny?
Jenny. My interest would prevent me.
Jenk. Upon that security any woman may, I think, be trusted. I must after him, though. [*Exit.*
Jenny. I knew the time when Mr Jenkins would not have left me so hastily: 'tis odd, that the same cause that increases the passion in one sex should destroy it in the other; the reason is above my reach, but the fact I am a severe witness of: heigh-ho!

Enter Hartop (*Still as Sir* Penurious Trifle) *and Sir Gregory* Gazette.

Hart. And so, you knight, says he; you know, knight, what low dogs the ministers were then; how does your pot; a pot, you, that they put over the fire to broil broth and meat in; you have seen a pot, you knight? how does your pot boil these troublesome times? hey, you! God, my lord, says he, I don't know, I seldom go into my kitchen; a kitchen, you knight, is a place where they dress victuals! roast and boil, and so forth; God, says he, I seldom go into the kitchen; but, I suppose, the scum is uppermost still; hey, you knight!—What, God, hey! but where's your son, Sir Gregory?
Sir Greg. Good now, good now! where's Tim, Miss Sukey? lack-a-day! what's become of Tim?
Jenny. Gone out a tiny bit; he'll be here presently.
Sir Greg. Wonderful! good now, good now! well, and how, Miss Sukey, has Tim —— Has he —— Well, and what, you have —— Wonderful!

Enter a Servant with a letter.

Serv. Sir, I was commanded to deliver this into your own hands by Mr Jenkins.
Hart. Hey, you? what, a letter? God so! any answer, you? hey!
Serv. None, Sir. *Exit.*
Sir Greg. Lack-a-day, Sir Penurious is busy! Well, Miss, and did Tim do the thing?—did he please you?—come now, tell us the whole story! wonderful!—rare

news

news for Dame Winny!—ha! Tim's father's own son! but come, whisper!—ay!

Hart. [*Reads.*] "I have only time to tell you that your scheme is blasted: this instant I encountered Mrs Penelope Trifle with her niece: they will soon be with you."
——So then all's over! but let's see what expedition will do!——Well, you knight, hey! what, have they settled? Is the girl willing?

Sir Greg. Good now, good now! right as my leg! ah! Tim, little did I think——But, lack-a-day! I wonder where the boy is! let's seek him.

Hart. Agreed, you knight! hey! come.

Enter Jenkins.

Sir Greg. Lack-a-day! here's Mr Jenkins. Good now! have you seen Tim?

Jenk. Your curiosity shall be immediately satisfied; but I must first have a word with Sir Penurious.

Hart. Well, you! what, hey! any news, Dick?

Jenk. Better than you could hope! your rival is disposed of!

Hart. Disposed of! how?

Jenk. Married by this time, you rogue! the woman that wanted him was no other than Mally Pengrouse, she trudged it up all the way after him, as Tim says: I have recommended them to my chaplain, and before this the business is done.

Hart. Bravissimo! you rogue! but how shall I get off with the knight?

Jenk. Nay, that must be your contrivance.

Hart. I have it! Suppose I was to own the whole design to Sir Gregory, as our plan has not succeeded with his son, and, as he seems to have a tolerable regard for me, it is possible he may assist my scheme on Sir Penurious.

Jenk. 'Tis worth trying however:——but he comes.

Sir Greg. Well, good now! Mr Jenkins, have you seen Tim? I can't think where the boy——

Hart. 'Tis now time, Sir Gregory, to set you clear with respect to some particulars; I am now no longer Sir Penurious Trifle, but your friend and relation, Jack Hartop.

Sir Greg. Wonderful! good now, good now! cousin Hartop as I am a living man!——Hey!—well but, good now! how, Mr Jenkins, hey?

Vol. I.   L.   *Jenk.*

Jenk. The story, Sir Gregory, is rather too long to tell you now; but in two words, my friend Hartop has very long had a paſſion for Miſs Trifle, and was apprehenſive your ſon's application would deſtroy his views, which in order to defeat, he aſſumed the character of Sir Penurious; but he is ſo captivated with your integrity and friendſhip, that he rather chuſes to forego his own intereſt than interrupt the happineſs of your ſon.

Sir Greg. Wonderful! good now, good now! that's kind! who could have thought it, couſin Hartop? lack-a-day! well, but where's Tim? hey! good now! and who are you?

Jenk. This, Sir, is Jenny, the handmaid of the houſe.

Sir Greg. Wonderful! a peſtilent huſſey! Ah, Hartop, you are a wag! a pize of your pots and your royal oaks! lack-a-day! who could have thought—Ah! Jenny, you're a — [*Exit* Jenny.] But where's Tim?

Enter Robin.

Robin. Wounds, maſter never ſtir alive if maſter Tim has na gone and married Mally Pengrouſe!

Sir Greg. Wonderful! how, ſirrah, how? good now, good now! couſin Hartop.——Mally Pengrouſe! who the dickens is ſhe?

Robin. Maſter Timothy's ſweetheart in Cornwall.

Sir Greg. And how came ſhe here? lack-a-day, couſin!

Robin. She tramped it up after maſter: maſter Timothy is without, and ſays as how they be married: I wanted him to come in, but he's afraid you'll knock'n down.

Sir Greg. Knock'n down! good now! let me come at him! I'll——Ah, rogue! lack-a-day! couſin, ſhew me where he is! I'll——

Hart. Moderate your fury, good Sir Gregory; conſider, it is an evil without a remedy.

Sir Greg. But what will Dame Winny ſay? Good now! ſuch a diſparagement to——and then what will Sir Penu—us ſay? lack-a-day! I am almoſt diſtracted!—and you, ,ou lubberly dog! why did not you —— [*Exit* Robin.] I'll——ah! couſin Hartop, couſin Hartop! good now, good now!

Hart. Dear Sir, be calm; this is no ſuch ſurpriſing matter; we have ſuch inſtances in the newſpapers every day.

Sir Greg.

Sir Greg. Good now! no, coufin, no.

Hart. Indeed, Sir Gregory, it was but laſt week that Lord Lofty's fon married his mother's maid; and Lady Betty Forward run away, not a month ago, with her uncle's butler.

Sir Greg. Wonderful! what, in the news?——Good now, that's fome comfort, however;—but what will Sir Penurious——

Hart. As to that, leave him to me; I have a project to prevent his laughing at you, I'll warrant.

Sir Greg. But how? how, coufin Hartop, how?

Hart. Sir Gregory, d've think me your friend?

Sir Greg. Lack-a-day! ay, coufin, ay.

Hart. And would you, in return, ferve me in a circumſtance that can't injure yourſelf?

Sir Greg. Good now, to be ſure, coufin.

Hart. Will you then permit me to affume the figure of your fon, and fo pay my addreffes to Mifs Trifle?—I was pretty happy in the imitation of her father; and if I could impoſe upon your ſagacity, I ſhall find leſs difficulty with your brother knight.

Sir Greg. Good now! Tim! ah, you could not touch Tim.

Hart. I warrant you. But, fee, the young gentleman.

Enter Timothy.

Sir Greg. Ah, Tim, Tim! little did I——Good now, good now!

Tim. I could not help it now, fath and foul! but if you'll forgive me this time, I'll never do fo no more.

Sir Greg. Well, well, if thee can't forgive thyſelf, I can forgive thee; but thank my coufin Hartop.

Hart. Oh, Sir! if you are fatisfy'd, I am rewarded. I wiſh you joy; joy to you, child.

Sir Greg. Thanks, coufin Hartop.

Enter Waiter.

Wait. Sir, Mrs Penelope Trifle, with her niece, being come to town, and hearing your Worſhip was in the houſe, would be glad to pay you their compliments.

Sir Greg. Lack-a-day! wonderful!—here we are all topſy-turvey again!——What can be done now, coufin Hartop?

Hart.

Hart. Dick! shew the ladies in here; but delay them a little. The luckiest incident in the world, Sir Gregory!—If you will be kind enough to lend Jenkins your dress, and Master Timothy will lend me his, I'll make up matters in a moment.

Sir Greg. Ay, ay, cousin.

Tim. Faith and soul, you shall have mine sire——

Hart. No, no.—Step into the next room a minute, Sir Gregory.

Sir Greg. Ay, ay, where you will.

Tim. Faith, here will be choice sport. [*Exeunt.*

Enter Mrs Penelope and Suck, with Waiter.

Wait. The gentlemen will wait on you presently.—Would you chuse any refreshment?

Suck. A draught of ale, friend, for I'm main dry.

Mrs Pen. Fie! sie! niece! is that liquor for a young lady? don't disparage your family and breeding. The person is to be born that ever saw me touch any thing stronger than water till I was three-and-twenty.

Suck. Troth, aunt, that's so long ago, that I think there's few people alive who can remember what you did then.

Mrs Pen. How! gillflirt!—none of your fleers! I am glad here's a husband coming that will take you down: Your tantrums!—You are grown too headstrong and robust for me.

Suck. Gad, I believe you would be glad to be taken down the same way!

Mrs Pen. Oh! you are a pert——But see your lover approaches. Now Sukey, be careful, child: None of your——

Enter Jenkins as Sir Gregory, and Hartop as Tim.

Jenk. Lack-a-day, lady! I rejoice to see you! wonderful! and your niece!—Tim, the ladies.

Hart. Your servant, Mistress!—I am glad to see you, Miss Suck. [*Salutes her*]. Faith and soul, Mistress Suck's a fine young woman, more or less!

Suck. Yes, I am well enough, I believe.

Jenk. But, Lady, where's my brother Trifle! where is Sir Penurious?

Suck.

Suck. Father's at home, in expectation of you; and aunt and I be come to town to make preparations.

Jenk. Ay, wonderful!—Pray, Lady, shall I, good now! crave a word in private? Tim, will you and your sweetheart draw back a little?

Hart. Yes, father: Come, Miss, will you jog a tiny bit this way?

Suck. With all my heart.

Jenk. There is, Lady, a wonderful affair has happen'd, good now! Son Tim has fallen in love with a young woman at his uncle's, and 'tis partly to prevent bad consequences, that I am, lack-a-day! so hasty to match him: and one of my men, good now! tells me that he has seen the wench since we have been in town; she has follow'd us here, sure as a gun, lady! If Tim sees the girl, he'll never marry your niece.

Mrs Pen. It is indeed, Sir Gregory Gazette, a most critical conjuncture, and requires the most mature deliberation.

Jenk. ——Deliberation! lack-a-day, Lady, whilst we deliberate, the boy will be lost.

Mrs Pen. Why, Sir Gregory Gazette, what operations can we determine upon?

Jenk. Lack-a-day! I know but one.

Mrs Pen. Administer your proposition, Sir Gregory Gazette: you will have my concurrence, Sir, in any thing that does not derogate from the regulations of conduct; for it would be most preposterous in one of my character to deviate from the strictest attention.

Jenk. Lack-a-day, Lady, no such matter is wanted. But, good now, could not we tack the young couple together directly? your brother and I have already agreed.

Mrs Pen. Are the previous preliminaries settled, Sir Gregory Gazette?

Jenk. Good now! as firm as a rock, lady.

Mrs Pen. Why then, to preserve your son, and accomplish the union between our families, I have no objections to the acceleration of their nuptials, provided the child is inclined, and a minister may be procur'd.

Jenk. Wonderful! you are very good, good now! there has been one match already in the house to-day; we may have the same parson. Here! Tim! and young gentlewoman

woman!—Well, Mifs! wonderful, and how? has Tim? he, boy! Is not Mifs a fine young lady?

Hart. Fath and foul, father, Mifs is a charming young woman; all red and white, like Nelly—Hum!

Jenk. Hoih, Tim! Well, and Mifs, how does my boy? he's an honeft hearty lad? Has he, good now! had the art? How d'ye like him, young gentlewoman?

Seek. Likes? well enough, I think.

Jenk. Why then, Mifs, with your leave, your aunt and I here have agreed, if you are willing, to have the wedding over directly.

Seek. Ged! with all my heart. Afk the young man.

Hart. Fath and foul, juft as you pleafe; to-day, to-morrow, or when you will, more or lefs.

Jenk. Good now, good now! then get you in there, there you will find one to do your bufinefs; wonderful! matters will foon be managed within. Well, lady, this was, good now, fo kind! Lack-a-day! I verily believe if Dame Winny was dead, that I fhould be glad to lead up fuch another dance with you, lady.

Mrs Pen. You are, Sir, fomething too precipitate: Nor would there, did circumftances concur, as you infinuate, be fo abfolute a certitude, that I, who have rejected fo many matches, fhould inftantaneoufly fuccumb.

Jenk. Lack-a-day, lady, good now! I——

Mrs Pen. No, Sir; I would have you inftructed, that had not Penelope Trifle made irrefragable refolutions, fhe need not in long have preferved her family furname.

Jenk. Wonderful! why, I was only——

Mrs Pen. Nor has the title of Lady Gazette fuch refplendent charms, or fuch bewitching allurements, as to throw me at once into the arms of Sir Gregory.

Jenk. Good now! who fays——

Mrs Pen. Could wealth, beauty, or titles fuperior to perhaps——

Enter Sir Gregory, Roger, *and* Tim.

Tim. Yes, indeed, father; Mr Hartop knew on't as well as I, and Mr Jenkins got us a parfon.

Sir Greg. Good now, good now! a rare couple of friends! But I'll be even with them! I'll mar their market! Mafter Jenkins, you have fobb'd me finely.

Jenk. Lack-a-day, what's the matter now?

Sir Greg.

Sir Greg. Come, come, none of your lack-a-days! none of your gambols, nor your tricks to me: Good now, good now! give me my cloaths! here, take your tawdry trappings, I have found you out at last: I'll be no longer your property.

Jenk. Wonderful! what's all this, lady? Good now, good now! what's here! a ſtage play?

Sir *reg.* Play me no plays; but give me my wig ' and your precious friend my loving couſin (pize on the kindred) let 'n—

Jenk. Good now, good now! what are theſe folks? as ſure as a gun, they're mad.

Sir Greg. Mad! no, no; we are neither mad nor fools: no thanks to you, though.

Mrs Pen. What is all this? can you unravel this perplexity, untwine this myſtery, Sir Gregory Gazette?

Sir Greg. He Sir Gregory Gazette? Lack-a-day, lady! you are trick'd, impoſed upon, bamboozl'd: Good now, good now! 'tis I am Sir Gregory Gazette.

Mrs Pen. How!

Tim. Foth and foul, 'tis true, miſtreſs; and I am his ſon Tim, and will ſwear it.

Mrs Pen. Why is'nt Mr Timothy Gazette with my niece Suſannah Trifle?

Tim. Who, me! Lord, no, 'tis none of I, it is couſin Hartop in my cloaths.

Mrs Pen. What's this? and pray, who—

Jenk. Why, as I ſee the affair is concluded, you may, Madam, call me Jenkins. Come, Hartop, you may now throw off your diſguiſe; the knight had like to have embarraſſed us.

Mrs Pen. How, Mr Jenkins! and would you, Sir, participate of a plot to—

Hart. Madam, in the iſſue, your family will, I hope, have no great reaſon to repent. I always had the greateſt veneration for Miſs Penelope Trifle's underſtanding; the higheſt eſteem! for her virtues can entitle me to the honour of being regarded as her relation.

Mrs Pen. Sir, I ſhall determine on nothing, 'till I am appriſed of my brother's reſolution.

Hart. For that we muſt wait. Sir Gregory, I muſt intreat you and your ſon's pardon for ſome little liberties I have taken with you both. Mr Jenkins, I have the higheſt

obligation

obligation to your friendship; and, Miss, when we become a little better acquainted, I flatter myself the change will not prove unpleasing.

Sash. I know nothing at all about it.

Hart. Sir Gregory, we shall have your company at dinner?

Sir Greg. Lack-a-day, no, no, that boy has spoil'd my stomach—Come, Tim, fetch thy crib, and let us be jogging towards Wales ; but how thou wilt get off with thy mother——

Tim. Never fear, father——

Since you have been pleas'd our nuptial knot to bless,
We shall be happy all our lives—more or less——

THE

THE ENGLISHMAN
RETURNED FROM PARIS:

BEING THE SEQUEL TO

THE ENGLISHMAN IN PARIS.

A FARCE.

IN TWO ACTS.

PROLOGUE.

Spoken by Mr Foote.

OF all the passions that possess mankind,
The love of novelty rules most the mind.
In search of this, from realm to realm we roam,
Our fleets come fraught with every folly home.
From Lybia's deserts hostile brutes advance,
And dancing dogs in droves skip here from France.
From Indian lands gigantic forms appear,
Striking our British breasts with awe and fear,
As once the Lilliputians——Gulliver.
Not only objects that affect the sight,
In foreign arts and artists we delight.
Near to that spot where Charles bestrides a horse,
In humble prose the place is Charing Cross;
Close by the margin of a kennel's side,
A dirty dismal entry opens wide;
There, with hoarse voice, check shirt, and callous hand,
Duff's Indian English trader takes his stand,
Surveys each passenger with curious eyes,
And rustic Roger falls an easy prize;
Here's China porcelain that Chelsea yields,
And India handkerchiefs from Spitalfields;
With Turkey carpets that from Wilton came,
And Spanish rocks and blades from Birmingham.
Factors are forced to favour this deceit,
And English goods are smuggled through the street.
The rude to polish, and the fair to please,
'The hero of to-night has cross'd the seas:
Though to be born a Briton be his crime,
He's manufactur'd in another clime.
'Tis Buck begs leave once more to come before ye,
The little subject of a former story;
How chang'd, how fashion'd, whether brute or beau,
We trust the following scenes will fully shew.
For them and him we your indulgence crave,
'Tis ours still to fix on, and yours to save.

EPILOGUE.

EPILOGUE.

Spoken by Mrs Bellamy.

AMONG the arts to make a piece go down,
And fix the fickle favour of the town,
An Epilogue is deem'd the surest way
To atone for all the errors of the play.
Thus, when pathetic strains have made you cry,
In trips the Comic Muse, and wipes your eye.
With equal reason, when she has made you laugh,
Melpomene should send you snivelling off.
But our Bard, unequal to the task,
Rejects the dagger, and retains the mask.
Fain would he send you cheerful home to-night,
And harmless mirth by honest means excite;
Scorning with luscious phrase, or double sense,
To raise a laughter at the fair's expence.
What method shall we chuse your taste to hit?
Will no one lend our bard a little wit?
Thank ye, kind souls, I'll take it from the pit.
The piece concluded, and the curtain down,
Up starts that fatal phalanx, call'd The Town:
In full assembly weighs our author's fate,
And Surly thus commences the debate:
Pray, among friends, does not this poisoning scene
The sacred right of Tragedy profane?
If Farce may mimic thus her awful bowl;
Oh fie, all wrong, fark naught, upon my foul!
Then Buck cries, Billy, can it be in nature?
Not the least likeness in a single feature,
My Lord, Lord love him, 'tis a precious piece;
Let's come on Friday night and have a hiss.
To this a peroquier assents with joy,
Pas comme il affront les François, moi, ma foi.
In such distress, what can the poet do?
Where seek for shelter when those foes pursue?
He dares demand protection, Sirs, from you.

DRAMATIS

DRAMATIS PERSONÆ.

At Covent-Garden.

Buck,	— —	Mr Booth.
Crab,	—	Mr Shuter.
Lord John,	—	Mr Waite.
Macrothen,	—	Mr Saville.
Racket,	— —	Mr Cushing.
Tallyhoe,	—	Mr Cautherly.
Latitat,	— —	Mr Dunstall.
Sergeon,	—	Mr Wignell.
Lucinda,	— —	Mrs Bulkley.

La Jaquet, La Loire, Beaumie, and Servants.

ACT I.

Crab discovered reading.

"AND I do constitute my very good friend, Giles Crab, Esq. of St Martin in the Fields, executor to this my will; and do appoint him guardian to my ward Lucinda; and do submit to his direction the management of all my affairs, till the return of my son from his travels; whom I do intreat my said executor, in consideration of our ancient friendship, to advise, to counsel, &c. &c.

John Buck.

A good, pretty legacy! Let's see, I find myself heir, by this generous devise of my very good friend, to ten actions at common law, nine suits in Chancery, the conduct of a boy, bred a booby at home, and finished a fop abroad; together with the direction of a marriageable, and therefore an unmanageable wench; and all this to an old fellow of sixty-six, who heartily hates business, is tired of the world, and despises every thing in it. Why, how the devil came I to merit——

Enter Servant.

Ser. Mr Latitat, of Staple's Inn.
Crab. So, here begin my plagues. Shew the hound in.

Enter Latitat, with a bag, &c.

Lat. I would, Mr Crab, have attended your summons immediately, but I was obliged to sign judgment in error at the Common Pleas; sue out of the Exchequer a writ of *quo minus*, and surrender in *banco regis* the defendant, before the return of the *sci fa*, to discharge the bail.

Crab. Prithee, man, none of thy unintelligible law jargon to me; but tell me in the language of common sense and thy country what I am to do.

Lat. Why, Mr Crab, as you are already possessed of a probat, and letters of administration *de bonis* are granted, you may sue, or, be sued; I hold it sound doctrine for no executor to discharge debts, without a receipt upon record: this can be obtained by no means but by an action. Now actions, Sir, are of various kinds, there are special actions,

tions, actions on the case, or *assumpsits*, actions of trover, actions of *clausum fregit*, actions of battery, actions of—

Crab. Hey, the devil, where's the fellow running now?—But hark'ee, Latitat, why I thought all our law proceedings were directed to be in English.

Lat. True, Mr Crab.

Crab. And what do you call all this stuff, ha?

Lat. English.

Crab. The devil you do.

Lat. Vernacular, upon my honour, Mr Crab. For as Lord Coke describes the common law to be the perfection—

Crab. So, here's a fresh deluge of impertinence. A truce to thy authorities, I beg; and as I find it will be impossible to understand thee without an interpreter, if you will meet me at five, at Mr Brief's chambers, why, if you have any thing to say, he will translate it for me.

Lat. Mr Brief, Sir, and translate, Sir!—Sir, I would have you to know, that no practitioner in Westminster-hall gives clearer——

Crab. Sir, I believe it; for which reason I have referred you to a man who never goes into Westminster-hall.

Lat. A bad proof of his practice, Mr Crab.

Crab. A good one of his principles, Mr Latitat.

Lat. Why, Sir, do you think that a lawyer——

Crab. Zounds, Sir, I never thought about a lawyer.—The law is an oracular idol, you are explanatory ministers; nor should any of my own private concerns have made me bow to your beastly *Baal*. I had rather lose a cause than contest it. And had not this old, doating dunce, Sir John Buck, plagued me with the management of his money, and the care of his booby boy, Bedlam should sooner have had me than the bar.

Lat. Bedlam, the bar! Since, Sir, I am provoked, I don't know what your choice may be, or what your friends may chuse for you; I wish I was your *prochein ami*: but I am under some doubts as to the sanity of the testator, otherwise he could not have chosen for his executor, under the sanction of the law, a person who despises the law. And the law, give me leave to tell you, Mr Crab, is the bulwark, the fence, the protection, the *sine qua non*, the *ne plus ultra*——

Crab. Mercy, good six and eight-pence.

Lat.

Lat. The defence and offence, the by which, and the whereby, the statute common and customary, or as Plowden classically and elegantly expresses it, 'tis

Mos communis vetus mores, consulta senatus,
Hæc tria jus statuunt terra Britanna tibi.

Crab. Zounds, Sir, among all your laws, are there none to protect a man in his own house?

Lat. Sir, a man's house is his *castellum*, his castle; and so tender is the law of any infringement of that sacred right, that any attempt to invade it by force, fraud, or violence, clandestinely, or *vi et armis*, is not only deemed *felonies*, but *burglarias*. Now, Sir, a burglary may be committed either upon the dwelling or out-house.

Crab. O lawd! O lawd!

Enter Servant.

Serv. Your clerk, Sir——The parties, he says, are all in waiting at your chambers.

Lat. I come. I will but just explain to Mr Crab the nature of a burglary, as it has been described by a late statute.

Crab. Zounds, Sir, I have not the least curiosity.
Lat. Sir, but every gentleman should know—
Crab. I won't know. Besides, your clients—
Lat. O, they may stay. I shan't take up five minutes, Sir—A burglary—
Crab. Not an instant.
Lat. By the common law—
Crab. I'll not hear a word.
Lat. It was but a *clausum fregit*.
Crab. Dear Sir, be gone.
Lat. But by the late acts of par——
Crab. Help, you dog. Zounds, Sir, get out of my house.

Serv. Your clients, Sir——

Crab. Push him out [*the lawyer talking all the while*]. So, ho! Hark'ee, rascal, if you suffer that fellow to enter my doors again, I'll strip and discard you the very minute. [*Exit Serv.*]—This is but the beginning of my torments. But that I expect the young whelp from abroad, every instant, I'd fly for it myself, and quit the kingdom at once.

Enter Servant.

Serv. My young mafter's travelling tutor, Sir, juft arrived.

Crab. Oh, then I fuppofe, the blockhead of a baronet is clofe at his heels. Shew him in. This bear-leader, I reckon now, is either the clumfy curate of the knight's own parifh church, or fome needy highlander, the out-caft of his country, who, with the pride of a German baron, the poverty of a French marquis, the addrefs of a Swifs foldier, and the learning of an academy ufher, is to give our heir apparent politenefs, tafte, literature; a perfect knowledge of the world, and of himfelf.

Enter Macrochen.

Mac. Maifter Crab, I am your devoted fervant.

Crab. Oh, a Britifh child, by the mefs.—Well, where's your charge?

Mac. O, the young baronet is o' the road. I was mighty afraid he had o'er ta'en me; for between Canterbury and Rochefter, I was ftopt, and robb'd by a highwayman.

Crab. Robb'd! what the devil could he rob you of?

Mac. In gude troth, not a mighty booty. Buchanan's hiftory, Lauder againft Milton, and two pound of high-dried Glafgow.

Crab. A travelling equipage. Well, and what's become of your cub? Where have you left him?

Mac. Mein you Sir Charles? I left him at Calais with another young nobleman, returning from his travels. But why caw ye him cub, Maifter Crab? In gude troth there's a meeghty alteration.

Crab. Yes, yes, I have a fhrewd guefs at his improvements.

Mac. He's quite a phenomenon.

Crab. Oh, a comet, I dare fwear, but not an unufual one at Paris. The Fauxbourg of St Germains fwarms with fuch, to the no fmall amufement of our very good friends the French.

Mac. Oh, the French were mighty fond of him.

Crab. But as to the language, I fuppofe he's a perfect mafter of that.

Mac.

Mac. He cancew for eught that he need, but he is na quite maister of the accent.

Crab. A most astonishing progress!

Mac. Suspend your judgement awhile, and you'll find him all you wish, allowing for the sallies of juvenility; and must take the vanity to myself of being, in a great measure, the author.

Crab. Oh, if he be but a faithful copy of the admirable original, he must be a finished piece.

Mac. You are pleased to compliment.

Crab. Not a whit. Well, and what—I suppose you, and your—what's your name?

Mac. Mocrothm, at your service.

Crab. Macrothen! Hum! You and your pupil agreed very well?

Mac. Perfectly. The young gentleman is of an amiable disposition.

Crab. Oh, ay: and it would be wrong to sour his temper. You knew your duty better, I hope, than to contradict him.

Mac. It was na for me, Maister Crab.

Crab. Oh, by no means, Maister Macruthen; all your business was to keep him out of 'frays; to take care, for the sake of his health, that his wine was genuine, and his mistresses as they should be. You pimp'd for him I suppose?

Mac. Pimp for him! D'ye mean to affront—

Crab. To suppose the contrary would be the affront, Mr Tutor. What, man, you know the world. 'T..s not by contradiction, but by compliance, that men make their fortunes. And was it for you to thwart the humour of a lad upon the threshold of ten thousand pounds a year?

Mac. Why, to be sure, great allowances must be made.

Crab. No doubt, no doubt.

Mac. I see, Maister Crab, you know mankind, you are Sir John Buck's executor.

Crab. True.

Mac. I have a little thought that may be useful to us both.

Crab. As how?

Mac. Could na we contrive to make a hond o' the young baronet?

Crab. Explain,

Mac.

Mac. Why you, by the will, have the care o' the cash: and I can make a shift to manage the lad.

Crab. Oh, I conceive you. And so between us both, we may contrive to ease him of that inheritance which he knows not how properly to employ; and apply it to our own use. You do know how.

Mac. Ye ha hit it.

Crab. Why what a superlative rascal art thou, thou inhospitable villain! Under the roof, and in the presence, of thy benefactor's representative, with almost his ill-bestowed bread in thy mouth, art thou plotting the perdition of his only child! And, from what part of my life didst thou derive a hope of my compliance with such a hellish scheme?

Mac. Maister Crab, I am of a nation——

Crab. Of known honour and integrity; I allow it. The kingdom you have quitted, in consigning the care of its monarch, for ages, to our predecessors, in preference to its proper subjects, has given you a brilliant panegyric, that no other people can parallel.

Mac. Why, to be sure——

Crab. And one happiness it is, that though national glory can beam a brightness on particulars, the crimes of individuals can never reflect a disgrace upon their country. Thy apology but aggravates thy guilt.

Mac. Why, Maister Crab, I——

Crab. Guilt and confusion choak thy utterance. Avoid my sight. Vanish!—[*Exit Mac.*]—A fine fellow this, to protect the person, inform the inexperience, direct and moderate the desires of an unbridled boy! But can it be strange, whilst the parent negligently accepts a superficial recommendation to so important a trust, that the person whose wants perhaps, more than his abilities make desirous of it, should confider the youth as a kind of property, and not consider what to make him, but what to make of him; and thus prudently lay a foundation for his future sordid hopes, by a criminal compliance with the lad's present prevailing passions? But vice and folly rule the world. Without, there!—[*Enter Serv.*]—Rascal, where d'you run, blockhead? Bid the girl come hither.—Fresh instances, every moment, fortify my abhorrence, my detestation of mankind. This turn may be term'd misanthropy; and imputed to chagrin and disappointment. But it can only be be by those fools, who, through softness or ignorance, regard the faults of others, like their own, through the wrong end of the perspective.

Enter Lucinda.

So, what, I suppose your spirits are all afloat. You have heard your fellow's coming.

Luc. If you had your usual discernment, Sir, you would distinguish, in my countenance, an expression very different from that of joy.

Crab. Oh, what, I suppose your monkey has broke his chain, or your parrot died in moulting.

Luc. A person less censorious than Mr Crab might assign a more generous motive for my distress.

Crab. Distress! a pretty, poetical phrase. What motive canst thou have for distress? Has not Sir John Buck's death assured thy fortune? and art not thou——

Luc. By that very means, a helpless, unprotected orphan.

Crab. Pho', prithee, wench, none of thy romantic cant to me. What, I know the sex: the objects of every woman's wish are property and power. The first you have, and the second you won't be long without; for here's a puppy riding post to put on your chains.

Luc. It would appear affectation not to understand you. And, to deal freely, it was upon that subject I wish'd to engage you.

Crab. Your information was needless; I knew it.

Luc. Nay, but why so severe? I did flatter myself that the very warm recommendation of your deceased friend would have abated a little of that rigour.

Crab. No wheedling, Lucy. Age and contempt have long shut these gates against flattery and dissimulation. You have no sex for me. Without preface, speak your purpose.

Luc. What then, in a word, is your advice with regard to my marrying Sir Charles Buck?

Crab. And do you seriously want my advice?

Luc. Most sincerely.

Crab. Then you are a blockhead. Why, where could you mend yourself? Is not he a fool, a fortune, and in love? —Look'ee, girl.—[*Enter Servant*]—Who sent for you, Sir?

Serv. Sir, my young master's post chaise is broke down,

at the corner of the street, by a coal cart. His cloaths are all dirt, and he swears like a trooper.

Crab. Ay! Why then carry the chaise to the coach-maker's, his coat to a scowrer's, and him before a justice.—Prithee, why dost trouble me? I suppose you would not meet your gallant.

Luc. Do you think I should?

Crab. No, retire. And if this application for my advice is not a copy of your countenance, a mask; if you are obedient, I may yet set you right.

Luc. I shall, with pleasure, follow your directions.

[*Exit.*

Crab. Yes, so long as they correspond with your own inclination. Now we shall see what Paris has done for this puppy. But here he comes; light as the cork in his heels, or the feather in his hat.

Enter Buck, *Lord* John, La Loire, Bearnois, *and* Macrothen.

Buck. Not a word, mi Lor, jurais, it is not to be supported!——after being rompu tout vif, disjointed by that execrable pavé, to be tumbled into a kennel by a filthy charbonnier; a dirty retailer of sea-coal, morbleu!

Ld. J. An accident that might have happened any where, Sir Charles.

Buck. And then the hideous hootings of that canaille, that murderous mob, with the barbarous—Monsieur in the mud, huzza! Ah, *pais sauvage, barbare, inhospitable!* ah, uh, *qu'est ce que nous avons?* Who?

Mar. That is Maister Crab, your father's executor.

Buck. Ha, ha. *Serviteur très humble, monsieur.* Eh bien! What! is he dumb? Mac, my Lor, *mort de ma vie,* the veritable *Jack-Roast-beef* of the French comedy. Ha, ha, how do you do, *Monsieur-Jack-Roast-beef,* ha, ha?

Crab. Prithee take a turn or two round the room.

Buck. A turn or two! *Volontiers.* Eh bien! Well, have you, in your life, seen any thing so, ha, ha, hey!

Crab. Never. I hope you had not many spectators of your tumble.

Buck. Pourquoi? Why so?

Crab. Because I would not have the public curiosity forestalled. I can't but think, in a country so fond of

Strange

strange sights, if you were kept up a little, you would bring a great deal of money.

Buck. I don't know, my dear, what my person would produce in this country, but the counter-part of your very grotesque figure has been extremely beneficial to the comedians from whence I came. *N'est ce pas vrai, mi Lor?* Ha, ha.

Ld. J. The resemblance does not strike me. Perhaps I may seem singular; but the particular customs of particular countries, I own, never appeared to me as proper objects of ridicule.

Buck. Why so?

Ld. J. Because in this case it is impossible to have a rule for your judgement. The forms and customs which climate, constitution, and government have given to our kingdom can never be transplanted with advantage to another, founded on different principles. And thus, though the habits and manners of different countries may be directly opposite, yet, in my humble conception, they may be strictly, because naturally, right.

C. ab. Why there are some glimmerings of common sense about this young thing. Harkee, child, by what accident did you stumble upon this blockhead?—[*to* Buck.]—I suppose the line of your understanding is too short to fathom the depth of your companion's reasoning.

Buck. My dear. [*gapes.*]

Crab. I say, you can draw no conclusion from the above premises.

Buck. Who I? Damn your premises, and conclusions too. But this I conclude from what I have seen, my dear, that the French are the first people in the universe; that, in the arts of living, they do or ought to give laws to the whole world; and that whosoever would either eat, drink, dress, dance, fight, sing, or even sneeze, *avec elegance*, must go to Paris to learn it. This is my creed.

Crab. And these precious principles you are come here to propagate.

Buck. C'est vrai, Monsieur Crab: and with the aid of these brother missionaries, I have no doubt of making a great many proselytes. And now for a detail of their qualities. *Brownois, avancez.* This is an officer of my household, unknown to this country.

Crab. And what may he be?—I'll humour the puppy.

Buck.

Buck. This is my Swiſs Porter. *Tenez vous droit, Bearnois.* There's a fierce figure to guard the gate of an hotel.

Crab. What, do you ſuppoſe we have no porters?

Buck. Yes, you have dunces that open doors; a drudgery that this fellow does by deputy. But for intrepidity in denying a diſagreeable viſiter; for politeneſs in introducing a miſtreſs, acuteneſs in diſcerning, and conſtancy in excluding a dun, a greater genius never came from the Cantons.

Crab. Aſtoniſhing qualities!

Buck. Retirez, *Bearnois.* But here's a *bijou,* here's a jewel indeed! *Venez ici, mon cher La Loire. Comment trouvez vous à Paris ici?*

La L. Très bien.

Buck. Very well. Civil creature! This, Monſieur Crab, is my cook *La Loire,* and for *hors d'oeuvres, entre rôtis, ragouts, entremets,* and the diſpoſition of a deſert, Paris never ſaw his parallel.

Crab. His wages, I ſuppoſe, are proportioned to his merit.

Buck. A bagatelle, a trifle. Abroad but a bare two hundred. Upon his cheerful compliance, in coming hither into exile with me, I have indeed doubled his ſtipend.

Crab. You could do no leſs.

Buck. And now, Sir, to complete my equipage, *regardez* Monſieur *La Jonquil,* my firſt *valet de chambre,* excellent in every thing; but *pour l'accommodage,* for decorating the head, inimitable. In one word, *La Jonquil* ſhall, for fifty to five, knot, twiſt, tye, frize, cut, curl, or comb with any *garçon perruquier,* from the Land's End to the Orkneys.

Crab. Why, what an infinite fund of public ſpirit muſt you have, to drain your purſe, mortify your inclination, and expoſe your perſon, for the mere improvement of your countrymen?

Buck. Oh, I am a very Roman for that. But at preſent I had another reaſon for returning.

Crab. Ay, what can that be?

Buck. Why, I find there is a likelihood of ſome little fracas between us. But, upon my ſoul, we muſt be very brutal to quarrel with the dear agreeable creatures for a trifle.

Crab.

Crab. They have your affections then.

Buck. De tout mon cœur. From the infinite civility shewn to us in France, and their friendly professions in favour of our country, they can never intend us an injury.

Crab. Oh, you have hit their humour to a hair. But I can have no longer patience with the puppy. Civility and friendship, you booby! Yes, their civility at Paris has not left you a guinea in your pocket, nor would their friendship to your nation leave it a foot of land in the universe.

Buck. Lord John, this is a strange old fellow. Take my word for it, my dear, you mistake this thing egregiously. But all you English are constitutionally sullen.— November fogs, with salt boil'd beef, are most cursed recipes for good-humour, or a quick apprehension. Paris is the place. 'Tis there men laugh, love, and live! *Vive l'amour! Sans amour, et sans jes désirs, on cœur est bien moins heureux qu'il ne pense.*

Crab. Now would not any soul suppose that this yelping hound had a real relish for the country he has quitted?

Buck. A mighty unnatural supposition, truly.

Crab. Foppery and affectation all.

Buck. And you really think Paris a kind of purgatory, ha, my dear?

Crab. To thee the most solitary spot upon earth, my dear.—Familiar puppy!

Buck. Whimsical enough. But come, *pour passer le tems*, let us, old Diogenes, enter into a little debate. Mi Lor, and you, Macruthen, determine the dispute between that source of delights, *ce paradis de plaisirs*, and this cave of ears, this seat of scurvy and the spleen.

Mac. Let us heed them weal, my Lord. Maister Crab has met with his match.

Buck. And first for the great pleasure of life, the pleasure of the table; ah, *quelle différence!* The eafe, the wit, the wine, the *badinage*, the *persifflage*, the *double entendre*, the *chansons à boire*. Oh, what delicious moments have I pass'd *chez madame la duchesse de Barbouillac*.

Crab. Your mistress, I suppose.

Buck. Who, I! *Fi donc!* How is it possible for a woman of her rank to have a *penchant* for me? Hey, Mac.

Mac. Sir Charles is too much a man of honour to blab.
But,

But, to say truth, the whole city of Paris thought as much.

Crab. A precious fellow this!

Buck. Taisez vous, Mac. But we lose the point in view. Now, Monsieur Crab, let me conduct you to what you call an entertainment. And first, the melancholy mistress is fixed in her chair, where, by the bye, she is condemned to do more drudgery than a dray-horse. Next proceeds the master, to marshal the guests, in which is much caution is necessary as at a coronation, with, "My lady, sit here," and, "Sir Thomas, sit there," till the length of the ceremony, with the length of the grace, have destroyed all apprehensions of the meat burning your mouths.

Mac. Bravo, bravo! Did I na' say Sir Charles was a phœnomenon?

Crab. Peace, puppy.

Buck. Then, in solemn silence, they proceed to demolish the substantials, with, perhaps, an occasional interruption, of, "Here's to you friends," "Hob or nob," "Your love and mine." Pork succeeds to beef, pies to puddings; the cloth is removed; madam, drenched with a bumper, drops a curtesy, and departs; leaving the jovial host, with his sprightly companions, to tobacco, port, and politics. *Voilà un repas à la mode d'Angleterre,* Monfieur Crab.

Crab. It is a thousand pities that your father is not a living witness of these prodigious improvements.

Buck. C'est vrai à propos, he is dead, as you say, and you are——

Crab. Against my inclination, his executor.

Buck. Peut être; well, and——

Crab. Oh, my task will soon determine. One article, indeed, I am strictly enjoined to see performed, your marriage with your old acquaintance Lucinda.

Buck. Ha, ha, la petite Lucinde! Et comment—

Crab. Prithee, peace, and hear me. She is bequeathed conditionally, that if you refuse to marry her, twenty thousand pounds; and if she rejects you, which I suppose she will have the wisdom to do, only five.

Buck. Reject me! Very probable, hey, Mac! But could we not have an *entrevûe?*

Crab. Who's there? Let Lucinda know we expect her.

Mac. Had na' ye better, Sir Charles, equip yourself in a more suitable garb, upon a first visit to your mistress?

Crab.

Crab. Oh, such a figure and address can derive no advantage from dress.
Buck. Serviteur. But, however, Mac's hint may not be so *mal à propos. Allons, Jonquil, je m'en vais m'habiller.* Mi Lor, shall I trespass upon your patience. My toilet is but the work of ten minutes. Mac, dispose of my domestics *à leur aise*, and then attend me with my portfeuille, and read, while I dress, those remarks I made in my last voyage from Fontainbleau to Compeigne.

   Serviteur, Messieurs;
    Car le bon vin
     Du matin
   Sortant du tonneau,
   Vaut bien mieux que
     Le Latin
   De toute la Sorbonne.   [*Exit.*

Crab. This is the most consummate coxcomb! I told the fool of a father what a puppy Paris would produce him; but travel is the word, and the consequence, an importation of every foreign folly; and thus the plain persons and principles of old England are so confounded and jumbled with the excrementitious growth of every climate, that we have lost all our ancient characteristic, and are become a bundle of contradictions, a piece of patch-work, a mere harlequin's coat.

Ld. J. Do you suppose then, Sir, that no good may be obtained——

Crab. Why, prithee, what have you gained?

Ld. J. I should be sorry my acquisitions were to determine the debate. But do you think, Sir, the shaking off some native qualities, and the being made more sensible, from comparison of certain national and constitutional advantages, objects unworthy the attention?

Crab. You shew the favourable side, young man; but how frequently are substituted for national prepossessions, always harmless, and often happy, guilty and unnatural prejudices!—Unnatural!—For the wretch who is weak and wicked enough to despise his country, sins against the most laudable laws of nature; he is a traitor to the community where Providence has placed him; and should be denied those social benefits he has rendered himself unworthy to partake. But sententious lectures are ill calculated for your time of life.

            Ld. J.

Ld. J. I differ from you here, Mr Crab. Principles that call for perpetual prastice cannot be too soon received. I sincerely thank you, Sir, for this communication, and should be happy to have always near me so moral a monitor.

Crab. You are indebted to France for her flattery. But I leave you with a lady where it will be better employed.

Enter Lucinda.

Crab. This young man waits here till your puppy is powdered. You may ask him after your French acquaintance. I know nothing of him; but he does not seem to be altogether so great a fool as your fellow. [*Exit.*

Luc. I'm afraid, Sir, you have had but a disagreeable tête-à-tête.

Ld. J. Just the contrary, Madam. By good sense, tinged with singularity, we are entertained as well as improved. For a lady, indeed, Mr Crab's manners are rather too rough.

Luc. Not a jot; I am familiarized to 'em, I know his integrity, and can never be disobliged by his sincerity.

Ld. J. This declaration is a little particular, from a lady who must have received her first impressions in a place remarkable for its delicacy to the fair sex. But good sense can conquer even early habits.

Luc. This compliment I can lay no claim to. The former part of my life procured me but very little indulgence. The pittance of knowledge I possess was taught me by a very severe mistress, Adversity. But you, Sir, are too well acquainted with Sir Charles Buck not to have known my situation.

Ld. J. I have heard your story, Madam, before I had the honour of seeing you. It was affecting: you'll pardon the declaration; it now becomes interesting. However, it is impossible I should not congratulate you on the near approach of the happy catastrophe.

Luc. Events that depend upon the will of another a thousand unforeseen accidents may interrupt.

Ld. J. Could I hope, Madam, your present critical condition would acquit me of temerity, I should take the liberty to presume, if the suit of Sir Charles be rejected—

Enter Crab.

Crab. So, youngster! what I suppose you are already practising

practising one of your foreign lessons. Perverting the affections of a friend's mistress, or debauching his wife, are mere peccadilloes in modern morality. But at present you are my care. That way conducts you to your fellow traveller.—[*Exit. Ld. J.*]—I would speak with you in the library. [*Exit.*

Luc. I shall attend you, Sir. Never was so unhappy an interruption. What could my Lord mean? But be it what it will, it ought not, it cannot concern me. Gratitude and duty demand my compliance with the dying wish of my benefactor, my friend, my father. But am I then to sacrifice all my future peace? But reason not, rash girl; obedience is thy province.

*Tho' hard the task, be it my part to prove
That sometimes duty can give birth to love.* [*Exit.*

ACT II.

Buck *at his toilet, attended by three* valets de chambre *and* Macruthen.

Mac. NOtwithstanding aw his plain dealing, I doubt whether Maister Crab is so honest a man.

Buck. Prithee, Mac, name not the monster. If I may be permitted a quotation from one of their paltry poets,

Who is knight of the shire represents 'em all.

Did ever mortal see such *mirroirs*, such looking glasses as they have here, too! One might as well address oneself, for information, to a bucket of water. *La Jonquil, mettes sous le rouge, offes. Eh bien, Mac, miserable!* Hey!

Mac. It's very becoming.

Buck. Aye, it will do for this place; I really could have forgiven my father's living a year or two longer, rather than be compelled to return to this—[*Enter Ld. John*]— My dear Lord, *je demande mille pardons*, but the terrible fracas in my chaise has so *glaced* and disordered my hair, that it required an age to adjust it.

Ld. J. No apology, Sir Charles, I have been entertained very agreeably.

Buck. Who have you had, my dear Lord, to entertain you?
Ld. J.

Ld. J. The very individual lady that's foon to make you a happy hufband.

Buck. A happy who? hufband! What two very oppofite ideas, confounded *enfemble!* In my confcience, I believe there's contagion in the clime, and my Lor is infected. But pray, my dear Lord, by what accident have you difcovered that I was upon the point of becoming that happy—Oh, *un mari! Diable?*

Ld. J. The lady's beauty and merit, your inclinations, and your father's injunctions, made me conjecture that.

Buck. And can't you fuppofe that the lady's beauty may be poffefs'd, her merit rewarded, and my inclinations gratified, without an abfolute obedience to that fatherly injunction?

Ld. J. It does not occur to me.

Buck. No, I believe not, my Lor. Thofe kind of talents are not given to every body. *Donnez moi mon manchon.* And now you fhall fee me manage the lady.

Enter Servant.

Serv. Young Squire Racket, and Sir Toby Tallyhoe, who call themfelves your honour's old acquaintances.

Buck. Oh the brutes! By what accident could they difcover my arrival! My dear, dear Lor, aid me to efcape this embarras.

Racket *and* Tallyhoe *without.*

Hoic a boy, hoic a boy.

Buck. Let me die if I do not believe the Hottentots have brought a whole hundred of hounds with them. But they fay, forms keep fools at a diftance. I'll receive 'em *en cérémonie.*

Enter Racket *and* Tallyhoe.

Tally. Hey boy, hoix, my little Buck.

Buck. Monfieur le Chevalier votre très humble ferviteur.

Tally. Hey.

Buck. Monfieur Racket, je fuis charmé de vous voir.

Rack. Anon what!

Buck. Ne m'entendez vous? Don't you underftand French?

Rack. Know French! No, nor you neither, I think, Sir Toby,

Toby, foregad I believe the Papiftes ha' bewitch'd him in foreign parts.

Tally. Bewitch'd and transformed him too. Let me perifh, Racket, if I don't think he's like one of the folks we ufed to read of at fchool, in Ovid's Metamorphis; and that they have turned him into a beaft.

Rack. A beaft! No, a bird, you fool. Lookee, Sir Toby, by the Lord Harry, here are his wings.

Tally. Hey! ecod and fo they are, ha, ha. I reckon, Racket, he came over with the wood-cocks.

Buck. Voilà des véritables Anglois. The ruftic rude ruffians!

Rack. Let us fee what the devil he has put upon his pole, Sir Toby.

Tally. Aye.

Buck. Do, dear favage, keep your diftance.

Tally. Nay, fore George we will have a fcrutiny.

Rack. Aye, aye, a fcrutiny.

Buck. En grace, La Jonquil, my Lor, protect me from thefe pirates.

Ld. J. A little compaffion, I beg, gentlemen. Confider, Sir Charles is on a vifit to his bride.

Tally. Bride! zounds, he's fitter for a band-box. Racket, hocks the heels.

Rack. I have 'em, Knight. Foregad he is the very reverfe of a bantam cock; his comb's on his feet, and his feathers on his head. Who have we got here! What are thefe fellows, paftry-cooks?

Enter Crab.

Crab. And is this one of your newly acquired accomplifhments, letting your miftrefs languifh for a—— but you have company, I fee.

Buck. O, yes, I have been inexpreffibly happy. Thefe gentlemen are kind enough to treat me, upon my arrival, with what I believe they call in this country a rout. My dear Lor, if you don't favour my flight. But fee if the toads a'n't tumbling my toilet.

Ld. J. Now's your time, fteal off; I'll cover your retreat.

Buck. Mac, let La Jonquil follow to re-fettle my *cheveux.—Je vous remercie mille, mille fois, mon cher* my Lor.

Rack. Hola, Sir Toby, ftole away!

Buck.

Buck. O mon Dieu.

Tally. Poh, rot him, let him alone. He'll never do for our purpose. You must know we intend to kick up a riot to-night at the play-house, and we wanted him of the party; but that fop would swoon at the sight of a cudgel.

Ld. J. Pray, Sir, what is your cause of contention?

Tally. Cause of contention, hey, faith, I know nothing of the matter. Racket, what is it we are angry about?

Racket. Angry about! Why you know we are to demolish the dancers.

Tally. True, true, I had forgot. Will you make one?

Ld. J. I beg to be excused.

Rack. May hap you are a friend to the French.

Ld. J. Not I, indeed, Sir. But if the occasion will permit me a pun, though I am far from being a well-wisher to their arms, I have no objection to the being entertained by their legs.

Tally. Aye! Why then if you'll come to-night, you'll split your sides with laughing, for I'll be rot if we don't make them caper higher, and run faster, than ever they have done since the battle of Blenheim. Come along, Racket.
[*Exit.*

Ld. J. Was there ever such a contrast?

Crab. Not so remote as you imagine; they are scions from the same stock, set in different soils. The first shrub, you see, flowers most prodigally, but matures nothing; the tall slip, though stunted, bears a little fruit; crabbed, 'tis true, but still the growth of the clime. Come, you'll follow your friend. [*Exeunt.*

Enter Lucinda, *with a Servant.*

Luc. When Mr Crab, or Sir Charles, enquire for me, you will conduct them hither. [*Exit. Serv.*] How I long for an end to this important interview! Not that I have any great expectations from the issue; but still, in my circumstances, a state of suspence is, of all situations, the most disagreeable. But hush, they come.

Enter Sir Charles, Macrathen, Ld. John, *and* Crab.

Buck. Mac, announce me.

Mac. Madam, Sir Charles Buck craves the honour of kissing your hand.

Buck. Très humble serviteur. Et comment se porte Mademoiselle.

demoiselle. I am ravished to see thee, *ma chere petite Ly-
biade.—Eh bien, ma reine!* Why you look divinely, child.
But, *mon enfant*, they have dressed you most diabolically.
Why, what a *coiffure* must you have, and, *ah mon Dieu*,
a total absence of rouge. But, perhaps, you are out. I had
a cargo from Deffreney the day of my departure; shall I
have the honour to supply you?

Luc. You are obliging, Sir, but I confess myself a convert to the chaste customs of this country, and with a commercial people, you know, Sir Charles, all artifice—

Buck. Artifice! You mistake the point, *ma chere*. A
proper proportion of red is an indispensable part of your
dress; and, in my private opinion, a woman might as well
appear in public, without powder, or a petticoat.

Crab. And, in my private opinion, a woman, who puts
on the first, would make very little difficulty in pulling off
the last.

Buck. Oh, Monsieur Crab's judgment must be decisive
in dress. Well, and what amusements, what spectacles,
what parties, what contrivances, to conquer father time,
that foe to the fair? I fancy one must *ennuier considérable-
ment* in your London here.

Luc. Oh, we are in no distress for diversions. We have
an opera.

Buck. Italien, I suppose, *pitoiable*, shocking, *assommant!*
Oh, there is no supporting their *bi, bi, bi, bi. Ah mon
Dieu! Ah, chaste brillant soleil,*

> *Brillant soleil,*
> *A-t-on jamais veu ton pareil?*

There's music and melody.

Luc. What a fop!

Buck. But proceed, *ma princesse*.

Luc. Oh, then we have plays.

Buck. That I deny, child.

Luc. No plays!

Buck. No.

Luc. The assertion is a little whimsical.

Buck. Aye that may be; you have here dramatic things,
farcical in their composition, and ridiculous in their repre-
sentation.

Luc. Sir, I own myself unequal to the controversy;
but,

but, surely Shakespeare—my Lord, this subject calls upon you for its defence.

Crab. I know from what fountain this fool has drawn his remarks; the author of the Chinese Orphan, in the preface to which Mr Voltaire calls the principal works of Shakespeare monstrous farces.

Ld. J. Mr Crab is right, Madam. Mr Voltaire has stigmatized with a very unjust and a very invidious appellation the principal works of that great master of the passions; and his apparent motive renders him the more inexcusable.

Luc. What could it be, my Lord?

Ld. J. The preventing his countrymen from becoming acquainted with our author; that he might be at liberty to pilfer from him with the greater security.

Luc. Ungenerous, indeed!

Buck. Palpable defamation.

Luc. And as to the exhibition, I have been taught to believe, that for a natural pathetic, and a spirited expression, no people upon earth——

Buck. You are imposed upon, child, the Lequesne, the Lanoue, the Grandval, the Dumesnil, the Gauffin, what dignity, what action! But, *à propos*, I have myself wrote a tragedy in French.

Luc. Indeed!

Buck. En verité, upon Voltaire's plan.

Crab. That must be a precious piece of work.

Buck. It is now in repetition at the French comedy. Grandval and La Gauffin perform the principal parts. Oh, what an *eclat*! What a burst will it make in the parterre, when the King of Anamaboe refuses the person of the Princess of Cochineal!

Luc. Do you remember the passage?

Buck. Entire; and I believe I can convey it in their manner.

Luc. That will be delightful.

Buck. And first the King.

> Ma chere princess, je vous aime, c'est vrai;
> De ma femme vous portez les charmants attraits.
> Mais ce n'est pas bonnête pour un homme tel que moi,
> De tromper ma femme, ou de rompre ma foi.

Luc. Inimitable!

Buck.

Buck. Now the Princess; she is, as you may suppose, in extreme distress.
Luc. No doubt.
*Buck. Mon grand roy, mon cher adorable,
Ayez pitié de moi; je suis inconsolable.*

[Then he turns his back upon her, at which she in a fury]
*Monstre, ingrat, affreux, horrible, funeste,
Ob que je vous aime, ab que je vous déteste!*

[Then he]
*Penfez vous, madame, à me donner la loi,
Votre haine, votre amour, font les mêmes chofes à moi.*

Luc. Bravo!
Ld. J. Bravo, bravo!
Buck. Aye, there's passion and poetry, and reason and rhime. Oh how I detest blood, and blank verse! There is something so soft, so musical, and so natural, in the rich rhimes of the *Theatre François!*
Ld. J. I did not know Sir Charles was so totally devoted to the *belles lettres.*
Buck. Oh, entirely. 'Tis the ton, the taste, I am every night at the *Caffè* * *Procope,* and had not I had the misfortune to be born in this curs'd country, I make no doubt but you would have seen my name among the foremost of the French academy.
Crab. I should think you might easily get over that difficulty, if you will be but so obliging as publicly to renounce us. I dare engage not one of your countrymen shall contradict or claim you.
Buck. No!—Impossible. From the barbarity of my education, I must ever be taken for an *Anglois.*
Crab. Never.
Buck. En verité!
Crab. En verité.
Buck. You flatter me.
Crab. But common justice.
Mac. Nay, Maister Crab is in the right, for I have often heard the French themselves say, Is it possible that gentleman can be British?

* A coffee house opposite the French Comedy, where the wits assemble every evening.

Buck.

Buck. Obliging creatures! And you concur with them.
Crab. Entirely.
Luc. Entirely.
Ld. J. Entirely.
Buck. How happy you make me!
Crab. Egregious puppy! But we lose time. A truce to this trumpery. You have read your father's will.
Buck. No; I read no English. When Mac has turned it into French, I may run over the items.
Crab. I have told you the part that concerns the girl. And as your declaration upon it will difcharge me, I leave you to what you will call an *eclairciffement*. Come, my Lord.
Buck. Nay, but Monfieur Crab, my Lor, Mac.
Crab. Along with us. [*Exit.*
Buck. A comfortable fcrape I am in! What the deuce am I to do? In the language of the place, I am to make love, I fuppofe. A pretty employment!
Luc. I fancy my hero is a little puzzled with his part. But now for it.
Buck. A queer creature, that Crab, *ma petite*. But, *à propos*, How d'ye like my Lord.
Luc. He feems to have good fenfe and good breeding.
Buck. *Pas trop.* But don't you think he has fomething of a foreign kind of air about him?
Luc. Foreign?
Buck. Aye, fomething fo Englifh in his manner.
Luc. Foreign and Englifh! I don't comprehend you.
Buck. Why, that is, he has not the eale, the *je ne fçai quoi*, the *bon ton*.—In a word, he does not refemble me, now.
Luc. Not in the leaft.
Buck. Ah, I thought fo. He is to be pitied, poor devil, he can't help it. But, *entre nous, ma chere*, the fellow has a fortune.
Luc. How does that concern me, Sir Charles?
Buck. Why, *je penfe, ma reine*, that your eyes have done execution there.
Luc. My eyes execution!
Buck. Aye, child, is there any thing fo extraordinary in that? *Ma foi*, I thought by the vivacity of his praife, that he had already fummoned the garrifon to furrender.
Luc. To carry on the allufion, I believe my Lord is

too

too good a commander, to commence a fruitless siege. He could not but know the condition of the town.

Buck. Condition! Explain, ma chere.

Luc. I was in hopes your interview with Mr Crab had made that unneceffary.

Buck. Oh, aye, I do recollect fomething of a ridiculous article about marriage, in a will. But what a plot againft the peace of two poor people! Well, the malice of fome men is amazing! Not content with doing all the mifchief they can in their life, they are for entailing their malevolence, like their eftates, to lateft pofterity.

Luc. Your contempt of me, Sir Charles, I receive as a compliment. But the infinite obligations I owe to the man, who had the misfortune to call you fon, compel me to infift, that in my prefence, at leaft, no indignity be offered to his memory.

Buck. Heyday! What, in heroics, ma reine!

Luc. Ungrateful, unfilial wretch! So foon to trample on his afhes, whofe fond heart, the greateft load of his laft hours, were his fears for thy future welfare.

Buck. Ma foi, elle eft folle, fhe is mad, fans doute.

Luc. But I am to blame. Can he who breaks through one facred relation regard another? Can the monfter who is corrupt enough to contemn the place of his birth, reverence thofe who gave him being?——impoffible.

Buck. Ah, a pretty monologue, a fine foliloquy this, child.

Luc. Contemptible. But I am cool.

Buck. I am mighty glad of it. Now we fhall underftand one another, I hope.

Luc. We do underftand one another. You have already been kind enough to refufe me. Nothing is wanting but a formal rejection under your hand, and fo concludes our acquaintance.

Buck. Vous allez trop vite, you are too quick, ma chere. If I recollect, the confequence of this rejection is my paying you twenty thoufand pounds.

Luc. True.

Buck. Now that have not I the leaft inclination to do.

Luc. No, Sir? Why you own that marriage—

Buck. Is my averfion. I'll give you that under my hand, if you pleafe; but I have a prodigious love for the Louis.

Luc.

Luc. Oh, we'll foon fettle that difpute; the law——

Buck. But hold, *ma reine*. I don't find that my provident father has precifely determined the time of this comfortable conjunction. So, tho' I am condemned, the day of execution is not fixed.

Luc. Sir!

Buck. I fay, my foul, there goes no more to your dying a maid than my living a bachelor.

Luc. O, Sir, I fhall find a remedy.

Buck. But now fuppofe, *ma belle*, I have found one to your hand?

Luc. As how? Name one.

Buck. I'll name two. And firft, *mon enfant*; tho' I have an irrefiftible antipathy to the conjugal knot, yet I am by no means blind to your perfonal charms; in the poffeffion of which, if you pleafe to place me, not only the aforefaid twenty thoufand pounds, but the whole *terre* of your devoted fhall fall at your——

Luc. Grant me patience!

Buck. Indeed you want it, my dear. But if you donnee, I fly.

Luc. Quick, Sir, your other. For this is——

Buck. I grant, not quite fo fafhionable as my other. It is then, in a word, that you would let this lubberly lord make you a lady, and appoint me his affiftant, his private friend, his *cicifbei*. And as we are to be joint partners of your perfon, let us be equal fharers in your fortune, *ma belle*.

Luc. Thou mean, abject, mercenary thing. Thy miftrefs! Gracious heaven! Univerfal empire fhould not bribe me to be thy bride. And what apology, what excufe could a woman of the leaft fenfe or fpirit make for fo unnatural a connection!

Buck. Fort bien!

Luc. Where are thy attractions? Canft thou be weak enough to fuppofe thy frippery drefs, thy affectation, thy grimace, could influence beyond the borders of a brothel?

Buck. Très bien!

Luc. And what are thy improvements? Thy air is a copy from thy barber: For thy drefs, thou art indebted to thy tailor. Thou haft loft thy native language, and brought home none in exchange for it.

Buck. Extrêmement bien!

Luc.

Luc. Had not thy vanity so soon exposed thy villainy, I might in reverence to that name, to which thou art a disgrace, have taken a wretched chance with thee for life.

Buck. I am obliged to you for that. And a pretty pacific partner I should have had. Why, look'ee child, you have been, to be sure, very eloquent, and upon the whole, not unentertaining: Tho' by the bye, you have forgot, in your catalogue, one of my foreign acquisitions; *c'est-à-dire*, that I can, with a most intrepid *sang froid*, without a single emotion, support all this storm of female fury. But, *adieu, ma belle*. And when a cool hour of reflection has made you sensible of the propriety of my proposals, I shall expect the honour of a card.

Luc. Be gone for ever.

Buck. Pour jamais! Foregad she would make an admirable actress. If I once get her to Paris, she shall play a part in my piece. [*Exit.*

Luc. I am ashamed, this thing has had the power to move me thus. Who waits there? Dear Mr Crab——

Enter Lord John *and* Crab.

Ld. J. We have been unwillingly, Madam, silent witnesses to this shameful scene. I blush that a creature, who wears the outward mark of humanity, should be in his morals so much below——

Crab. Prithee, why didst thou not call thy maids, and toss the booby in a blanket?

Ld. J. If I might be permitted, Madam, to conclude what I intended saying, when interrupted by Mr Crab——

Luc. My Lord, don't think me guilty of affectation. I believe, I guess at your generous design; but my temper is really so ruffled, besides I am meditating a piece of female revenge on this coxcomb.

Ld. J. Dear Madam, can I assist?

Luc. Only by desiring my maid to bring hither the tea. ——My Lord, I am confounded at the liberty, but——

Ld. J. No apology. You honour me, Madam.

Crab. And prithee, wench, what is thy scheme?

Luc. Oh, a very harmless one, I promise you.

Crab. Zounds, I am sorry for it. I long to see the puppy severely punished, methinks.

Luc. Sir Charles, I fancy, can't be yet got out of the house. Will you desire him to step hither?

Crab.

Crab. I'll bring him.
Luc. No, I wiſh to have him alone.
Crab. Why then I'll ſend him. [*Exit.*

Enter Lettice.

Luc. Place theſe things on the table, a chair on each ſide: very well. Do you keep within call. But hark, he is here. Leave me, Lettice. [*Exit Lettice.*

Enter Buck.

Buck. So, ſo, I thought ſhe would come to; but, I confeſs not altogether ſo ſoon. Eh bien, ma belle, ſee me ready to receive your commands.
Luc. Pray be ſeated, Sir Charles. I am afraid the natural warmth of my temper might have hurried me into ſome expreſſions not altogether ſo ſuitable.
Buck. Ah bagatelle. Name it not.
Luc. Voulez-vous du thé, Monſieur?
Buck. Volontiers. This tea is a pretty innocent kind of beverage; I wonder the French don't take it. I have ſome thoughts of giving it a faſhion next winter.
Luc. That will be very obliging. It is of extreme ſervice to the ladies this ſide the water, you know.
Buck. True, it promotes parties, and infuſes a kind of ſpirit of converſation, and that—
Luc. En voulez-vous encore?
Buck. Je vous rends mille graces. But what has occaſioned me, ma reine, the honour of your meſſage by Mr Crab?
Luc. The favours I have received from your family, Sir Charles, I thought, demanded from me, at my quitting your houſe, a more decent and ceremonious adieu, than our laſt interview would admit of.
Buck. Is that all, ma chere? I thought your flinty heart had at laſt relented. Well, ma reine, adieu.
Luc. Can you then leave me?
Buck. The fates will have it ſo.
Luc. Go then, perfidious traitor, be gone; I have this conſolation, however, that if I cannot legally poſſeſs you, no other woman ſhall.
Buck. Hey, how, what?
Luc. And though the pleaſure of living with you is denied me, in our deaths at leaſt we ſhall ſoon be united.
Buck.

Buck. Soon be united in death? When, child?

Luc. Within this hour.

Buck. Which way?

Luc. The fatal draught's already at my heart. I feel it here; it runs through every pore. Pangs, pangs unutterable! The tea we drank, urged by despair and love—Oh!

Buck. Well!

Luc. I poison'd—

Buck. The devil!

Luc. And as my generous heart would have shared all with you, I gave you half—

Buck. Oh, curse your generosity!

Luc. Indulge me in the cold comfort of a last embrace.

Buck. Embrace! O confound you! But it mayn't be too late. Macruthen, Jonquil! physicians, apothecaries, oil and antidotes. Oh! *je meu s, je mes s.* Ah, la diableffe! [*Exit.*

Enter Lord John *and* Crab.

Crab. A brave wench. I could kifs thee for this contrivance.

Ld. J. He really deserves it all.

Crab. Deserves it? Hang him. But the fenfible resentment of this girl has almost reconciled me to the world again. But stay, let us see—Can't we make a further use of the puppy's punishment? I suppose, we may very safely depend on your contempt of him?

Luc. Most securely.

Crab. And this young thing here has been breathing passions and protestations. But I'll take care, my girl sha'nt go a beggar to any man's bed. We must have this twenty thousand pound, Lucy.

Ld. J. I regard it not. Let me be happy, and let him be—

Crab. Psha, don't scorch me with thy flames. Referve your raptures; or, if they must have vent, retire into that room, whilst I go plague the puppy. [*Exeunt.*

Enter Buck, Macruthen, Jonquil, Bearnois, La Loire, Phyfician, Surgeon. Buck *is a cap and night gown.*

Surg. This copious phlebotomy will abate the inflammation, and if the fix blisters on your head and back rife, why there may be hopes.

Buck. Cold comfort, I burn, I burn, I burn—Ah, there's a shoot. And now, again, I freeze.
Mac. Aye, they are symptoms of a strong poison.
Buck. Oh, I am on the rack.
Mrs. Oh, if it be got to the vitals, a fig for aw antidotes.

Enter Crab.

Crab. Where is this miserable devil? What's he alive still?
Mac. In gude troth, and that's aw.
Buck. Oh!
Crab. So you have made a pretty piece of work on't, young man!
Buck. O what could provoke me to return from Paris?
Crab. Had you never been there, this could not have happened.

Enter Racket and Tallyhoe.

Rack. Where is he?—He's a dead man, his eyes are fix'd already.
Buck. Oh!
Tally. Who poison'd him, Racket?
Rack. Gad I don't know. His French cook, I reckon.
Crab. Were there a possibility of thy reformation, I have yet a secret to restore thee.
Buck. Oh give it, give it.
Crab. Not so fast. It must be on good conditions.
Buck. Name 'em. Take my estate, my—save but my life, take all.
Crab. First then renounce thy right to that lady, whose just resentment has drawn this punishment upon thee; and, to which she is an unhappy partaker.
Buck. I renounce her from my soul.
Crab. To this declaration you are witnesses. Next, your tawdry trappings, your foreign foppery, your washes, pa', rs, pomades, must blaze before your door.
Buck. What, all?
Crab. All; not a rag shall be reserved. The execution of that part of your sentence shall be assigned to your old friends here.
Buck. Well, take 'em.

Tally-

Tally. Huzza, come Racket, let's rummage.

(Exeunt Racket and Tallyhoe.

Crab. And, lastly, I'll have these exotic attendants, these instruments of your luxury, these panders to your pride, pack'd in the first cart, and sent post to the place from whence they came.

Buck. Spare me but *La Jonquil.*

Crab. Not an instant. The importation of these puppies makes a part of the politics of your old friends the French; unable to resist you whilst you retain your ancient roughness, they have recourse to these minions, who would first, by unmanly means, sap and soften all your native spirit, and then deliver you an easy prey to their employers.

Buck. Since then it must be so, *adieu, à la Jonquil.*

(Exeunt Jonquil *and* Bearnois.

Crab. And now to the remedy. Come forth, Lucinda.

Enter Lucinda *and* Lord John.

Buck. Hey, why, did not she swallow the poison?
Crab. No; nor you neither, you blockhead.
Buck. Why, did not I leave you in pangs?
Luc. Aye, put on. The tea was innocent, upon my honour, Sir Charles. But you allow me to be an excellent actress.
Buck. Oh, curse your talents!
Crab. This fellow's public renunciation has put your person and fortune in your own power; and if you were sincere in your declaration of being directed by me, bestow it there.
Luc. As a proof of my sincerity, my Lord, receive it.
Ld. J. With more transport, than Sir Charles the news of his safety.
Luc. to Buck. You are not, at present, in a condition to take possession of your post.
Buck. What?
Luc. Oh, you recollect; my Lord's private friend; his assistant, you know.
Buck. Oh, ho!
Mrs. But, Sir Charles, as I find the affair of the poison was but a joke, had na'ye better withdraw, and tack off your blisters?
Crab. No, let 'em stick. He wants 'em. And now concludes my care. But before we close the scene, receive,
                                                                young

young man; this laſt advice from the old friend of your
father; as it is your happineſs to be born a Briton, let it
be your boaſt; know that the bleſſings of liberty are your
birth-right, which while you preſerve, other nations may
envy or fear, but can never conquer or command you. Believe, that French faſhions are as ill ſuited to the genius,
as their politics are pernicious to the peace of your native
land.

A recourſe to theſe ſacred truths, you'll find,
That poiſon, ſo your puniſhment deſign'd,
Will prove a wholeſome medicine to your mind.

(*Exeunt omnes.*

THE AUTHOR;

A COMEDY,

OF TWO ACTS.

PROLOGUE.

Written and Spoken by Mr Foote.

SEVERE their taste, who, in this critic age,
With fresh materials furnish out the stage!
Not that our fathers drain'd the comic store;
Fresh characters spring up as heretofore——
Nature with novelty does still abound;
On every side fresh follies may be found.
But then the taste of every guest to hit,
To please at once the gallery, box, and pit,
Requires at least—no common share of wit.
   Those, who adorn the orb of higher life,
Demand the lively rake, or modish wife;
Whilst they, who in a lower circle move,
Yawn at their wit, and slumber at their love.
If light, low mirth employs the comic scene,
Such mirth as drives from vulgar minds the spleen;
The polish'd critic damns the wretched stuff,
And cries—" 'Twill please the galleries well enough."
Such jarring judgments who can reconcile,
Since fops will frown, where humble traders smile!
   To dash the poet's ineffectual claim,
And quench his thirst for universal fame,
The Grecian fabulist, in moral lay,
Has thus address'd the writers of this day.
   Once on a time, a Son and Sire, we're told,
The stripling tender, and the father old,
Purchas'd a jack-ass at a country fair,
To ease their limbs, and hawk about their ware:
But as the sluggish animal was weak,
They fear'd, if both should mount, his back would break:
Up gets the boy; the father leads the ass,
And through the gazing crowd attempts to pass;
Forth from the throng the grey-beards hobble out,
And hail the cavalcade with feeble shout.
" Thus the respect to reverend age you shew!
And this the duty you to parents owe!
He beats the hoof, and you are set astride;
Sirrah! get down, and let your father ride."
As Grecian lads were seldom void of grace,
The decent, duteous youth, resign'd his place.
Then a fresh murmur through the rabble ran;
Boys, girls, wives, widows, all attack the man.

" Sure

"Sure never was brute beast so void of nature!
Have you no pity for the pretty creature?
To your own babe can you be unkind?
Here—Sake, Bib, Baty—put the child behind."
Old Dapple next the clown's compassion claim'd;
" 'Tis wonderment, them boobies ben't asham'd.
Two at a time upon a poor dumb beast!
They might as well have carried he at least."
The pair, still pliant to the partial voice,
Dismount and bear the ass—Then what a noise!—
Huzzas,—loud laughs, low gibes, and bitter jokes,
From the yet silent fire these words provoke.
Proceed, my boy, nor heed their farther call,
Vain his attempt who strives to please them all!".

EPILOGUE.

EPILOGUE.

Written by a Lady, and spoken by Mrs Clive.

WELL—thank my stars, that I have done my talk,
And now throw off this awkward, ideot mask.
Cou'd we suppose this circle so refin'd,
Who seek those pleasures that improve the mind,
Cou'd from such vulgarisms feel delight;
Or laugh at characters so unpolite?
Who come to plays, to see and to be seen;
Not to hear things that shock, or give the spleen;
Who then an opera, when they hear 'tis thin.
" Lord! do you know?" says Lady Bell—" I'm told
That Jacky Dapple got so great a cold
Last Tuesday night—There wa'n't a creature there;
Not a male thing to hand one to one's chair.
Divine Mingotti! what a swell has she!
O! such a *sostenuto* upon E!
Ma'am, when she's quite in voice, she'll go to C!"
" Lord," says my Lady English—" here's a pother!
Go where she will, I'll never see another."
Her Ladyship, half choak'd with London air,
And brought to town to see the sights—and stare.
" Fine singing that!—I'm sure it's more like screaming:
To me, I vow, they're all a pack of women!
Oh barbare!—Inhumane!—Tramontane!——
Does not this creature come from Pudding-Lane?
Look, look, my Lord!—She goggles!—Ha, ha, pray be quiet;
Dear Lady Bell, for shame! You'll make a riot.
Why will they mix with us to make a rout?
Bring in a bill, my Lord, to keep 'em out."
" We'll have a Test Act, faith!"—my Lord replied;
" And shut out all that are not qualified."
Thus ridicule is bounded like a ball,
Struck by the great, then answer'd by the small;
While we, at times, return it to you all.
A skilful hand will ne'er your rage provoke;
For though it hits you, you'll applaud the stroke;
Let it but only glance, you'll never frown;
Nay, you'll forgive, tho't knocks your neighbour down.

Vol. I. 8 DRAMATIS

DRAMATIS PERSONÆ.

At Drury-Lane, 1759.

Governor Cape,	—	Mr Wrighten.
Young Cape,	— —	Mr Arne.
Sprightly,	— —	Mr R. Palmer.
Cadwallader,	—	Mr Bannister.
Post,	— —	Mr Waldron.
Vamp,	—	Mr Moody.
Prince's Devil,	—	Mr Bearon,
Robin,	—	Mr Chaplin.
Mrs Cadwallader,	—	Mrs Wrighten.
Miss Arabella,	— —	Mrs Smith.

ACT I.

Governor Cape and Robin.

Gov. AND he believes me dead, Robin?
Rob. Most certainly.
Gov. You have given him no intimation that his fortunes might mend.
Rob. Not a distant hint.
Gov. How did he receive the news?
Rob. Calmly enough: When I told him that his hopes from abroad were at an end, that the friend of his deceased father thought he had done enough in putting it in his power to earn his own livelihood, he replied 'twas no more than he had long expected; charged me with his warmest acknowledgments to his conceal'd benefactor; thanked me for my care, sigh'd, and left me.
Gov. And how has he lived since?
Rob. Poorly, but honestly: To his pen he owes all his subsistence. I am sure my heart bleeds for him: Consider, Sir, to what temptations you expose him.
Gov. The severer his trials, the greater his triumph. Shall the fruits of my honest industry, the purchase of many perils, be lavish'd on a lazy luxurious booby, who has no other merit than being born five and twenty years after me? No, no, Robin; him, and a profusion of debts, were all that the extravagance of his mother left me.
Rob. You loved her, Sir.
Gov. Fondly.—Nay, foolishly, or necessity had not compell'd me to seek for shelter in another climate. 'Tis true, fortune has been favourable to my labours, and when George convinces me that he inherits my spirit, he shall share my property; not else.
Rob. Consider, Sir, he has not your opportunities.
Gov. Nor had I his education.
Rob. As the world goes, the worst you con'd have given him. Lack-a-day, learning, learning, Sir, is no commodity for this market; nothing makes money here, Sir, but money; or some certain fashionable qualities that you would not wish your son to possess.
Gov. Learning useless? Impossible!—Where are the Oxfords,

Oxfords, the Halifaxes, the great protectors and patrons of the liberal arts?

Rob. Patron!—The word has loft its use; a guinea subscription at the request of a lady, whose chambermaid is acquainted with the author, may be now and then pick'd up—Protectors! Why I dare believe there's more money laid out upon Iflington turnpike in a month, than upon all the learned men in Great Britain in seven years.

Gov. And yet the press groans with their productions. How do they all exist?

Rob. In garrets, Sir; as, if you will step to your son's apartments in the next street, you will see.

Gov. But what apology shall we make for the visit?

Rob. That you want the aid of his profession; a well penn'd address now, from the subjects of your late government, with your gracious reply, to put into the news-papers.

Gov. Aye; is that part of his practice?—Well, lead on, Robin.

Scene draws and discovers Young Cape *with the Printer's Devil.*

Cape. Prythee go about thy business—Vanish, dear Devil.

Devil. Master bid me not come without the proof; he says as how there are two other answers ready for the press, and if your's don't come out a Saturday 'twon't pay for the paper; but you are always so lazy: I have more plague with you—There's Mr Guzzle, the translator, never keeps me a minute—unless the poor gentleman happens to be fuddled.

Cape. Why, you little footy, fniv'ling, diabolical puppy, is it not sufficient to be plagu'd with the stupidity of your absurd master, but I must be pester'd with your impertinence?

Devil. Impertinence!—Marry, come up, I keep as good company as your worship every day in the year—There's Master Clench, in Little Britain, does not think it beneath him to take part of a pot of porter with me, though he has wrote two volumes of lives in quarto, and has a folio a coming out in numbers.

Cape. Harky', Sirrah, if you don't quit the room this inflant, instant, I'll shew you a shorter way into the street than the stairs.

Devil. I shall save you the trouble—Give me the French book that you took the story from for the last Journal.

Cape. Take it—[*throws it at him.*]

Devil. What, d'ye think it belongs to the circulating library, or that it is one of your own performances, that you—

Cape. You shall have a larger—[*Exit. Devil.*] 'Sdeath! a pretty situation I am in! And are these the fruits I am to reap from a long, laborious, and expensive—

Re-enter Devil.

Devil. I had like to have forgot, here's your week's pay for the newspaper, five and five pence, which with the two-and-a-penny, Master pass'd his word for to Mrs Suds, your washer-woman, makes the three half crowns.

Cape. Lay it on the table.

Devil. Here's a man on the stairs wants you; by the sheepishness of his looks, and the shabbiness of his dress, he's either a pick-pocket, or poet—Here, walk in, Mr What-d'ye-call-'um, the gentleman's at home.

[*Surveys the figure, laughs, and exit.*]

Enter Poet.

Poet. Your name, I presume, is Cape.

Cape. You have hit it, Sir.

Poet. Sir, I beg pardon; you are a gentleman that writes?

Cape. Sometimes.

Poet. Why, Sir, my case, in a word, is this; I, like you, have long been a retainer of the muses, as you may see by their livery.

Cape. They have not discarded you, I hope.

Poet. No, Sir, but their upper servants, the booksellers, have. I printed a collection of jests upon my own account, and they have ever since refused to employ me; you, Sir, I hear, are in their graces: Now I have brought you, Sir, three imitations of Juvenal in prose; Tully's Oration for Milo, in blank verse; two Essays on the British Herring Fishery, with a large collection of Rebuses; which, if you will dispose of to them, in your own name, we'll divide the profits.

Cape. I am really, Sir, sorry for your distress, but I have a larger cargo of my own manufacturing than they chuse to engage in.

Poet. That's pity; you have nothing in the compiling or index way, that you wou'd intrust to the care of another?

Cape. Nothing.

Poet. I'll do it at half price.

Cape. I'm concerned it is not in my power at present to be useful to you; but if this trifle—

Poet. Sir, your servant, shall I leave you any of my—

Cape. By no means.

Poet. An essay or an ode?

Cape. Not a line.

Poet. Your very obedient.— [*Exit.* Poet.

Cape. Poor fellow! and how far am I removed from his condition! Virgil had his Pollio; Horace his Mecænas; Martial his Pliny: My protectors are Title Page, the publisher; Vamp, the bookseller; and Index, the printer. A most noble triumvirate; and the rascals are as proscriptive and arbitrary, as the famous Roman one, into the bargain.

Enter Sprightly.

Spri. What! in soliloquy, George? Reciting some of the pleasantries, I suppose, in your new piece.

Cape. My disposition has, at present, very little of the vis comica.

Spri. What's the matter?

Cape. Survey that mass of wealth upon the table; all my own, and earn'd in little more than a week.

Spri. Why, 'tis an inexhaustible mine!

Cape. Ay, and delivered to me, too, with all the soft civility of Billingsgate, by a printer's prime minister, call'd a Devil.

Spri. I met the imp upon the stairs; but I thought these midwives to the muses were the idolizers of you, their favourite son.

Cape. Our tyrants, Tom. Had I, indeed, a posthumous piece of infidelity, or an amorous novel, decorated with luscious copper-plates, the slaves would be civil enough.

Spri. Why don't you publish your own works?

Cape. What! and paper my room with 'em! no, no, that will never do; there are secrets in all trades; ours is one
great

great mystery, but the explanation would be too tedious at present.

Spri. Then why don't you divert your attention to some other object?

Cape. That subject was employing my thoughts.

Spri. How have you resolved?

Cape. I have, I think, at present two strings to my bow; if my comedy succeeds, it buys me a commission; if my mistress, my Laura, proves kind, I am settled for life; but if both my cords snap, adieu to the quill, and welcome the musquet.

Spri. Heroically determined!—But *à propos*—how proceeds your honourable passion?

Cape. But slowly—I believe I have a friend in her heart, but a most potent enemy in her head: You know, I am poor, and she is prudent. With regard to her fortune too, I believe her brother's consent essentially necessary—But you promised to make me acquainted with him.

Spri. I expect him here every instant. He may, George, be useful to you in more than one capacity; if your comedy is not crowded, he is a character, I can tell you, that will make no contemptible figure in it.

Cape. His sister gave me a sketch of him last summer.

Spri. A sketch can never convey him. His peculiarities require infinite labour and high finishing.

Cape. Give me the outlines.

Spri. He is a compound of contrarieties; pride and meanness; folly and archness: At the same time that he wou'd take the wall of a Prince of the Blood, he would not scruple eating a fry'd sausage at the Meusgate. There is a minuteness, now and then, in his descriptions; and some whimsical, unaccountable turns in his conversation, that are entertaining enough: But the extravagance and oddity of his manner, and the boast of his birth, complete his character.

Cape. But how will a person of his pride and pedigree, relish the humility of this apartment?

Spri. Oh, he is prepar'd—You are, George, though prodigiously learn'd and ingenious, an abstracted being, odd and whimsical; the case with all you great geniuses: You love the snug, the chimney corner of life; and retire to this obscure nook, merely to avoid the importunity of the great.

Cape.

Cape. Your servant——But what attraction can a character of this kind have for Mr Cadwallader?

Spri. Infinite! next to a Peer, he honours a poet: and modestly imputes his not making a figure in the learned world himself to the neglect of his education—hush! he's on the stairs—on with your cap, and open your book; Remember great dignity and absence.

Enter Vamp.

Cape. Oh, no; 'tis Mr Vamp: Your commands, good Sir?

Vamp. I have a word, Master Cape, for your private ear.

Cape. You may communicate; this gentleman is a friend.

Vamp. An author?

Cape. Voluminous.

Vamp. In what way?

Cape. Universal.

Vamp. Bless me! he's very young, and exceedingly well rigg'd; what, a good subscription, I reckon.

Cape. Not a month from Leyden; an admirable theologist! he study'd it in Germany; if you shou'd want such a thing now, as ten or a dozen manuscript sermons, by a deceas'd clergyman, I believe he can supply you.

Vamp. No.

Cape. Warranted originals.

Vamp. No, no, I don't deal in the sermon way, now; I lost money by the last I printed, for all 'twas wrote by a Methodist; but, I believe, Sir, if they be'nt long, and have a good deal of Latin in 'em, I can get you a chap.

Spri. For what, Sir?

Vamp. The manuscript sermons you have wrote, and want to dispose of.

Spri. Sermons that I have wrote?

Vamp. Ay, ay; Master Cape has been telling me—

Spri. He has; I am mightily oblig'd to him.

Vamp. Nay, nay, don't be afraid; I'll keep council; old Vamp had not kept a shop so long at the Turnstile, if he did not know how to be secret; why, in the year forty-five, when I was in the treasonable way, I never squeak'd; I never gave up but one author in my life, and he was dying of a consumption, so it never came to a trial.

Spri. Indeed!

Vamp.

Vamp. Never———look here [*Shews the sole of his hand*] crop'd close!—bare as a board!—and for nothing in the world but an innocent book of bawdy, as I hope for mercy: Oh! the laws are very hard, very severe upon us.

Spri. You have given me, Sir, so positive a proof of your secrefy that you may rely upon my communication.

Vamp. You will be safe—but gusso, we must mind business, though; here, Master Cape, you must provide me with three taking titles for these pamphlets, and if you can think of a pat Latin motto for the largest—

Cape. They shall be done.

Vamp. Do so, do so. Books are like women, Master Cape; to strike, they must be well-drefs'd; fine feathers make find birds; a good paper, an elegant type, a handsome motto, and a catching title, has drove many a dull treatife through three editions—Did you know Harry Handy?

Spri. Not that I recollect.

Vamp. He was a pretty fellow; he had his Latin *ad unguem*, as they say; he would have turn'd you a fable of Dryden's, or an epistle of Pope's into Latin verfe in a twinkling; except Peter Hasty, the voyage-writer, he was as great a lofs to the trade as any within my memory.

Cape. What carried him off?

Vamp. A halter; hang'd for clipping and coining, Master Cape; I thought there was fomething the matter by his not coming to our shop for a month or two: he was a pretty fellow!

Spri. Were you a great lofer by his death?

Vamp. I can't fay:—As he had taken to another courfe of living, his execution made a noife; it fold me feven hundred of his tranflations, befides his laft dying fpeech and confeffion; I got it; he was mindful of his friends in his laft moments: he was a pretty fellow!

Cape. You have no farther commands, Mr Vamp?

Vamp. Not at prefent; about the fpring I'll deal with you, if we can agree for a couple of volumes in octavo.

Spri. Upon what fubject?

Vamp. I leave that to him; Mafter Cape knows what will do, though novels are a pretty light fummer reading, and do very well at Tunbridge, Briftol, and the other watering places: no bad commodity for the Weft India trade neither; let 'em be novels, Mafter Cape.

Cape. You shall be certainly supply'd.

Vamp. I doubt not; pray how does Index go on with your Journal?

Cape. He does not complain.

Vamp. Ah, I knew the time—but you have over-stock'd the market. Titlepage and I had once lik'd to have engag'd in a paper. We had got a young Cantab for the essays; a pretty historian from Aberdeen; and an attorney's clerk for the true intelligence; but I don't know how, it drop'd for want of a politician.

Cape. If in that capacity I can be of any—

Vamp. No, thank you, Master Cape; in half a year's time, I have a grandson of my own that will come in; he's now in training as a waiter at the Cocoa-tree coffeehouse; I intend giving him the run of Jonathan's for three months to understand trade and the funds; and then I'll start him—no, no, you have enough on your hands; stick to your business: and d'ye hear, 'ware clipping and coining; remember Harry Handy; he was a pretty fellow!

[*Exit.*

Spri. And I'm sure thou art a most extraordinary fellow! But prythee, George, what cou'd provoke thee to make me a writer of sermons?

Cape. You seem'd desirous of being acquainted with our business, and I knew old Vamp wou'd let you more into the secret in five minutes, than I cou'd in as many hours.

(*Knocking below, loud.*)

Spri. Cape, to your post; here they are e'faith, a coachful! Let's see, Mr and Mrs Cadwallader, and your flame, the sister, as I live.

(*Cadwallader without*). Pray, by the bye, han't you a poet above?

(*Without*). Higher up.

Cad. Egad, I wonder what makes your poets have such an aversion to middle floors—they are always to be found in the extremities; in garrets, or cellars—

Enter Mr and Mrs Cadwallader and Arabella.

Cad. Ah, Sprightly!

Spri. Hush!

Cad. Hey, what's the matter?

Spri. Hard at it; unwilling some knotty point; totally absorb'd!

Cad.

Cad. Godfo, what, that's ho! Beck, Bell, there he is, egad, as great a poet, and as ingenious a——what's he about?—Hebrew?
Spri. Weaving the whole Æneid into a tragedy: I have been here this half hour, but he has not mark'd me yet.
Cad. Cou'd not I take a peep?
Spri. An earthquake wou'd not rouze him.
Cad. He feems in a damn'd paffion.
Cape. The belt of Pallas! nor prayers, nor tears, nor fupplicating gods fhall fave thee now.
Cad. Hey! zounds, what the devil? who?
Cape. ——*Pallas! te hoc vulnere, Pallas Immolat, & pœnam fcelerato ex fanguine fumit.*
Cad. Damn your palace; I wifh I was well out of your garret.
Cape. Sir, I beg ten thoufand pardons: ladies, your moft devoted. You will excufe me, Sir, but being juft on the cataftrophe of my tragedy, I am afraid the poetic furor may have betray'd me into fome indecency.
Spri. Oh, Mr Cadwallader is too great a genius himfelf, not to allow for thefe intemperate fallies of a heated imagination.
Cad. Genius! Look ye hear, Mr What's-your-name?
Cape. Cape.
Cad. Cape! True; though by the bye here, hey! You live devilifh high; but perhaps you may chufe that for exercife, hey! Sprightly! Genius! Look'e here, Mr Cape, I had as pretty natural parts, as fine talents!—but between you and I, I had a damn'd fool of a guardian, an ignorant, illiterate, ecod—he cou'd as foon pay the national debt as write his own name, and fo was refolved to make his ward no wifer than himfelf, I think.
Spri. Oh! fye, Mr Cadwallader, you don't do yourfelf juftice.
Cape. Indeed, Sir, we muft contradict you, we can't fuffer this defamation. I have more than once heard Mr Cadwallader's literary acquifitions loudly talk'd of.
Cad. Have you?—no, no, it can't be, hey! though let me tell you, laft winter, before I had the meafles, I cou'd have made as good a fpeech upon any fubject, in Italian, French, German—but I am all unhing'd; all—Oh! Lord, Mr Cape, this is Becky; my dear Becky, child, this is a great poet—ah, but fhe does not know what that

is—a little foolish or so, but of a very good family—here, Becky, child, won't you ask Mr Cape to come and see you?

Mrs Cad. As Dicky says, I shall be glad to see you at our house, Sir.

Cape. I have too great a regard for my own happiness, Ma'am, to miss so certain an opportunity of creating it.

Mrs Cad. Hey! What?

Cape. My inclinations, as well as my duty, I say, will compel me to obey your kind injunctions.

Mrs Cad. What does he say, our Bell?

Arab. Oh, that he can have no greater pleasure than waiting on you.

Mrs Cad. I'm sure that's more his goodness than my desert; but when you be'nt better engag'd we shou'd be glad of your company of an evening to make one with our Dicky, sister Bell, and I, at whisk and swabbers.

Cad. Hey, ecod do, Cape, come and look at her grotto and shells, and see what she has got—well, he'll come, Beck, —ecod do, and she'll come to the third night of your tragedy, hey! won't you, Beck?—is'nt she a fine girl? hey, you; humour her a little, do;—hey, Beck; he says you are as fine a woman as ever he—ecod who knows but he may make a copy of verses on you?—there, go, and have a little chat with her, talk any nonsense to her, no matter what; she's a damn'd fool, and won't know the difference—there, go, Beck—well, Sprightly, hey! what are you and Bell like to come together? Oh, ecod, they tell me, Mr Sprightly, that you have frequently Lords and Viscounts, and Earls, that take a dinner with you; now I shou'd look upon it as a very particular favour, if you would invite me at the same time, hey! will you?

Spri. You may depend on it.

Cad. Will you? Gad, that's kind; for between you and I, Mr Sprightly, I am of as ancient a family as the best of them, and people of fashion shou'd know one another, you know.

Spri. By all means of means.

Cad. Hey! shou'd not they so? When you have my Lord, or Baron, nay egad, if it be but a Baronet, or a Member of Parliament, I shou'd take it as a favour.

Spri. You will do them honour; they must all have heard of the antiquity of your house.

Cad. Antiquity! hey! Beck, where's my pedigree?

Mrs Cad.

Mrs Cad. Why, at home, lock'd up in the butler's pantry.

Cad. In the pantry! What the devil, how often have I bid you never to come out without it?

Mrs Cad. Lord! what signifies carrying such a lumb'ring thing about?

Cad. Signifies! You are a fool, Beck; why, suppose we should have any disputes when we are abroad, about precedence, how the devil shall we be able to settle it? But you shall see it at home. Oh Becky, come hither, we will refer our dispute to———— [*They go apart.*

Arab. Well, Sir, your friend has prevail'd; you are acquainted with my brother; but what use you propose—

Cape. The pleasure of a more frequent admission to you.

Arab. That all?

Cape. Who knows but a strict intimacy with Mr Cadwallader may in time incline him to favour my hopes?

Arab. A sandy foundation! Cou'd he be prevail'd upon to forgive your want of fortune; the obscurity, or at least uncertainty of your birth, will prove an unsurmountable bar.

Cad. Hold, hold, hold, Beck; zounds! you are so—

Spri. Well, but hear him out, Ma'am.

Cape. Consider we have but an instant. What project? what advice?

Arab. O fye! You would be ashamed to receive succour from a weak woman! Poetry is your profession, you know; so that plots, contrivances, and all the powers of imagination are more peculiarly your province.

Cape. Is this a season to rally?

Cad. Hold, hold, hold; ask Mr Cape.

Arab. To be serious then; if you have any point to gain with my brother, your application must be made to his better part.

Cape. I understand you; plough with the heifer.

Arab. A delicate allusion, on my word; but take this hint—Amongst her passions, admiration, or rather adoration, is the principal.

Cape. Oh! that is her foible?

Arab. One of them; against that fort you must plant your batteries—But here they are.

Mrs Cad. I tell you, you are a nonsense man, and I won't

won't agree to any such thing: Why, what signifies a Parliament man? You make such a rout indeed.

Cad. Hold, Becky, my dear, don't be in a passion now, hold; let us reason the thing a little, my dear.

Mrs Cad. I tell you I won't; what's the man an oaf? I won't reason, I hate reason, and so there's an end on't.

Cad. Why then you are obstinate eood, perverse, hey! But my dear, now, Becky, that's a good girl: Hey! come, hold, hold—Egad, we'll refer it to Mr Cape.

Mrs Cad. Defer it to who you will, it will signify nothing.

Cape. Bless me, what's the matter, Madam? Sure, Mr Cadwallader, you must have been to blame; no inconsiderable matter cou'd have ruffled the natural softness of that tender and delicate mind.

Cad. Pretty well commenced.

Mrs Cad. Why, he's always a fool, I think; he wants to send our little Dicky to school, and make him a Parliament man.

Cape. How old is Master, Ma'am?

Mrs Cad. Three years and a quarter come Lady-day.

Cape. The intention is rather early.

Cad. Hey! early, hold, hold; but Becky mistakes the thing, egad I'll tell you the whole affair.

Mrs Cad. You had better hold your chattering, so you had.

Cad. Nay, prythee, my dear; Mr Sprightly, do, stop her mouth, hold, hold; the matter, Mr Cape, is this. Have you ever seen my Dicky?

Cape. Never.

Cad. No? hold, hold, egad he's a fine, a sensible child; I tell Becky he's like her, to keep her in humour; but between you and I he has more sense already than all her family put together. Hey! Becky! is not Dicky the picture of you? He's a sweet child! Now, Mr Cape, you must know, I want to put little Dicky to school; now between—hey! you, hold, you, hold, the great use of a school is, hey! egad, for children to make acquaintances, that may hereafter be useful to them; for between you and I, as to what they learn there does not signify twopence.

Cape. Not a farthing.

Cad. Does it, hey? Now this is our dispute, whether poor

poor little Dicky, he's a sweet boy, shall go to Mr Quæ Genius's at Edgware, and make an acquaintance with my young Lord Knap, the eldest son of the Earl of Frize, or to Doctor Ticklepitcher's at Barnet, to form a friendship with young Stocks, the rich broker's only child.

Cape. And for which does the lady determine?

Cad. Why I have told her the case; says I, Becky, my dear; who knows, if Dicky goes to Quæ Genius's, but my Lord Knap may take such a fancy to him, that upon the death of his father, and he comes to be Earl of Frize, he may make poor little Dicky a Member of Parliament? Hey! Cape?

Mrs Cad. Ay, but then if Dicky goes to Ticklepitcher's, who can tell but young Stocks, when he comes to his fortune, may lend him money if he wants it?

Cad. And if he does not want it, he won't take after his father, hey! well, what's your opinion, Master Cape?

Cape. Why, Sir, I can't but join with the lady, money is the main article; it is that that makes the mare to go.

Cad. Hey! egad, and the Alderman too, you; so Dicky may be a Member, and a fig for my Lord: Well, Becky, be quiet, he shall stick to Stocks.

Mrs Cad. Ay let'n; I was sure as how I was right.

Cad. Well, hush Becky. Mr Cape, will you eat a bit with us to-day, hey! will you?

Cape. You command me.

Cad. That's kind; why then Becky and Bell shall step and order the cook to toss up a little, nice—Hey! will you, Becky? Do, and I'll bring Cape.

Mrs Cad. Ay, with all my heart. Well, Mr What-d'ye-call'um, the poet; ecod the man's well enough—Your servant.

Cape. I am a little too much in dishabille to offer your Ladyship my hand to your coach.

Cad. Pshaw! never mind, I'll do it—Here you have company coming. [*Exeunt* Mr *and* Mrs Cad. *and* Arch.

Enter Governor and Robin.

Cape. Ah, Master Robin!

Robin. Why, you have a great levee this morning, Sir.

Cape. Ay, Robin, there's no obscuring extraordinary talents.

Rob.

Rob. True, Sir; and this friend of mine begs to claim the benefit of them.

Cape. Any friend of yours; but how can I be serviceable to him?

Rob. Why, Sir, he is lately returned from a profitable government; and, as you know the unsatisfied mind of man, no sooner is one object possess'd, but another starts up to——

Cape. A truce to moralizing, dear Robin, to the matter; I am a little busy.

Rob. In a word, then, this gentleman, having a good deal of wealth, is desirous of a little honour.

Cape. How can I confer it?

Rob. Your pen may.

Cape. I don't understand you.

Rob. Why touch him up a handsome complimentary address from his colony, by way of praising the prudence of his administration, his justice, valour, benevolence, and——

Cape. I am sorry 'tis impossible for me now to misunderstand you. The obligations I owe you, Robin, nothing can cancel; otherwise this won'd prove our last interview. —Your friend, Sir, has been a little mistaken, in recommending me as a person fit for your purpose. Letters have been always my passion, and indeed are now my profession; but though I am the servant of the public, I am not the prostitute of particulars: As my pen has never been ting'd with gall, to gratify popular resentment, or private pique, so it shall never sacrifice its integrity to flatter pride, impose falsehood, or palliate guilt. Your merit may be great, but let those, Sir, be the heralds of your worth who are better acquainted with it.

Gov. Young man, I like your principles and spirit; your manly refusal gives me more pleasure than any honours your papers could have procured me.

Spri. Now this business is dispatch'd, let us return to our own affairs—You dine at Cadwallader's?

Cape. I do.

Spri. Wou'd it not be convenient to you to have him out of the way?

Cape. Extremely.

Spri. I have a project, that I think will prevail.

Cape. Of what kind?

Spri.

Spri. Bordering upon the dramatic; but the time is so pressing, I shall be at a loss to procure performers. Let's see—Robin is a sure card—A principal may easily be met with, but where the duce can I get an interpreter?

Rob. Offer yourself, Sir; it will give you an opportunity of more closely inspecting the conduct of your son.

Gov. True. Sir, though a scheme of this sort may ill suit with my character and time of life, yet from a private interest I take in that gentleman's affairs, if the means are honourable——

Spri. Innocent upon my credit.

Gov. Why then, Sir, I have no objection, if you think me equal to the task——

Spri. Most happily fitted for it. I shou'd not have taken the liberty—but hush! He's return'd.

Enter Cadwallader.

Spri. My dear friend! the luckiest circumstance!
Cad. Hey! how? Stay, hey!
Spri. You see that gentleman?
Cad. Well, hey!
Spri. Do you know who he is?
Cad. Not I.
Spri. He is Interpreter to Prince Potowowsky.
Cad. Wowsky? who the devil is he?
Spri. Why, the Tartarian Prince, that's come over Ambassador from the Cham of the Calmucks.
Cad. Indeed!
Spri. His Highness has just sent me an invitation to dine with him; now every body that dines with a Tartarian Lord, has a right to carry with him what the Latins called his *Umbra*; in their language it is *Jablanowsky*.
Cad. *Jablanowsky!* well?
Spri. Now, if you will go in that capacity, I shall be glad of the honour.
Cad. Hey! why, wou'd you carry me to dine with his Royal Highness?
Spri. With pleasure.
Cad. My dear friend, I shall take it as the greatest favour, the greatest obligation—I shall never be able to return it.
Spri. Don't mention it.

Cad. Hey! but hold, hold, how the devil shall I get off with the poet? You know I have ask'd him to dinner.

Spri. Oh, the occasion will be apology sufficient; besides, there will be the ladies to receive him.

Cad. My dear Mr Cape, I beg ten thousand pardons, but here your friend is invited to dinner with Prince—— what the devil is his name?——

Spri. Potowowski.

Cad. True; now, Sir, ecod he has been so kind as to offer to carry me as his Jablanousky, wou'd you be so good to excuse——

Cape. By all means; not a word, I beg.

Cad. That is exceeding kind; I'll come to you after dinner; hey! stay, but is there any ceremony to be used with his Highness?

Spri. You dine upon carpets cross-legg'd.

Cad. Hey! hold, hold, cross-legg'd, zounds! that's odd, well, well, you shall teach me.

Spri. And his Highness is particularly pleased with those amongst his guests that do honour to his country soup.

Cad. Oh! let me alone for that; but should not I dress?

Spri. No, there's no occasion for it.

Cad. Dear friend, forgive me; nothing should take me from you, but being a Hobblin Wissy. Well, I'll go and study to sit cross-legg'd, 'till you call me.

Spri. Do so.

Cad. His Highness Potowowsky! This is the luckiest accident! [*Exit.*

Cape. Hah! hah! hah! but how will you conduct your enterprize?

Spri. We'll carry him to your friend Robin's; dress up one of the under actors in a ridiculous habit; this gentleman shall talk a little gibberish with him. I'll compose a soup of some nauseous ingredients; let me alone to manage. But do you chuse, Sir, the part we have assign'd?

Goo. As it seems to be but a harmless piece of mirth, I have no objection.

Spri. Well then let us about it; come, Sir.

Cape. Mr Sprightly!

Spri. What's the matter?

Cape. Wou'd it not be right to be a little spruce, a little smart upon this occasion?

Spri.

Spri. No doubt; drefs, drefs, man; no time is to be loft.

Cape. Well, but Jack, I cannot fay that at prefent I—

Spri. Prythee explain. What would you fay?

Cape. Why then, I cannot fay, that I have any other garments at home.

Spri. Oh, I underftand you, is that all? Here, here, take my—

Cape. Dear Sprightly, I am quite afham'd, and forry.

Spri. That's not fo obliging, George; what, forry to give me the greateft pleafure that——But I have no time for fpeeches; I muft run to get ready my foup. Come, gentlemen.

Rob. Did you obferve, Sir?

Geo. Moft feelingly! But it will foon be over.

Rob. Courage, Sir; times perhaps may change.

Cape. A poor profpect, Robin! But this fcheme of life at leaft muft be changed; for what fpirit, with the leaft fpark of generofity, can fupport a life of eternal obligation, and difagreeable drudgery? Inclination not confulted, genius cramp'd, and talents mifapply'd.

What profpect have thofe authors to be read,
Whofe daily writings earn their daily bread? [*Exeunt.*

ACT II.

Young Cape and Mrs Cadwallader at cards.

Mrs Cad. YOU want four, and I two, and my deal: Now, knave noddy——no, hearts be trumps.

Cape. I beg.

Mrs Cad. Will you ftock 'em?

Cape. Go on, if you pleafe, Madam.

Mrs Cad. Hearts again—One, two, three; one, two, —hang 'em, they won't flip, three. Diamonds——the two: Have you higher than the Queen?

Cape. No, Madam.

Mrs Cad. Then there's higheft—and loweft, by golh. Games are over; you are to deal.

Cape. Pfhaw, hang cards; there are other amufements better

better suited to a tête-a-tête, than any the four aces can afford us.

Mrs Cad. What pastimes be they?—We ben't enough for hunt the whistle, nor blind-man's buff: but I'll call our Bell, and Robin the butler. Dicky will be here anbye.

Cape. Hold a minute. I have a game to propose, where the presence of a third person, especially Mr Cadwallader's, wou'd totally ruin the sport.

Mrs Cad. Ay, what can that be?

Cape. Can't you guess?

Mrs Cad. Not I; questions and commands, mayhap.

Cape. Not absolutely that——some little resemblance; for I am to request, and you are to command.

Mrs Cad. Oh daisy; that's charming, I never play'd at that in all my born days; come, begin then.

Cape. Can you love me?

Mrs Cad. Love you! But is it in jest or earnest?

Cape. That is as you please to determine.

Mrs Cad. But mayn't I ask you questions too?

Cape. Doubtless.

Mrs Cad. Why, then, do you love me?

Cape. With all my soul.

Mrs Cad. Upon your sayso.

Cape. Upon my sayso.

Mrs Cad. I'm glad on't with all my heart. This is the rarest pastime!

Cape. But you have not answer'd my question.

Mrs Cad. Hey? that's true. Why, I believe there's no love lost.

Cape. So; our game will soon be over; I shall be up at a deal. I wish I mayn't be engaged to play deeper here than I intended though. [*Aside.*

Mrs Cad. Well, now 'tis your turn.

Cape. True; aye; but zooks you are too hasty; the pleasure of this play, like hunting, does not consist in immediately chopping the prey.

Mrs Cad. No! How then?

Cape. Why first I am to start you, then run you a little in view, then lose you, then unravel all the tricks and doubles you make to escape me.

You

You fly o'er hedge and ſtile,
I purſue for many a mile,
You grow tir'd at laſt and quat,
Then I catch you, and all that.

Mrs Cad. Dear me, there's a deal on't! I ſhall never be able to hold out long; I had rather be taken in view.

Cape. I believe you.

Mrs Cad. Well, come, begin and ſtart me, that I may come the ſooner to quatting.—Huſh! here's ſiſter; what the deuce brought her? Bell will be for learning this game too, but don't you teach her for your life, Mr Poet.

Enter Arabella.

Arab. Your mantuamaker, with your new ſack, ſiſter.

Mrs Cad. Is that all? She might have ſtay'd, I think.

Arab. What? You were better engaged? But don't be angry, I am ſorry I interrupted you.

Mrs Cad. Hey! Now will I be hang'd if ſhe be'nt jealous of Mr Poet; but I'll liſten, and ſee the end on't, I'm reſolved.   [*Aſide* and *Exit.*

Arab. Are you concern'd at the interruption too?

Cape. It was a very ſeaſonable one, I promiſe you; had you ſtay'd a little longer, I don't know what might have been the conſequence.

Arab. No danger to your perſon, I hope.

Cape. Some little attacks upon it.

Arab. Which were as feebly reſiſted.

Cape. Why, conſider, my dear Bell; tho' your ſiſter is a fool, ſhe is a fine woman, and fleſh is frail.

Arab. Dear Bell! And fleſh is frail! We are grown ſtrangely familiar, I think.

Cape. Heydey! In what corner ſits the wind now?

Arab. Where it may poſſibly blow ſtrong enough to overſet your hopes.

Cape. That a breeze of your breath can do.

Arab. Affected!

Cape. You are obliging, Madam; but pray, what is the meaning of all this?

Arab. Aſk your own guilty conſcience.

Cape. Were I inclined to flatter myſelf, this little paſſion wou'd be no bad preſage.

Arab.

Arab. You may prove a false prophet.

Cape. Let me die, if I know what to—But to descend to a little common sense; what part of my conduct——

Arab. Look'e, Mr Cape, all explanations are unnecessary: I have been lucky enough to discover your disposition before it is too late; and so you know there's no occasion—but however, I'll not be any impediment to you; my sister will be back immediately; I suppose my presence will only—But consider, Sir, I have a brother's honour——

Cape. Which is as safe from me, as if it was lock'd up in your brother's closet: But surely, Madam, you are a little capricious here; have I done any thing but obey your directions?

Arab. That was founded upon a supposition that—— but no matter.

Cape. That what?

Arab. Why, I was weak enough to believe, what you was wicked enough to protest——

Cape. That I loved you; and what reason have I given you to doubt it?

Arab. A pretty situation I found you in at my entrance.

Cape. An assumed warmth, for the better concealing the fraud.

Mrs Cad. What's that? [*Aside, listening.*

Cape. Surely if you doubted my constancy, you must have a better opinion of my understanding.

Mrs Cad. Mighty well. [*Aside.*

Cape. What, an ideot, a driveller! no consideration upon earth, but my paving the way to the possession of you, could have prevailed upon me to support her folly a minute.

Enter Mrs Cadwallader.

Mrs Cad. Soh! Mr Poet, you are a pretty gentleman, indeed; ecod, I'm glad I have caught you. I'm not such a fool as you think for, man: but here will be Dicky presently, he shall hear of your tricks, he shall: I'll let him know what a pretty person he has got in his house.

Cape. There's no parrying this; had not I better decamp.

Arab. And leave me to the mercy of the enemy: My brother's brother's temper is so odd, there's no knowing in what light he'll see this.

Mrs Cad. Oh, he's below, I hear him. Now we shall hear what he'll say to you, Madam.

Enter Cadwallader, Governor, Sprightly, *and* Robin.

Cad. No, pray walk in, Mr Interpreter, between you and I, I like his Royal Highness mightily; he's a polite, pretty, well-bred gentleman———but damn his soup.

Gov. Why, Sir, you eat as if you lik'd it.

Cad. Lik'd it! hey, egad, I would not eat another mess to be his master's prime minister; as bitter as gall, and as black as my hat; and there have I been sitting these two hours with my legs under me till they are both as dead as a herring.

Cape. Your dinner displeas'd you?

Cad. Displeas'd! hey! Look'e, Mr Sprightly, I'm mightily obliged to you for the honour; but hold, hold, you shall never persuade me to be a Hobblinwisky again, if the great Cham of the Calmucks were to come over himself. Hey! and what a damn'd language has he got? Whee, haw, haw! But you speak it very fluently.

Gov. I was long resident in the country.

Cad. May be so, but he seems to speak it better; you have a foreign kind of an accent, you don't sound it through the nose so well as he. Hey! well Becky, what, and how have you entertained Mr Cape?

Mrs Cad. Oh! here have been fine doings since you have been gone.

Cape. So, now comes on the storm.

Cad. Hey! hold, hold, what has been the matter?

Mrs Cad. Matter! why, the devil is in the poet, I think.

Cad. The devil! hold.

Mrs Cad. Why here he has been making love to me like bewitch'd.

Cad. How, which way?

Mrs Cad. Why, some on't was out of his poetry, I think.

Cad. Hey! hold, hold, egad I believe he's a little mad; this morning he took me for King Turnus, you; now who can tell, but this afternoon he may take you for Queen Dido?

Mrs

Mrs Cad. And there he told me I was to run, and to double, and quat, and there he was to catch me, and all that.

Cad. Hold, hold, catch you? Mr Cape, I take it very unkindly; it was, d'ye see, a very unfriendly thing to make love to Becky in my absence.

Cape. But, Sir.

Cad. And it was the more ungenerous, Mr Cape, to take this advantage, as you know she is but a foolish woman.

Mrs Cad. Ay, me; who am but a foolish woman.

Cape. But hear me.

Cad. A poor ignorant, illiterate, poor Becky! And for a man of your parts to attack——

Cape. There's no——

Cad. Hold, hold, evod, it is just as if the Grand Signor, at the head of his Janisaries, was to kick a chimney-sweeper.

Mrs Cad. Hey! what's that you say, Dicky; what, be I like a chimney-sweeper?

Cad. Hey! hold, hold. Zounds! no, Beck.; hey! no: That's only by way of simile, to let him see I understand your tropes, and figures, as well as himself, egad! and therefore——

Spri. Nay, but Mr Cadwallader——

Cad. Don't mention it, Mr Sprightly; he is the first poet I ever had in my house, except the bellman for a Christmas-box.

Spri. Good Sir.

Cad. And hold, hold, I am resolved he shall be the last.

Spri. I have but one way to silence him.

Cad. And let me tell you——

Spri. Nay, Sir, if I must tell him; he owes his reception here to my recommendation; any abuse of your goodness, any breach of hospitality here, he is answerable to me for.

Cad. Hey! hold, hold, so he is, evod; at him; give it him home.

Spri. Ungrateful monster! and is this your return for the open, generous treatment——

Mrs Cad. As good fry'd cow-heel, with a roast fowl and saufages, as ever came to a table.

Cad.

Cad. Hufh, Beck, hufh!

Spri. And cou'd you find no other object, but Mr Cadwallader; a man, perhaps, poffefs'd of a genius superior to your own——

Cad. If I had had a Univerfity education——

Spri. And of a family as old as the creation.

Cad. Older; Beck, fetch the pedigree.

Spri. Thus far relates to this gentleman; but now, Sir, what apology can you make me, who was your paffport, your fecurity?

Cad. Zounds, none; fight him.

Spri. Fight him?

Cad. Ay, do; I'd fight him myfelf, if I had not had the meafles left winter; but ftay till I get out of the room.

Spri. No, he's fure of a protection here, the prefence of the ladies.

Cad. Pfhaw, pox! they belong to the family, never mind them.

Spri. Well, Sir, are you dumb? No excufe? No palliation?

Cad. Ay, no palliation?

Mrs Cad. Ay, no tribulation? It's a fhame, fo it is.

Cape. When I have leave to fpeak——

Cad. Speak! what the devil can you fay?

Cape. Nay, Sir——

Spri. Let's hear him, Mr Cadwallader, however.

Cad. Hold, hold; come, begin then.

Cape. And firft to you, Mr Spightly, as you feem moft interefted; pray does this charge correfpond with any other action of my life, fince I have had the honour to know you?

Spri. Indeed, I can't fay that I recollect, but ftill as the fcholiafts fay—*Nemo repente fuit turpiffimus.*

Cad. Hold, hold, what's that?

Spri. Why, that is as much as to fay, this is bad enough.

Mrs Cad. By gofh! and fo it is.

Cad. Ecod, and fo it is: Speak a little more Latin to him; if I had been bred at the Univerfity, you fhou'd have it both fides of your ears.

Cape. A little patience, gentlemen; now, to you; you were pleafed yourfelf to drop a few hints of your lady's

Vol. I. U weaknefs;

weakness; might not she take too seriously what was meant as a mere matter of merriment?

Cad. Hey! hold, hold.

Spri. A paltry excuse; can any woman be such a fool as not to know when a man has a design upon her person?

Cad. Answer that, Mr Cape, hey! answer that.

Cape. I can only answer for the innocency of my own intentions; may not your lady, apprehensive of my becoming too great a favourite, contrive this charge with a view of destroying the connexion——

Spri. Connexion!

Cad. Hey! hold, hold, connexion.

Spri. There's something in that——

Cad. Hay! is there? hold, hold, hey! egad, he is right ——You're right, Mr Cape; hold, Becky, my dear, how the devil cou'd you be so wicked, hey! child; ecod, hold, hold, how could you have the wickedness to attempt to destroy the connexion?

Mrs Cad. I don't know what you say.

Cad. D'ye hear? you are an incendiary, but you have miss'd your point; the connexion shall be only the stronger: My dear friend, I beg ten thousand pardons, I was too hasty; but ecod, Becky's to blame.

Cape. The return of your favour has effaced every other impression.

Cad. There's a good-natured creature!

Cape. But if you have the least doubts remaining, this lady, your sister, I believe, will do me the justice to own——

Mrs Cad. Ay, ask my fellow, if I be a thief.

Cad. What the devil is Becky at now?

Mrs Cad. She's as bad as he.

Cad. Bad as he? hey! how; what the devil, she did not make love to you too? stop, hey! hold, hold, hold.

Mrs Cad. Why no, foolish, but you are always running on with your riggmonrowles, and won't stay to hear a body's story out.

Cad. Well, Beck, come let's have it.

Mrs Cad. Be quiet then; why, as I was telling you, first he made love to me, and wanted me to be a hare.

Cad. A hare! hold, ecod, that was whimsical; a hare! hey! oh ecod, that might be because he thought you a little hair-brain'd already: Becky, a damn'd good story. Well, Beck, go on, let's have it out.

Mrs

Mrs Cad. No, I won't tell you no more, so I won't.
Cad. Nay, prythee, Beck.
Mrs Cad. Hold your tongue then: And so there he was going on with his nonsense, and so in come our Bell; and so——
Cad. Hold, hold, Becky; damn your so's; go on, child, but leave out your so's; it's a low——hold, hold, vulgar ——but go on.
Mrs Cad. Why, how can I go on, when you stop me every minute? well, and then our Bell came in and interrupted him, and methought she looked very frumpish and jealous.
Cad. Well.
Mrs Cad. And so I went out and listen'd.
Cad. So, what you staid and listen'd?
Mrs Cad. No; I tell you upon my staying, she went out; no——upon my going out, she staid.
Cad. This is a damn'd blind story, but go on, Beck.
Mrs Cad. And then at first she scolded him roundly for making love to me; and then he said as how she advised him to it; and then she said no; and then he said——
Cad. Hold, hold; we shall never understand all these he's and she's; this may all be very true, Beck, but, hold, hold; as I hope to be saved, thou art the worst teller of a story——
Mrs Cad. Well, I have but a word more; and then he said as how I was a great fool,
Cad. Not much mistaken in that. (*Aside.*)
Mrs Cad. And that he wou'd not have stay'd with me a minute, but to pave the way to the possession of she.
Cad. Well, Beck, well?
Mrs Cad. And so——that's all.
Cad. Make love to her, in order to get possession of you?
Mrs Cad. Love to me, in order to get she.
Cad. Hey! Oh, now I begin to understand. Hey! what's this true, Bell? hey! hold, hold, hold; ecod, I begin to smoke, hey! Mr Cape?
Cape. How shall I act?
Rob. Own it, Sir, I have a reason.
Cad. Well, what say you, Mr Cape? let's have it, without equivocation; or, hold, hold, hold, mental reservation. Guilty, or not?

Cape.

Cape. Of what, Sir?
Cad. Of what? hold, hold, of making love to Bell.
Cape. Guilty.
Cad. Hey! how? hold, zounds! no, what, not with an intention to marry her?
Cape. With the lady's approbation, and your kind consent.
Cad. Hold, hold, what, my consent to marry you!
Cape. Ay, Sir.
Cad. Hold, hold, hold, what our Bell? to mix the blood of the Cadwalladers with the puddle of a poet?
Cape. Sir?
Cad. A petty, paltry, ragged, rhiming——
Spri. But Mr——
Cad. A scribbling, hold, hold, hold——garretteer? that has no more cloaths than backs, no more heads than hats, and no shoes to his feet.
Spri. Nay, but——
Cad. The offspring of a dunghill! born in a cellar, hold, hold, and living in a garret; a fungus, a mushroom.
Cape. Sir, my family——
Cad. Your family! hold, hold, hold; Peter, fetch the pedigree; I'll shew you——your family! a little obscure ——hold, hold, I don't believe you ever had a grandfather.

Enter Peter *with the Pedigree.*

There it is; there; Peter, help me to stretch it out: There's seven yards more of lineals, besides three of collaterals, that I expect next Monday from the Herald's Office; d'ye see, Mr Sprightly?
Spri. Prodigious!
Cad. Nay, but look'e, there's Welch Princes, and Ambassadors, and Kings of Scotland, and Members of Parliament: hold, hold, eed, I no more mind an Earl or a Lord in my pedigree, hold, hold, than Kouli Khan would a serjeant in the train'd bands.
Spri. An amazing descent!
Cad. Hey, is it not? and for this low, lousy son of a shoemaker, to talk of families——hold, hold, get out of my house.
Rob. Now is your time, Sir.
Cad. Mr Sprightly, turn him out.
Geo. Stop, Sir, I have a secret to disclose, that may make you alter your intentions.
Cad. Hold, hold: how, Mr Interpreter?

Geo.

Gov. You are now to regard that young man in a very different light, and consider him as my son.

Cape. Your son, Sir?

Gov. In a moment, George, the mysteries shall be explain'd.

Cad. Your son? hold, hold; and what then?

Gov. Then! why then he is no longer the scribbler, the mushroom you have described, but of birth and fortune equal to your own.

Cad. What! the son of an interpreter equal to me! a fellow that trudges about, teaching of languages to foreign courts!

Gov. A teacher of languages!

Cad. Stay; ecod, a runner to monsieurs and marquisses!

Spri. You are mistaken, Sir.

Cad. A jack-pudding! that takes fillips on the nose for six-pence a piece? hold, hold, acod, give me eighteen-penny worth, and change for half a crown.

Gov. Stop, when you are well.

Cad. A sponger at other men's tables! that has jallop put into his beer, and his face black'd at Christmas for the diversion of children!

Gov. I can hold no longer. 'Sdeath, Sir; who is it you dare treat in this manner?

Cad. Hey! zounds, Mr Sprightly, lay hold of him.

Spri. Calm your choler. Indeed, Mr Cadwallader, nothing cou'd excuse your behaviour to this gentleman but your mistaking his person.

Cad. Hold, hold. Is not he interpreter to——

Spri. No.

Cad. Why, did not you tell——

Spri. That was a mistake. This gentleman is the Prince's friend; and, by a long residence in the Monarch's country, is perfect master of the language.

Cad. But who the devil is he then?

Spri. He is Mr Cape, Sir; a man of unblemish'd honour, capital fortune, and late governor of one of our most considerable settlements.

Cad. Governor! hold, hold, and how came you father to——hey!——

Gov. By marrying his mother.

Cape. But how am I to regard this?

Gov. As a solemn truth; that foreign friend, to whom you

you owe your education, was no other than myself; I had my reasons, perhaps capricious ones, for concealing this; but now they cease, and I am proud to own my son.

Cape. Sir; it is not for me (*kneeling*)—but if gratitude, duty filial—

Gov. Rise, my boy; I have ventured far to fix thy fortune, George; but to find thee worthy of it more than o'erpays my toil; the rest of my story shall be reserved till we are alone.

Cad. Hey! hold, hold, hold; ecod, a good sensible old fellow this; but, hark'e, Sprightly, I have made a damn'd blunder here: Hold, hold, Mr Governor, I ask ten thousand pardons; but who the devil cou'd have thought that the interpreter to Prince Potowowsky—

Gov. Oh, Sir, you have in your power sufficient means to atone for the injuries done us both.

Cad. Hold, how?

Gov. By bestowing your sister, with, I flatter myself, no great violence to her inclinations, here.

Cad. What, marry Bell? hey! hold, hold; zounds, Bell, take him, do; 'ecod, he is a good likely—hey! will you?

Arab. I shan't disobey you, Sir.

Cad. Shan't you? that's right. Who the devil knows but he may come to be a governor himself; hey! hold, hold; come here then, give me your hands both (*joins their hands*); there, there, the business is done: and now, brother Governor—

Gov. And now, brother Cadwallader,

Cad. Hey, Beck! here's something new for my pedigree; we'll pop in the governor to-morrow.

Mrs Cad. Hark'e, Mr Governor, can you give me a black boy and a monkey?

Cad. Hey! ay, ay, you shall have a black boy, and a monkey, and a parrot too, Beck.

Spri. Dear George, I am a little late in my congratulations; but—

Gov. Which if he is in acknowledging your disinterested friendship, I shall be sorry I ever own'd him. Now, Robin, my cares are over, and my wishes full; and if George remains as untainted by affluence, as he has been untempted by distress, I have given the poor a protector, his country an advocate, and the world a friend.

[*Exeunt Omnes.*

THE
MAYOR OF GARRAT;

A COMEDY,

IN TWO ACTS.

DRAMATIS PERSONÆ.

Major Sturgeon.	—	Mr Barrister.
Sir Jacob Jollup.		Mr Watson.
Bruin.	— —	Mr Wright.
Ultra.	— —	Mr Wilkinson.
Rigid.	=	Mr Hollisott.
Mob.		Mess. Hales, Nash, &c.
Snuffle.	—	Mr Booth.
Crispin Heel-Tap.	—	Mr Griffiths.
Jerry Sneak.		Mr Dodd.
Mrs Bruin.	—	Miss Sherrey.
Mrs Sneak.	— =	Mrs Webster.

ACT I. SCENE I.

SCENE *Sir Jacob's House at Garrat.*

Enter Sir Jacob.

Sir Jac. ROGER—

Enter Roger.

Rog. Anan, Sir—

Sir Jac. Sir, sirrah! and why not Sir Jacob, you rascal? Is that all your manners? Has his Majesty dubb'd me a knight for you to make me a mister? Are the candidates near upon coming?

Rog. Nic Goose, the tailor, from Putney, they say, will be here in a 'crack, Sir Jacob.

Sir Jac. Has Margery fetch'd in the linen?

Rog. Yes, Sir Jacob.

Sir Jac. Are the pigs and the poultry lock'd up in the barn?

Rog. Safe, Sir Jacob.

Sir Jac. And the plate and spoons in the pantry?

Rog. Yes, Sir Jacob.

Sir Jac. Then give me the key; the mob will soon be upon us; and all is fish that comes to their net. Has Ralph laid the cloth in the hall?

Rog. Yes, Sir Jacob.

Sir Jac. Then let him bring out the turkey and chine, and be sure there is plenty of mustard; and, d'ye hear, Roger, do you stand yourself at the gate, and be careful who you let in.

Rog. I will, Sir Jacob. [*Exit Rog.*

Sir Jac. So, now I believe things are pretty secure: but I can't think what makes my daughters so late ere they— [*Knocking at the gate.*
Who is that, Roger?

Roger without. Master Lint, the potter-carrier, Sir Jacob.

Sir Jac. Let him in. What the deuce can he want?

Enter Lint.

Sir Jac. Well, Master Lint, your will?

Lint. Why, I come, Sir Jacob, partly to enquire after your health; and partly, as I may say, to settle the business of the day.

Sir Jac. What business?

Lint. Your Worship knoweth, this being the day of election, the rabble may be riotous; in which case, maims, bruises, contusions, dislocations, fractures simple and compound, may likely ensue: now your Worship need not be told, that I am not only a pharmacopolist, or vender of drugs, but likewise chirurgeon, or healer of wounds.

Sir Jac. True, Master Lint, and equally skilful in both.

Lint. It is your Worship's pleasure to say so, Sir Jacob: Is it your Worship's will that I lend a ministring hand to the maim'd?

Sir Jac. By all means.

Lint. And to whom must I bring in my bill?

Sir Jac. Doubtless, the vestry.

Lint. Your Worship knows, that, kill or cure, I have contracted to physic the parish-poor by the great: but this must be a seperate charge.

Sir Jac. No, no; all under one: come, Master Lint, don't be unreasonable.

Lint. Indeed, Sir Jacob, I can hardly afford it. What with the dearness of drugs, and the number of patients the peace has procured me, I can't get salt to my porridge.

Sir Jac. Bad this year, the better the next—We must take things rough and smooth as they run.

Lint. Indeed I have a very hard bargain.

Sir Jac. No such matter; we are, neighbour Lint, a little better instructed. Formerly, indeed, a fit of illness was very expensive; but now, physic is cheaper than food.

Lint. Marry, heaven forbid!

Sir Jac. No, no; your essences, elixirs, emetics, sweats, drops, and your pastes, and your pills, have silenced your pestles and mortars. Why, a fever, that would formerly have cost you a fortune, you may now cure for twelve penn'orth of powder.

Lint. Or kill, Sir Jacob.

Sir Jac. And then as to your scurvies, and gouts, rheumatisms,

matisms, consumptions, coughs, and catarrhs, tar-water and turpentine will make you as sound as a roach.

Lint. Nostrums!

Sir Jac. Specifics, specifics, Master Lint.

Lint. I am very sorry to find a man of your Worship's ——Sir Jacob, a promoter of puffs; an encourager of quacks, Sir Jacob.

Sir Jac. Regulars, Lint, regulars; look at their names—Roger, bring me the news—not a soul of them but is either P.L. or M.D.

Lint. Plaguy liars! Murderous dogs!

Roger *brings the news.*

Sir Jac. Liars! Here, look at the list of their cures. The oath of Margery Squab, of Ratcliff-Highway, spinster.

Lint. Perjuries.

Sir Jac. And see, here, the churchwardens have signed it.

Lint. Fictitious, Sir Jacob.

Sir Jac. Sworn before the worshipful Mr Justice Drowsy, this thirteenth day of——

Lint. Forgery.

Sir Jac. Why, harkye, sirrah, do you think Mr Justice Drowsy would set his hand to a forgery?

Lint. I know, Sir Jacob, that woman; she has been cured of fifty diseases in a fortnight, and every one of 'em mortal.

Sir Jac. You impudent——

Lint. Of a dropsy, by West——

Sir Jac. Audacious——

Lint. A cancer, by Cleland——

Sir Jac. Arrogant——

Lint. A palsy, by Walker——

Sir Jac. Impertinent——

Lint. Gout and sciatic, by Rock——

Sir Jac. Insolent——

Lint. Consumption, by Stevens's drops——

Sir Jac. Paltry——

Lint. And squinting, by the Chevalier Taylor——

Sir Jac. Pill-gilding puppy!

Lint. And as to the Justice, so the affidavit brings him a shilling——

Sir Jac. Why, harkye, rascal, how dare you abuse the commission?

commission?—You blood-letting, tooth-drawing, corn-
cutting, worm-killing, blistering, glistering——

Lint. Bless me, Sir Jacob, I did not think to—

Sir Jac. What, sirrah, do you insult me in my office?
Here, Roger, out with him—turn him out.

Lint. Sir, as I hope to be——

Sir Jac. Away with him. You scoundrel, if my clerk
was within, I'd send you this instant to Bridewell. Things
are come to a pretty pass, indeed, if, after all my reading
in Wood, and Nelson, and Burn; if after twenty years
attendance at turnpike-meetings, sessions petty and quarter; if after settling of rates, licencing ale-houses, and
committing of vagrants—But all respect to authority is lost,
and *suus quorum* now-a-days is no more regarded than a
petty constable. [*Knocking.*] Roger, see who is at the
gate? Why, the fellow is deaf.

Rog. Justice Sturgeon, the fishmonger, from Brentford.

Sir Jac. Gad's my life! and Major to the Middlesex
militia. Usher him in, Roger.

Enter Major Sturgeon.

Sir Jac. I could have wish'd you had come a little sooner, Major Sturgeon.

Maj. Why, what has been the matter, Sir Jacob?

Sir Jac. There has, Major, been here an impudent pill-
monger, who has dar'd to scandalize the whole body of the
bench.

Maj. Insolent companion! had I been here, I would have
mittimus'd the rascal at once.

Sir Jac. No, no, he wanted the Major more than the
Magistrate; a few smart strokes from your cane would
have fully answer'd the purpose—Well, Major, our wars
are done; the rattling drum, and squeaking fife, now wound
our ears no more.

Maj. True, Sir Jacob, our corps is disembodied, so
the French may sleep in security.

Sir Jac. But, Major, was it not rather late in life for
you to enter upon the profession of arms?

Maj. A little awkward in the beginning, Sir Jacob:
the great difficulty they had was, to get me to turn out
my toes; but use, use reconciles all them kind of things:
why, after my first campaign, I no more minded the noise
of the guns than a flea-bite.

Sir

Sir Jac. No!

Maj. No. There is more made of these matters than they merit. For the general good, indeed, I am glad of the peace; but as to my single self—And yet, we have had some desperate duty, Sir Jacob.

Sir Jac. No doubt.

Maj. Oh! such marchings and counter-marchings, from Brentford to Elin, from Elin to Acton, from Acton to Uxbridge; the dust flying, sun scorching, men sweating—Why, there was our last expedition to Honslow, that day's work carried off Major Molasses. Bunhill-fields never saw a braver commander! He was an irreparable loss to the service.

Sir Jac. How came that about?

Maj. Why, it was partly the Major's own fault; I advised him to pull off his spurs before he went upon action; but he was resolute, and would not be rul'd.

Sir Jac. Spirit; zeal for the service.

Maj. Doubtless—But to proceed: In order to get our men in good spirits, we were quartered at Thistleworth the evening before; at day-break, our regiment form'd at Honslow town's end, as it might be about here. The Major made a fine disposition: on we march'd, the men all in high spirits, to attack the gibbet where Gardel is hanging; but turning down a narrow lane to the left, as it might be about there, in order to possess a pig's stye, that we might take the gallows in flank, and, at all events, secure a retreat, who should come by but a drove of fat oxen for Smithfield. The drums beat in the front, the dogs bark'd in the rear, the oxen set up a gallop; on they came thundering upon us, broke through our ranks in an instant, and threw the whole corps in confusion.

Sir Jac. Terrible!

Maj. The Major's horse took to his heels; away he scour'd over the heath. That gallant commander stuck both his spurs into the flank, and for some time held by his mane: but in crossing a ditch, the horse threw up his head, gave the Major a dowse in the chops, and plump'd him into a gravel-pit, just by the powder-mills.

Sir Jac. Dreadful!

Maj. Whether from the fall or the fright, the Major mov'd off in a month—Indeed it was an unfortunate day for us all.

Sir

Sir Jac. As how?

Maj. Why, as Captain Cucumber, Lieutenant Parrypan, Enſign Tripe, and myſelf, were returning to town in the Turnham-Green ſtage, we were ſlopp'd near the Hammerſmith turnpike, and robb'd and ſtripp'd by a footpad.

Sir Jac. An unfortunate day, indeed!

Maj. But in ſome meaſure to make me amends, I got the Major's commiſſion.

Sir Jac. You did?

Maj. O yes. I was the only one of the corps that could ride; otherwiſe, we always ſucceeded of courſe; no jumping over heads; no underhand work among us; all men of honour; and I muſt do the regiment the juſtice to ſay, there never was a ſet of more amiable officers.

Sir Jac. Quiet and peaceable.

Maj. As lambs, Sir Jacob. Excepting one boxing bout at the Three Compaſſes in Acton, between Captain Sheers and the Colonel, concerning a game at All-fours, I don't remember a ſingle diſpute.

Sir Jac. Why, that was mere mutiny; the Captain ought to have been broke.

Maj. He was; for the Colonel not only took away his cockade, but his cuſtom; and I don't think Captain Sheers has done a ſtitch for him ſince.

Sir Jac. But you ſoon ſupplied the loſs of Modeſtes?

Maj. In part only: no, Sir Jacob, he had great experience; he was train'd up to arms from his youth: at ſixteen he trail'd a pike in the artillery-ground; at eighteen got a company in the Smithfield pioneers; and by the time he was twenty, was made aid-de-camp to Sir Jeffery Grub, Knight, Alderman, and Colonel of the Yellow.

Sir Jac. A rapid riſe!

Maj. Yes, he had a genius for war; but what I wanted in practice, I made up by doubling my diligence. Our porter at home had been a ſerjeant of marines; ſo after ſhop was ſhut up at night, he us'd to teach me my exerciſe; and he had not to deal with a duncе, Sir Jacob.

Sir Jac. Your progreſs was great.

Maj. Amazing. In a week I could ſhoulder, and reſt, and poiſe, and turn to the right, and wheel to the left; and in leſs than a month I could fire without winking or blinking.

Sir

Sir Jac. A perfect Hannibal!

Maj. Ah, and then I learnt to form lines, and hollows, and squares, and evolutions, and revolutions: let me tell you, Sir Jacob, it was lucky that Monsieur kept his myrmidons at home, or we should have pepper'd his flat bottom'd boats.

Sir Jac. Ay, marry, he had a marvellous escape.

Maj. We would a taught him what a Briton can do, who is fighting *pro arois* and *focus*.

Sir Jac. Pray now, Major, which do you look upon as the best disciplin'd troops, the London regiments, or the Middlesex militia?

Maj. Why, Sir Jacob, it does not become me to say; but lack-a-day, they have never seen any service—Holiday soldiers! Why, I don't believe, unless indeed upon a Lord Mayor's day, and that mere matter of accident, that they were ever wet to the skin in their lives.

Sir Jac. Indeed!

Maj. No! soldiers for sun-shine, cockneys; they have not the appearance, the air, the freedom, the *je ne sçai* that—Oh, could you but see me salute! you have never a spontoon in the house?

Sir Jac. No; but we could get you a shove-pike.

Maj. No matter. Well, Sir Jacob, and how are your fair daughters, sweet Mrs Sneak, and the lovely Mrs Bruin; is she as lively and as brilliant as ever?

Sir Jac. Oh, oh, now the murder is out; this visit was intended for them: come, own now, Major, did not you expect to meet with them here? You officers are men of such gallantry!

Maj. Why, we do tickle up the ladies, Sir Jacob; there is no resisting a red coat.

Sir Jac. True, true, Major.

Maj. But that is now all over with me. "Farewell to the plumed steeds and neighing troops," as the black man says in the play; like the Roman Censurer, I shall retire to my Savine field, and there cultivate cabbages.

Sir Jac. Under the shade of your laurels.

Maj. True; I have done with the Major, and now return to the Magistrate; *cedant arma togæ.*

Sir Jac. Still in the service of your country.

Maj. True; man was not made for himself; and so, thinking

thinking that this would prove a busy day in the justicing way, I am come, Sir Jacob, to lend you a hand.

Sir Jac. Done like a neighbour.

Maj. I have brought, as I suppose most of our business will be in the battery way, some warrants and mittimuses ready fill'd up, with all but the names of the parties, in order to save time.

Sir Jac. A provident magistrate.

Maj. Pray, how shall we manage as to the article of swearing; for I reckon we shall have oaths as plenty as hops.

Sir Jac. Why, with regard to that branch of our business, to-day, I believe, the law must be suffer'd to sleep.

Maj. I should think we might pick up something that's pretty that way.

Sir Jac. No, poor rascals, they would not be able to pay; and as to the stocks, we should never find room for their legs.

Maj. Pray, Sir Jacob, is Matthew Marrowbone, the butcher of your town, living or dead?

Sir Jac. Living.

Maj. And swears as much as he used?

Sir Jac. An alter'd man, Major; not an oath comes out of his mouth.

Maj. You surprize me; why, when he frequented our town of a market day, he has taken out a guinea in oaths—and quite chang'd?

Sir Jac. Entirely; they say his wife has made him a Methodist, and that he preaches at Kennington-Common.

Maj. What a deal of mischief those rascals do in the country—Why then we have entirely lost him?

Sir Jac. In that way; but I got a brace of bind-overs from him last week for a couple of bastards.

Maj. Well done, Master Matthew—but pray now, Sir Jacob— [*Mob without huzza!*

Sir Jac. What's the matter now, Roger?

Enter Roger.

Rog. The electors desire to know, if your Worship has any body to recommend?

Sir Jac. By no means; let them be free in their choice: I shan't interfere.

Rog. And if your Worship has any objection to Crispin Heeltap the cobler's being returning officer?

Sir

Sir Jac. None, provided the rafcal can keep himfelf fober: Is he there?

Rog. Yes, Sir Jacob: make way there; ftand farther off from the gate: here is Madam Sneak in a chair, along with her hufband.

Maj. Gad-fo, you will permit me to convey her in?
[*Exit Major.*

Sir Jac. Now here is one of the evils of war. This Sturgeon was as pains-taking a Billingfgate broker as any in the bills of mortality. But the fifh is got out of his element; the foldier has quite demolifhed the citizen.

Enter Mrs Sneak, handed by the Major.

Mrs Sneak. Dear Major, I demand a million of pardons. I have given you a profufion of trouble; but my hufband is fuch a goofe-cap, that I can't get no good out of him at home or abroad—Jercy, Jerry Sneak!—Your bleffing, Sir Jacob.

Sir Jac. Daughter, you are welcome to Garret.

Mrs Sneak. Why, Jerry Sneak! I fay.

Enter Sneak, with a band-box, a hoop-petticoat under his arm, and cardinal, &c. &c. &c. &c.

Sneak. Here, lovy.

Mrs Sneak. Here, booby: there, lay thefe things in the hall; and then go and look after the horfe: are you fure you have got all the things out of the chaife?

Sneak. Yes, chuck.

Mrs Sneak. Then give me my fan.

Jerry drops the things in fearching his pocket for the fan.

Mrs Sneak. Did ever mortal fee fuch a—I declare, I am quite afham'd to be feen with him abroad: go, get you gone out of my fight.

Sneak. I go, lovy: good-day to my father-in-law.

Sir Jac. I am glad to fee you, fon Sneak: but where is your brother Bruin and his wife?

Sneak. He will be here anon, father Sir Jacob; he did but juft ftep into the Alley to gather how tickets were fold.

Sir Joc. Very well, fon Sneak. [*Exit Snr.*].

Mrs Sneak. Son! yes, and a pretty fon you have provided.

Sir Jac. I hope all for the beft: why, what terrible work there would have been, had you married fuch a one

as your filter? one houfe could never have contain'd you—
now, I thought this meek mate——
Mrs Sneak. Meek! a mufhroom! a milkfop!
Sir Jac. Lookye, Molly, I have married you to a man;
take care you don't make him a monfter. [*Exit Sir Jacob.*
Mrs Sneak. Monfter! why, Major, the fellow has no
more heart than a moufe! had my kind ftars indeed allot-
ted me a military man, I fhould, doubtlefs, have deported
myfelf in a befeemingly manner.
Maj. Unqueftionably, Madam.
Mrs Sneak. Nor would the Major have found, had it
been my fortune to intermarry with him, that Molly
Jollup would have difhonoured his cloth.
Maj. I fhould have been too happy.
Mrs Sneak. Indeed, Sir, I reverence the army; they
are all fo brave, fo polite, fo every thing a woman can
wifh—
Maj. Oh! Madam—
Mrs Sneak. So elegant, fo genteel, fo obliging: and
then the rank; why, who would dare to affront the wife
of a Major?
Maj. No man with impunity; that I take freedom to
fay, Madam.
Mrs Sneak. I know it, good Sir: oh! I am no ftranger
to what I have mifs'd.
Maj. Oh, Madam!—let me die, but fhe has infinite
merit. [*Afide.*
Mrs Sneak. Then to be join'd to a fneaking flovenly
cit; a paltry, praying, pitiful pin-maker!
Maj. Melancholy!
Mrs Sneak. To be joftled and cramm'd with the croud;
no refpect, no place, no precedence; to be choak'd with
the fmoke of the city; no country jaunts but to Illington;
no balls but at Pewterers-hall.
Maj. Intolerable!
Mrs Sneak. I fee, Sir, you have a proper fenfe of my
fufferings.
Maj. And would fhed my beft blood to relieve them.
Mrs Sneak. Gallant gentleman!
Maj. The brave muft favour the fair.
Mrs Sneak. Intrepid Major!
Maj. Divine Mrs Sneak!
Mrs Sneak. Obliging commander!

Maj.

Maj. Might I be permitted the honour—
Mrs Sneak. Sir—
Maj. Just to ravish a kiss from your hand.
Mrs Sneak. You have a right to all we can grant.
Maj. Courteous, condescending, complying—hum—ha!

Enter Sneak.

Sneak. Chuck, my brother and sister Bruin are just turning the corner; the Clapham stage was quite full, and so they came by water.
Mrs Sneak. I wish they had all been souss'd in the Thames—a praying impertinent puppy!
Maj. Next time I will clap a centinel to secure the door.
Mrs Sneak. Major Sturgeon, permit me to withdraw for a moment; my dress demands a little repair.
Maj. Your ladyship's most entirely devoted.
Mrs Sneak. Ladyship! he is the very Broglio and Belleisle of the army!
Sneak. Shall I wait upon you, dove?
Mrs Sneak. No, dolt; what, would you leave the Major alone? is that your manners, you mongrel?
Maj. Oh, Madam, I can never be alone; your sweet idera will be my constant companion.
Mrs Sneak. Mark that: I am sorry, Sir, I am obligated to leave you.
Maj. Madam—
Mrs Sneak. Especially with such a wretched companion.
Maj. Oh, Madam—
Mrs Sneak. But as soon as my dress is restored, I shall fly to relieve your distress.
Maj. For that moment I shall wait with the greatest impatience.
Mrs Sneak. Courteous commander.
Maj. Paragon of women!
Mrs Sneak. Adieu!
Maj. Adieu! [*Exit Mrs* Sneak.
Sneak. Notwithstanding, Sir, all my chicken has said, I am special company when she is not by.
Maj. I doubt not, Master Sneak.
Sneak. If you would but come one Thursday night to our club, at the Nag's-head, in the Poultry, you would meet some roaring, rare boys, i'faith: there's Jemmy Perkins,

kins, the packer; little Tom Simkins, the grocer; honest Master Muzzle, the mid-wife—

Maj. A goodly company!

Sneak. Ay, and then sometimes we have the choice spirits from Comus's court, and we crack jokes, and are so jolly and funny: I have learnt myself to sing "An old woman clothed in grey." But I durst not sing out loud, because my wife would overhear me; and she says as how I bawl worser than the broom-man.

Maj. And you must not think of disobliging your lady.

Sneak. I never does: I never contradicts her, not I.

Maj. That's right: she is a woman of infinite merit.

Sneak. O, a power: and don't you think she is very pretty withal?

Maj. A Venus!

Sneak. Yes, werry like Wenus—mayhap you have known her some time?

Maj. Long.

Sneak. Belike before she was married?

Maj. I did Master Sneak.

Sneak. Ay, when she was a virgin. I thought you was an old acquaintance by your kissing her hand; for we ben't quite so familiar as that—but then, indeed, we han't been married a year.

Maj. The mere honey-moon.

Sneak. Ay, ay, I suppose we shall come to it by degrees.

Bruin. [within] Come along, Jane; why you are as surly and lazy, you jade—

Enter Bruin *and* Wife; Bruin *with a cotton cap on; his Wife with his wig, great-coat, and fishing-rod.*

Bruin. Come, Jane, give me my wig; you slut, how you have tousled the curls? Master Sneak, a good morning to you. Sir I am your humble servant, unknown.

Enter Roger.

Rog. Mrs Sneak begs to speak with the Major.

Maj. I will wait on the lady immediately.

Sneak. Don't tarry an instant; you can't think how impatient she is. [*Exit* Major.

Sneak. A good morrow to you, brother Bruin; you have had a warm walk across the fields.

Mrs Bruin. Good lord, I am all in a muck—

Bruin.

Bruin. And who may you thank for it, huffy? If you had got up time enough, you might have fecur'd the fare; but you are a lazy lie-a-bed.

Mrs Bruin. There's Mr Sneak keeps my fifter a chay.

Bruin. And fo he may; but I know better what to do with my money: indeed, if the war had but continued a-while, I don't know what mought ha' been done; but this plaguy peace, with a pox to't, has knock'd up all the trade of the Alley.

Mrs Bruin. For the matter of that, we can afford it well enough as it is.

Bruin. And how do you know that? who told you as much, Mrs Blixen? I hope I know the world better than to truft my concerns with a wife: no, no, thank you for that, Mrs Jane.

Mrs Bruin. And pray who is more fitterer to be trufted?

Bruin. Hey-day! why, the wench is bewitch'd: come, come, let's have none of your palaver here—take twelve-pence and pay the waterman.—But firft fee if he has broke none of the pipes—and, d'ye hear, Jane, be fure to lay the fifhing-rod fafe. [*Exit Mrs Bruin.*

Sneak. Ods me, how finely fhe's manag'd! what would I give to have my wife as much under!

Bruin. It is all your own fault, brother Sneak.

Sneak. D'ye think fo? fhe is a fweet pretty creature.

Bruin. A vixen.

Sneak. Why, to fay the truth, fhe does now and then hector a little; and, between ourfelves, domineers like the devil: O Lord, I lead the life of a dog: why, fhe allows me but two fhillings a week for my pocket.

Bruin. No!

Sneak. No, man; 'tis fhe that receives and pays all: and then I am forc'd to trot after her to church, with her cardinal, pattens, and prayer-book, for all the world as if I was ftill a 'prentice.

Bruin. Zounds! I would houfe them all in the kennel.

Sneak. I durft not—And then, at table, I never gets what I loves.

Bruin. The devil!

Sneak. No; fhe always helps me herfelf to the tough drumfticks of turkies, and the damn'd fat flaps of fhoulders of mutton; I don't think I have eat a bit of under-cruft since we have been married: you see, brother Bruin, I am almost as thin as a lath.

Bruin. An absolute skeleton!

Sneak. Now, if you think I could carry my point, I would so swinge and leather my lambkin; God, I would so curry and claw her.

Bruin. By the lord Harry, she richly deserves it.

Sneak. Will you, brother, lend me a lift?

Bruin. Command me at all times.

Sneak. Why then, I will verily pluck up a spirit; and the first time she offers to—

Mrs Sneak. [*within.*] Jerry, Jerry Sneak!

Sneak. Gad's my life, sure as a gun that's her voice: look-ye, brother, I don't chuse to breed a disturbance in another body's house; but as soon as ever I get home—

Bruin. Now is your time.

Sneak. No, no; it would not be decent.

Mrs Sneak. [*within.*] Jerry? Jerry!—

Sneak. I come, lovy. But you will be sure to stand by me?

Bruin. Trot, nincompoop.

Sneak. Well, if I don't—I wish—

Mrs Sneak. [*within.*] Where is this lazy puppy a-loitering?

Sneak. I come, chuck, as fast as I can—Good Lord, what a sad life do I lead! [*Exit Sneak.*

Bruin. Ex quovis lignum: Who can make a silk purse of a sow's ear?

Enter Sir Jacob.

Sir Jac. Come, son Bruin, we are all seated at table, man; we have but just time for a snack: the candidates are near upon coming.

Bruin. A poor, paltry, mean spirited—Damn it, before I would submit to such a—

Sir Jac. Come, come, man; don't be so crusty.

Bruin. I follow, Sir Jacob: Damme, when once a man gives up his prerogative, he might as well give up—But, however, it is no bread and butter of mine—Jerry, Jerry! —Zounds, I would Jerry and jerk her too. [*Exit.*

ACT

ACT II.

SCENE continues.

Sir Jacob, Major Sturgeon, Mr and Mrs Bruin, Mr and Mrs Sneak, discovered.

Mrs Sneak. INDEED, Major, not a grain of curiosity. Can it be thought that we, who have a Lord Mayor's show every year, can take any pleasure in this?

Maj. In time of war, Madam, these meetings are not amiss; I fancy a man might pick up a good many recruits: but in these piping times of peace, I wonder Sir Jacob permits it.

Sir Jac. It would, Major, cost me my popularity to quash it: the common people are as fond of their customs as the barons were of their *Magna Charta*: besides, my tenants make some little advantage.

Enter Roger.

Rog. Crispin Heel-Tap, with the electors, are set out from the Adam and Eve.

Sir Jac. Gad-so, then they will soon be upon us: Come, good folks, the balcony will give us the best view of the whole. Major, you will take the ladies under protection.

Maj. Sir Jacob, I am upon guard.

Sir Jac. I can tell you, this Heel-Tap is an arch rascal.—

Sneak. And plays the best game at cribbage in the whole corporation of Garrat.

Mrs Sneak. That puppy will always be a-chattering.

Sneak. Nay, I did but—

Mrs Sneak. Hold your tongue, or I'll send you home in an instant—

Sir Jac. Pr'ythee, daughter!—You may to-day, Major, meet with something that will put you in mind of more important transactions.

Maj. Perhaps so.

Sir Jac. Lack-a-day, all men are alike; their principles exactly the same: for tho' art and education may disguise

or

or polish the manners, the same motives and springs are universally planted.

Maj. Indeed!

Sir Jac. Why, in this mob, this group of plebeians, you will meet with materials to make a Sylla, a Cicero, a Solon, or a Cæsar: let them but change conditions, and the world's great lord had been but the best wrestler on the green.

Maj. Ay, ay, I could have told these things formerly; but since I have been in the army, I have entirely neglected the classes. [*Mob without huzza.*

Sir Ja. But the heroes are at hand, Major.

Snuff. Father Sir Jacob, might not we have a tankard of flingo above?

Sir Jac. By all means.

Snuff. D'ye hear, Roger. [*Exeunt into the balcony.*

SCENE, *a Street.*

Enter Mob, *with* Heel-Tap *at their head; some crying a* Goose; *others a* Mug; *others a* Primmer.

Heel-Tap. Silence, there; silence!

1st Mob. Hear neighbour Heel-Tap.

2d Mob. Ay, ay, hear Crispin.

3d Mob. Ay, ay, hear him, hear Crispin: he will put us into the model of the thing at once.

Heel-Tap. Why then, silence! I say.

All. Silence.

Heel-Tap. Silence, and let us proceed, neighbours, with all the decency and confusion usual upon these occasions.

1st Mob. Ay, ay, there is no doing without that.

All. No, no, no.

Heel-Tap. Silence then, and keep the peace: what, is there no respect paid to authority? am not I the returning officer?

All. Ay, ay, ay.

Heel-Tap. Chosen by yourselves, and approved of by Sir Jacob?

All. True, true.

Heel-Tap. Well then, be silent and civil; stand back there, that gentleman without a shirt, and make room for your betters: Where's Simon Snuffle the sexton?

Snuffle. Here.

Heel-Tap.

Heel-Tap. Let him come forward; we appoint him our Secretary: for Simon is a scoll'ard, and can read written hand; and so let him be respected accordingly.

2d Mob. Room for Master Snuffle.

Heel-Tap. Here, stand by me: and let us, neighbours, proceed to open the premunire of the thing: but first, your reverence to the lord of the manor: a long life and a merry one to our landlord Sir Jacob! Huzza!

Mob. Huzza!

Sneak. How fares it, honest Crispin?

Heel-Tap. Servant, Master Sneak.—Let us now open the premunire of the thing, which I shall do briefly, with all the loquacity possible; that is, in a medium way; which, that we may the better do it, let the secretary read the names of the candidates, and what they say for themselves; and then we shall know what to say of them: Master Snuffle, begin.

Snuffle. "To the worthy inhabitants of the ancient corporation of Garrat: Gentlemen, your votes and interest are humbly requested in favour of Timothy Goose, to succeed your late worthy mayor, Mr Richard Dripping, in the said office, he being"——

Heel-Tap. This Goose is but a kind of gosling, a sort of sneaking scoundrel: who is he?

Snuffle. A journeyman tailor, from Putney.

Heel-Tap. A journeyman tailor! A rascal, has he the impudence to transpire to be mayor? D'ye consider, neighbours, the weight of this office? Why, it is a burden for the back of a porter; and can you think that this cross-legg'd cabbage-eating son of a cucumber, this whey-fac'd ninny, who is but the ninth part of a man, has strength to support it?

1st Mob. No Goose! no Goose!

2d Mob. A Goose!

Heel-Tap. Hold your hissing, and proceed to the next.

Snuffle. "Your votes are desired for Matthew Mug."

1st Mob. A Mug! A Mug!

Heel-Tap. Oh, oh, what you are all ready to have a touch of the tankard: but, fair and soft, good neighbours, let us taste this Master Mug, before we swallow him; and, unless I am mistaken, you will find him a damn'd bitter draught.

1st Mob. A Mug! a Mug!

2d Mob. Hear him; hear Master Heel-Tap.
1st Mob. A Mug! a Mug!
Heel-Tap. Harkye, yon fellow, with your mouth full of Mug, let me ask you a question: bring him forward: pray is not this Matthew Mug a victualler?
3d Mob. I believe he may.
Heel-Tap. And lives at the sign of the Adam and Eve?
3d Mob. I believe he may.
Heel-Tap. Now answer upon your honour, and as you are a gentleman, what is the present price of a quart of home-brew'd at the Adam and Eve?
3d Mob. I don't know.
Heel-Tap. You lie, sirrah: en't it a groat?
3d Mob. I believe it may.
Heel-Tap. Oh, may be so: now, neighbours, here's a pretty rascal; this same Mug, because, d'ye see, state affairs would not jog glibly without laying a farthing a quart upon ale; this scoundrel, not contented to take things in a a medium way, has had the impudence to raise it a penny.
Mob. No Mug! no Mug!
Heel-Tap. So, I thought I should crack Mr Mug. Come, proceed to the next, Simon.
Snuffle. The next upon the list is Peter Primmer, the schoolmaster.
Heel-Tap. Ay, neighbours, and a sufficient man: let me tell you, Master Primmer is the man for my money; a man of learning; that can lay down the law; why, adzooks, he is wise enough to puzzle the parson: and then, how you have heard him oration at the Adam and Eve of a Saturday night, about Russia and Prussia: Ecod, George Gage the exciseman is nothing at all to un.
4th Mob. A Primmer!
Heel-Tap. Ay, if the folks above did but know him; why, lads, he will make us all Statesmen in time.
2d Mob. Indeed!
Heel-Tap. Why, he swears as how all the miscarriages are owing to the great people's not learning to read.
3d Mob. Indeed!
Heel-Tap. For, says Peter, says he, if they would but once submit to be learned by me, there is no knowing to what a pitch the nation might rise.
1st Mob. Ay, I wish they would.
Sneak. Crispin, what, is Peter Primmer a candidate?
Heel-Tap.

THE MAYOR OF GARRAT.   179

Heel-Tap. He is, Master Sneak.

Sneak. Lord, I know him, man, as well as my mother; why, I used to go to his lectures to Pewterers-hall long with Deputy Firkin.

Heel-Tap. Like enough.

Sneak. Odds me, brother Bruin, can you tell what is become of my wife?

Bruin. She is gone off with the Major.

Sneak. Mayhap to take a walk in the garden; I will go and take a peep at what they are doing. [*Exit.* Sneak.

Mob without huzza.

Heel-Tap. God-fo! the candidates are coming. Come, neighbours, range yourselves to the right and left, that you may be canvass'd in order; let us see who comes first?

1st Mob. Master Mug.

Heel-Tap. Now, neighbours, have a good caution that this Master Mug does not cajole you; he is a damn'd palavering fellow.

Enter Matthew Mug.

Mug. Gentlemen, I am the lowest of your slaves: Mr Heel-Tap, have the honour of kissing your hand.

Heel-Tap. There, did not I tell you?

Mug. Ah, my very good friend, I hope your father is well?

1st Mob. He is dead.

Mug. So he is. Mr Grub, if my wishes prevail, your very good wife is in health.

2d Mob. Wife! I never was married.

Mug. No more you were. Well, neighbours and friends! Ah! what honest Dick Bennet.

3d Mob. My name is Gregory Gubbins.

Mug. You are right, it is so; and how fares it with good Master Gubbins?

3d Mob. Pretty tight, Master Mug.

Mug. I am exceedingly happy to hear it.

4th Mob. Harkye, Master Mug.

Mug. Your pleasure, my very dear friend.

4th Mob. Why as how, and concerning our young one at home.

Mug. Right; she is a prodigious promising girl.

4th Mob. Girl! Zooks, why 'tis a boy.

Mug.

Mug. True; a fine boy! I love and honour the child.

4th Mob. Nay, 'tis none such a child; but you promised to get us a place.

Mug. A place! what place?

4th Mob. Why, a gentleman's service, you know.

Mug. It is done; it is fix'd; it is settled.

4th Mob. And when is the lad to take oo?

Mug. He must go in a fortnight at farthest.

4th Mob. And is it a pretty goodish birth, Master Mug?

Mug. The best in the world; head butler to Lady Barbara Bounce.

4th Mob. A lady!

Mug. The wages are not much, but the vails are amazing.

4th Mob. Barbara Bounce?

Mug. Yes; she has routs on Tuesdays and Sundays, and he gathers the tables; only he finds candles, cards, coffee, and tea.

4th Mob. Is Lady Barbara's work pretty tight?

Mug. As good as a sine-cure; he only writes cards to her company, and dresses his mistress's hair.

4th Mob. Hair! Zounds, why Jack was bred to dressing of horses.

Mug. True; but he is suffered to do that by deputy.

4th Mob. May be so.

Mug. It is so. Harkye, dear Heel-Tap, who is this fellow? I should remember his face.

Heel-Tap. And don't you?

Mug. Not I, I profess.

Heel-Tap. No!

Mug. No.

Heel-Tap. Well said, Master Mug; but come, time wears: have you any thing more to say to the corporation?

Mug. Gentlemen of the Corporation of Garrat.

Heel-Tap. Now, twig him; now, mind him: mark how he hawls his muscles about.

Mug. The honour I this day solicit, will be to me the most honourable honour that can be conferr'd; and, should I succeed, you, gentlemen, may depend on my using my utmost endeavours to promote the good of the borough; for which purpose, the encouragement of your trade and manufactories will most principally tend. Garrat, it must

be

be own'd, is an inland town, and has not, like Wandſ-
worth, and Fulham, and Putney, the glorious advantage
of a port; but what nature has denied, induſtry may ſupply: cabbage, carrots, and colly-flowers, may be deemed,
at preſent, your ſtaple commodities; but why ſhould not
your commerce be extended? Were I, gentlemen, worthy to adviſe, I ſhould recommend the opening a new
branch of trade; ſparagraſs, gentlemen, the manufacturing
of ſparagraſs: Batterſea, I own, gentlemen, bears, at preſent, the belle; but where lies the fault? In ourſelves,
gentlemen: let us, gentlemen, but exert our natural
ſtrength, and I will take upon me to ſay, that a hundred
of graſs from the Corporation of Garrat, will in a ſhort
time, at the London market, be held, at leaſt, as an equi-
valent to a Batterſea bundle.

Mob. A Mug! a Mug!

Heel-Tap. Damn the fellow, what a tongue he has! God,
I muſt ſtep in, or he will carry the day. Harkye, Maſter Mug!

Mug. Your pleaſure, my very good friend?

Heel-Tap. No flummering me; I tell thee, Matthew,
'twon't do: why, as to this article of ale here, how comes
it about that you have rais'd it a penny a quart?

Mug. A word in your ear, Criſpin; you and your
friends ſhall have it at three pence.

Heel-Tap. What, ſirrah, d'ye offer a bribe! D'ye dare
to corrupt me, you ſcoundrel!

Mug. Gentlemen——

Heel-Tap. Here, neighbours; the fellow has offer'd to
bate a penny a quart, if ſo be as how I would be conſent-
ing to impoſe upon you.

Mob. No Mug! no Mug!

Mug. Neighbours, friends——

Mob. No Mug!

Mug. I believe this is the firſt borough that ever was
loſt by the returning officer's refuſing a bribe. [*Exit Mug.*

Mob. Let us go and pull down his ſign.

Heel-Tap. Hold, hold, no riot: but that we may not
give Mug time to pervert the votes and carry the day, let
us proceed to the election.

Mob. Agreed! agreed! [*Exit Heel-Tap and Mob.*

Sir

Sir Jacob, Bruin, and Wife, come from the balcony.

Sir Jac. Well, son Bruin, how d'ye relish the Corporation of Garrat?

Bruin. Why, lookye, Sir Jacob, my way is always to speak what I think: I don't approve on't at all.

Mrs Bruin. No!

Sir Jac. And what's your objection?

Bruin. Why, I was never over-fond of your May-games; besides, corporations are too serious things; they are edge-tools, Sir Jacob.

Sir Jac. That they are frequently tools, I can readily grant: but I never heard much of their edge.

Mrs Bruin. Well now, I protest, I am pleas'd with it mightily.

Bruin. And who the devil doubts it?—You women folks are easily pleas'd.

Mrs Bruin. Well, I like it so well, that I hope to see one every year.

Bruin. Do you? Why then you will be damnably bit; you may take your leave I can tell you, for this is the last you shall see.

Sir Jac. Fye, Mr Bruin, how can you be such a bear: is that a manner of treating your wife?

Bruin. What, I suppose you would have me such a sniveling sot as your son-in-law Sneak, to truckle and cringe, to fetch and to—

Enter Sneak, in a violent hurry.

Sneak. Where's brother Bruin? O Lord! brother, I have such a dismal story to tell you—

Bruin. What's the matter?

Sneak. Why, you know I went into the garden to look for my wife and the Major, and there I hunted and hunted as sharp as if it had been for one of my own minikens; but the deuce a Major or Madam could I see: at last, a thought came into my head to look for them up in the summer-house.

Bruin. And there you found them?

Sneak. I'll tell you, the door was lock'd; and then I look'd thro' the key-hole: and, there, Lord a mercy upon us! [*Whispers*] as sure as a gun.

Bruin.

Bruin. Indeed! Zounds, why did not you break open the door?

Sneak. I durſt not: what, would you have me ſet my wit to a ſoldier? I warrant, the Major would have knock'd me down with one of his boots; for I could ſee they were both of them off.

Bruin. Very well! pretty doings! You ſee, Sir Jacob, theſe are the fruits of indulgence: you may call me bear, but your daughter ſhall never make me a beaſt.

Mob huzzas.

Sir Jac. Hey-day! What, is the election over already?

Enter Criſpin, &c.

Heel-Tap. Where is Maſter Sneak?
Sneak. Here, Criſpin.
Heel-Tap. The ancient Corporation of Garat, in conſideration of your great parts and abilities, and out of reſpect to their landlord, Sir Jacob, have unanimouſly choſen you mayor.

Sneak. Me! huzza! good Lord, who would have thought it: but how came Maſter Primmer to loſe it?

Heel-Tap. Why, Phill Fleam had told the electors, that Maſter Primmer was an Iriſhman; and ſo they would none of them give their vote for a foreigner.

Sneak. So then, I have it for certain: Huzza! Now, brother Bruin, you ſhall ſee how I'll manage my madam: Gad, I'll make her know I am a man of authority; ſhe ſhan't think to bullock and domineer over me.

Bruin. Now for it, Sneak; the enemy's at hand.
Sneak. You promiſe to ſtand by me, brother Bruin.
Bruin. Tooth and nail.
Sneak. Then now for it; I am ready, let her come when ſhe will.

Enter Mrs Sneak.

Mrs Sneak. Where is the puppy?
Sneak. Yes, yes, ſhe is axing for me.
Mrs Sneak. So, ſot; what, is this true that I hear?
Sneak. May be 'tis, may be 'tan't: I don't chuſe to truſt my affairs with a woman. Is that right, brother Bruin?
Bruin. Fine! don't bate her an inch.
Sneak. Stand by me.

N₃7

Mrs Sneak. Hey-day! I am amaz'd! Why, what is the meaning of this?

Sneak. The meaning is plain, that I am grown a man, and vil do what I please, without being accountable to nobody.

Mrs Sneak. Why, the fellow is surely bewitch'd.

Sneak. No, I am unwitch'd, and that you shall know to your cost; and since you provoke me, I will tell you a bit of my mind: what, I am the husband, I hope?

Bruin. That's right: at her again.

Sneak. Yes; and you shan't think to hector and domineer over me as you have done; for I'll go to the club when I please, and stay out as late as I list, and row in a boat to Putney on Sundays, and wisk my friends at Vitfontide, and keep the key of the till, and help myself at table to what vittles I like, and I'll have a bit of the brown.

Bruin. Bravo, brother! Sneak, the day's your own.

Sneak. An't it! why, I did not think it was in me: shall I tell her all I know?

Bruin. Every thing; you see she is struck dumb.

Sneak. As an oyster: besides, Madam, I have something furder to tell you: oons, if some folks go into gardens with Majors, mayhap other people may go into garrets with maids.—There, I gave it her home, brother Bruin.

Mrs Sneak. Why, doodle! jackanapes! harkye, who am I?

Sneak. Come, don't go to call names: am I? vhy my vife, and I am your master.

Mrs Sneak. My master! you paltry, puddling puppy; you sneaking, shabby, scrubby, sniveling whelp!

Sneak. Brother Bruin, don't let her come near me.

Mrs Sneak. Have I, sirrah, demean'd myself to wed such a thing, such a reptile as thee! Have I not made myself a bye-word to all my acquaintance! Don't all the world cry, Lord, who would have thought it! Miss Molly Jollup to be married to Sneak! to take up at last with such a noodle as he!

Sneak. Ay, and glad enough you could catch me: you know, you was pretty near your last legs.

Mrs Sneak. Was there ever such a confident cur? My last legs! Why, all the country knows, I could have pick'd and chus'd where I would: did not I refuse 'Squire Ap-Griffith from Wales? did not Counsellor Crab come a-courting a-courting a twelvemonth? did not Mr Wort, the great brewer of Brentford, make an offer that I should keep my post chay?

Sneak. Nay, brother Bruin, she has had very good proffers, that is certain.

Mrs Sneak. My last legs!—but I can rein my passion no longer; let me get at the villain.

Bruin. O fye, sister Sneak.

Sneak. Hold her fast.

Mrs Sneak. Mr Bruin, unhand me: when, it is you that have stirred up these coals then; he is set on by you to abuse me.

Bruin. Not I; I would only have a man behave like a man.

Mrs Sneak. What, and are you to teach him, I warrant—but here comes the Major.

Enter Major Sturgeon.

Oh Major! such a riot and rumpus! Like a man indeed! I wish people would mind their own affairs, and not meddle with matters that does not concern them: but all in good time; I shall one day catch him alone, when he has not his bullies to back him.

Sneak. Adod, that's true, brother Bruin; what shall I do when she has me at home, and nobody by but ourselves?

Bruin. If you get her once under, you may do with her whatever you will.

Major. Look ye, Master Bruin, I don't know how this behaviour may suit with a citizen; but, were you an officer, and Major Sturgeon upon your court-martial—

Bruin. What then?

Major. Then! why then you would be broke.

Bruin. Broke! and for what?

Major. What? read the articles of war: but these things are out of your sphear; points of honour are for the sons of the sword.

Sneak. Honour! if you come to that, where was your honour when you got my wife in the garden?

Major. Now, Sir Jacob, this is the curse of our cloth: all suspected for the faults of a few.

Sneak. Ay, and not without reason; I heard of your tricks at the King of Bohemy, when you was campaining about, I did: father Sir Jacob, he is as wicious as an old ram.

Major. Stop whilst you are fafe, Mafter Sneak; for the fake of your amiable lady, I pardon what is paft—But for you—

Bruin. Well.

Major. Dread the whole force of my fury.

Bruin. Why, lookye, Major Sturgeon, I don't much care for your poppers and fharps, because why, they are out of my way; but if you will doff with your boots, and box a couple of bouts—

Major. Box! box! blades! bullets! Bagfhot!

Mrs Sneak. Not for the world, my dear Major! oh, rifk not fo precious a life. Ungrateful wretches! and is this the reward for all the great feats he has done? After all his marchings, his foufings, his fweatings, his fwimmings; muft his dear blood be fpilt by a broker!

Major. Be satisfy'd, fweet Mrs Sneak; thefe little fracafos we foldiers are fubject to; trifles, bagatailes, Mrs Sneak: But that matters may be conducted in a military manner, I will get our chaplain to pen me a challenge. Expect to hear from my adjutant.

Mrs Sneak. Major, Sir Jacob; what, are you all leagu'd againft his dear—A man! yes, a very manly action indeed to fet married people a quarrelling, and ferment a difference between hufband and wife: if you were a man, you would not ftand by and fee a poor woman beat and abus'd by a brute, you would not.

Sneak. Oh Lord, I can hold out no longer! why, brother Bruin, you have fet her a veeping: my life, my lovy, don't veep: did I ever think I fhould have made my Molly to veep?

Mrs Sneak. Laft lags! you lubberly— [*Strikes him.*

Sir Jac. Oh, fye! Molly.

Mrs Sneak. What, are you leagu'd againft me, Sir Jacob?

Sir Jac. Prithee, don't expofe yourfelf before the whole parifh: but what has been the occafion of this?

Mrs Sneak. Why, has not he gone and made himfelf the fool of the fair? Mayor of Garrat indeed? oood, I could trample him under my feet.

Sneak. Nay, why fhould you grudge me my parfarment?

Mrs

Mrs Sneak. Did you ever hear such an oaf? why, thee wilt be pointed at wherever thou goeft: lookye, Jerry, mind what I fay; go, get 'em to chufe fomebody elfe, or never come near me again.

Sneak. What fhall I do, father Sir Jacob?

Sir Jac. Nay, daughter, you take this thing in too ferious a light; my honeft neighbours thought to compliment me: but come, we'll fettle the bufinefs at once. Neighbours, my fon Sneak being feldom amongft us, the duty will never be done, fo we will get our honeft friend Heel-Tap to execute the office; he is, I think, every way qualified.

Mob. A Heel-Tap!

Heel-Tap. What d'ye mean, as Mafter Jeremy's deputy?

Sir Jac. Ay, ay, his *locum tenens*.

Sneak. Do, Crifpin; do be my *locum tenens*.

Heel-Tap. Give me your hand, Mafter Sneak, and to oblige you I will be the *locum tenens*.

Sir Jac. So, that is fettled; but now to heal the other breach: come, Major, the gentlemen of your cloth feldom bear malice; let me interpofe between you and my fon.

Major. Your fon-in-law, Sir Jacob, does deferve a caftigation; but, on recollection, a cit would but fully my arms. I forgive him.

Sir Jac. That's right: as a token of amity, and to celebrate our feaft, let us call in the fiddles. Now if the Major had but his fhoes, he might join in a country-dance.

Major. Sir Jacob, no fhoes, a Major muft be never out of his boots; always ready for action. Mrs Sneak will find me lightfome enough.

Sneak. What are all the women engaged? why then my *locum tenens* and I will jig together. Forget and forgive, Major.

Major. Freely.

   Nor be it faid, that, after all my toil,
   I ftain'd my regimentals by a broil.
   To you I dedicate boots, fword, and fhield,

Sir Jac. As harmlefs in the chamber as the field.

THE ORATORS;

A COMEDY,

OF

THREE ACTS.

LECTURER, = Mr Boote.

PUPILS, 14. {
Mr Weston,
Mr Finn,
Mr Grice,
Mr Boynton,
Mr Davis,
Mr Loveday,
Mr Carter,
Mr Palmer,
Mr Strange,
Mr Smith,
Mr Pearce,
Mr Kent,
Mr Gardner,
Mr Newton,
Mr Souter.
}

ACT I.

Enter Will Tirehack, and Harry Scamper, booted, with whips in their hands, into a side-box.

Scamper. PSHAW! zounds! prithee, Will, let us go; what signifies our staying here?

Tirehack. Nay, but tarry a little; besides, you know we promised to give Poll Baylifs and Bett Skinner the meeting.

Scamper. No matter, we shall be sure to find them at three at the Shakspeare.

Tirehack. But as we are here, Harry, let us know a little what it's about?

Scamper. About! Why lectures, you fool! Have not you read the bills? and we have plenty of them at Oxford you know!

Tirehack. Well, but for all that, there may be fun.

Scamper. Why then, stay and enjoy it yourself; and I'll step to the Bull and Gate, and call upon Jerry Lack-Latin, and my horse. We shall see you at three. [*Rising.*

Tirehack. Nay, but prithee, stay.

Scamper. Rot me if I do. [*Going out of the box.*

Tirehack. Halloo, Harry! Harry—

Scamper. Well, what's the matter now? [*Returning.*

Tirehack. Here's Poll Baylifs come into the gallery.

Scamper. No—

Tirehack. She is, by—

Scamper. [*looking.*] Yes faith! It is she sure enough.— How goes it, Poll?

Tirehack. Well now, we shall have you, I hope?

Scamper. Ay, if I thought we should get any fun.

Tirehack. I'll make an enquiry. Halloo! snuffers, snuffers!

Enter Candle-snuffer.

Your pleasure, Sir?

Tirehack. What is all this business about here?

Snuffer. Can't say, Sir.

Scamper. Well but you could if you would, let us into the secret.

Snuffer.

Snuffer. Not I, upon my honour!

Tireback. Your honour, you son of a whore! D'ye hear, bid your master come hither, we want to ask him a question.

Snuffer. I will— [*Exit.*

Tireback. Scamper, will you ask him, or shall I?

Scamper. Let me alone to him—

Enter Foote.

Tireback. O! here he is—

Foote. Your commands with me, gentlemen?

Scamper. Why, you must know Will and I here are upon a scheme from Oxford; and because cash begins to run low—How much have you, Will?

Tireback. Three and twenty shillings, besides the crown I paid at the door.

Scamper. And I eighteen, now, as this will last us but to-night, we are willing to husband our time; let us see, Will, how are we engaged?

Tireback. Why at three, with Bett and Poll, there, at the Shakspeare; after that to the coronation; for you know we have seen it but nine times—

Scamper. And then back to the Shakspeare again; where we sup, and take horse at the door.

Tireback. So there's no time to be lost, you see; we desire, therefore, to know what sort of a thing this affair here of yours is? What, is it damn'd funny and comical?

Foote. Have you seen the bills?

Scamper. What, about the lectures? ay, but that's all flam, I suppose; no, no. No tricks upon travellers; no, we know better—What, are there any more of you; or do you do it all yourself?

Foote. If I was in want of comedians, you, gentlemen, are kind enough to lend me a lift; but upon my word, my intentions, as the bill will inform you, are serious——

Tireback. Are they? then I'll have my money again. What, do you think we come to London to learn any thing?—Come Will. [*Going.*

Foote. Hold, gentlemen, I would detain you if possible. What is it you expect?

Scamper. To be jolly, and laugh, to be sure—

Foote. At what?

Tireback.

Tireback. At what —— damme, I don't know—at you, and your frolicks and fancies—

Foote. If that is all you defire, why, perhaps we fhan't difappoint you—

Scamper. Shan't you?—why, that is an honeft fellow—, come, begin—

Foote. But you'll be fo kind as not to interrupt me?

Scamper. Never fear——

Foote. Ladies and gentlemen——

[Suds *from the oppofite box calls to* Foote, *and ftops him fhort.*

Suds. Stop a minute; may I be permitted to fpeak?

Foote. Doubtlefs, Sir.

Suds. Why the affair is this: My wife Alice—for you muft know my name is Ephraim Suds, I am a foap-boiler in the city,—took it into her head, and nothing would ferve her turn, but that I muft be a common-council man, this year; for, fays Alice, *fays fhe,* it is the *eafieft* way to rife in the world.

Foote. A juft obfervation—you fucceeded?

Suds. Oh! there was no danger of that—yes, yes, I got it all hollow; but now to come to the marrow of the bufinefs. Well, Alice, fays I, now I am chofen, what's next to be done? " Why now, fays Alice, *fays fhe*, thee muft learn to make fpeeches; why doft not fee what pur- ferment neighbour Grogram has got; why man, 'tis all brought about by his *fpeechifying*. I tell thee what, Ephraim, if thee can't but once learn to lay down the law, there's no knowing to what thee may'ft rife.——"

Foote. Your lady had reafon.

Suds. Why I thought fo too; and, as good luck would have it, who fhould come into the city, in the very nick of time, but Mafter Profeffor along with his lectures—Adod, away, in a hurry, Alice and I danced to Pewterers-hall.

Foote. You improved, I hope?

Suds. O Lud! it is unknown what knowledge we got; we can read—Oh! we never ftop to fpell a word now— and then he told us fuch things about verbs, and nouns, and adverbs, that never entered our heads before, and emphafis, and accent; heaven blefs us, I did not think there had been fuch things in the world.

Foote. And have you *fpeechified* yet?

Suds. Soft; foft and fair; we muft walk before we can

Vol. I.   B b   run

run—I think I have laid a pretty foundation. The manfion-houfe was not built in a day, Mafter Foote. But to go on with my tale, my dame one day looking over the papers, came running to me; now, Ephraim, fays fhe, thy bufinefs is done; rare news, lad; here is a man at the other end of the town, that will make thee a *fpeecher* at once, and out fhe pull'd your propofals. Ah, Alice, fays I, then he'ft but a fool, why I know that man, he is all upon his fun; he lectures—why, 'tis all but a bam— Well, 'tis but feeing fays fhe, fo, *widnes nokus*, fhe would have me come hither; now, if fo be you be ferious, I fhall think my money wifely beftowed; but if it be only your comical works, I can tell you, you fhall fee me no more.

Foote. Sir, I fhould be extremely forry to lofe; if I knew but what would content you?

Suds. Why, I want to be made an orator of; and to fpeak fpeeches, as I tell you, at our meetings, about politics, and peace, and addreffes, and the new bridge, and all thefe kind of things.

Foote. Why with your happy talents I fhould think much might be done.

Suds. I am proud to hear you fay fo. Indeed I am. I did *fpeechify* once at a veftry concerning new lettering the church buckets, and came off cutely enough; and, to fay the truth, that was the thing that provoked me to go to Pewterers-hall. [*Sits down again.*

Foote. Well, Sir, I flatter myfelf, that in proportion to the difference of abilities in your two inftructors, you will here make a tolerable progrefs. But now, Sir, with your favour, we will proceed to explain the nature of our defign, and I hope, in the procefs, you gentlemen, will find entertainment, and you, Sir, information.

Mr Foote then proceeded in his lecture.

My plan, gentlemen, is to be confidered as a fuperftructure on that admirable foundation laid by the modern profeffor of Englifh, both our labours tending to the fame general end, the perfectioning of our countrymen in a moft effential article, the right ufe of their native language.

But what he has happily begun, I have the vanity to think I have as happily finifhed; he has, it is true, introduced you into the body of the church, but I conduct you into the choir of the cathedral: or, to explain myfelf by a more familiar allusion, though he is the Poitier who teaches you the ſtep and the grounds ; yet I am the Gallini who gives you the air, and the grace of the minuet.

His aim is propriety alone; mine, propriety with elegance.

For though reading, ſo ſhamefully neglected, not only by thoſe of tender years, but the adult; not only by children, but even by grown men and women ; not only in our private ſeminaries, but in our public univerſities ; is allowed to be a neceſſary ingredient towards the formation of an orator; yet, a great many other rules, a great many other precepts are requiſite to obtain this perfection.

Nay, perhaps we might, to ſupport an argument without the danger of a defeat, at leaſt if we may truſt obſervation, that of all the profeſſions that require a verbal intercourſe with the public, there is no one to which reading is of ſo little utility as that of oratory.

I need not inſiſt upon this head, as I believe every gentleman's experience will furniſh him with inſtances of men eminent in oratory, who, from an early vivacity have neglected, or the indulgence of their parents have been emancipated from the attention and application neceſſary, it is true, to acquire this rugged art, but at the ſame time ſo ill-ſuited to their tender years, and ſo oppoſite to thoſe innocent amuſements in which children are known univerſally to delight. *Thwart not a child, for you ſpoil his temper*—is, or at leaſt ought to be, an Engliſh proverb, as it is an univerſal practice.

I would not here be underſtood to depreciate the uſefulneſs of reading, or to detract from the exceeding merit of the profeſſor's plan ; no, my meaning is only juſt to drop a hint that I may occaſionally uſe him as a walking ſtick ; a kind of an *elegantly clouded Mocoa*, or an *airy Anamaboo*; yet, that it is by no means my intention to depend upon him as a *ſupport*, or lean upon him as a *crutch ;* in a word, he will be rather ornamental than neceſſary to me.

But uſeleſs as is his plan to me, I ſincerely wiſh it ſucceſs for the ſake of the public ; and if my influence was equal to my inclination, I would have a law enacted, upon the plan of the militia bill, that annually, or biennially, draughts ſhould be made from every pariſh of two, three, or more, as in that act of able-bodied, ſo in this of intelligent perſons, who at the expence of the ſeveral counties, ſhould be ſent to the capital, and there compelled to go

through

through as many courses of the professor's lectures as he shall deem sufficient: thus, by those periodical rural detachments, the whole nation will, in a few years, be completely served, and a stock of learning laid in, that will last till time shall be no more.

Would our rulers but adopt this scheme! how superior would England be even to the most illustrious periods of Greece and Rome! what an unrivalled happiness for us, what an eternal fund of fame for them! Ye Solons, ye Lycurgus's, ye Numa's, hide your diminished heads; see what a revolution two laws in a few years have produced; see a whole people, sunk in more than Gothic ignorance, accustomed to no other iron implements than the pacific plough-share, or the harmless spade, start out at once profound scholars and veteran soldiers: if at this happy period, a Frenchman, thinking any thing out of his own country worthy his attention, should condescend to pay this kingdom a visit, methinks, I anticipate the account he will give of us at his return (like his countrymen of old, who, at the taking of Rome, bursting into the Capitol, and there finding the senate fixed and immovable in their seats, declared them an assembly of kings), so will he at once pronounce the whole British nation to be an army of generals, and one congregation of doctors. Happy country! where the *Arma* & *Toga* are so fortunately blended as to prevent all contention for the pre-eminence.

I know but one objection that can be made to this plan, and that merely a temporary one; that the culture of our lands will sustain an infinite injury, if such a number of peasants were to deparochiate, there being already scarce hands sufficient, from the recruits constantly made for Germany, &c. &c. &c. to carry on the common business of husbandry.

But what are riches, perishable commodities, glittering, transitory, fallacious goods, when compared to the substantial, incorruptible endowments of the mind! this truth is indeed happily inculcated by an old English adage;

" *When lands and goods are gone and spent,*
" *Then learning is most excellent.*"

This sensible and poetical distich, I would recommend to Mr Professor, as a motto for his intended treatise; but I suppose he is already well provided with an apt *Latin*,

THE ORATORS.

if not a *Greek* one, to either of which I must yield the preference.

But to wave this ethical argument; I can easily foil the force of this objection, by a natural and obvious *succedaneum*. Suppose a clause was to be added to the bill for the importation of tallow, raw hides, and live cattle from Ireland, that, during this literary emigration, a sufficient number of inhabitants of that country may be transported hither to supply the vacancy: but here it must be observed, that for this purpose an act of parliament is indispensably necessary; for though it would be difficult, if not impossible, for us, in our present condition, to get in even our harvests, without the aid of hands annually exported for that purpose from Ireland; yet this is at best but an illicit trade, and the men themselves are to be considered under the article of smuggled goods; a very heavy penalty being laid by statute on all masters of vessels, who shall venture to import any of the above-cited commodity into this realm, without special licence; to this purpose I recollect a case in point, the fifth of William and Mary, Ban. Reg. The King contra Odearry. Vide V. Rep. vol. iii. chap. 9. page 4.

But if this should be thought by the people in power too great an indulgence to the Irish, as we have never been remarkably profuse in our favours to our loyal and affectionate sister, I see no other method of redressing the imaginary evil, than by exempting from this service all the unsies till a general peace, and accepting, in their room, a suitable number of discreet middle-aged females; and these, when they have been properly perfected in the mysteries of our language, may be returned to their several parishes, and there form little infantine communities of literati, which will be a stock for the succeeding generation; and, indeed, upon consideration, I don't know whether this won't prove the best method for the introduction and universal propagation of the plan.

For the English common people, naturally sullen and obstinate, and religiously attached to their old customs, might be shocked and scandalized to see, at one bold stroke, the *festues* and *falces*, which have been, from time immemorial, consigned to one, or more matron in every village, ravished at once from their hands, and delivered over to the administration of the opposite sex.

But

But to return to my own subject, from which my zeal for Mr Professor's success has tempted me to make rather too long a digression:

When I ventured to affirm that the profession of an orator might exist independently of an accurate knowledge of the arrangement, and different combinations of the four-and-twenty letters, so far as (*in the words of the professor*) they relate to their being the arbitrary marks of meaning upon paper; yet, I would not be understood to affect this generally, as to every species of oratory, but to confine myself to those particular branches only, where the orator's own mind suggests the matter that his own mouth discharges: for instance, now, as when affairs of state are weighed at a common-council, religious points militated at the Robin-Hood, the arts and sciences handled in the Strand, or politics debated near Westminster-abbey; here the arguments and words given are supposed to arise from the immediate impulse of the giver; but where they are concurrent agents, as in the oratory peculiar to the pulpit and the stage, where one individual furnishes the matter, and another administers the manner, the case is widely different.

In the first instance, a tolerable proficiency in reading is indispensably requisite, as scarce any memory but the late Mr Heydegger's could retain, to any degree of certainty, the various parts of the Liturgy, the Old and New Testament, briefs, faculties, excommunications, &c. &c. &c. and a lapse on those solemn occasions might be attended with very awkward circumstances; nor would I here be supposed to insinuate, that the pieces of oratory delivered from the pulpit are not the composition of the deliverer; no—This is so far from being generally the case, that I have often heard complaints made against particular agents, that they have forced upon their congregations their own crude and insipid productions, when, at the same time, their native language would furnish them with so extensive and noble a collection of admirable materials. But here the auditor, unless he be well read in theology, may be led into a mistake; for there are some men, who, by a particular happiness in their manner, have the address to make the works of other men so absolutely their own, that there is no distinguishing the difference; as this the poet hints in his *Mask dum recitat*, &c. For these various reasons, I think a warm application to the art of reading

cannot

cannot be too strongly recommended to the professors of this kind of oratory.

With regard to the professors of the stage, though reading is undoubtedly useful, yet, as the performer is to repeat, and not to read, the deficiency may be supplied by the introduction of a third agent, viz. a person to read to him till the words are rooted in his memory. This expedient, though tedious, I have known frequently practised with good success: little blunders will now and then unavoidably arise, either from the misapprehension of the second agent, or the ignorance or waggery of the third; but these slips are generally unobserved, or, through inattention or indulgence, overlooked by an audience. But to return to the consideration of my own plan, from which no temptation shall, for the future, seduce me to digress:

We will first, then, consider the utility of oratory.

Secondly, the distinct and various kinds, or species, of that science, as they are practised at this day in this kingdom.

Thirdly, we will demonstrate, that every branch of English oratory is peculiarly our own, owes its rise, progress, and perfection to this country, and was not only unknown to the ancients, but is entirely repugnant to all those principles they have endeavoured to establish.

Fourthly, that any rhetorical system now existing, instead of a cross in the hands, with letters to direct you on your road, will prove only but a Will in the Wisp, to confound, perplex, and bewilder you.

Fifthly, from hence will result a necessity for the immediate establishment of an academy, for the promulgation and inculcation of modern oratory.

To which academy, the author of these proposals does hope, sixthly, that he shall be appointed perpetual professor.

Perhaps it may not be impertinent here to observe, that the author has industriously avoided, and will, in the course of this treatise, avoid all poetical allusion, all grandeur of expression, all splendour of diction; in short, renounce every rhetorical prop, as knowing that, on didactic subjects, order, simplicity, and perspicuity, are the means to gain his end, which is not to gratify the imagination, but to improve and polish the understanding of my countrymen.

First, then, we are to demonstrate the utility of oratory: and this, we flatter ourselves, will, in a great measure,

be

be evident from the confideration of its univerfality, and
the diftinctions it procures, both lucrative and honourable,
to any man eminent in the art.

There is, by the conftitution of this kingdom, an affembly of many individuals, who, as the feventh fon of a
feventh fon is born a phyfician, are orators by hereditary
right; that is, by birth they are enabled to give their opinions and fentiments on all fubjects, where the intereft of
their country is concerned: To this we are to add another affembly, confifting of 558 individuals, where, though
the fame privilege is enjoyed as in the firft inftance, yet
this advantage is not poffeffed in virtue of any inherent natural right, but is obtained in confequence of an annual,
triennial, or feptennial deputation from the whole body of
the people; if then we add to this lift the number of all
thofe candidates who are ambitious of this honour, with
the infinite variety of changes that a revolution of twenty
years will produce, we cannot eftimate thofe fands of national orators, in *effe*, *poffe*, and *velle*, to a fmaller quantity than 20,000; and this, I believe, by the difciples of
Demoivre, will be thought a very moderate computation.

The two orders of the long robe next demand our attention; and as the pre-eminence is unqueftionably due
to the priefthood, let us confider what number of perfons
is neceffary to fupply that fervice? England is divided into nine thoufand nine hundred and thirteen parifhes: now,
if we fuppofe two paftors for every parifh, this learned
body will be found to confift of nineteen thoufand eight
hundred and twenty-fix individuals: but as the moft facred characters are no more exempted from that fatal ftroke
that puts a temporary period to our exiftence, than the
profane, it is neceffary that a provifion fhould be made of
fit and able perf'ns; fo that at all events there be no lack
of labourers in this plentiful vineyard: nor has the policy
of this nation been fo blinded as not to guard againft this
poffible contingency, by erecting fchools, feminaries, and
univerfities, in which a convenient quantity of our youth
are properly trained, in order to fill up chafms which may
be occafionally made by the infatiable fcythe of death. If
then we eftimate this corps de referve at the half only of
the ftanding force, we fhall find the army entire amount
to 29,739.

I forefee that an objection will be made to this calculation,

tion, viz. That two pastors to every parish is a most exorbitant and improbable charge; for that many parishes, from impropriations, appropriations, and other accidents, instead of two, are scarce able to support one pastor; and that this complaint is almost general throughout the whole principality of Wales, where many individuals of this respectable order, to the great damage of their dignity, are obliged to have recourse to very unclerical professions for the support of themselves and families.

This objection we will allow its full force; but then if it be considered that, in our original estimate, we omitted all deans, canons, prebends, heads and fellows of colleges, chaplains to ships, regiments, and private families, together with the whole body of dissenting ministers of all denominations, field-preachers, and parish clerks, I believe we shall be thought rather to have diminished than exaggerated the real quantity.

As I have not been able to get admittance to the archives of the several inns of court in this metropolis, I am afraid we shall not be able to determine, with the same degree of certainty, the exact number of those who have devoted their lives and labours to the explanation and due execution of our municipal laws: I am, therefore, obliged to depend on circumstantial evidence, which, in some cases is admitted, even in our courts, to have equal force with proof positive.

And here the reason of the law (as the law is the perfection of reason) is extremely clear. To illustrate this by an instance:

A swears a robbery against *B*; *A* may lie, or at least be mistaken; but if the goods stolen from *A*, and previously described by him, are found, with their marks, in the possession of *B*, *B* not being able to account for such possession, that circumstance shall be deemed of at least equal weight against *B*, as if *A* was to swear positively to the personal identity of *B*. This being the practice of the courts we shall proceed, with all possible expedition (which, indeed, is not the practice of the courts), to produce our proofs circumstantial. As in the former instance we have grounded our calculation on the number of parishes, we shall in this derive our computation from the number of houses in the kingdom.

To any man tolerably acquainted with the country of England, it is unnecessary to observe, that not only in every town, but almost in every hamlet through which he travels, his eyes are constantly caught by the appearance of a smart house, prefaced with white rails, and prologued by a red door, with a brass knocker; when you desire to be acquainted with the name and quality of the owner of this mansion, you are always told that it belongs to lawyer such a one: now, if a hamlet containing thirty houses, with perhaps an environ of an equal number, where labour and the fruits of the earth are the only sources of wealth, can support one attorney in this rural magnificence, what an infinite number of lawyers can a commercial capital sustain? But because I would rather retrench than exceed, I will only quarter one attorney upon fifty houses. The number of houses in the reign of George the First (since which time the quantity has been considerably encreased), was computed at 1,175,951. The number of attorneys then will be 23,518; and, if we reckon one barrister to twenty attorneys, the sum total is 24,693.

I know it will be here objected, that but one small part of this numerous body can be benefited by my plan, the privilege of speaking publicly being permitted to the superior order, the barristers alone: but this criticism is confined to the observation of what passes merely in Westminster-hall, without considering that, at every quarter and petty session at all county courts, courts-leet, courts-baron, &c. &c. &c. full power of pleading is permitted to every practitioner of the law.

As the number of those who incorporate themselves to promote, not only with their cash, but their counsel, the progress of the arts and sciences, is unlimited, it will be impossible for any fixed period to ascertain their quantity: nor can we, with any certainty, as the Court Register has been silent to the members of common-council, determine the amount of the city orators; besides, as what has been already offered is more than sufficient to prove the utility of our scheme from its universality, we shall not trouble our readers nor ourselves with any further calculations; for though they are replete with great depth of knowledge, are the result of intense application, and the vehicles of mathematical truths, yet to the million the disquisition is but dry and tedious, and our purpose always was, and is, to mix with our instruction a proper portion of delectation.

We will, therefore, for these reasons, hasten to the consideration of the second point proposed, viz. An inquiry into the various kinds of oratory now exiſting in this country. And we ſhall not, on this occaſion, trouble ourſelves with the inveſtigation of all the ſmaller branches of this art; but, like the profeſſors in anatomy, contenting ourſelves with the diſſection of the noble parts, remit the examination of the ignoble ones to the care of ſubaltern artiſts. Leaving, then, to the minute philoſophers of the age all the orators of veſtries, clubs, and coffee-houſes, *Paſco minora canamus*; and for the better illuſtration of this head, permit me, reader, to be a little fanciful. We will ſuppoſe oratory to be one large tree, of which true ſcience is the *radix*; eloquence the trunk; from which trunk ſprout nine diſtinct ramifications; from which ramifications depends a fruit peculiar to each. But to make this clearer, we will preſent thee with the tree itſelf, not enigmatically hieroglyfied, but plainly and palpably pourtrayed.

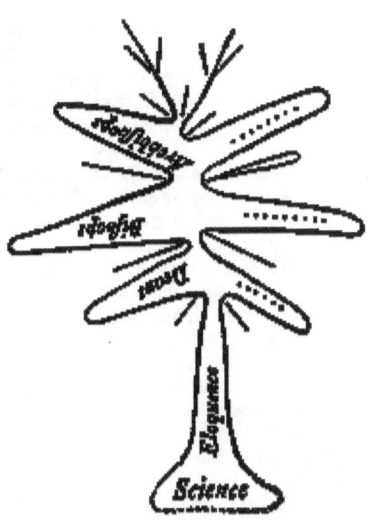

But here, reader, let me not arrogate to myſelf the merit of this happy explication; I own the hint was firſt given me with my grammar. The ingenious, profound Lilly,

Lilly, after he has led his pupils through the various and almost impervious provinces of nouns, pronouns, verbs, participles, and adverbs, conducts them to the foot of that arduous and stupendous mountain *Pæi mihi*: here, dreading lest their youthful ardour might be damped with the steep ascent, he reanimates their slackened nerves with the mystic picture of an apple-tree, the access of whose boughs, though tedious and difficult, will yet be amply rewarded by leave to revel uncontrouled through the whole region of pippins. May the luscious fruit sprouting from the apex of each of my ramifications prove an equal spur to every beardless orator!

I don't know whether the mentioning another order of orators, as they are not at present existing in this kingdom, may not be deemed an impropriety. But as I am a sincere lover of my country, I can't help recommending an immediate importation of some of those useful and able artists. Sir William Temple, in his Essay on Poetry, has recorded their virtues; and as the race was not extinguished in his time, it is to be hoped that it still remains.

In Ireland, says Sir William, the great men of their septs, among many officers of their family, had not only a physician, a huntsman, a smith, and such like, but a poet and tale-teller.

The first recorded and sung the actions of their ancestors, and entertained the company at feasts; the latter amused them with tales, when they were melancholy and could not sleep: and a very gallant gentleman has told me, of his own experience, that in his wolf-hunting there, when he used to be abroad in the mountains two or three days together, and lie very ill at nights, so as he could not well sleep, they would bring one of those tale-tellers, that when he lay down would begin a story of a king, or a giant, a dwarf and a damsel, and continue all night long in such an even tone that you heard him going on whenever you awakened; and he believed nothing any physicians could give had so good and so innocent an effect to make men sleep in any pains or distempers of body or mind. These are Sir William Temple's words, which contain an amazing instance of the power of those orators over the passions, it requiring full as much art and address to assuage and quell, as to blow up and excite a tumult in the mind.

In a bill not long since depending in Parliament, for the
better

better regulating the city watch, a clause was recommended, by a late respectable magistrate, that, to prevent the watchmen from sleeping at nights on bulks (the source of many disorders), the said watchmen should be compelled to sleep six hours in the day; an arch member seconded the motion, and begged to be included in this clause; for that being grievously afflicted with the gout, he could not for many days sleep a single wink; now if he could be compelled to take a six hours sleep every day, he apprehended that his fits would be of a much shorter duration. Upon this dry comment, the motion was rashly rejected; but if the house had received the least intimation of the astonishing abilities of the *rockers* (for by that appellation I chose to distinguish this order of orators), I am convinced that the above clause would not only have been received, but that proper encouragement would have been given, by Parliament, for the introduction and establishment of this useful oratorical sect.

Nor, indeed, considering the vast addition to our customary cares, from the unaccountable fluctuation of our funds, the cause of concern to many thousand individuals, do I think a visit from a convenient quantity of those artists would be now out of season; but how this honour is to be obtained, whether any of these great men are now residing amongst us, under the disguise of chairmen and hackney coachmen; or whether it would not be more adviseable to employ those gentlemen who have so lately and successfully rummaged the Highlands of Scotland and Ireland for the remains of Runic poetry in search of the ablest professors; is submitted to the society for the encouragement of arts.

I am aware that, on this occasion, some arch wag, possessed of the same spirit with the above senator, will object to my scheme of importation, by alleging, that we have of our own growth an ample provision of rockers, and refer us for proof to our several churches and chapels, during the hours of eleven and two on a Sunday, where the sleep-compelling power will be experimentally demonstrated to exist in its full force against us; but not to derogate from the abilities of my countrymen, surely the shortness of the time, the cause of the nap, rarely continuing above fifteen or sixteen minutes, will not admit of a proper experiment: besides, how can one orator supply

ply a whole parish, unless, indeed, our churches were to be converted into dormitories, which I can't think will happen, as this would be attended with inconveniencies too obvious to need a recital.

Abstracted from this last order, the English orators are to be divided into four distinct classes, the pulpit, the senate, the bar, and the stage; with the first of these branches, the pulpit, I shan't interfere, and, indeed, so few people now of consequence and consideration frequent the churches, that the art is scarce worth cultivation. The bar—

Scamper. Phaw! there's enough of this dull prosing; come, give us a little of something that's funny; you talked about pupils. Could not we see them?

Foote. Rather too precipitate, Sir; but, however, in some measure to satisfy you, and demonstrate the success of our scheme; give me leave to introduce to you a most extraordinary instance, in the person of a young Highlander. It is not altogether a year since this astonishing subject spoke nothing but Erse. Encouraged by the prodigies of my brother professor's skill, whose fame, like the Chevalier Taylor's, pierces the remotest regions, his relations were tempted to send this young genius to Edinburgh; where he went through a regular course of the professor's lectures to finish his studies; he has been about six weeks under my care, and, considering the time, I think you will be amazed at his progress. Donald!—

Enter Donald.

What's yer wull, Sir?

Foote. Will you give these ladies and gentlemen a proof of your skill?

Donald. Ah, ye wud ha' a specimen of my oratorical art.

Foote. If you please.

Donald. In gude troth on ye sal; wol ye gi' me a topic?

Foote. O! chuse for yourself.

Donald. Its aw one to Donald.

Foote. What think you of a short panegyric on the science we are treating of?

Donald. On oratory? wi' aw my heart.

Foote. Mind your action; let that accompany your words—

Donald.

Donald. Dunna heed, mon—the topic I presum to handle, is the miraculous gifts of an orator, wha' by the bare power of his words, he leads men, women, and bairns as he lifts—

Scamper. And who?

Donald. [*tartly.*] Men, women, and bairns.

Scamper. Bairns; who are they?

Foote. Oh! children—his meaning is obvious enough.

Donald. Ay, ay; men, women, and bairns, wherever he lifts; and first for the antiquity of the art—Ken ye, my lads, wha was the first orator?—Mayhap, ye think it was Tully the Latinest; ye are wide o' the mark; or Demosthenes the Greek? In gude troth, ye're as far off as before—Wha was it then? It was e'en that arch-chiel, the Deevil himsel—

Scamper. [*Hastily.*] The devil it was; how do you prove that?

Donald. Gods zounds, mon, ye brake the thrid of my hurrang; an ye'll but ha'd yer tongue, I'se prove it as plain as a pike-staff.

Tireback. Be quiet, Will, and let him go on.

Donald. I say it was that arch-chiel, the Deevil himsel. Ye ken weel, my lads, how Adam and Eve were planted in Eden, wi' plenty o' bannocks and cail, and aw that they wished, but were prohibited the eating of pippins—

Scamper. Apples—

Donald. Weel, weel, and are' na pippins and apples aw the same thing?

Foote. Nay, pray, gentlemen, hear him out. Go on with your pippins—

Donald. Prohibited the eating of pippins; upon which what does me the orator Satan, but he whispers a saft speech in her lug; egad our grannum fell to in an instant, and eat a pippin without staying to pare it—(*Addresses himself to the Oxonians.*) Ken ye, lads, wha was the first orator, now?

Tireback. [*to Scamper.*] What say you to that?

Scamper. By my soul, the fellow's right—

Donald. Ay, but ye wan'na ha' patience—ye wan'na ha' patience, lads—

Tireback. Hold your jaw, and go on—

Donald. Now, we come to the definition of an orator; and it is from the Latin words *oro, orare*, to entreat, or perswad;

perſwad; and how? by the means o' elocution, or argument, which argument confiſts o' letters, which letters joined mak ſyllables, which ſyllables compounded mak words, which words combined mak ſentences, or periods, or which aw together mak an orator, ſo the firſt gift of an orator is words—

Scamper. Here, Donald, you are out.

Donald. How ſo?

Scamper. Words, the firſt gift of an orator! no, Donald, no, at ſchool I learned better than that: do'ſt not remember, Will, what is the firſt perfection of an orator? Action. The ſecond, action. The third, action.

Tireback. Right, right, Harry, as right as my nail; there, Donald, I think he has given you a doſe—

Donald. An ye ſtay me, i' the midſt o' my argument—

Scamper. Why don't you ſtick to truth?

Donald. I tell ye, I can *logically.*

Tireback Damn your logic—

Donald. Mighty weel—Maiſter Foote, how ca' ye this uſage?

Foote. Oh! never mind them—proceed.

Donald. In gude troth, I'le nat ſay ane word mare.

Foote. Finiſh, finiſh, Donald—

Donald. Ah! they have jumbled aw my ideas together; but an they will enter into a fair argumentation, I'le convince 'em that Donald Macgregor is mare than a match.

Scamper. You be—

Donald. Very weel—

Foote. Nay, but my dear Donald—

Donald. Hands aff, Maiſter Foote—I ha' finiſhed my tale, the De'el a word mare ſal ye get out o' Donald—yer fervant, Sir. [*Exit.*

Foote. You ſee, gentlemen, what your impatience has loſt us.

Scamper. Rot him, let him go; but is this fellow one of your *pupils?* why, what a damnable twang he has got, with his men, women, and bairns!—

Foote. His pronunciation is, I own, a little irregular; but then conſider he is but merely a novice; why, even in his preſent condition, he makes no bad figure for his five minutes at the *Robin Hood*; and in a month or two, we ſhan't be aſhamed to ſtart him in a more *reſpectable place.*

But

But now, gentlemen, we are to descend to the peculiar essential qualities of each distinct species of oratory; and first for the bar—but as no didactic rules can so well convey, or words make a proper impression, we will have recourse to more palpable means, and endeavour, by a lively imitation, to demonstrate the extent of our art. We must, for this end, employ the aid of our pupils; but as some preparation is necessary, we hope you will indulge us in a short interruption.

ACT II.

SCENE, *A Hall of Justice.*

Enter Foote.

THE first species of oratory we are to demonstrate our skill in is that of the bar; and, in order to give our lecture an air of reality, you are to suppose this a court of justice, furnished with proper ministers to discharge the necessary functions. But, to supply these gentlemen with business, we must likewise institute an imaginary cause; and, that the whole may be ideal, let it be the prosecution of an imaginary being; I mean the phantom of Cock-lane, a phœnomenon that has puzzled the brains, and terrified the minds of many of our fellow-subjects.

You are to consider, ladies and gentlemen, that the language of the bar is a species of oratory distinct from every other. It has been observed, that the ornaments of this profession have not shone with equal lustre in an assembly near their own hall; the reason assigned, though a pleasant, is not the true one. It has been hinted, that these gentlemen were in want of their briefs; but was that the disease, the remedy would be easy enough: they need only have recourse to the *artifice* successfully practised by some of their colleagues; instead of having their briefs in their hands, to hide them at the bottom of their hats.

[*Calls to his pupils, who enter dressed as a justice, a clerk, a serjeant at law, and a counsellor.*]

You will remember, gentlemen, your proper pauses, repetitions, hums, ha's, and interjections: now seat yourselves, and you the counsel remember to be mighty dull, and you the justice to fall asleep. I must prepare to appear in this cause as a witness. [*Exit*.

Justice. Clerk, read the indictment.

Clerk *reads*.

Middlesex, to wit.

Fanny Phantom, you are indicted, that on or before the first day of January 1762, you the said Fanny did, in a certain house, in a certain street, called Cock-lane, in the county of Middlesex, maliciously, treacherously, wickedly, and wilfully, by certain thumpings, knockings, scratchings, and flutterings against doors, walls, wainscots, bedsteads, and bedposts, disturb, annoy, assault, and terrify divers innocent, inoffensive, harmless, quiet, simple people, residing in, at, near or about the said Cock-lane, and elsewhere, in the said county of Middlesex, to the great prejudice of said people in said county. How say you, guilty, or—

Counsellor *stops the Clerk short*.

May it please your Worship—hem—I am counsel in this cause for the ghost—hem—and before I can permit her to plead, I have an objection to make, that is—hem—I shall object to her pleading at all.—Hem—it is the standing law of this country—hem—and has—hem—always been so allowed, deemed, and practised, that—hem—all criminals should be tried *par pares*, by their equals—hem—that is—hem—by a jury of equal rank with themselves. Now, if this be the case, as the case it is; I—hem—I should be glad to know how my client can be tried in this here manner. And first, who is my client? she is in the indictment called a phantom, a ghost; what is a ghost? a spirit. What is a spirit? a spirit is a thing that exists independently of, and is superior to flesh and blood. And can any man go for to think, that I can advise my client to submit to be tried by people of an inferior rank to herself? certainly no—I therefore, humbly move to squash this indictment, unless a jury of ghosts be first had and obtained; unless a jury of ghosts be first had and obtained. [*Sits down*.

Serjeant. I am, in this cause, counsel against Fanny Phantom the ghost;—eh—and notwithstanding the rule laid down by Mr Prosequi, be—eh—right in the main, yet here it can't avail his client a whit. We allow—eh —we do allow, please your Worship, that Fanny *qu*oad Phantom,

Phantom,—eh—had originally a right to a jury of ghosts; but—eh—if she did, by any act of her own, forfeit this right, her plea cannot be admitted. Now, we can prove, please your Worship, prove by a cloud of witnesses, that said Fanny did, as specified in the indictment, scratch, knock, and flutter;—eh—which said scratchings, knockings, and flutterings—eh—being operations, merely peculiar to flesh, blood, and body—eh—we do humbly apprehend—eh—that by condescending to execute the aforesaid operations, she has waved her privilege as a ghost, and may be tried in the ordinary form, according to the statute so made and provided in the reign of, &c. &c. &c.

Your Worship's opinion.

Tarebach. Smoke the justice, he is as fast as a church.

Scamper. I fancy he has touched the tankard too much this morning; he'll know a good deal of what they have been saying.

Justice. [*Is awaked by the Clerk, who tells him they have pleaded.*] Why the objection—oh—brought by Mr Prosequi, is (*whispers the clerk*) doubtless provisionally a valid objection; but then, if the culprit has, by an act of her own, defeated her privilege, as asserted in Mr Serjeant's replication; we conceive she may be legally tried—oh,—besides—oh,—besides. I, I, I can't well see how we could impannel a jury of ghosts; or—oh—how twelve spirits, who have no body at all, can be said to take a corporal oath, as required by law—unless, indeed, as in case of the peerage, the prisoner may be tried on their honour.

Counsellor. Your Worship's distinction is just; knockings, scratchings, &c. as asserted by Mr Serjeant—

Serjeant. Asserted—Sir, do you doubt my instructions?

Counsellor. No interruptions, if you please, Mr Serjeant; I say as asserted, but can assertions be admitted as proofs? certainly no—

Serjeant. Our evidence is ready—

Counsellor. To that we object, to that we object, as it will anticipate the merits—your Worship—

Serjeant. Your Worship—

Justice. Why, as you impeach the ghost's privilege, you must produce proofs of her scratchings.

Serjeant. Call Shadrach Bodkin.

Clerk. Shadrach Bodkin, come into court.

Enter

Enter Bodkin.

Serjeant. Pray, Mr Bodkin, where do you live?
Bodkin. I fojourn in Lukener's-lane.
Serjeant. What is your profeffion.
Bodkin. I am a *teacher of the word*, and a *tailor*.
Scamper. Zounds, Will, it is a methodift.
Tireback. No, fure!
Stamper. By the lord Harry, it is.
Clerk. Silence.
Serjeant. Do you know any thing of Fanny the Phantom?
Bodkin. Yea—I do.
Serjeant. Can you give any account of her thumpings, fcratchings, and flutterings?
Bodkin. Yea—manifold have been the fcratchings and knockings that I have heard.
Serjeant. Name the times.
Bodkin. I have attended the fpirit *Fanny* from the firft day of her flutterings, even to the laft fcratch fhe gave.
Serjeant. How long may that be?
Bodkin. Five weeks did fhe flutter, and fix weeks did fhe fcratch.
Scamper. Six weeks—damn it, I wonder fhe did not wear out her nails.
Clerk. Silence.
Serjeant. I hope the court is convinced.
Counfellor. Hold, Mafter Bodkin, you and I muft have a little difcourfe. A tailor, you fay. Do you work at your bufinefs?
Bodkin. No—
Counfellor. Look upon me, look upon the court—then your prefent trade is your teaching?
Bodkin. It is no trade.
Counfellor. What is it then, a calling?
Bodkin. No, it is no calling—it is rather—as I may fay —a *forcing*—a *compelling*—
Counfellor. By whom?
Bodkin. By the fpirit that is within me—
Scamper. It is an evil fpirit, I believe; and needs muft when the devil drives, you know, Will.
Tireback. Right, Harry—

Counfellor.

Counsellor. When did you first feel these spiritual motions?

Bodkin. In the town of Norwich, where I was born;—One day as I was sitting cross-legged on my shop-board, new-seating a cloth pair of breeches of Mr Alderman Crape's—I felt the spirit within me, moving upwards and downwards, and this way and that way, and tumbling and jumbling—at first I thought it was the cholic—

Counsellor. And how are you certain it was not?

Bodkin. At last I heard a voice whispering within me, crying, Shadrach, Shadrach, Shadrach, cast away the things that belong to thee, thy thimble and sheers, and do the things that I bid thee.

Counsellor. And you did?

Bodkin. Yes, verily.

Counsellor. I think I have heard a little of you, Master Bodkin; and so you quitted your business, your wife, and your children?

Bodkin. I did.

Counsellor. You did—But then you communed with other mens wives?

Bodkin. Yes, and with widows, and with maidens.

Counsellor. How came that about, Shadrach?

Bodkin. I was moved thereunto by the spirit.

Counsellor. I should rather think by the flesh—I have been told, friend Bodkin, that twelve became pregnant—

Bodkin. Thou art deceived—They were barely but nine.

Counsellor. Why, this was an active spirit.

Serjeant. But to the point, Mr Profequi.

Counsellor. Well, then—you say you have heard those scratchings and knockings?

Bodkin. Yes——

Counsellor. But why did you think they came from a spirit?

Bodkin. Because the very same thumps, scratches, and knocks, I have felt on my breast-bone from the spirit within me——

Counsellor. And those noises you are sure you heard on the first of January?

Bodkin. Certain—

Serjeant. But to what do all those interrogatories tend?

Counsellor. To a most material purpose; your Worship observes,

observes, that Bodkin is positive as to the noise made on the first day of January by Fanny the Phantom: now if we can prove an *alibi*, that is, that, on that very day, at that very time, the said Fanny was scratching and fluttering any where else, we apprehend that we destroy the credit of this witness—Call Peter Paragraph.

Clerk. Peter Paragraph, come into court.

Counsellor. This gentleman is an eminent printer, and has collected, for the public information, every particular relative to this remarkable story; but as he has the misfortune to have but one leg, your Worship will indulge him in the use of a chair.

Clerk. Peter Paragraph, come into court.

Enter Paragraph.

Counsellor. Pray, Mr Paragraph, where was you born?

Paragraph. Sir, I am a native of Ireland, and born and bred in the city of Dublin.

Counsellor. When did you arrive in the city of London?

Paragraph. About the last autumnal equinox; and now I recollect, my Journal makes mention of my departure for England in the Balborough packet, Friday, October the tenth, N. S. or new stile.

Counsellor. Oh! then the Journal is yours?

Paragraph. Please your Worship, it is; and relating thereto I believe I can give you a pleasant conceit—Last week I went to visit a Peer, for I know Peers, and Peers know me. Quoth his Lordship to me, Mr Paragraph, with respect to your Journal, I would wish that your paper was whiter, or your ink blacker. Quoth I to the Peer by way of *reply*, I hope you will own there is enough for the money; his Lordship was pleased to laugh. It was such a pretty repartee, ha, he, he, he——

Justice. Pray, Mr Paragraph, what might be your business in England?

Paragraph. Hem——a little love affair, please your Worship.

Counsellor. A wife, I suppose—

Paragraph. Something tending that way; even so long ago as January 1739-40, there past some amorous glances between us; she is the daughter of old Vamp of the Turnstile;

stile: but at that time I stifled my passion, Mrs Paragraph being then in the land of the living.

Counsellor. She is now dead?

Paragraph. Three years and three quarters, please your Worship: We were exceeding happy together; she was, indeed, a little apt to be jealous.

Counsellor. No wonder—

Paragraph. Yes: they can't help it, poor souls; but notwithstanding, at her death, I gave her a prodigious good character in my Journal.

Counsellor. And how proceeds the present affair?

Paragraph. Just now, we are quite at a stand—

Counsellor. How so?

Paragraph. The old scoundrel her father has played me a slippery trick.

Counsellor. Indeed!

Paragraph. As he could give no money in hand, I agreed to take her *fortune* in *copies*; I was to have the Wits Vade Mecum entire; four hundred of News from the invisible world, in sheets; all that remained of Glanvil upon Witches; Hill's Bees, Bardana, Brewing, and Balsam of Honey, and three eighths of Robinson Crusoe.

Counsellor. A pretty fortune!

Paragraph. Yes; they are things that stir in the trade; but you must know that we agreed to go halves in Fanny the Phantom. But whilst I and two authors, whom I had hired to ask questions, at nine shillings a-night, were taking notice of the knockings at the house of Mr Parsons himself, that old rascal Vamp had privately printed off a thousand eighteenpenny scratchings, purchased of two Methodist preachers, at the public house over the way—

Counsellor. Now we come to the point—look upon this evidence; was he present at Mr Parsons' knockings?

Paragraph. Never; this is one of the rascally Methodists—Harkee, fellow, how could you be such a scoundrel to sell for genuine your counterfeit scratchings to Vamp?

Bodkin. My scratchings were the true scratchings—

Paragraph. Why, you lying son of a whore, did not I buy all my materials from the girl's father himself?

Bodkin. What the spirit commanded, that did I.

Paragraph. What spirit?

Bodkin. The spirit within me—

Paragraph. If I could but get at you, I would soon try what

what fort of a fpirit it is—ſtop, you villain.—[*Exit* Bodkin.]—The rogue has made his eſcape—but I will dog him, to find out his haunts, and then return for a warrant—His ſcratchings! a ſcoundrel; I will have juſtice, or I'll turn his tabernacle into a pigſtye. [*Exit* Paragraph.

Counſellor. I hope, pleaſe your Worſhip, we have ſufficiently eſtabliſhed our *alibi*.

Juſtice. You are unqueſtionably entitled to a jury of ghoſts.

Counſellor. Mr Serjeant, you will provide us a liſt?

Serjeant. Let us ſee—you have no objection to Sir George Villars; the evil genius of Brutus; the ghoſt of Banquo; Mrs Veal.

Counſellor. We object to a woman—your Worſhip—

Juſtice. Why, it is not the practice: this, it muſt be owned, is an extraordinary caſe. But, however, if, on conviction, the Phantom ſhould plead pregnancy, Mrs Veal will be admitted into the jury of matrons.

Serjeant. I thank your Worſhip: then the court is adjourned.

Terence *and* Dermot *in an upper box*.

Terence. By my ſhoul but I will ſpake.

Dermot. Arrah, be quiet, Terence.

Terence. Dibble burn me but I will; but, but, not ſpake, what ſhould ail me? harkee you, Mr Juſtice—

Scamper Halloo, what's the matter now, Will?

Dermot. Leave off, honey Terence, now you are well—

Terence. Dermot, be eaſy—

Scamper. Hear him—

Tireback. Hear him—

Terence. Ay, hear him, hear him; why the matter is this, Mr Juſtice, that little hopping fellow there, that Dublin Journal man, is as great a liar as ever was born—

Tireback. How ſo?

Terence. Ay, prithee, don't bodder me; what, d'ye learn no more manners at Oxford College, than to ſtop a gentleman in the midſt of his ſpeech before he begins? oh, for ſhame of yourſelf—Why, the matter is this, Mr Juſtice, that there what the debble d'ye call him, Pra-Praragraf, but by my ſhoul, that is none of his name neither, I know the little baſtard as well as myſelf; as to Fanny the Phantom,

long

THE ORATORS.

long life to the poor gentlewoman, he knows no more of her than the mother that bore her—

Suds. Indeed! good Lord, you surprise me!

Terence. Arrah, now honey Suds, spake when you are spoke to; you arn't upon the jury, my jewel, now; by my shoul you are a little too fat for a ghost.

Tireback. Prithee, friend Ephraim, let him go on; let's hear a little what he would be at—

Terence. I say, he knows nothing about the cafe that is litigated here, d'ye fee, at all, at all; becaufe why, I han't ha been from Dublin above four weeks, or a month; and I faw him in his shop every day; fo how could he be here and there too? unless, indeed, he used to fly backwards and forwards, and that you fee is impossible, because why, he has got a wooden leg.

Scamper. What the devil is the fellow about?

Tireback. I smoke him—harkee, Terence, who do you take that lame man to be?

Terence. Oh, my jewel, I know him well enough sure by his person, for all he thought to conceal himself by changing his name—

Scamper. Why, it is Foote, you fool.

Terence. Arrah, who?

Tireback. Foote.

Terence. Fot, what the lecture-man? P—

Tireback. Yes.

Terence. Arrah, be easy, honey—

Scamper. Nay, enquire of Suds.

Suds. Truly I am minded 'twas he.

Terence. Your humble servant yourself, Mr Suds; by my shoul, I'll wager you three thirteens to a rap, that it is no fuch matter at all, at all.

Scamper. Done—and be judged by the company.

Terence. Done—I'll ask the orator himself—here he comes;

Enter Foote.

harkee, honey Fot; was it yourself that was hopping about here but now!

Foote. I have heard your debate, and must give judgment against you—

Terence. What, yourself, yourself!

Foote. It was—

Terence.

Terence. Then, faith, I have loft my thirteens—Arrah, but Fox, my jewel, why are you after playing fuch pranks to bring an honeft jontleman into company where he is nat —But what is this felling of lectures a thriving profeffion?

Foote. I can't determine as yet; the public have been very indulgent; I have not long opened.

Terence. By my fhoul, if it anfwers, will you be my pupil and learn me the trade?

Foote. Willingly—

Terence. That's an honeft fellow, long life to you, lad.
[*Sits down.*

Enter M'George.

M'George. Here is Doctor Friſcamo without.

Foote. Friſcamo—who is he?

M'George. The German phyfician from James-ftreet.

Foote. Well; what is his bufinefs with me?

M'George. He is in danger of lofing his trade.

Foote. How fo?

M'George. He fays, laft fummer, things went on glibly enough, for then he had the market all to himfelf; but this year there is an Italian fellow ftarted up in the garden, that with his face and grimace has taken all his patients away.

Foote. That's hard.

M'George. Dreadful—if you was to hear the poor man's terrible tale, you would really be moved to compaffion: he fays that his bleeding won't find him in bread; and as to the tooth trade, excepting two ftumps, for fixpence a piece, 'tis a month fince he looked in a mouth—

Foote. How can I help him?

M'George. Why, he thinks oratory will do all with the Englifh; and if you would but teach him to talk, he fhould get all his cuftom again—

Foote. Can he read?

M'George. Oh Lord! poor man, no.

Foote. We'll let him attend here on—

M'George. He hopes that you will quickly difpatch him, for if he finds he can't do as a doctor, he intends to return to the curing of horfes again.

Foote. Well, tell him he may reft affured, he fhall either bleed or fhoe in a fortnight. [*Exit* M'George.

Foote. Having thus completed our lecture on the eloquence

quence peculiar to the bar, we shall produce one great group of orators, in which will be exhibited specimens of every branch of the art. You will have at one view, the choleric, the placid, the voluble, the frigid, the frothy, the turgid, the calm, and the clamorous; and as a proof of our exquisite skill, our subjects are not such as a regular education has prepared for the reception of this sublime science, but a set of illiterate mechanics, whom you are to suppose assembled at the Robin-Hood in the Butcher-row, in order to discuss and adjust the various systems of Europe; but particularly to determine the separate interest of their own mother country.

ACT III.

SCENE, *The Robin-Hood.*

The PRESIDENT.

Dermot O'Droheda, *a chairman;* Tim Twist, *a tailor;* Strap, *a shoemaker;* Anvil, *a smith;* Sam Slaughter, *a butcher;* Catchpole, *a bailiff. All with pewter pots before them.*

Pres. SILENCE, gentlemen; are your pots replenished with porter?

All. Full, Mr President.

Pres. We will then proceed to the business of the day; and let me beg, gentlemen, that you will, in your debates, preserve that decency and decorum that is due to the importance of your deliberations, and the dignity of this illustrious assembly—[*Gets up, pulls off his hat, and reads the motion.*]—Motion made last Monday to be debated today, " That, for the future, instead of that vulgar potation called porter, the honourable members may be supplied with a proper quantity of Irish usquebagh.

" Dermot O'Droheda + his mark."

O'Droheda. [*Gets up.*] That's I myself.

Pres. Mr O'Droheda.

O'Droheda. Mr President, the case is this; it is not becase I am any great lover of that same usquebagh that I have set my mark to the motion; but becase I did not think it was decent for a number of gentlemen that were,

d'ye

d'ye see, met to settle the affairs of the nation, to be guzzling a pot of porter; to be sure the liquor is a pretty sort of a liquor enough when a man is hot with trotting between a couple of poles; but this is another guess matter; becase why, the head is concerned; and if it was not for the malt and the hops, dibble burn me but I would as soon take a drink from the Thames as your porter. But as to usquebaugh; ah, long life to the liquor—it is an exhilirator of the bowels, and a stomatic to the head; I say, Mr Prefident, it invigorates, it stimulates, it—in short it is the onliest liquor of life, and no man alive will die whilst he drinks it.

[*Sits down.* Twist *gets up, having a piece of paper, containing the heads of what he says, in his hat.*

Pref. Mr Timothy Twist.

Tim Twist. Mr Prefident, I second Mr O'Droheda's motion; and, Sir, give me leave—I say, Mr Prefident—[*looks in his hat*]—give me leave to observe, that, Sir, though it is impossible to add any force to what has been advanced by my honourable friend in the straps; yet, Sir, —[*looks in his hat again*]—it may, Sir, I say, be necessary to obviate some objections that may be made to the motion; and first, it may be thought—I say, Sir, some gentleman may think, that this may prove pernicious to our manufacture—[*looks in his hat*]—and the duty doubtless it is of every member of this illustrious assembly to have a particular eye unto that; but, Mr Prefident—Sir—[*looks in his hat, is confused, and sits down.*]

Pref. Mr Twist, O pray finish, Mr Twist.

Twist. [*Gets up.*] I say, Mr Prefident, that, Sir, if, Sir, it be considered that—as—I say—[*looks in his hat*]—I have nothing farther to say. [*Sits down, and Strap gets up.*

Pref. Mr Strap.

Strap. Mr Prefident, it was not my intention to trouble the assembly upon this occasion, but when I hear insinuations thrown out by gentlemen, where the interest of this country is so deeply concerned, I own I cannot sit silent; and give me leave to say, Sir, there never came before this assembly a point of more importance than this; it strikes, Sir, at the very root of your constitution; for, Sir, what does this motion imply? It implies that porter, a wholesome, domestic manufacture, is to be prohibited at once. And for what, Sir? for a foreign pernicious commodity. I had, Sir, formerly the honour, in conjunction with my
learned

learned friend in the leather apron, to expel sherbet from amongst us, as I looked upon lemons as a fatal and foreign fruit; and can it be thought, Sir, that I will sit silent to this? No, Sir, I will put my shoulders strongly against it; I will oppose it *manibus totibus*. For should this proposal prevail, it will not end here: fatal, give me leave to say, will, I foresee, be the issue; and I shan't be surprised, in a few days, to hear from the same quarter, a motion for the expulsion of gin, and a premium for the importation of whisky.

[*A buzz of approbation, with significant nods and winks from the other members. He sits down; and* Anvil *and another member get up together; some cry* Anvil, *others* Jacobs.]

Pres. Mr Anvil.

Anvil. Mr President, Sir—

[*The members all blow their noses, and cough;* Anvil *talks all the while, but is not heard.*]

Pres. Silence, gentlemen; pray, gentlemen. A worthy member is up.

Anvil. I say, Mr President, that if we consider this case in its utmost extent—[*All the members cough, and blow their noses again*]—I say, Sir, I will. Nay, I insist on being heard. If any gentleman has any thing to say any where else, I'll hear him.

[*Members all laugh, and* Anvil *sits down in a passion, and* Slaughter *gets up*.]

Pres. Mr Samuel Slaughter.

Slaughter. Sir, I declare it, at the bare hearing of this here motion, I am all over in a sweat; for my part, I can't think what gentlemen mean by talking in that there manner; not but I likes that every man should deliver his mind; I does mine; it has been ever my way; and when a member opposes me, I like him the better for it; it's right; I am pleased; he can't please me more; it is as it should be; and though I differ from the honourable gentleman in the flannel night-cap, over the way, yet I am pleased to hear him say what he thinks; for, Sir, as I said, it is always my rule to say what I think, right or wrong —[*a loud laugh*]—ay, ay, gentlemen may laugh, with all my heart, I am used to it, I don't mind it a farthing; but, Sir, with regard to that there motion, I entirely agree with my worthy friend with the pewter-pot at his mouth.

Now,

Now, Sir, I would fain ask any gentleman this here question; can any thing in nature be more natural for an Englishman, than porter? I declare, Mr President, I think it the most wholesomest liquor in the world. But if it must be a change, let us change it for rum, a wholesome palatable liquor, a liquor that—in short, Mr President, I don't know such a liquor. Ay, gentlemen may stare; I say, and I say it upon my conscience, I don't know such a liquor. Besides, I think there is in this here affair a point of law, which I shall leave to the consideration of the learned, and for that there reason, I shall take up no more of your time.

[*He sits down, Catchpole gets up.*

Pres. Mr Catchpole.

Catchpole. I get up to the point of law. And though, Sir, I am bred to the business, I can't say I am prepared for this question. But though this usquebagh, as a dram, may not (by name) be subject to a duty, yet, it is my opinion, or rather belief, it will be considered, as in the case of horses, to come under the article of dried goods—but I move that another day this point be debated.

Slaughter. I second the motion.

[*Catchpole gives a paper to the President, who reads it.*

Pres. Hear your motion.

" That it be debated next Thursday, whether the dram ufquebagh is subject to a particular duty; or, as in the case of horses, to be considered under the article of dried goods."

All. Agreed, agreed.

Foote. And, now, ladies and gentlemen, having produced to you glaring proofs of our great ability in every species of oratory, having manifested, in the persons of our pupils, our infinite address in conveying our knowledge to others, we shall close our morning's lecture, instituted for public good, with a proposal for the particular improvement of individuals. We are ready to give private instructions to any reverend gentleman in his probationary sermon for a lectureship; to young barristers who have causes to open, or motions to make; to all candidates of the sock or buskin; or to the new members of any of those oratorical societies with which this metropolis is at present so plentifully stocked. [*Exeunt omnes.*

THE

THE MINOR;

A COMEDY;

OF

THREE ACTS.

PERSONS IN THE INTRODUCTION.

Foote.
Canker.
Shank.
Prompter.

IN THE COMEDY.

Sir William Wealthy,	=	Mr Baddeley.
Mr Richard Wealthy,		Mr Wrighten.
Sir George Wealthy,	=	Mr Aickin.
Shift,	— =	Mr Bannister.
Loader,	=	Mr Brandsby.
Dick,	— —	Mr Burton.
Trusty,	=	Mr Parsons.
Smirk,	— —	Mr Bannister.
The Baron, assumed,		Mr Baddeley.
Mrs Cole,	—.	Mr Bannister.
Lucy,	— —	Miss Hopkins.

TO HIS GRACE

WILLIAM DUKE OF DEVONSHIRE,

LORD CHAMBERLAIN OF HIS MAJESTY'S
HOUSEHOLD.

My Lord,

THE Minor, who is indebted for his appearance on the stage to your Grace's indulgence, begs leave to desire your farther protection, at his entering into the world.

Though the allegiance due from the whole dramatic people to your Grace's station, might place this address in the light of a natural tribute; yet, my Lord, I should not have taken that liberty with the Duke of Devonshire, if I could not at the same time plead some little utility in the design of my piece; and add, that the public approbation has stamped a value on the execution.

The law, which threw the stage under the absolute government of a Lord Chamberlain, could not fail to fill the minds of all the objects of that power with very gloomy apprehensions; they found themselves (through their own licentiousness, it must be confess'd) in a more precarious dependent state than any other of his Majesty's subjects. But when their direction was lodged in the hands of a nobleman whose ancestors had so successfully struggled for national liberty, they ceased to fear for their own. It was not from a patron of the liberal arts they were to expect an oppressor; it was not from the friend of freedom, and of man, they were to dread partial monopolies, or the establishment of petty tyrannies.

Their warmest wishes are accomplished; none of their rights have been invaded, except what, without the first poetic authority, I should not venture to call a right, the *jus noceudi*.

Your tenderness, my Lord, for all the followers of the Muses, has been in no instance more conspicuous, than in your late favour to me, the meanest of their train; your Grace has thrown open (for those who are denied admittance into the palaces of Parnassus) a cottage on its borders, where the unhappy migrants may be, if not magnificently, at least hospitably, entertained.

I shall detain your Grace no longer, than just to echo the public voice, that, for the honour, progress, and perfection of letters,

Vol. I.   F   your

your Grace may long continue their much-loved Castor, who have always been their generous protector.

I have the honour, my Lord, to be, with the greatest respect and gratitude,

Your Grace's most dutiful,

most obliged,

and obedient servant,

Edgbro, July 8, 1760.

SAMUEL FOOTE.

INTRODUCTION.

INTRODUCTION.

Enter Canker *and* Smart.

Smart. BUT are you sure he has leave?
Cank. Certain.
Smart. I'm damn'd glad on't. For now we shall have a laugh either with him, or at him, it does not signify which.
Cank. Not a farthing.
Smart. D'you know his scheme?
Cank. Not I. But is not the door of the Little Theatre open?
Smart. Yes. Who is that fellow that seems to stand centry there?
Cank. By his tatter'd garb and meagre visage, he must be one of the troop.
Smart. I'll call him. Holo, Mr ——

Enter Pearl.

What, is there any thing going on over the way?
Pear. A rehearsal.
Smart. Of what?
Pear. A new piece.
Smart. Foote's?
Pear. Yes.
Cank. Is he there?
Pear. He is.
Smart. Zounds, let's go and see what he is about.
Cank. With all my heart.
Smart. Come along then. [*Exeunt.*

Enter Foote *and an* Actor.

Foote. Sir, this will never do; you must get rid of your high notes, and country cant. Oh, 'tis the true strolling.

Enter Smart *and* Canker.

Smart. Ha, ha, ha! what, hard at it, my boy!—Here's your old friend Canker and I come for a peep. Well, and hey, what is your plan?
Foote. Plan?

Smart.

Smart. Ay, what are your characters? Give us your groupe; how is your cloth fill'd?

Foote. Characters!

Smart. Ay.—Come, come, communicate. What, man, we will lend thee a lift. I have a damn'd fine original for thee, an aunt of my own, just come from the North, with the true Newcastle bur in her throat; and a nose and a chin. I am afraid she is not well enough known; but I have a remedy for that. I'll bring her the first night of your piece, place her in a confpicuous ftation, and whifper the fecret to the whole houfe. That will be damn'd fine, won't it?

Foote. Oh, delicious!

Smart. But don't name me. For if fhe fmokes me for the author, I fhall be dafh'd out of her codicil in a hurry.

Foote. Oh, never fear me. But I fhou'd think your uncle Tom a better character.

Smart. What, the politician?

Foote. Aye; that every day, after dinner, as foon as the cloth is remov'd, fights the battle of Minden, batters the French with cherry ftones, and purfues 'em to the banks of the Rhine in a ftream of fpilt port.

Smart. Oh, damn it, he'll do.

Foote. Or what fay you to your father-in-law, Sir Timothy? who, though as broken-winded as a Hounflow poft-horfe, is eternally chaunting Venetian ballads. *Kara cara cara bigeia.*

Smart. Admirable! by heavens!—Have you got 'em?

Foote. No.

Smart. Then in with 'em my boy.

Foote. Not one.

Smart. Pr'ythee why not?

Foote. Why, look'e, Smart, though you are, in the language of the world, my friend, yet there is one thing you, I am fure, love better than any body.

Smart. What's that?

Foote. Mifchief.

Smart. No, pr'ythee——

Foote. How now am I fure that you, who fo readily give up your relations, may not have fome defign upon me?

Smart. I don't underftand you.

Foote. Why, as foon as my characters begin to circulate a little fuccefsfully, my mouth is ftopp'd in a minute, by

the

the clamour of your relations,—Oh, damme,—'tis a shame,—it should not be,—people of distinction brought upon the stage. And so out of compliment to your cousin, I am to be beggar'd for treating the public with the follies of your family, at your own request.

Smart. How can you think I would be such a dog? What the devil, then, are we to have nothing personal? Give us the actors however.

Foote. Oh, that's stale. Besides, I think they have, of all men, the best right to complain.

Smart. How so?

Foote. Because, by rendering them ridiculous in their profession, you, at the same time, injure their pockets. Now, as to the other gentry, they have providentially something besides their understanding to rely on; and the only injury they can receive is, that the whole town is then diverted with what before was only the amusement of private parties.

Cant. Give us then a national portrait; a Scotchman or an Irishman.

Foote. If you mean merely the dialect of the two countries, I can't think it either a subject of satire or humour; it is an accidental unhappiness, for which a man is no more accountable than the colour of his hair. Now affectation I take to be the true comic object. If, indeed, a North Briton, struck with a scheme of reformation, should advance from the banks of the Tweed, to teach the English the true pronunciation of their own language, he would, I think, merit your laughter: nor would a Dublin mechanic, who, from heading the liberty-boys in a skirmish on Ormond Quay, should think he had a right to prescribe military laws to the first commander in Europe, be a less ridiculous object.

Smart. Are there such?

Foote. If you mean that the blunders of a few peasants, or the partial principles of a single scoundrel, are to stand as characteristical marks of a whole country; your pride may produce a laugh, but, believe me, it is at the expence of your understanding.

Cant. Heyday, what a system is here! Laws for laughing! And pray, sage Sir, instruct us when we may laugh with propriety?

Foote. At an old beau, a superannuated beauty, a military

litary coward, a stuttering orator, or a gouty dancer. In short, whoever affects to be what he is not, or strives to be what he cannot, is an object worthy the poet's pen, and your mirth.

Smart. Pha, I don't know what you mean by your is nots and cannots—damn'd abstrufe jargon. Ha, Canker!

Cank. Well, but if you will not give us persons, let us have things. Treat us with a modern amour, and a stare intrigue, or a——

Foote. And so amufe the public ear at the expence of private peace. You muft excufe me.

Cank. And with thefe principles you expect to thrive on this fpot?

Smart. No, no, it won't do. I tell thee the plain roaft and boil'd of the theatres will never do at this table. We muft have high feafoned ragouts and rich sauces.

Foote. Why, perhaps, by way of defert, I may produce fomething that may hit your palate.

Smart. Your bill of fare?

Foote. What think you of one of thofe itinerant field orators, who, though at declar'd enmity with common fenfe, have the addrefs to poifon the principles, and at the fame time pick the pockets of half our induftrious fellow fubjects?

Cank. Have a care. Dangerous ground. *Ludere cum facris*, you know.

Foote. Now I look upon it in a different manner. I confider thefe gentlemen in the light of public performers, like myfelf; and whether we exhibit at Tottenham-court, or the Hay-market, our purpofe is the fame, and the place is immaterial.

Cank. Why, indeed, if it be confidered—

Foote. Nay, more, I muft beg leave to affert, that ridicule is the only antidote againft this pernicious poifon. This is a madnefs that argument can never cure: and fhould a little wholefome feverity be applied, perfecution would be the immediate cry: where then can we have recourfe, but to the comic Mufe? Perhaps, the archnefs and feverity of her fmile may redrefs an evil, that the laws cannot reach, or reafon reclaim.

Cank. Why, if it does not cure thofe already diftemper'd, it may be a means to ftop the infection.

Smart.

Smart. But how is your scheme conducted?

Foote. Of that you may judge. We are just going upon a repetition of the piece. I should be glad to have your opinion.

Smart. We will give it you.

Foote. One indulgence: as you are Englishmen, I think, I need not beg, that as from necessity most of my performers are new, you will allow for their inexperience, and encourage their timidity.

Smart. But reasonable.

Foote. Come, then, prompter, begin.

Pear. Lord, Sir, we are all at a stand.

Foote. What's the matter?

Pear. Mrs O-Schohnefy has resus'd the part of the baw'd; she says she is a gentlewoman, and it would be a reflection on her family to do any such thing!

Foote. Indeed!

Pear. If it had been only a whore, says she, I should not have minded it; because no lady need be ashamed of doing that.

Foote. Well, there is no help for it; but these gentlemen must not be disappointed. Well, I'll do the character myself.

ACT I.

Sir William Wealthy, and Mr Richard Wealthy.

Sir Will. COME, come, brother, I know the world. People who have their attention eternally fixed upon one object, can't help being a little narrow in their notions.

R. Weal. A sagacious remark that, and highly probable, that we merchants, who maintain a constant correspondence with the four quarters of the world, should know less of it than your fashionable fellows, whose whole experience is bounded by Westminster bridge.

Sir Will. Nay, brother, as a proof that I am not blind to the benefit of travelling, George, you know, has been in Germany these four years.

R. Weal. Where he is well grounded in gaming and gluttony;

gluttony; France has furnished him with fawning and flattery; Italy equip'd him with capriols and cantatas: and thus accomplish'd, my young gentleman is return'd with a cargo of whores, cooks, valets de chambre, and fiddlesticks; a most valuable member of the British commonwealth.

Sir Will. You dislike then my system of education?

R. Weal. Most sincerely.

Sir Will. The whole?

R. Weal. Every particular.

Sir Will. The early part, I should imagine, might merit your approbation.

R. Weal. Least of all. What, I suppose, because he has run the gauntlet through a public school, where, at sixteen, he had practised more vices than he would otherwise have heard of at sixty.

Sir Will. Ha, ha, prejudice!

R. Weal. Then, indeed, you remov'd him to the university; where, lest his morals should be mended, and his understanding improv'd, you fairly set him free from the restraint of the one, and the drudgery of the other, by the privileg'd distinction of a silk gown and a velvet cap.

Sir Will. And all these evils, you think, a city education would have prevented?

R. Weal. Doubtless.—Proverbs, proverbs, brother William, convey wholesome instruction. Idleness is the root of all evil. Regular hours, constant employment, and good example, can't fail to form the mind.

Sir Will. Why truly, brother, had you stuck to your old civic vices, hypocrisy, contempt, and avarice, I don't know whether I might not have committed George to your care; but you cockneys now beat us suburbians at our own weapons. What, old boy, times are chang'd since the date of thy indentures; when the sleek, crop-ear'd 'prentice us'd to dangle after his mistress, with the great Bible under his arm, to St Bride's, on a Sunday; bring home the text, repeat the civilions of the discourse, dine at twelve, and regale, upon a gaudy day, with buns and beer at Illington, or Mile-End.

R. Weal. Wonderfully facetious!

Sir Will. Our modern lads are of a different metal. They have their gaming clubs in the Garden, their little lodgings, the snug depositories of their rusty swords, and occasionally bag-wigs; their horses for the turf; ay, and

their

their commiſſions of bankruptcy too, before they are well out of their time.

R. Weal. Infamous aſperſion!

Sir Will. But the laſt meeting at Newmarket, Lord Lofty receiv'd at the hazard-table, the identical note from the individual tailor to whom he had paid it but the day before for a new ſet of liveries.

R. Weal. Invention!

Sir Will. Theſe are anecdotes you will never meet with in your weekly travels from Gateſton-ſtreet to your boarded box in Clapham, brother.

R. Weal. And yet that boarded box, as your prodigal ſpendthrift proceeds, will ſoon be the only ſeat of the family.

Sir Will. May be not. Who knows what a reformation our projeƈt may produce!

R. Weal. I do. None at all.

Sir Will. Why ſo?

R. Weal. Becauſe your means are ill-proportion'd to their end. Were he my ſon, I would ſerve him——

Sir Will. As you have done your daughter. Diſcard him. But conſider, I have but one.

R. Weal. That would weigh nothing with me: for, was Charlotte to ſet up a will of her own, and rejeƈt the man of my choice, ſhe muſt expeƈt to ſhare the fate of her ſiſter. I conſider families as a ſmaller kind of kingdoms, and would have diſobedience in the one as ſeverely puniſhed as rebellion in the other. Both cut off from their reſpeƈtive ſocieties.

Sir Will. Poor Lucy! But ſurely you begin to relent. Mayn't I intercede?

R. Weal. Look'e, brother, you know my mind. I will be abſolute. If I meddle with the management of your ſon, it is at your own requeſt; but if, direƈtly or indireƈtly, you interfere with my baniſhment of that wilful, head-ſtrong, diſobedient huſſy, all ties between us are broke; and I ſhall no more remember you as a brother, than I do her as a child.

Sir Will. I have done. But to return. You think there is a probability in my plan?

R. Weal. I ſhall attend the iſſue.

Sir Will. You will lend your aid, however?

R. Weal. We ſhall ſee how you go on.

Vol. I.   G g   *Enter*

THE MINOR.

Enter Servant.

Serv. A letter, Sir.
Sir Will. Oh, from Capias, my attorney. Who brought it?
Serv. The person is without, Sir.
Sir Will. Bid him wait. [*Reads.*] [*Exit Serv.*

"Worthy Sir,
"The bearer is the person I promis'd to procure. I thought it was proper for you to examine him *viva voce.* So if you administer a few interrogatories, you will find, by cross-questioning him, whether he is a competent person to prosecute the cause you wot of. I wish you a speedy issue: and as there can be no default in your judgment, am of opinion it should be carried into immediate execution. I am, Worthy Sir, &c.
TIMOTHY CAPIAS."

"P.S. The party's name is Samuel Shift. He is an admirable mime, or mimic, and most delectable company; as we experience every Tuesday night at our club, the Magpye and Horse-shoe, Fetter-lane."

Very methodical indeed, Mr Capias! John.

Enter Servant.

Bid the person who brought this letter walk in. [*Exit Serv.*] Have you any curiosity, brother?
R. Weal. Not a jot. I must to the 'Change. In the evening you may find me in the counting-house, or at Jonathan's. [*Exit R. Wealthy.*
Sir Will. You shall hear from me.

Enter Shift *and* Servant.

Shut the door, John, and remember, I am not at home. [*Exit Serv.*] You came from Mr Capias?
Shift. I did, Sir.
Sir Will. Your name, I think, is Shift?
Shift. It is, Sir.
Sir Will. Did Mr Capias drop any hint of my business with you?
Shift. None. He only said, with his spectacles on his nose, and his hand upon his chin, Sir William Wealthy is a respectable personage, and my client; he wants to retain

you

you in a certain affair, and will open the case, and give you your brief himself: if you adhere to his instructions, and carry your cause, he is generous, and will discharge your bill without taxation.

Sir Will. Ha! ha! my friend Capias to a hair! Well, Sir, this is no bad specimen of your abilities. But see that the door is fast. Now, Sir, you are to——

Shift. A moment's pause, if you please. You must know, Sir William, I am a prodigious admirer of forms. Now Mr Capias tells me, that it is always the rule, to administer a retaining fee before you enter upon the merits.

Sir Will. Oh, Sir, I beg your pardon!

Shift. Not that I question'd your generosity; but forms, you know——

Sir Will. No apology, I beg. But as we are to have a closer connection, it may not be amiss, by way of introduction, to understand one another a little. Pray, Sir, where was you born?

Shift. At my father's.

Sir Will. Hum!——And what was he?

Shift. A gentleman.

Sir Will. What was you bred?

Shift. A gentleman.

Sir Will. How do you live?

Shift. Like a gentleman.

Sir Will. Cou'd nothing induce you to unbosom yourself?

Shift. Look'e, Sir William, there is a kind of something in your countenance, a certain openness and generosity, a *je ne scai quoi* in your manner, that I will unlock: You shall see me all.

Sir Will. You will oblige me.

Shift. You must know then, that Fortune; which frequently delights to raise the noblest structures from the simplest foundations; who from a tailor made a pope, from a gin-shop an empress, and many a prime minister from nothing at all, has thought fit to raise me to my present height from the humble employment of Light your Honour——A link boy.

Sir Will. A pleasant fellow.——Who were your parents?

Shift. I was produced, Sir, by a left-handed marriage, in the language of the news-papers, between an Illustrious lamp-lighter lamp-lighter and an eminent itinerant cat and dog butcher. —Cat's meat, and dog's meat.——I dare say, you have heard my mother, Sir. But as to this happy pair I owe little besides my being, I shall drop them where they dropt me——in the street.

Sir Will. Proceed.

Shift. My first knowledge of the world I owe to a school, which has produced many a great man; the avenues of the play-house. There, Sir, leaning on my extinguish'd link, I learn'd dexterity from pick-pockets, connivance from constables, politics and fashions from footmen, and the art of making and breaking a promise, from their masters. Here, sirrah, light me a-cross the kennel.——I hope your Honour will remember poor Jack.——You ragged rascal, I have no half-pence——I'll pay you the next time I see you.—— But, lack-a-day, Sir, that time I saw as seldom as his tradesmen.

Sir Will. Very well.

Shift. To these accomplishments from without the theatre, I must add one that I obtain'd within.

Sir Will. How did you gain admittance there?

Shift. My merit, Sir, that, like my link, threw a radiance round me.——A detachment from the head-quarters here, took possession, in the summer, of a country corporation, where I did the honours of the barn, by sweeping the stage, and clipping the candles. There my skill and address was so conspicuous, that it procur'd me the same office the ensuing winter, at Drury-Lane, where I acquir'd intrepidity; the crown of all my virtues.

Sir Will. How did you obtain that?

Shift. By my post. For I think, Sir, he that dares stand the shot of the gallery in lighting, snuffing, and sweeping, the first night of a new play, may bid defiance to the pillory, with all its customary compliments.

Sir Will. Some truth in that.

Shift. But an unlucky crab-apple, apply'd to my right eye, by a patriot gingerbread-baker from the Borough, who would not suffer three dancers from Switzerland, because he hated the French, forced me to a precipitate retreat.

Sir Will. Poor devil!

Shift. Broglio and Contades have done the same. But as it happen'd, like a tennis-ball, I rose higher than the rebound.

Sir

Sir Will. How fo?

Shift. My misfortune, Sir, mov'd the compassion of one of our performers, a whimsical man, he took me into his service. To him I owe, what I believe, will make me useful to you.

Sir Will. Explain.

Shift. Why, Sir, my master was remarkably happy in an art, which, however disesteem'd at present, is, by Tully, reckon'd amongst the perfections of an orator; mimicry.

Sir Will. Why, you are deeply read, Mr Shift!

Shift. A smattering—But as I was saying, Sir, nothing came amiss to my master. Bipeds, or quadrupeds; rationals, or animals; from the clamour of the bar, to the cackle of the barn-door; from the soporific twang of the tabernacle of Tottenham-Court, to the melodious bray of their long-ear'd brethren in Bunhill-Fields; all were objects of his imitation, and my attention. In a word, Sir, for two whole years, under this professor, I study'd and starv'd, impoverish'd my body, and pamper'd my mind; till thinking myself pretty near equal to my master, I made him one of his own bows, and set up for myself.

Sir Will. You have been successful, I hope.

Shift. Pretty well, I can't complain. My art, Sir, is a *paſſe-par-tout*. I seldom want employment. Let's see how stand my engagements. [*Pulls out a pocket-book.*] Hum, —hum, Oh! Wednesday at Mrs Gammut's near Hanover-square; there, there, I shall make a meal upon the Mingotti; for her ladyship is in the opera interest; but, however, I shall revenge her cause upon her rival Mattei. Sunday evening at Lady Suſſiusto's concert. Thursday I dine upon the actors, with ten Templars, at the Mitre in Fleet-street. Friday I am to give the amorous parly of two intriguing cats in a gutter, with the disturbing of a hen-roost, at Mr Deputy Sugarsops, near the Monument. So, Sir, you see my hands are full. In short, Sir William, there is not a buck or turtle devoured within the bills of mortality, but there I may, if I please, stick a napkin under my chin.

Sir Will. I'm afraid, Mr Shift, I must break in a little upon your engagements; but you shall be no loser by the bargain.

Shift. Command me.

Sir Will. You can be secret as well as serviceable?

Shift.

Shift. Mute as a mackrel.
Sir Will. Come hither then. If you betray me to my son——
Shift. Scalp me.
Sir Will. Enough.—You must know, then, the hopes of our family are, Mr Shift, center'd in one boy.
Shift. And I warrant, he is a hopeful one.
Sir Will. No interruption, I beg. George has been abroad these four years, and from his late behaviour, I have reason to believe, that had a certain event happened, which I am afraid he wished,—my death——
Shift. Yes; that's natural enough.
Sir Will. Nay, pray,—there wou'd soon be an end to an ancient and honourable family.
Shift. Very melancholy indeed. But families, like bosoms, will wear to the stumps, and finally fret out, as you say.
Sir Will. Pr'ythee peace for five minutes.
Shift. I am tongue-ty'd.
Sir Will. Now I have projected a scheme to prevent this calamity.
Shift. Ay, I should be glad to hear that.
Sir Will. I am going to tell it you.
Shift. Proceed.
Sir Will. George, as I have contriv'd it, shall experience all the misery of real ruin, without running the least risque.
Shift. Ay, that will be a *coup de maître*.
Sir Will. I have prevail'd upon his uncle, a wealthy citizen——
Shift. I don't like a city plot.
Sir Will. I tell thee it is my own.
Shift. I beg pardon.
Sir Will. My brother, I say, some time since wrote him a circumstantial account of my death; upon which he is returned, in full expectation of succeeding to my estate.
Shift. Immediately.
Sir Will. No; when at age. In about three months.
Shift. I understand you.
Sir Will. Now, Sir, guessing into what hands my headless boy would naturally fall on his return, I have, in a feign'd character, associated myself with a set of rascals, who will spread every bait that can flatter folly, inflame extravagance,

extravagance, allure inexperience, or catch credulity.—
And when, by their means, he thinks himself reduc'd to
the laſt extremity; loſt even to the moſt diſtant hope——
    Shift. What then?
    Sir Will. Then will I ſtep in, like his guardian-angel,
and ſnatch him from perdition. If mortify'd by miſery,
he becomes conſcious of his errors, I have ſav'd my ſon;
but if, on the other hand, gratitude can't bind, nor ruin
reclaim him, I will caſt him out, as an alien to my blood,
and truſt for the ſupport of my name and family to a re-
moter branch.
    Shift. Bravely reſolv'd. But what part am I to ſuſtain
in this drama?
    Sir Will. Why, George, you are to know, is already
ſtript of what money he could command by two ſharpers:
but as I never truſt them out of my ſight, they can't deceive me.
    Shift. Out of your ſight!
    Sir Will. Why, I tell thee, I am one of the knot: an a-
dept in their ſcience, can ſlip, ſhuffle, cog, or cut with the
beſt of 'em.
    Shift. How do you eſcape your ſon's notice?
    Sir Will. His firm perſuaſion of my death, with the ex-
travagance of my diſguiſe.——Why, I wou'd engage to
elude your penetration, when I am beau'd out for the baron. But of that by and by. He has recourſe, after his
ill ſucceſs, to the cent. per cent. gentry, the uſurers, for a
further ſupply.
    Shift. Natural enough.
    Sir Will. Pray do you know,—I forgot his name,—a
wrinkled old fellow, in a thread-bare coat? He ſits every
morning, from twelve till two, in the laſt corner of Lloyd's
coffee-houſe; and every evening, from five till eight, under the clock, at the Temple-exchange.
    Shift. What, little Transfer the broker!
    Sir Will. The ſame. Do you know him?
    Shift. Know him! Ay, rot him. It was but laſt Eaſ-
ter Tueſday, he had me turn'd out at a feaſt, in Leather-
ſeller's Hall, for ſinging Room for Cuckold's, like a parrot; and vow'd it meant a reflection upon the whole body
corporate.
    Sir Will. You have reaſon to remember him.
    Shift. Yes, yes, I recommended a minor to him myſelf,
for

for the loan only of fifty pounds; and wou'd you believe it, as I hope to be sav'd, we din'd, supp'd, and wasted five-and-thirty guineas upon tick, in meetings at the Cross-keys, in order to settle the terms; and after all, the scoundrel would not lend us a stiver.

Sir Will. Cou'd you personate him?

Shift. Him! Oh, you shall see me shift into his shamble in a minute; and, with a wither'd face, a bit of a purple nose, a cautionary stammer, and a sleek silver head, I would undertake to deceive even his banker. But to speak the truth, I have a friend that can do this inimitably well. Have not you something of more consequence for me?

Sir Will. I have. Cou'd not you, Master Shift, assume another shape? You have attended auctions?

Shift. Auctions! a constant puff. Deep in the mystery; a professed connoisseur, from a Niger to a nautilus, from the Apollo Belvidere to a butterfly.

Sir Will. One of these infinuating, oily orators I will get you to personate: for we must have the plate and jewels in our possession, or they will soon fall into other hands.

Shift. I will do it.

Sir Will. Within I'll give you farther instructions.

Shift. I'll follow you.

Sir Will. [*Going, returns.*] You will want materials.

Shift. Oh, my dress I can be furnish'd with in five minutes. [*Exit Sir Will.*] A whimsical old blade this. I shall laugh if this scheme miscarries. I have a strange mind to lend it a lift—never had a greater—Pho, a damn'd unnatural connection this of mine! What have I to do with fathers and guardians! a parcel of preaching, prudent, careful, curmudgeonly—dead to pleasures themselves, and the blasters of it in others——Mere dogs in a manger—No, no, I'll veer, tack about, open my budget to the boy, and join in a counter-plot. But hold, hold, friend Stephen, see first how the land lies. Who knows whether this German-iz'd genius has parts to comprehend, or spirit to reward thy merit. There's danger in that, ay, marry is there. 'Egad before I shift the helm, I'll first examine the coast; and then, if there be but a bold shore, and a good bottom, have a care, old Square Toes, you will meet with your match. [*Exit.*

Enter

THE MINOR:

Enter Sir George, Loader, and Servant.

Sir Geo. Let the Martin pannels for the vis-a-vis be carried to Long-Acre, and the pye-balls sent to Hall's to be bitted——You will give me leave to be in your debt till the evening, Mr Loader. I have just enough left to discharge the baron; and we must, you know, be punctual with him, for the credit of the country.

Load. Fire him, a fouls-nos'd son of a bitch. Levant me, but he got enough last night to purchase a principality amongst his countrymen, the High-dutchiens and Hungarians.

Sir Geo. You had your share, Mr Loader.

Load. Who, I! Lurch me at four, but I was mark'd to the top of your trick, by the baron, my dear. What, I am no cinque and quarter man. Come, shall we have a dip in the history of the Four Kings this morning?

Sir Geo. Rather too early. Besides, it is the rule abroad, never to engage a-fresh, till our old scores are discharg'd.

Load. Capot me, but those lads abroad are pretty fellows, let 'em say what they will. Here, Sir, they will vowel you, from father to son, to the twentieth generation. They wou'd as soon now-a-days pay a tradesman's bill, as a play debt. All sense of honour is gone, not a stiver stirring. They cou'd as soon raise the dead as two pounds two; nick me, but I have a great mind to tie up, and ruin the rascals—What, has Transfer been here this morning?

Enter Dick.

Sir Geo. Any body here this morning, Dick?

Dick. No body, your Honour.

Load. Repique the rascal. He promis'd to be here before me.

Dick. I beg your Honour's pardon. Mrs Cole from the Piazza was here, between seven and eight.

Sir Geo. An early hour for a lady of her calling.

Dick. Mercy on me! The poor gentlewoman is mortally alter'd since we us'd to lodge there, in our jaunts from Oxford: wrapt up in flannels: all over the rheumatism.

Load. Ay, ay, old Moll is at her last stake.

242   THE MINOR.

Dick. She bade me say, she just stopt in her way to the Tabernacle; after the exhortation, she says, she'll call again.

Sir Geo. Exhortation! Oh, I recollect. Well, whilst they only make proselytes from that profession, they are heartily welcome to them. She does not mean to make me a convert?

Dick. I believe she has some such design upon me; for she offer'd me a book of hymns, a shilling, and a dram, to go along with her.

Sir Geo. No bad scheme, Dick. Thou hast a fine sober psalm-singing countenance; and when thou hast been some time in their trammels, may'st make as able a teacher as the best of 'em.

Dick. Laud, Sir, I want learning.

Sir Geo. Oh, the spirit, the spirit will supply all that, Dick, never fear.

Enter Sir William as a German baron.

My dear baron, what news from the Haymarket? What says the Florenza? Does she yield? Shall I be happy? Say yes, and command my fortune.

Sir Will. I was never did see so fine a woman since I was leave Hamburgh; dere was all de colours, all red and white, dat was quite natural; point d'artifice. Then she was dance and sing—I vow to heaven, I was never see de like!

Sir Geo. But how did she receive my embassy? What hopes?

Sir Will. Why dere was, Monsieur le Chevalier, when I first enter, dree or four damn'd queer people? ah, ah, thought I, by gad I guess your business. Dere was one fat big woman's, dat I know long time: le valet de chambre was tell me dat she came from a grand marchand; ha, ha, dought I, by your leave, Sick, to your shop; or, if you must leave de pritty girl, dere is de play-hous, dat do very well for you; but for de opera, pardonnez, by gar dat is meat for your master.

Sir Geo. Infolent mechanic!—but she despis'd him!

Sir Will. Ah, may for, he is damn'd rich, has beaucoup de guineas; but after de fat woman was go, I was tell the signora, Madam, der is one certain Chevalier of dis country, who has travell'd, see de world, bien fait, well made, beaucoup d'esprit, a great deal of monies,
                                                                    who

who beg, by gar, to have de honour to drow himself at your feet.

Sir Geo. Well, well, baron.

Sir Will. She aſks your name; as foon as I tell her, ſhe, by gar, dans an inſtant, ſhe melt like de lomp of ſugar: ſhe run to her bureau, and, in de minute, return vid de paper.

Sir Geo. Give it me. [*Reads.*

Les preliminaires d'une traite entre le Chevalier Wealthy, and le Signor Diamenti.

A bagatelle, a trifle: ſhe ſhall have it.

Load. Hark'e, knight, what is all that there outlandiſh ſtuff?

Sir Geo. Read, read! The eloquence of angels, my dear baron!

Load. Slom me, but the man's mad! I don't underſtand their gibberiſh.—What is it in Engliſh?

Sir Geo. The preliminaries of a ſubſidy treaty, between Sir G. Wealthy, and Signora Florenza; that the ſaid Signora will reſign the poſſeſſion of her perſon to the ſaid Sir George, on the payment of three hundred guineas monthly for equipage, table, domeſtics, dreſs, dogs, and diamonds; her debts to be duly diſcharged, and a note advanced of five hundred by way of entrance.

Load. Zounds, what a cormorant! She muſt be deviliſh handſome.

Sir Geo. I am told ſo.

Load. Told ſo! Why, did you never ſee her?

Sir Geo. No; and poſſibly never may, but from my box at the opera.

Load. Hey-day! Why, what the devil—

Sir Geo. Ha, ha, you ſtare, I don't wonder at it. This is an elegant refinement, unknown to the groſs voluptuaries of this part of the world. This is, Mr Loader, what may be called a debt to your dignity: for an opera girl is as eſſential a piece of equipage for a man of faſhion as his coach.

Load. The devil!

Sir Geo. 'Tis for the vulgar only to enjoy what they poſſeſs: the diſtinction of ranks and conditions are, to have hounds, and never hunt; cooks, and dine at taverns; houſes you never inhabit; miſtreſſes you never enjoy—

Load.

Load. And debts you never pay. Egad, I am not surpriz'd at it; if this be your trade, no wonder that you want money for necessaries, when you give such a damn'd deal for nothing at all.

Enter Servant.

Serv. Mrs Cole, to wait upon your Honour.

Sir Geo. My dear baron, run, difpatch my affair, conclude my treaty, and thank her for the very reafonable conditions.

Sir Will. I shall.

Sir Geo. Mr Loader, shall I trouble you to introduce the Lady? She is, I think, your acquaintance.

Load. Who, old Moll? Ay, ay, she's your marketwoman. I wou'd not give fixpence for your Signoras. One armful of good wholefome British beauty, is worth a ship-load of their trapfing, tawdry trollops. But hark'e, baron, how much for the table? Why, she must have a devilish large family, or a monftrous ftomach.

Sir Will. Ay, ay, dare is her modes, la complaifante to walk in de park, and to go to de play; two broders, deux valets, drec Spanish lap-dogs, and de monkey.

Load. Strip me, if I won'd fet five shillings against the whole gang. May my partner renounce with the game in his hand, if I were you, knight, if I would not——

[*Exit.* Bar.

Sir Geo. But the Lady waits. [*Exit.* Load.] A ftrange fellow this! What a whimfical jergon he talks! Not an idea abftracted from play! To fay truth, I am fincerely fick of my acquaintance: But, however, I have the firft people in the kingdom to keep me in countenance. Death and the dice level all diftinctions.

Enter Mrs Cole, *fupported by* Loader *and* Dick.

Mrs Cole. Gently, gently, good Mr Loader.

Load. Come along, old Moll. Why, you jade, you look as rofy this morning, I must have a fmack at your muns. Here, tafte her, she is as good as old hock to get you a ftomach.

Mrs Cole. Fye, Mr Loader, I thought you had forgot me.

Load. I forget you! I would as foon forget what is trumps.

Mrs

Mrs Cole. Softly, softly, young man. There, there, mighty well. And how does your Honour do? I han't seen your Honour, I can't tell the—Oh! mercy on me, there's a twinge—

Sir Geo. What is the matter, Mrs Cole?

Mrs Cole. My old diforder, the rheumatife; I han't been able to get a wink of——Oh la! what, you have been in town thefe two days?

Sir Geo. Since Wednefday.

Mrs Cole. And never once call'd upon old Cole. No, no, I am worn out, thrown by and forgotten, like a tatter'd garment, as Mr Squintum fays. Oh, he is a dear man! But for him I had been a loft fheep; never known the comforts of the new birth; no,—There's your old friend, Kitty Carrot, at home ftill. What, fhall we fee you this evening? I have kept the green room for you ever fince I heard you were in town.

Load. What, fhall we take a fnap at old Moll's. Hey, beldam, have you a good batch of burgundy abroach?

Mrs Cole. Bright as a ruby; and for flavour! You know the Colonel—He and Jenny Cummins drank three flafks, hand to fift, laft night.

Load. What, and bilk thee of thy fhare?

Mrs Cole. Ah, don't mention it, Mr Loader. No, that's all over with me. The time has been, when I cou'd have earn'd thirty fhillings a-day by my own drinking, and the next morning was neither fick nor forry: But now, O land, a thimbleful turns me topfy-turvy.

Load. Poor old girl!

Mrs Cole. Ay, I have done with thefe idle vanities; my thoughts are fix'd upon a better place. What, I fuppofe, Mr Loader, you will be for your old friend the black-ey'd girl, from Rofemary-lane. Ha, ha! Well, 'tis a merry little tit. A thoufand pities fhe's fuch a reprobate! —But fhe'll mend; her time is not come: all fhall have their call, as Mr Squintum fays, fooner or later; regeneration is not the work of a day. No, no, no,—Oh!

Sir Geo. Not worfe, I hope.

Mrs Cole. Rack, rack, gnaw, gnaw, never eafy, a-bed or up, all's one. Pray, honeft friend, have you any clary or mint-water in the houfe?

Dick. A cafe of French drams.

Mrs

Mrs Cole. Heaven defend me! I would not touch a dram for the world.

Sir Geo. They are but cordials, Mrs Cole. Fetch 'em you blockhead. [*Exit Dick.*

Mrs Cole. Ay, I am a going; a wafting and a wafting, Sir George. What will become of the house when I am gone, Heaven knows.—No.—When people are miss'd, then they are mourned. Sixteen years have I liv'd in the Garden, comfortably and creditably; and, though I say it, could have got bail any hour of the day: Reputable tradesmen, Sir George, neighbours, Mr Loader knows; no knock-me-down doings in my house. A set of regular, sedate, sober customers. No rioters. Sixteen did I say— Ay, eighteen years I have paid scot and lot in the parish of St Paul's, and during the whole time, no body have said, Mrs Cole, why do you so? Unless twice that I was before Sir Thomas De Val, and three times in the Round House.

Sir Geo. Nay, don't weep, Mrs Cole.

Load. May I lose deal, with an honour at bottom, if old Moll does not bring tears into my eyes.

Mrs Cole. However, it is a comfort after all, to think one has past through the world with credit and character. Ay, a good name, as Mr Squintum says, is better than a gallipot of ointment.

Enter Dick with a dram.

Load. Come, bafte, Dick, hafte; sorrow is dry. Here, Moll, shall I fill thee a bumper?

Mrs Cole. Hold, hold, Mr Loader? Heaven help you, I could as soon swallow the Thames. Only a sip, to keep the gout out of my stomach.

Load. Why, then, here's to thee. Levant me, but it is supernaculum. Speak when you have enough.

Mrs Cole. I won't trouble you for the glass; my hands do so tremble and shake, I shall but spill the good creature.

Load. Well pull'd. But now to business. Pr'ythee, Moll, did not I see a tight young wench in a linen gown, knock at your door this morning?

Mrs Cole. Ay; a young thing from the country.

Load. Could we not get a peep at her this evening?

Mrs Cole. Impossible! she is engag'd to Sir Timothy Totter. I have taken earnest for her these three months.

Load.

Load. Pho, what signifies such a fellow as that! tip him an old trader, and give her to the knight.

Mrs Cole. Tip him an old trader!—mercy on us, where do you expect to go when you die, Mr Loader?

Load. Crop me, but this Squintum has turn'd her brains.

Sir Geo. Nay, Mr Loader, I think the gentleman has wrought a most happy reformation.

Mrs Cole. Oh, it was a wonderful work. There had I been tossing in a sea of sin, without rudder or compass. And had not the good gentleman piloted me into the harbour of grace, I must have struck against the rocks of reprobation, and have been quite swallow'd up in the whirlpool of despair. He was the precious instrument of my spiritual sprinkling. But however, Sir George, if your mind be set upon a young country thing, to-morrow night I believe, I can furnish you.

Load. As how?

Mrs Cole. I have advertis'd this morning, in the register-office, for servants under seventeen; and ten to one but I light on something that will do.

Load. Pillory me, but it has a face.

Mrs Cole. Truly, confidently with my conscience, I wou'd do any thing for your Honour.

Sir Geo. Right, Mrs Cole, never lose sight of that monitor. But pray how long has this heavenly change been wrought in you?

Mrs Cole. Ever since my last visitation of the gout.— Upon my first fit, seven years ago, I began to have my doubts, and my waverings; but I was lost in a labyrinth, and no body to shew me the road. One time, I thought of dying a Roman, which is truly a comfortable communion enough for one of us: but it wou'd not do.

Sir Geo. Why not?

Mrs Cole. I went one summer over to Boulogne to repent; and, wou'd you believe it, the bare-footed, bald-pate beggars would not give me absolution, without I quitted my business—did you ever hear of such a set of scabby—Besides, I cou'd not bear their barbarity. Would you believe it, Mr Loader, they lock up for their lives, in a nunnery, the prettiest, sweetest, tender, young things! —Oh, six of them, for a season, would finish my business here,

here, and then I shou'd have nothing to do but to think of hereafter.

Load. Brand me, what a country!

Sir Geo. Oh, scandalous!

Mrs Cole. O no, it would not do. So, in my last illness, I was wish'd to Mr Squintum, who slept in with his saving grace, got me with the new birth, and I became, as you see, regenerate, and another creature.

Enter Dick.

Dick. Mr Transfer, Sir, has sent to know if your Honour be at home.

Sir Geo. Mrs Cole, I am mortify'd to part with you. But bus'ness, you know—

Mrs Cole. True, Sir George. Mr Loader, your arm—gently, oh, oh!

Sir Geo. Won'd you take another thimbleful, Mrs Cole?

Mrs Cole. Not a drop—I shall see you this evening?

Sir Geo. Depend upon me.

Mrs Cole. To-morrow I hope to snit you—we are to have, at the Tabernacle, an occasional hymn, with a thanksgiving sermon for my recovery. After which I shall call at the register office, and see what goods my advertisement has brought in.

Sir Geo. Extremely obliged to you, Mrs Cole.

Mrs Cole. Or if that should not do, I have a tid bit at home, will suit your stomach. Never brush'd by a beard. Well, heaven bless you—softly, have a care, Mr Loader—: Richard, you may as well give me the bottle into the chair, for fear I should be taken ill on the road. Gently—so, so!

[*Exit Mrs Cole and Loader.*

Sir Geo. Dick, shew Mr Transfer in—ha, ha, what a hodge podge! how the jade has jumbled together the carnal and the spiritual; with what ease she reconciles her new birth to her old calling!—No wonder these preachers have plenty of proselytes, whilst they have the address so comfortably to blend the hitherto jarring interests of the two worlds.

Enter Loader.

Well, knight I have hous'd her; but they want you within, Sir.

Sir Geo. I'll go to them immediately.

ACT

ACT II.

Enter Dick, introducing Transfer.

Dick. MY master will come to you presently.

Enter Sir George.

Sir Geo. Mr Transfer, your servant.

Tranf. Your Honour's very humble. I thought to have found Mr Loader here.

Sir Geo. He will return immediately. Well, Mr Transfer—but take a chair—you have had a long walk. Mr Loader, I presume, open'd to you the urgency of my bus'ness.

Tranf. Ay, ay, the general cry, money, money? I don't know, for my part, where all the money is flown to. Formerly a note, with a tolerable endorsement, was as current as cash. If your uncle Richard now wou'd join in this security—

Sir Geo. Impossible.

Tranf. Ay, like enough. I wish you were of age.

Sir Geo. So do I. But as that will be consider'd in the premium—

Tranf. True, true,—I see you understand bus'ness—and what sum does your Honour lack at present?

Sir Geo. Lack!—how much have you brought?

Tranf. Who, I? dear me! none.

Sir Geo. Zounds, none!

Tranf. Lack-a-day, none to be had, I think. All the morning have I been upon the hunt. There, Ephraim Barebones the tallow chandler, in Thames-street, us'd to be a never-failing chap; not a guinea to be got there. Then I totter'd away to Nebuchadnezzar Zebulon, in the Old Jewry, but it happen'd to be Saturday; and they never touch on the Sabbath, you know.

Sir Geo. Why what the devil can I do?

Tranf. Good me, I did not know your Honour had been so press'd.

Sir Geo. My honour press'd! yes, my honour is not only press'd, press'd, but ruin'd, unless I can raise money to redeem it. That blockhead Loader, to depend upon this old dozing—

Transf. Well, well, now I declare, I am quite sorry to see your Honour in such a taking.

Sir Geo. Damn your sorrow.

Transf. But come, don't be cast down: tho' money is not to be had, money's worth may, and that's the same thing.

Sir Geo. How, dear Transfer?

Transf. Why I have, at my warehouse in the city, ten casks of whale-blubber, a large cargo of Dantzick dowlas, with a curious sortment of Birmingham hafts, and Whitney blankets for exportation.

Sir Geo. Hey!

Transf. And stay, stay, then, again, at my country-house, the bottom of Gray's-inn-Lane, there's a hundred tun of fine old hay, only damag'd a little last winter, for want of thatching; with forty load of flint stones.

Sir Geo. Well.

Transf. Your Honour may have all these for a reasonable profit, and convert them into cash.

Sir Geo. Blubber and blankets? Why, you old rascal, do you banter me?

Transf. Who I? O law, marry heaven forbid.

Sir Geo. Get out of my—you stuttering scoundrel.

Transf. If your Honour wou'd but hear me—

Sir Geo. Troop, I say, unless you have a mind to go a shorter way than you came. [*Exit Transf.*] And yet there is something so uncommonly ridiculous in his proposal, that were my mind more at ease.—[*Enter Loader.*] So, Sir, you have recommended me to a fine fellow.

Load. What's the matter?

Sir Geo. He can't supply me with a shilling! and wants, besides, to make me a dealer in dowlas.

Load. Ay, and a very good commodity too. People that are upon ways and means, must not be nice, knight. A pretty piece of work you have made here! thrown up the cards, with the game in your hands.

Sir Geo. Why, pr'ythee, of what use wou'd his—

Load. Use! of every use. Procure you the spankers, my boy. I have a broker, that, in a twinkling, shall take off your bargain.

Sir Geo. Indeed!

Load. Indeed! ay, indeed. You sit down to hazard and

but

not know the chances! I'll call him back. Holo, Transfer. A pretty little, busy, bustling—you may travel miles, before you will meet with his match. If there is one pound in the city, he will get it. He creeps, like a ferret, into their bags, and makes the yellow boys bolt again.

Enter Transfer.

Come hither, little Transfer; what, man, our Minor was a little too hasty; he did not understand trap: knows nothing of the game, my dear.

Transf. What I said, was to serve Sir George; as he seem'd—

Load. I told him so; well, well, we will take thy commodities, were they as many more. But try, pr'ythee, if thou cou'dst not procure us some of the ready, for present spending.

Transf. Let me consider.

Load. Ay, do, come: shuffle thy brains; never fear the barmest. To let a lord of lands want shiners; 'tis a shame.

Transf. I do recollect, in this quarter of the town, an old friend, that us'd to do things in this way.

Load. Who?

Transf. Statute, the scrivener.

Load. Slam me, but he has nick'd the chance.

Transf. A hard man, Master Loader!

Sir Geo. No matter.

Transf. His demands are exorbitant.

Sir Geo. That is no fault of ours.

Load. Well said, knight!

Transf. But to save time, I had better mention his terms.

Load. Unnecessary.

Transf. Five per cent. legal interest.

Sir Geo. He shall have it.

Transf. Ten, the premium.

Sir Geo. No more words.

Transf. Then, as you are not of age, five more for ensuring your life.

Load. We will give it.

Transf. As for what he will demand for the risque—

Sir Geo. He shall be satisfy'd.

Transf. You pay the attorney.

Sir Geo. Amply, amply; Loader, dispatch him.

Load.

Load. There, there, little Transfer; now every thing is settled. All terms shall be comply'd with, reasonable or unreasonable. What, our principal is a man of honour. [*Exit Transfer.*] Hey, my knight, this is doing business. This peach is a sure card.

Re-enter Transfer.

Tranf. I had forgot one thing. I am not the principal; you pay the brokerage.
Load. Ay, ay; and a handsome present into the bargain, never fear.
Tranf. Enough, enough.
Load. Hark'e, Transfer, we'll take the Birmingham hafts and Whitney wares.
Tranf. They shall be forthcoming.——You would not have the hay, with the flints?
Load. Every pebble of 'em. The magistrates of the Borough's borough are infirm and gouty. He shall deal them as new pavement. [*Exit Transfer.*] So, that's settled. I believe, knight, I can lend you a helping hand as to the last article. I know some traders that will truck: fellows with finery. Not commodities of such clumsy conveyance as old Transfer's.
Sir Geo. You are obliging.
Load. I'll do it, boy; and get you, into the bargain, a bonny auctioneer, that shall dispose of 'em all in a crack.
[*Exit.*

Enter Dick.

Dick. Your uncle, Sir, has been waiting some time.
Sir Geo. He comes in a lucky hour. Shew him in.—
[*Exit Dick.*] Now for a lecture. My situation shu'n't sink my spirits, however. Here comes the musty trader, running over with remonstrances. I must banter the cit.

Enter Richard Wealthy.

R. W'eal. So, Sir, what, I suppose, this is a spice of your foreign breeding, to let your uncle kick his heels in your hall, whilst your presence chamber is crouded with pimps, bawds, and gamesters.
Sir Geo. Oh, a proof of my respect dear nuncle. Would it have been decent now, uncle, to have introduced you into such company?
R. Weal.

R. Weal. Wonderfully confiderate! Well, young man, and what do you think will be the end of all this? Here I have received, by the laft mail, a quire of your draughts from abroad. I fee you are determin'd our neighbours fhould tafte of your magnificence.

Sir Geo. Yes, I think I did fome credit to my country.

R. Weal. And how are all thefe to be paid?

Sir Geo. That I fubmit to you, dear nuncle.

R. Weal. From me!——Not a foufe to keep you from the Counter.

Sir Geo. Why then let the fcoundrels ftay. It is their duty. I have other demands, debts of honour, which muft be difcharg'd.

R. Weal. Here's a diabolical diftinction! Here's a proftitution of words!—Honour! 'fdeath, that a rafcal, who has pick'd your pocket, fhall have his crime gilded with the moft facred diftinction, and his plunder punctually paid, whilft the induftrious mechanic, who minifters to your very wants, fhall have his debt delay'd, and his demand treated as infolent.

Sir Geo. Oh! a truce to this thread-bare trumpery, dear nuncle.

R. Weal. I confefs my folly; but make yourfelf eafy; you won't be troubled with many more of my vifits. I own I was weak enough to defign a fhort expoftulation with you; but as we in the city know the true value of time, I fhall take care not to fquander away any more of it upon you.

Sir Geo. A prudent refolution.

R. Weal. One commiffion, however, I can't difpenfe with myfelf from executing——It was agreed between your father and me, that as he had but one fon, and I one daughter——

Sir Geo. Your gettings fhould be added to his eftate, and my coufin Margery and I fquat down together in the comfortable ftate of matrimony.

R. Weal. Puppy! Such was our intention. Now his laft will claims this contract.

Sir Geo. Difpatch, dear nuncle.

R. Weal. Why then, in a word, fee me here demand the execution.

Sir Geo. What d'ye mean? For me to marry Margery?

R. Weal. I do.

Sir Geo.

Sir Geo. What, moi-me?

R. Weal. You, you——Your answer, ay or no?

Sir Geo. Why then concisely and briefly, without evasion, equivocation, or further circumlocution,—No.

R. Weal. I am glad of it.

Sir Geo. So am I.

R. Weal. But pray, if it wou'd not be too great a favour, what objections can you have to my daughter? Not that I want to remove 'em, but merely out of curiosity. What objections?

Sir Geo. None. I neither know her, have seen her, enquir'd after her, or ever intend it.

R. Weal. What, perhaps, I am the stumbling block?

Sir Geo. You have hit it.

R. Weal. Ay, now we come to the point. Well, and pray——

Sir Geo. Why it is not so much a dislike to your person, though that is exceptionable enough, but your profession, dear nuncle, is an insuperable obstacle.

R. Weal. Good lack! And what harm has that done, pray?

Sir Geo. Done! So stain'd, polluted, and tainted the whole mass of your blood, thrown such a blot on your 'scutcheon, as ten regular successions can hardly efface.

R. Weal. The duce!

Sir Geo. And cou'd you now, consistently with your duty as a faithful guardian, recommend my union with the daughter of a trader?

R. Weal. Why, indeed, I ask pardon; I am afraid I did not weigh the matter as maturely as I ought.

Sir Geo. Oh, a horrid, barbarous scheme!

R. Weal. But then I thought her having the honour to partake of the same flesh and blood with yourself, might prove in some measure a kind of fullers-earth, to scour out the dirty spots contracted by commerce.

Sir Geo. Impossible!

R. Weal. Besides, here it has been the practice even of peers.

Sir Geo. Don't mention the unnatural intercourse!— Thank heav'n, Mr Richard Wealthy, my education has been in another country, where I have been too well instructed in the value of nobility, to think of intermixing it with

the

the offspring of a Bourgeois. Why, what apology cou'd I make to my children, for giving them such a mother?

R. Weal. I did not think of that. Then I must despair, I am afraid.

Sir Geo. I can afford but little hopes. Though, upon recollection——Is the grisette pretty?

R. Weal. A parent may be partial: She is thought so.

Sir Geo. Ah la jolie petite Bourgeoise! Poor girl, I sincerely pity her. And I suppose, to procure her emersion from the mercantile mud, no consideration wou'd be spar'd.

R. Weal. Why, to be sure, for such an honour one wou'd strain a point.

Sir Geo. Why, then, not totally to destroy your hopes, I do recollect an edict in favour of Britanny; that when a man of distinction engages in commerce, his nobility is suffer'd to sleep.

R. Weal. Indeed!

Sir Geo. And upon his quitting the contagious connection, he is permitted to resume his rank.

R. Weal. That's fortunate.

Sir Geo. So, nuncle Richard, if you will sell out of the stocks, shut up your counting-house, and quit St Mary Ax for Grosvenor-square——

R. Weal. What then?

Sir Geo. Why, when your rank has had time to rouse itself, for I think your nobility, nuncle, has had a pretty long nap, if the girl's person is pleasing, and the purchase-money is adequate to the honour, I may in time be prevail'd upon to restore her to the right of her family.

R. Weal. Amazing condescension!

Sir Geo. Good nature is my foible. But, upon my soul, I wou'd not have gone so far for any body else.

R. Weal. I can contain no longer. Hear me, spendthrift, prodigal, do you know that, in ten days, your whole revenue won't purchase you a feather to adorn your empty head?——

Sir Geo. Hey dey, what's the matter now?

R. Weal. And that you derive every acre of your boasted patrimony from your great uncle, a soap-boiler!

Sir Geo. Infamous aspersion!

R. Weal. It was his bags, the fruits of his honest industry, that preserv'd your lazy, beggarly nobility. His

wealth

wealth repair'd your tottering hall, from the ruins of which even the race had run.

Sir Geo. Better our name had perish'd! Insupportable! soap-boiling, uncle!

R. Weal. Traduce a trader in a country of commerce! It is treason against the community; and, for your punishment, I wou'd have you restor'd to the sordid condition from whence we drew you, and, like your predecessors, the Picts, stript, painted, and fed upon hips, haws, and blackberries.

Sir Geo. A truce, dear haberdasher.

R. Weal. One pleasure I have, that to this goal you are upon the gallop; but have a care, the sword hangs but by a thread. When next we meet, know me for the master of your fate. [*Exit.*

Sir Geo. Insolent mechanic! But that his Bourgeois blood wou'd have soil'd my sword——

Enter Baron and Loader.

Sir Will. What is de matter?

Sir Geo. A fellow here, upon the credit of a little affinity, has dar'd to upbraid me with being sprang from a soap-boiler.

Sir Will. Vat, you from the boiler of soap?

Sir Geo. Me.

Sir Will. Aha, begar, dat is anoder ting——And harke you, mister monsieur, be——how dare a you have d'affrontary——

Sir Geo. How!

Sir Will. De impertinence to sit down, play wid me?

Sir Geo. What is this?

Sir Will. A beggarly Bourgeois vis-a-vis, a baron of twenty descents.

Load. But, baron——

Sir Will. Bygar, I am almost asham'd to win of such a low, dirty——Give me my mouies, and let me never see your face.

Load. Why, but baron, you mistake this thing, I know the old buck this fellow prates about.

Sir Will. May be.

Load. Pigeon me, as true a gentleman as the grand signior. He was, indeed, a good-natur'd, obliging, friendly fellow; and being a great judge of soap, tar, and train-oil,

he

he ni'd to have it home to his houfe, and fell it to his acquaintance for ready money, to ferve them.

Sir Will. Was dat all?

Load. Upon my honour.

Sir Will. Oh, dat, dat is anoder ting. Bygar I was a-
fraid he was negotiant.

Load. Nothing like it.

Enter Dick.

Dick. A gentleman to enquire for Mr Loader.

Load. I come—A pretty fon of a bitch, this baron!
pimps for the man, picks his pocket, and then wants to
kick him out of company, becaufe his uncle was an oil-
man.   [*Exit.*

Sir Will. I beg pardon, chevalier, I was miftake.

Sir Geo. Oh, don't mention it; had the fam been fact,
your behaviour was natural enough.

Enter Loader.

Load. Mr Smirk, the auctioneer.

Sir Geo. Shew him in, by all means.   [*Exit Loader.*

Sir Will. You have affair.

Sir Geo. If you'll walk into the next room, they will be
finifhed in five minutes.

Enter Loader, with Shift as Smirk.

Load. Here, Mafter Smirk, this is the gentleman.—
Hark'e, knight, did I not tell you, old Moll was your
mark? Here fhe has brought a pretty piece of mens meat
already; as fweet as a nofegay, and as ripe as a cherry,
you rogue. Difpatch him, mean time we'll manage the
girl.   [*Exit.*

Smirk. You are the principal.

Sir Geo. Even fo. I have, Mr Smirk, fome things of
a confiderable value, which I want to difpofe of immediately.

Smirk. You have?

Sir Geo. Could you affift me?

Smirk. Doubtlefs.

Sir Geo. But directly?

Smirk. We have an auction at twelve. I'll add your
cargo to the catalogue.

Sir Geo. Can that be done?

Vol. I.   K k   *Smirk.*

Smirk. Every day's practice: it is for the credit of the fale. Laft week, amongft the valuable effects of a gentleman going abroad, I fold a choice collection of china, with a curious fervice of plate; though the real party was never mafter of above two Delft dishes, and a dozen of pewter, in all his life.

Sir Geo. Very artificial. But this muft be conceal'd.

Smirk. Bury'd here. Oh, many an aigrette and folitaire have I fold, to difcharge a lady's play-debt. But then we muft know the parties; otherwife it might be knockt down to the hufband himfelf. Hu, ha—Hey ho!

Sir Geo. True. Upon my word, your profeffion requires parts.

Smirk. No body's more. Did you ever hear, Sir George, what firft brought me into the bufinefs?

Sir Geo. Never.

Smirk. Quite an accident, as I may fay. You muft have known my predeceffor, Mr Prig, the greateft man in the world, in his way, ay, or that ever was, or ever will be; quite a jewel of a man; he would touch you up a lot; there was no refifting him. He wou'd force you to bid whether you wou'd or no. I fhall never fee his equal.

Sir Geo. You are modeft, Mr Smirk.

Smirk. No, no, but his fhadow. Far be it from me to vie with great men. But as I was faying, my predeceffor, Mr Prig, was to have a fale as it might be on a Saturday. On Friday, at noon, I fhall never forget the day, he was fuddenly feiz'd with a violent cholic. He fent for me to his bed-fide, fqueez'd me by the hand; Dear Smirk, faid he, what an accident! You know what is to-morrow; the greateft fhew this feafon; prints, pictures, bronzes, butterflies, medals, and minionettes; all the world will be there; lady Dy Jofs, Mrs Nankyn, the Duchefs of Dupe, and every body at all: You fee my ftate, it will be impoffible for me to mount. What can I do?—It was not for me, you know, to advife that great man.

Sir Geo. No, no.

Smirk. At laft, looking wifhfully at me, Smirk, fays he, d'you love me?—Mr Prig, can you doubt it?——I'll put it to the teft, fays he; fupply my place to-morrow.—I, eager to fhew my love, rafhly and rapidly replied, I will.

Sir Geo. That was bold.

Smirk. Abfolute madnefs. But I had gone too far to recede.

recede. Then the point was, to prepare for the aweful occasion. The first want that occurred to me was a wig; but this was too material an article to depend on my own judgment. I resolved to consult my friends. I told them the affair——You hear, gentlemen, what has happen'd; Mr Prig, one of the greatest men in his way the world ever saw, or ever will, quite a jewel of a man, taken with a violent fit of the cholic; to-morrow, the greatest shew this season; prints, pictures, bronzes, butterflies, medals, and mizionettes; every body in the world to be there; Lady Dy Jols, Mrs Nankyn, Duchess of Dupe, and all mankind; it being impossible he should mount, I have consented to sell——They star'd—It is true, gentlemen. Now I should be glad to have your opinions as to a wig. They were divided: some recommended a tye, others a bag: one mention'd a bob, but was soon over-rul'd. Now, for my part, I own, I rather inclin'd to the bag; but to avoid the imputation of rashness, I resolv'd to take Mrs Smirk's judgment, my wife, a dear good woman, fine in figure, high in taste, a superior genius, and knows old china like a Nabob.

Sir Geo. What was her decision?

Smirk. I told her the case—My dear, you know what has happen'd. My good friend, Mr Prig, the greatest man in the world, in his way, that ever was, or ever will be, quite a jewel of a man, a violent fit of the cholic——the greatest shew this season, to-morrow, pictures, and every thing in the world; all the world will be there: now, as it is impossible he should, I mount in his stead. You know the importance of a wig; I have ask'd my friends—some recommended a tye, others a bag—what is your opinion? Why, to deal freely, Mr Smirk, says she, a tye for your round, regular, smiling face would be rather too formal, and a bag too boyish, deficient in dignity for the solemn occasion; were I worthy to advise, you should wear a something between both.—I'll be hang'd, if you don't mean a major. I jumpt at the hint, and a major it was.

Sir Geo. So, that was fixt.

Smirk. Finally. But next day, when I came to mount the rostrum, then was the trial. My limbs shook, and my tongue trembled. The first lot was a chamber-utensil, in Chelsea china, of the pea-green pattern. It occasioned a great laugh; but I got through it. Her Grace, indeed, gave

gave me great encouragement. I overheard her whisper to Lady Dy, Upon my word, Mr Smirk does it very well. Very well, indeed, Mr Smirk, addressing herself to me. I made an acknowledging bow to her Grace, as in duty bound. But one flower flounced involuntarily from me that day, as I may say. I remember, Dr Trifle call'd it enthusiastic, and pronounc'd it a presage of my future greatness.

Sir Geo. What was that?

Smirk. Why, Sir, the lot was a Guido; a single figure, a marvellous fine performance; well preserv'd, and highly finish'd. It stuck at five and forty; I, charm'd with the picture, and piqu'd at the people, A going for five and forty, no body more than five and forty?——Pray, ladies and gentlemen, look at this piece, quite flesh and blood, and only wants a touch from the torch of Prometheus, to start from the canvas and fill a bidding. A general plaudit ensu'd; I bow'd, and in three minutes knock'd it down at sixty-three, ten.

Sir Geo. That was a stroke at least equal to your master.

Smirk. O dear me! You did not know the great man, alike in every thing. He had as much to say upon a ribbon as a Raphael. His manner was inimitably fine. I remember they took him off at the play-house some time ago; pleasant, but wrong. Public characters shou'd not be sported with—They are sacred——But we lose time.

Sir Geo. Oh, in the lobby, on the table, you will find the particulars.

Smirk. We shall see you. There will be a world of company. I shall please you. But the great nicety of our art is, the eye. Mark how mine skims round the room.—Some bidders are shy, and only advance with a nod; but I nail them. One, two, three, four, five. You will be surpriz'd—Ha, ha, ha,—heigh ho!   [*Exit.*

ACT

ACT III.

Enter Sir George and Loader.

Sir Geo. A Most infernal run. Let's see [*Pulls out a card.*] Loader a thousand, the baron two, Tally——Enough to beggar a banker. Every shilling of Transfer's supply exhausted! nor will even the sale of my moveables prove sufficient to discharge my debts. Death and the Devil! In what a complication of calamities has a few days plung'd me! And no resource?

Load. Knight, here's old Moll come to wait on you; she has brought the tid-bit I spoke of. Shall I bid her send her in?

Sir Geo. Pray do. [*Exit Loader.*

Enter Mrs Cole and Lucy.

Mrs Cole. Come along, Lucy. You bashful baggage, I thought I had silenc'd your scruples. Don't you remember what Mr Squintum said? A woman's not worth saving, that won't be guilty of a swinging sin; for then they have matter to repent upon. Here, your Honour, I leave her to your management. She is young, tender, and timid; does not know what is for her own good: but your Honour will soon teach her. I wou'd willingly stay, but I must not lose the lecture. *Exit.*

Sir Geo. Upon my credit, a fine figure! Aukward—— Can't produce her publicly as mine; but she will do for private amusement——Will you be seated, Miss?——Dumb! quite a picture! She too wants a touch of the Promethean torch——Will you be so kind, Ma'am, to walk from your frame and take a chair?——Come, pr'ythee, why so coy? Nay, I am not very adroit in the custom of this country. I suppose I must conduct you——Come, Miss.

Lucy. O, Sir.

Sir Geo. Child!

Lucy. If you have any humanity, spare me.

Sir Geo. In tears! What can this mean? Artifice. A project to raise the price, I suppose. Look'e, my dear, you may save this piece of pathetic for another occasion. It won't won't do with me; I am no novice—So, child, a truce to your tragedy, I beg.

Lucy. Indeed you wrong me, Sir; indeed you do.

Sir Geo. Wrong you! how came you here, and for what purpose?

Lucy. A shameful one. I know it all, and yet believe me, Sir, I am innocent.

Sir Geo. Oh, I don't question that. Your pious patroness is a proof of your innocence.

Lucy. What can I say to gain your credit? And yet, Sir, strong as appearances are against me, by all that's holy, you see me here, a poor distress'd, involuntary victim.

Sir Geo. Her style's above the common class; her tears are real.—Rise, child.—How the poor creature trembles!

Lucy. Say then I am safe.

Sir Geo. Fear nothing.

Lucy. May Heaven reward you. I cannot.

Sir Geo. Pr'ythee, child, collect yourself, and help me to unravel this mystery. You came hither willingly? There was no force?

Lucy. None.

Sir Geo. You know Mrs Cole.

Lucy. Too well.

Sir Geo. How came you then to trust her?

Lucy. Mine, Sir, is a tedious, melancholy tale,

Sir Geo. And artless too?

Lucy. As innocence.

Sir Geo. Give it me.

Lucy. It will tire you.

Sir Geo. Not if it be true. Be just, and you will find me generous.

Lucy. On that, Sir, I rely'd in venturing hither.

Sir Geo. You did me justice. Trust me with all your story. If you deserve, depend upon my protection.

Lucy. Some months ago, Sir, I was consider'd as the joint heiress of a respectable wealthy merchant; dear to my friends, happy in my prospects, and my father's favourite.

Sir Geo. His name.

Lucy. There you must pardon me. Unkind and cruel though he has been to me, let me discharge the duty of a daughter, suffer in silence, nor bring reproach on him who gave me being.

Sir

THE MINOR.

Sir Geo. I applaud your piety.

Lucy. At this happy period, my father, judging an addition of wealth must bring an increase of happiness, resolved to unite me with a man, sordid in his mind, brutal in his manners, and riches his only recommendation. My refusal of this ill-suited match, though mildly given, enflamed my father's temper, naturally choleric, alienated his affections, and banish'd me his house, distressed and destitute.

Sir Geo. Wou'd no friend receive you?

Lucy. Alas, how few are friends to the unfortunate! Besides, I knew, Sir, such a step wou'd be considered by my father as an appeal from his justice. I therefore retir'd to a remote corner of the town, trusting, as my only advocate, to the tender calls of nature, in his cool, reflecting hours.

Sir Geo. How came you to know this woman?

Lucy. Accident plac'd me in a house, the mistress of which profess'd the same principles with my infamous conductress. There, as enthusiasm is the child of melancholy, I caught the infection. A constant attendance on their assemblies procured me the acquaintance of this woman, whose extraordinary zeal and devotion first drew my attention and confidence. I trusted her with my story, and in return, receiv'd the warmest invitation to take the protection of her house. This I unfortunately accepted.

Sir Geo. Unfortunately indeed!

Lucy. By the decency of appearances, I was some time imposed upon. But an accident, which you will excuse my repeating, reveal'd all the horror of my situation. I will not trouble you with a recital of all the arts us'd to seduce me: Happily they hitherto have fail'd. But this morning I was acquainted with my destiny; and no other election left me, but immediate compliance, or a jail. In this desperate condition, you cannot wonder, Sir, at my chusing rather to rely on the generosity of a gentleman, than the humanity of a creature insensible to pity, and void of every virtue.

Sir Geo. The event shall justify your choice. You have my faith and honour for your security. For though I can't boast of my own goodness, yet I have an honest feeling for afflicted virtue; and, however unfashionable, a spirit that dares afford it protection. Give me your hand.

As

As soon as I have dispatch'd some pressing business here, I will lodge you in an asylum, sacred to the distresses of your sex; where indigent beauty is guarded from temptations, and deluded innocence retrieved from infamy.

[*Exeunt.*

Enter Shift.

Zooks, I have toil'd like a horse; quite tir'd, by Jupiter. And what shall I get for my pains? The old fellow here talks of making me easy for life. Easy! And what does he mean by easy? He'll make me an exciseman, I suppose, and so with an ink-horn at my button-hole, and a taper switch in my hand, I shall run about gauging of beer-barrels. No, that will never do. This lad here is no fool. Foppish, indeed. He does not want parts, no, nor principles neither. I overheard his scene with the girl. I think I may trust him. I have a great mind to venture it. It is a shame to have him dup'd by this old don. It must not be, I'll in and unfold—Ha!— Egad, I have a thought too, if my heir apparent can execute. I shall still lie conceal'd, and perhaps be rewarded on both sides.

I have it,—'tis engender'd, piping hot,
And now, Sir Knight, I'll match you with a plot. [*Exit.*

Enter Sir William *and* Richard Wealthy.

R. Weal. Well, I suppose, by this time, you are satisfied what a scoundrel you have brought into the world, and are ready to finish your foolery.

Sir Will. Got to the catastrophe, good brother.

R. Weal. Let us have it over then.

Sir Will. I have already alarmed all his tradesmen. I suppose we shall soon have him here, with a legion of bailiffs and constables.—Oh, you have my will about you?

R. Weal. Yes, yes.

Sir Will. It is almost time to produce it, or read him the clause that relates to his rejecting your daughter. That will do his business. But they come. I must return to my character.

Enter Shift.

Shift. Sir, Sir, we are all in the wrong box; our scheme
is

is blown up; your son has detected Loader and Tally, and is playing the very devil within.

Sir Will. Oh, the bunglers!

Shift. Now for it, youngster.

Enter Sir George, driving in Loader and another.

Sir Geo. Rascals, robbers, that, like the locust, mark the road you have taken, by the ruin and desolation you leave behind you.

Load. Sir George!

Sir Geo. And can youth, however cautious, be guarded against such deep-laid, complicated villany? Where are the rest of your diabolical crew? your auctioneer, usurer, and——O Sir, art you here?—I am glad you have not escaped us, however.

Sir Will. What de devil is de matter?

Sir Geo. Your birth, which I believe an imposition, preserves you, however, from the discipline those rogues have receiv'd. A baron, a nobleman, a sharper! O shame! It is enough to banish all confidence from the world. On whose faith can we rely, when those, whose honour is held as sacred as an oath, unmindful of their dignity, descend to rival pick-pockets in their infamous arts. What are these [*pulls out dice*] pretty implements? The fruits of your leisure hours! They are dextrously done. You have a fine mechanical turn.—Dick, secure the door.

Mrs Cole, speaking as entering.

Mrs Cole. Here I am, at last. Well, and how is your Honour, and the little gentlewoman?—Bless me! what is the matter here?

Sir Geo. I am, Madam, treating your friends with a cold collation, and you are opportunely come for your share. The little gentlewoman is safe, and in much better hands than you designed her. Abominable hypocrite! who, tottering under the load of irreverent age and infamous diseases, inflexibly proceed in the practice of every vice, impiously prostituting the most sacred institutions to the most infernal purposes.

Mrs Cole. I hope your Honour——

Sir Geo. Take her away. As you have been singular in your penitence, you ought to be distinguish'd in your penance;

penance; which, I promise you, shall be most publicly
and plentifully bestow'd. [*Exit Cole.*

Enter Dick.

Dick. The constables, Sir.
Sir Geo. Let them come in, that I may consign these
gentlemen to their care. [*To Sir William*]. Your letters
of nobility you will produce in a court of justice. Though,
if I read you right, you are one of those indigent, itinerant nobles of your own creation, which our reputation
for hospitality draws hither in shoals, to the shame of our
understanding, the impairing of our fortunes, and, when
you are trusted, the betraying of our designs. Officers, do
your duty.
Sir Will. Why, don't you know me?
Sir Geo. Just as I guess'd. An impostor. He has re-
cover'd the free use of his tongue already.
Sir Will. Nay, but George.
Sir Geo. Insolent familiarity! away with him.
Sir Will. Hold, hold, a moment. Brother Richard,
set this matter to rights.
R. Weal. Don't you know him?
Sir Geo. Know him? The very question is an affront.
R. Weal. Nay, I don't wonder at it. 'Tis your father,
you fool.
Sir Geo. My father! Impossible!
Sir Will. That may be, but 'tis true.
Sir Geo. My father alive! Thus let me greet the bles-
sing.
Sir Will. Alive! Ay, and I believe I shan't be in a
hurry to die again.
Sir Geo. But, dear Sir, the report of your death——
and this disguise——to what——
Sir Will. Don't ask any questions. Your uncle will tell
you all. For my part, I am sick of the scheme.
R. Weal. I told you what would come of your politics.
Sir Will. You did so. But if it had not been for those
clumsy scoundrels, the plot was as good a plot——O,
George, such discoveries I have to make. Within I'll un-
ravel the whole.
Sir Geo. Perhaps, Sir, I may match 'em.
Shift. Sir. [*Pulls him by the sleeve.*
Sir Geo. Never fear. It is impossible, gentlemen, to
determine

determine your fate, till this matter is more fully explain'd; till when, keep 'em in safe custody.—Do you know them, Sir?

Sir Will. Yes, but that's more than they did me. I can cancel your debts there, and, I believe, prevail on those gentlemen to refund too.—But you have been a sad profligate young dog, George.

Sir Geo. I can't boast of my goodness, Sir, but I think I could produce you a proof, that I am not so totally destitute of——

Sir Will. Ay! Why then pr'ythee do.

Sir Geo. I have, Sir, this day, refused a temptation, that greater pretenders to morality might have yielded to. But I will trust myself no longer, and must crave your interposition and protection——

Sir Will. To what?

Sir Geo. I will attend you with the explanation in an instant. [*Exit.*

Sir Will. Pr'ythee, Shift, what does he mean?

Shift. I believe I can guess.

Sir Will. Let us have it.

Shift. I suppose the affair I overheard just now, a prodigious fine elegant girl, faith, that, discarded by her family, for refusing to marry her grandfather, fell into the hands of the venerable lady you saw, who being the kind caterer for your son's amusements, brought her hither for a purpose obvious enough. But the young gentleman, touch'd with her story, truth, and tears, was converted from the spoiler of her honour to the protector of her innocence.

Sir Will. Look'e there, brother, did not I tell you that George was not so bad at the bottom?

R. Weal. This does indeed atone for half the——But they are here.

Enter Sir George and Lucy.

Sir Geo. Fear nothing, Madam, you may safely rely on the——

Lucy. My father!

R. Weal. Lucy!

Lucy. O, Sir, can you forgive your poor distrest unhappy girl? You scarce can guess how hardly I've been us'd, since my banishment from your paternal roof. Want, pining
want,

want, anguish and shame, have been my constant partners.

Sir Will. Brother!

Sir Geo. Sir!

Lucy. Father!

R. Weal. Rise, child, 'tis I must ask thee forgiveness. Canst thou forget the woes I've made thee suffer? Come to my arms once more, thou darling of my age.—What mischief had my rashness nearly completed. Nephew, I scarce can thank you as I ought, but——

Sir Geo. I am richly paid, in being the happy instrument.—Yet might I urge a wish——

R. Weal. Name it.

Sir Geo. That you would forgive my follies of to-day; and, as I have been providentially the occasional guardian of your daughter's honour, that you would bestow on me that right for life.

R. Weal. That must depend on Lucy; her will, not mine, shall now direct her choice—What says your father?

Sir Will. Me! Oh, I'll shew you in an instant. Give me your hands. There, children, now you are join'd, and the devil take him that wishes to part you.

Sir Geo. I thank you for us both.

R. Weal. Happiness attend you.

Sir Will. Now, brother, I hope you will allow me to be a good plotter. All this was brought to bear by my means.

Shift. With my assistance, I hope you'll own, Sir.

Sir Will. That's true, honest Shift, and thou shalt be richly rewarded; nay, George shall be your friend too. This Shift is an ingenious fellow, let me tell you, sirs.

Sir Geo. I am no stranger to his abilities, Sir. But if you please, we will retire. The various struggles of this fair sufferer require the soothing softness of a sister's love. And now, Sir, I hope your fears for me are over; for had I not this motive to restrain my follies, yet I now know the town too well to be ever its bubble, and will take care to preserve, at least,

Some more estate, and principles, and wit,
Than brokers, bawds, and gamesters shall think fit.

Shift,

THE MINOR.

Shift, addressing himself to Sir George.

And what becomes of your poor servant Shift?
Your father talks of lending me a lift—
A great man's promise, when his turn is serv'd!
Capons on promises wou'd soon be starv'd:
No, on myself alone, I'll now rely:
'Gad I've a thriving traffic in my eye—
Near the mad mansions of Moorfields I'll bawl;
Friends, fathers, mothers, sisters, sons, and all,
Shut up your shops and listen to my call.
With labour, toil, all second means dispense,
And live a rent-charge upon Providence.
Prick up your ears; a story now I'll tell,
Which once a widow, and her child befel,
I knew the mother, and her daughter well;
Poor, it is true, they were; but never wanted,
For whatsoe'er they ask'd, was always granted:
One fatal day, the matron's truth was try'd,
She wanted meat and drink, and fairly cry'd.
[*Child.*] Mother, you cry! [*Mother*]. Oh, child, I've got
no bread.
[*Child.*] What matters that? Why, Providence an't dead!
With reason good, this truth the child might say,
For there came in at noon, that very day,
Bread, greens, potatoes, and a leg of mutton,
A better sure a table ne'er was put on:
Ay, that might be, ye cry, with those poor souls;
But we ne'er had a rasher for the coals.
And d'ye deserve it? How d'ye spend your days?
In pastimes, prodigality, and plays!
Let's go see Foote! ah, Foote's a precious limb!
Old Nick will soon a football make of him!
For foremost rows in side-boxes you shove,
Think you to meet with side-boxes above,
Where gigling girls and powder'd fops may sit?
No, you will all be cramm'd into the pit,
And croud the house for Satan's benefit.
Oh, what you snivel? well, do so no more,
Drop, to atone, your money at the door,
And, if I please,—I'll give it to the poor.

THE

THE
LYAR;
A COMEDY,
OF
THREE ACTS.

PROLOGUE.

WHAT various revolutions in our art,
   Since Thespis first sung ballads in a cart!
By nature fram'd the witty war to wage,
And lay the deep foundations of the stage,
From his own soil that bard his pictures drew:
The gaping croud the mimic features knew,
And the broad jest with fire electric flew.
Succeeding times, more polish'd and refin'd,
To rigid rules the comic muse confin'd:
Robb'd of the nat'ral freedom of her song,
In artful measures now she floats along;
No sprightly sallies rouze the slumb'ring pit;
Thalia, grown mere architect in wit,
To doors and ladders has confin'd her cares,
Convenient closets, and a snug back-stairs;
'Twixt her and Satire has dissolv'd the league,
And jilted humour to enjoy intrigue.
To gain the suffrage of this polish'd age,
We bring to-night a stranger on the stage;
His sire De Vega; we confess this truth,
Lest you mistake him for a British youth.
Severe the censure on my feeble pen,
Neglecting manners, that she copies men:
Thus, if I hum or ha, or name report,
'Tis Serjeant Splitcause from the Inn of Court;
If, at the age that ladies cease to dance,
To romp at Ranelagh, or read romance,
I draw a dowager inclin'd to rant,
Or paint her rage for china or japan,
The true original is quickly known,
And Lady Squab proclaim'd throughout the town.
But in the following group let no man dare
To claim a limb, nay, not a single hair:
What gallant Briton would be such a sot
To own a child a Spaniard has begot.

Vol. I.   M   *EPILOGUE.*

EPILOGUE.

Between Miss Grantam and Old Wilding.

By a Man of Fashion.

M. Gr. HOLD, Sir,
    Our plot concluded, and strict justice done,
Let me be heard as counsel for your son.
Acquit I can't, I mean to mitigate:
Proscribe all lying, what would be the fate
Of this and every other earthly state?
Consider, Sir, if once you cry it down,
You'll shut up ev'ry coffeehouse in town:
The tribe of politicians will want food;
Ev'n now half famish'd—for the public good.
All Grub-street murderers of men and sense,
And every Office of intelligence,
All would be bankrupts, the whole lying race,
And no Gazette to publish their disgrace.
    O. Wild. Too mild a sentence, wou't the good and great
Patriots be wrong'd, that booksellers may eat?
    M. Gr. Your patience, Sir; yet hear another word.
Turn to the hall where justice wields her sword:
Think in what narrow limits you would draw,
By this proscription, all the sons of law:
For 'tis the fix'd, determin'd rule of courts,
Vyner will tell you, nay, ev'n Coke's Reports,
All pleaders may, when difficulties rise,
To gain one truth, expend a hundred lies.
    O. Wild. To curb this practice I am somewhat loath:
A lawyer has no credit but on oath.
    M. Gr. Then to the softer sex some favour shew:
Leave us possession of our modest No!
    O. Wild. Oh, freely, Ma'am, we'll that allowance give,
So that two Noes be held affirmative.
Provided over that your pish and fie,
On all occasions should be deem'd a lie.
    M. Gr. Hard terms!
On this rejoinder then I rest my cause:
Should all pay homage to Truth's sacred laws,
Let us examine what would be the case:
Why many a great man would be out of place.
                                            O. Wild.

EPILOGUE.

O. Wild. 'Twould many a virtuous character reftore.
M. Gr. But take a character from many more.
O. Wild. Though on the fide of bad the balance fill,
Better to find few good than fear for all.
M. Gr. Strong are your reafons; yet, ere I fubmit,
I mean to take the voices of the pit.
Is it your pleafure that we make a rule,
That ev'ry liar be proclaim'd a fool,
Fit fubjects for our author's ridicule?

DRAMATIS PERSONÆ.

Sir James Elliot,   —   Mr R. Palmer.
Old Wilding the father,   Mr Fearon.
Young Wilding,   —   Mr Palmer.
Papillion,   —   Mr Bannister.

Miss Grantam,   =   Mrs Hitchcock.
Miss Godfrey,   —   Miss Platt.
Kitty, the maid,   —   Mrs Bounty.

The Servant.

ACT I.

SCENE, *a Lodging.*

Young Wilding and Papillion discovered.

Y. Wild. AND I am now, Papillion, perfectly equipped.

Pap. Personne mieux. Nobody better.

Y. Wild. My figure?

Pap. Fait à peindre.

Y. Wild. My air?

Pap. Libre.

Y. Wild. My address?

Pap. Parisiene.

Y. Wild. My hat fits easily under my arm; not like the dragged tail of my tatter'd academical habit.

Pap. Ah, bien autre chose.

Y. Wild. Why then adieu, Alma Mater, and bien venue, la ville de Londre; farewell to the schools, and welcome the theatres; presidents, proctors, short commons with long graces, must now give place to plays, bagnios, long tavern-bills with no graces at all.

Pap. Ah, bravo, bravo!

Y. Wild. Well, but my dear Papillion, you must give me the chart du pays: This town is a new world to me; my provident papa, you know, would never suffer me near the smoke of London; and what can be his motive for permitting me now, I can't readily conceive.

Pap. Ni moi.

Y. Wild. I shall, however, take the liberty to conceal my arrival from him for a few days.

Pap. Vous avez raison.

Y. Wild. Well, my Mentor, and how am I to manage? direct my road: where must I begin? But the debate is, I suppose, of consequence?

Pap. Vraiment.

Y. Wild. How long have you left Paris, Papillion?

Pap. Twelve, thirteen year.

Y. Wild. I can't compliment you upon your progress in English.

Pap.

Pap. The accent is difficult.
Y. Wild. But here you are at home.
Pap. C'eſt vrai.
Y. Wild. No ſtranger to faſhionable places.
Pap. O faite!
Y. Wild. Acquainted with the faſhionable figure of both ſexes.
Pap. Sans doute.
Y. Wild. Well then, upon your lecture! And, d'ye hear, Papillion, as you have the honour to be promoted from the mortifying condition of an humble valet, to the important charge of a private tutor, let us diſcard all diſtance between us: ſee me ready to ſlack my thirſt at your fountain of knowledge, my Magnus Apollo.
Pap. Here then I diſcloſe my Helicon to my poetical pupil.
Y. Wild. Hey, Papillion!
Pap. Sir?
Y. Wild. What is this? why you ſpeak Engliſh!
Pap. Without doubt.
Y. Wild. But like a native.
Pap. To be ſure.
Y. Wild. And what am I to conclude from all this?
Pap. Logically thus, Sir: Whoever ſpeaks pure Engliſh is an Engliſhman; I ſpeak pure Engliſh; ergo, I am an Engliſhman. There's a categorical ſyllogiſm for you, major, minor, and conſequence. What, do you think, Sir, that whilſt you was buſy at Oxford, I was idle? no, no, no.
Y. Wild. Well, Sir, but notwithſtanding your pleaſantry, I muſt have this matter explain'd.
Pap. So you ſhall, my good Sir; but don't be in ſuch a hurry: you can't ſuppoſe I would give you the key, unleſs I meant you ſhould open the door.
Y. Wild. Why, then, prithee unlock.
Pap. Immediately. But by way of entering upon my poſt as preceptor, ſuffer me firſt to give you a hint: you muſt not expect, Sir, to find here, as at Oxford, men appearing in their real characters; every body there, Sir, knows that Dr Muffy is a fellow of Maudlin, and Tom Trifle a ſtudent of Chriſtchurch; but this town is one great comedy, in which not only the principles, but frequently the perſons are feigned.
Y. Wild. A uſeful obſervation.

Pap.

Pop. Why, now, Sir, at the first coffeehouse I shall enter you, you will perhaps meet a man from whose decent sable dress, placid countenance, infinuating behaviour, short sword, with the waiter's civil addition of "a dish of coffee for Dr Julap," you would suppose him to be a physician.

Y. Wild. Well!

Pop. Does not know diascordium from diaculum. An absolute French spy, concealed under the shelter of a huge medicinal periwig.

Y. Wild. Indeed!

Pop. A martial figure too, it is odds but you will encounter; from whose scars, title, dress, and address, you would suppose to have had a share in every action since the peace of the Pyrenees; runner to a gaming-table, and bully to a bawdy-house. Battles to be sure he has been in—with the watch; and frequently a prisoner too—in the round-house.

Y. Wild. Amazing!

Pop. In short, Sir, you will meet with lawyers who practise smuggling, and merchants who trade upon Hounslow-heath; reverend atheists, right honourable sharpers, and Frenchmen from the county of York.

Y. Wild. In the last list, I presume, you roll.

Pop. Just my situation.

Y. Wild. And pray, Sir, what may be your motive for this whimsical transformation?

Pop. A very harmless one, I promise you: I would only avail myself at the expence of folly and prejudice.

Y. Wild. As how?

Pop. Why, Sir—But, to be better understood, I believe it will be necessary to give you a short sketch of the principal incidents of my life.

Y. Wild. Prithee do.

Pop. Why then you are to know, Sir, that my former situation has been rather above my present condition, having once sustained the dignity of sub-preceptor to one of those cheap rural academies with which our county of York is so plentifully stocked.

Y. Wild. But to the point: why this disguise? why renounce your country?

Pop. There, Sir, you make a little mistake; it was my country that renounced me.

Y. Wild.

Y. Wild. Explain.

Pap. In an instant; upon quitting the school, and first coming to town, I got recommended to the compiler of the Monthly Review.

Y. Wild. What, an author too?

Pap. Oh, a voluminous one: the whole region of the belles lettres fell under my inspection; physic, divinity, and the mathematics, my mistress managed herself. There, Sir, like another Aristarch, I dealt out fame and damnation at pleasure. In obedience to the caprice and commands of my master, I have condemn'd books I never read, and applauded the fidelity of a translation, without understanding one syllable of the original.

Y. Wild. Ah! why I thought acuteness of discernment, and depth of knowledge, were necessary to accomplish a critic.

Pap. Yes, Sir, but not a monthly one. Our method was very concise: we copy the title-page of a new book; we never go any further: If we are ordered to praise it, we have at hand about ten words, which, scatter'd through as many periods, effectually does the business; as, "laudable design, happy arrangement, spirited language, nervous sentiment, elevation of thought, conclusive argument;" if we are to decry, then we have, "unconnected, flat, false, illiberal strictures, reprehensible, unnatural:" and thus, Sir, we pepper the author, and soon rid our hands of his work.

Y. Wild. A short recipe.

Pap. And yet, Sir, you have all the materials that are necessary: these are the arms with which we engage authors of every kind. To us all subjects are equal; plays or sermons, poetry or politics, music or midwifery, it is the same thing.

Y. Wild. How came you to resign this easy employment?

Pap. It would not suffice. Notwithstanding what we say, people will judge for themselves; our work hung upon hand, and all I could get from the publisher was four shillings a week, and my small beer. Poor pittance!

Y. Wild. Poor indeed.

Pap. Oh, half starv'd me!

Y. Wild. What was your next change?

Pap. I was mightily puzzled to chuse. Some would have had me turn player, and others methodist preacher: but

but as I had no money to build me a tabernacle, I did not think it could anſwer; and as to player—whatever might happen to me, I was determined not to bring a diſgrace upon my family, and ſo I reſolv'd to turn footman.

Y. Wild. Wiſely reſolv'd.

Pap. Yes, Sir, but not ſo eaſily executed.

Y. Wild. No!

Pap. Oh no, Sir. Many a weary ſtep have I taken after a place: here I was too old, there I was too young; here the laſt livery was too big, there it was too little; here I was aukward, there I was knowing; madam diſlik'd me at this houſe, her ladyſhip's woman at the next; ſo that I was as much puzzled to find out a place, as the great Cynic philoſopher to diſcover a man. In ſhort, I was quite in a ſtate of deſpair, when chance threw an old friend in my way that quite retrieved my affairs.

Y. Wild. Pray who might he be?

Pap. A little bit of a Swiſs genius, who had been French uſher with me at the ſame ſchool in the country. I opened my melancholy ſtory to him over three-pennyworth of beef-a-la-mode, in a cellar in St Ann's. My little foreign friend purs'd up his lanthorn jaws, and with a ſhrug of contempt, "Ah, maitre Jean, vous n'avez pas la politique; you have no fineſſe: to trive here you muſt ſtudy the folly of your own country." "How, Monſieur!" "Taiſez vous. Keep a your tongue! autre foy! I teach you ſpeak French, now I teach a you to forget Engliſh. Go vid me to my lodgement, I vil give you proper dreſs, den go preſent yourſelf to de ſame hotels, de very ſame houſe; you will find all de doors dat was ſhut in your face as footman Anglois, will fly open demſelves to a French valet de chambre."

Y. Wild. Well, Papillion?

Pap. Gad, Sir, I thought it was but an honeſt artifice; ſo I determin'd to follow my friend's advice.

Y. Wild. Did it ſucceed?

Pap. Better than expectation: my tawny face, long queu, and broken Engliſh, was a pas par tout. Beſides, when I am out of place, this diſguiſe procures me many reſources.

Y. Wild. As how?

Pap. Why, at a pinch, Sir, I am either a teacher of tongues, a friſeur, a dentiſt, or a dancing-maſter; theſe,

Vol. I.   N n   Sir,

Sir, are hereditary professions to Frenchmen. But now, Sir, to the point: as you were pleased to be so candid with me, I was determin'd to have no reserve with you. You have studied books, I have studied men; you want advice, and I have some at your service.

Y. Wild. Well, I'll be your customer.

Pap. But guard my secret: if I should be so unfortunate to lose your place, don't shut me out from every other.

Y. Wild. You may rely upon me.

Pap. In a few years I shall be in a condition to retire from business; but whether I shall settle at my family-seat, or pass over the continent, is as yet undetermined. Perhaps, in gratitude to the country, I may purchase a marquisate near Paris, and spend the money I have got by their means, generously amongst them.

Y. Wild. A grateful intention. But let us sally. Where do we open?

Pap. Let us see—one o'clock—it is a fine day: the Mall will be crouded.

Y. Wild. Alons.

Pap. But don't stare, Sir: survey every thing with an air of habit and indifference.

Y. Wild. Never fear.

Pap. But I would, Sir, crave a moment's audience, upon a subject that may prove very material to you.

Y. Wild. Proceed.

Pap. You will pardon my presumption; but you have, my good master, one little foible that I could wish you to correct.

Y. Wild. What is it?

Pap. And yet it is a pity too, you do it so very well.

Y. Wild. Prithee be plain.

Pap. You have, Sir, a lively imagination, with a most happy turn for invention.

Y. Wild. Well.

Pap. But now and then in your narratives you are hurry'd, by a flow of spirits, to border upon the improbable, a little given to the marvellous.

Y. Wild. I understand you: what, I am somewhat subject to lying.

Pap. Oh, pardon me, Sir; I don't say that; no, no, only a little apt to embellish, that's all. To be sure it is a fine gift; that there is no disputing: but men in general are

are so stupid, so rigorously attach'd to matter of fact——
And yet this talent of yours is the very soul and spirit of
poetry; and why it should not be the same in prose I can't
for my life determine.

Y. Wild. You would advise me, then, not to be quite so
poetical in prose?

Pap. Why, Sir, if you would descend a little to the
grovelling comprehension of the million, I think it would
be as well.

Y. Wild. I'll think of it.

Pap. Besides, Sir, people in this town are more snoaky
and suspicious. Oxford, you know, is the seat of the muses, and a man is naturally permitted more ornament and
garniture to his conversation than they will allow in this
latitude.

Y. Wild. I believe you are right. But we shall be late.
D'ye hear me, Papillion: if at any time you find me grow-
ing too poetical, give me a hint; your advice shan't be
thrown away. [*Exit.*

Pap. I wish it mayn't; but the disease is too rooted to
be quickly removed. Lord, how I have sweat for him!
yet he is as unembarrassed, easy, and fluent, all the time, as
if he really believed what he said. Well, to be sure he is
a great master; it is a thousand pities his genius could not
be converted to some public service: I think the government should employ him to answer the Brussels Gazette.
I'll be hanged if he is not too many for Monsieur Maubert,
at his own weapons. [*Exit.*

SCENE, *the Park.*

Enter Miss Grantam *and* Miss Godfrey, *and Servant.*

M. Gr. John, let the chariot go round to Spring-Gar-
dens, for your mistress and I shall call at Lady Bab's, Miss
Arabella Allnight's, the Countess of Crumple's, and the
tall man's, this morning. My dear Miss Godfrey, what
trouble I have had to get you out! why, child, you are as
tedious as a long morning. Do you know now, that of
all places of public rendezvous I honour the Park? forty
thousand million of times preferable to the play-house!
Don't you think so, my dear?

M. God. They are both well in their way.

M. Gr. Way! why the purpose of both is the same;
to

to meet company, is'n't it? what, d'ye think I go there for the plays, or come here for the trees? ha! ha! well that is well enough. But, O Gemini! I beg a million of pardons: you are a prude, and have no relish for the little innocent liberties with which a fine woman may indulge herself in public.

M. God. Liberties in public!

M. Gr. Yes, child, such as enchoring a song at an opera, interrupting a play in a critical scene of distress, hallooing to a pretty fellow cross the Mall, as loud as if you were calling a coach. Why, do you know now, my dear, that by a lucky stroke in dress, and a few high airs of my own making, I have had the good fortune to be gazed at and followed by as great a croud, on a Sunday, as if I was the Tripoli ambassador?

M. God. The good fortune, Ma'am! surely the wish of every decent woman is to be unnotic'd in public.

M. Gr. Decent! oh, my dear queer creature, what a phrase have you found out for a woman of fashion! Decency is, child, a mere Burgeois, plebeian quality, and fit only for those who pay court to the world, and not to us to whom the world pays court. Upon my word, you must enlarge your ideas: you are a fine girl, and we must not have you lost; I'll undertake you myself. But, as I was saying——Pray, my dear, what was I saying?

M. God. I profess I don't recollect.

M. Gr. Hey!——Oh, ah, the Park. One great reason for my loving the Park is, that one has so many opportunities of creating connections.

M. God. Ma'am.

M. Gr. Nay, don't look grave. Why, do you know that all my male friendships are form'd in this place?

M. God. It is an odd spot: but you must pardon me if I doubt the possibility.

M. Gr. Oh, I will convince you in a moment; for here seems to be coming a good smart figure that I don't recollect. I will throw out a lure.

M. God. Nay, for Heaven's sake!

M. Gr. I am determin'd, child: that is——

M. God. You will excuse my withdrawing.

M. Gr. Oh, please yourself, my dear.

[*Exit* Miss Godfrey.

Enter

Enter Young Wilding *with* Papillion.

Y. Wild. Your ladyship's handkerchief, Ma'am.

M. Gr. I am, Sir, concern'd at the trouble——

Y. Wild. A moſt happy incident for me, Madam; as chance has given me an honour in one lucky minute, that the moſt diligent attention has not been able to procure for me in the whole tedious round of a revolving year.

M. Gr. Is this meant to me, Sir?

Y. Wild. To whom elſe, Madam? ſurely you muſt have mark'd my reſpectful aſſiduity, my uninterrupted attendance; to plays, operas, balls, routs, and ridottos, I have purſued you like your ſhadow; I have beſieged your door for a glimpſe of your exit and entrance, like a diſtreſſed creditor, who has no arms againſt privilege but perſeverance.

Pap. So, now he is in for it; ſtop him who can.

Y. Wild. In ſhort, Madam, ever ſince I quitted America, which I take now to be about a year, I have as faithfully guarded the live-long night, your ladyſhip's portal, as a centinel the powder magazine in a fortified city.

Pap. Quitted America! well pull'd.

M. Gr. You have ſerv'd in America then?

Y. Wild. Full four years Ma'am: and during that whole time, not a ſingle action of conſequence but I had an opportunity to ſignalize myſelf; and I think I may, without vanity, affirm, I did not miſs the occaſion. You have heard of Quebec, I preſume?

Pap. What the deuce is he driving at now?

Y. Wild. The project to ſurprize that place was thought a happy expedient, and the firſt mounting the breach a gallant exploit. There, indeed, the whole army did me juſtice.

M. Gr. I have heard the honour of that conqueſt attributed to another name.

Y. Wild. The mere taking the town, Ma'am. But that's a triſle: ſieges now-a-days are reduc'd to certainties; it is amazing how minutely exact we, who know the buſineſs, are at calculation: for inſtance now, we will ſuppoſe the commander in chief, addreſſing himſelf to me, was to ſay, "Colonel, I want to reduce that fortreſs; what will be the expence?" "Why, pleaſe your highneſs, the reduction of that fortreſs will coſt you one thouſand and two lives,

lives, fixty-nine legs, ditto arms, fourfcore fractures, with about twenty dozen of flefh wounds."

M. Gr. And you fhall be near the mark?

Y. Wild. To an odd joint, Ma'am. But, Madam, it is not to the French alone that my feats are confin'd: Cherokees, Catabaws, with all the Aws and Ees of the continent, have felt the force of my arms.

Pap. This is too much, Sir.

Y. Wild. Hands off! Nor am I lefs adroit at a treaty, Madam, than terrible in battle. To me we owe the friendfhip of the Five Nations, and I had the firft honour of fmoaking the pipe of peace with the Little Carpenter.

M. Gr. And fo young!

Y. Wild. This gentleman, though a Frenchman and an enemy, I had the fortune to deliver from the Mohawks, whofe prifoner he had been for nine years. He gives a moft entertaining account of their laws and cuftoms: he fhall prefent you with the wampum belt, and a fcalping knife. Will you permit him, Madam, juft to give you a tafte of the military dance, with a fhort fpecimen of their warhoop.

Pap. For Heaven's fake!

M. Gr. The place is too public.

Y. Wild. In fhort, Madam, after having gathered as many laurels abroad as would garnifh a Gothic cathedral at Chriftmas, I returned to reap the harveft of the well-fought field. Here it was my good fortune to encounter you: then was the victor vanquifh'd; what the enemy could never accomplifh, your eyes in an inftant atchiev'd; prouder to ferve here then command in chief elfewhere; and more glorious in wearing your chains, than in triumphing over the vanquifh'd world.

M. Gr. I have got here a moft heroical lover; but I fee Sir James Elliot coming, and muft difmifs him. [*Afide*]. Well, Sir, I accept the tender of your paffion, and may find a time to renew our acquaintance; at prefent it is neceffary we fhould feparate.

Y. Wild. "Slave to your will, I live but to obey you." But may I be indulged with the knowledge of your refidence?

M. Gr. Sir?

Y. Wild. Your place of abode.

M. Gr. Oh, Sir, you can't want to be acquainted with that;

that, you have a whole year flood centinel at my ladyſhip's
portal.

Y. Wild. Madam, I—I—I—

M. Gr. Oh, Sir, your ſervant. Ha, ha, ha! What, you
are caught! Ha, ha, ha! Well, he has a more intrepid
aſſurance. Adieu, my Mars. Ha, ha, ha!   [*Exit.*

Pap. That laſt was an unlucky queſtion, Sir.

Y. Wild. A little mal-a-propos, I muſt confeſs.

Pap. A man ſhould have a good memory who deals
much in this poetical proſe.

Y. Wild. Poh! I'll ſoon re-eſtabliſh my credit. But I
muſt know who this girl is: Hark'e, Papillion, could not you
contrive to pump out of her footman—I ſee there he ſtands
—the name of his miſtreſs?

Pap. I will try.   [*Exit.*

[*Wilding retires to the back of the ſtage.*

Enter Sir James Elliot *and* Servant.

Sir Ja. Muſic and an entertainment?

Serv. Yes, Sir.

Sir Ja. Laſt night, upon the water?

Serv. Upon the water, laſt night.

Sir Ja. Who gave it?

Serv. That, Sir, I can't ſay.

To them Wilding.

Y. Wild. Sir James Elliot, your moſt devoted.

Sir Ja. Ah, my dear Wilding! you are welcome to
town.

Y. Wild. You will pardon my impatience; I interrupted you, you ſeem'd upon an intereſting ſubject.

Sir Ja. Oh, an affair of gallantry.

Y. Wild. Of what kind?

Sir Ja. A young lady regal'd laſt night by her lover,
on the Thames.

Y. Wild. As how?

Sir Ja. A band of muſic in boats.

Y. Wild. Were they good performers?

Sir Ja. The beſt. Then conducted to Marlbehall, where
ſhe found a magnificent collation.

Y. Wild. Well order'd?

Sir Ja. With elegance. After ſupper a ball; and to
conclude the night, a firework.

Y. Wild.

Y. Wild. Was the last well defign'd?
Sir Jo. Superb.
Y. Wild. And happily executed?
Sir Jo. Not a single faux pas.
Y. Wild. And you don't know who gave it?
Sir Jo. I can't even guefs.
Y. Wild. Ha, ha, ha!
Sir Jo. Why do you laugh?
Y. Wild. Ha, ha, ha! It was me.
Sir Jo. You!
Pap. You, Sir!
Y. Wild. Moi—me.
Pap. So, fo, fo; he is enter'd again.
Sir Jo. Why, you are fortunate, to find a miftrefs in fo fhort a fpace of time.
Y. Wild. Short! why, man, I have been in London thefe fix weeks.
Pap. O Lord, O Lord!
Y. Wild. It is true, not caring to encounter my father, I have rarely ventur'd out but at nights.
Pap. I can hold no longer. Dear Sir—
Y. Wild. Peace, puppy!
Pap. A curb to your poetical vein.
Y. Wild. I shall curb your impertinence.—But fince the ftory is got abroad, I will, my dear friend, treat you with all the particulars.
Sir Jo. I fhall hear it with pleafure.—This is a lucky adventure: But he muft not know he is my rival. [*Afide.*
Y. Wild. Why, Sir, between fix and feven my goddefs embark'd at Somerfet ftairs, in one of the companies barges, gilt and hung with damafk, expreflly for the occafion.
Pap. Mercy on us!
Y. Wild. At the cabin-door fhe was accofted by a beautiful boy, who, in the garb of a Cupid, paid her fome compliments in verfe of my own compofing: the conceits were pretty; allufions to Venus and the fea—the lady and the Thames—no great matter; but, however, well-tim'd, and what was better, well-taken.
Sir Jo. Doubtlefs.
Pap. At what a rate he runs!
Y. Wild. As foon as we had gained the center of the river, two boats full of trumpets, French horns, and other
martial

martial music, struck up their sprightly strains from the Surry-side, which were echo'd by a suitable number of lutes, flutes, and hautboys from the opposite shore. In this state, the oars keeping time, we majestically sail'd along, till the arches of the New Bridge gave a pause, and an opportunity for an elegant desert in Dresden china, by Robinson. Here the repast clos'd, with a few favourite airs from Eliza, Tenducci, and the Mattei.

Pap. Mercy on us!

Y. Wild. Opposite Lambeth I had prepared a naval engagement, in which Boscawen's victory over the French was repeated: the action was conducted by one of the commanders on that expedition, and not a single incident omitted.

Sir Ja. Surely you exaggerate a little.

Pap. Yes, yes, this battle will sink him.

Y. Wild. True to the letter, upon my honour, I shan't trouble you with a repetition of our collation, ball, feu d'artifice, with the thousand little incidental amusements that chance or design produc'd; it is enough to know, that all that could flatter the senses, fire the imagination, or gratify the expectation, was there produc'd in a lavish abundance.

Sir Ja. The sacrifice was, I presume, grateful to your deity.

Y. Wild. Upon that subject you must pardon my silence.

Pap. Modest creature!

Sir Ja. I wish you joy of your success.—For the present you will excuse me.

Y. Wild. Nay, but stay and hear the conclusion.

Sir Ja. For that I shall seize another occasion. [*Exit.*

Pap. Nobly perform'd, Sir.

Y. Wild. Yes, I think happily hit off.

Pap. May I take the liberty to offer one question?

Y. Wild. Freely.

Pap. Pray, Sir, are you often visited with these waking dreams?

Y. Wild. Dreams! what dost mean by dreams?

Pap. These ornamental reveries, these frolics of fancy, which, in the judgment of the vulgar, would be deem'd absolute flames.

Y. Wild. Why, Papillion, you have but a poor, narrow, circumscribed genius.

Vol. I.   O o   *Pap.*

Pap. I must own, Sir, I have no sublimity sufficient to relish the full fire of your Pindaric muse.

Y. Wild. No; a plebeian soul! But I will animate thy clay: mark my example, follow my steps, and in time thou may'st rival thy master.

Pap. Never, never, Sir, I have no talents to fight battles without blows, and give feasts that don't cost me a farthing. Besides, Sir, to what purpose are all these embellishments? Why tell the Lady you have been in London a year?

Y. Wild. The better to plead the length, and consequently the strength of my passion.

Pap. But why, Sir, a soldier.

Y. Wild. How little thou know'st of the sex! What, I suppose thou would'st have me attack them in mood and figure, by a pedantic, classical quotation, or a pompous parade of jargon from the schools. What, dost think that women are to be got like degrees?

Pap. Nay, Sir——

Y. Wild. No, no; the scavoir vivre is the science for them; the man of war is their man: they must be taken like towns, by lines of approach, counterscarps, angles, trenches, columns, and covert-ways; then enter sword in hand, pell-mell! oh, how they melt at the Gothic names of General Swappinback, Count Roufoumousky, Prince Montecuculi, and Marshal Fustinburgh! Men may say what they will of their Ovid, their Petrarch, and their Waller, but I'll undertake to do more business by the single aid of the London Gazette, than by all the sighing, dying, crying crotchets, that the whole race of rhymers have ever produced.

Pap. Very well, Sir; this is all very lively; but remember the travelling pitcher: if you don't one time or other, under favour, lye yourself into some confounded scrape, I will consent to be hanged.

Y. Wild. Do you think so, Papillion?—And whenever that happens, if I don't lye myself out of it again, why then I will be content to be crucify'd. And so, along after the Lady. [*Steps short, going out*]. Zounds, here comes my father! I must fly. Watch him, Papillion, and bring me word to the Cardigan. [*Exeunt separately.*

ACT

ACT II.

SCENE, *A Tavern.*

Young Wilding and Papillion rising from table.

Y. Wild. GAD, I had like to have run into the old gentleman's mouth.

Pap. It is pretty near the same thing; for I saw him join Sir James Elliot: so your arrival is no longer a secret.

Y. Wild. Why then I must lose my pleasure, and you your preferment: I must submit to the dull decency of a sober family, and you to the customary duties of brushing and powdering. But I was so flutter'd at meeting my father, that I forgot the fair; pr'ythee who is she?

Pap. There were two.

Y. Wild. That I saw?

Pap. From her footman I learnt her name was Godfrey.

Y. Wild. And her fortune!

Pap. Immense.

Y. Wild. Single, I hope?

Pap. Certainly.

Y. Wild. Then will I have her.

Pap. What, whether she will or no?

Y. Wild. Yes.

Pap. How will you manage that?

Y. Wild. By making it impossible for her to marry any one else.

Pap. I don't understand you, Sir.

Y. Wild. Oh, I shall only have recourse to that talent you so mightily admire. You will see, by the circulation of a few anecdotes, how soon I will get rid of my rivals.

Pap. At the expence of the Lady's reputation, perhaps.

Y. Wild. That will be as it happens.

Pap. And have you no qualms, Sir?

Y. Wild. Why, where's the injury?

Pap. No injury to ruin her fame!

Y. Wild. I will restore it to her again.

Pap. How?

Y. Wild. Turn tinker and mend it myself.

Pap.

Pap. Which way?

Y. Wild. The old way; folder it by marriage: that, you know, is the modern salve for every sore.

Enter Waiter.

Wait. An elderly gentleman to enquire for Mr Wilding.

Y. Wild. For me! what sort of a being is it?

Wait. Being, Sir!

Y. Wild. Ay; how is he drest?

Wait. In a tye-wig and snuff-colour'd coat.

Pap. Zooks, Sir, it is your father.

Y. Wild. Shew him up. [*Exit Waiter.*

Pap. And what must I do?

Y. Wild. Recover your broken English, but preserve your rank; I have a reason for it.

Enter Old Wilding.

O. Wild. Your servant, Sir: you are welcome to town.

Y. Wild. You have just prevented me, Sir: I was preparing to pay my duty to you.

O. Wild. If you thought it a duty, you should, I think, have sooner discharg'd it.

Y. Wild. Sir!

O. Wild. Was it quite so decent, Jack, to be six weeks in town, and conceal yourself only from me?

Y. Wild. Six weeks! I have scarce been six hours.

O. Wild. Come, come, I am better inform'd.

Y. Wild. Indeed, Sir, you are impos'd upon. This gentleman (who first give me leave to have the honour of introducing to you), this, Sir, is the Marquis de Chateau Briant, of an ancient house in Britanny; who, travelling through England, chose to make Oxford for some time the place of his residence, where I had the happiness of his acquaintance.

O. Wild. Does he speak English?

Y. Wild. Not fluently, but understands it perfectly.

Pap. Pray, Sir,——

O. Wild. Any services, Sir, that I can render you here you may readily command.

Pap. Beaucoup d'honeur.

Y. Wild. This gentleman, I say, Sir, whose quality and country are sufficient securities for his veracity, will assure you that yesterday we left Oxford together.

C. *Wild.*

O. Wild. Indeed!

Pap. C'est vrai.

O. Wild. This is amazing, I was, at the same time, inform'd of another circumstance too, that, I confess, made me a little uneasy, as it interfer'd with a favourite scheme of my own.

Y. Wild. What could that be, pray, Sir?

O. Wild. That you had conceiv'd a violent affection for a fair Lady.

Y. Wild. Sir!

O. Wild. And had given her very gallant and very expensive proofs of your passion.

Y. Wild. Me, Sir!

O. Wild. Particularly last night; music, collations, balls, and fireworks.

Y. Wild. Monsieur le Marquis!—And pray, Sir, who could tell you all this?

O. Wild. An old friend of yours.

Y. Wild. His name, if you please.

O. Wild. Sir James Elliot.

Y. Wild. Yes: I thought he was the man.

O. Wild. Your reason.

Y. Wild. Why, Sir, though Sir James Elliot has a great many good qualities, and is, upon the whole, a valuable man, yet he has one fault which has long determined me to drop his acquaintance.

O. Wild. What may that be?

Y. Wild. Why, you can't, Sir, be a stranger to his prodigious skill in the traveller's talent.

O. Wild. How!

Y. Wild. Oh, notorious to a proverb.—His friends, who are tender of his fame, gloss over his foible, by calling him an agreeable novelist: and so he is, with a vengeance. Why, he will tell you more lies in an hour, than all the circulating libraries, put together, will publish in a year.

O. Wild. Indeed!

Y. Wild. Oh, he is the modern Mandeville at Oxford; he was always distinguish'd by the facetious appellation of the Bouncer.

O. Wild. Amazing!

Y. Wild. Lord, Sir, he is so well understood in his own country, that at the last Hereford assize, a cause, as clear as the sun, was absolutely thrown away by his being merely mentioned as a witness.

O. Wild. A strange turn.

Y. Wild. Unaccountable. But there I think they went a little too far; for if it had come to an oath, I don't think he would have bounc'd neither; but in common occurrences there is no repeating after him. Indeed, my great reason for dropping him was, that my credit began to be a little suspected too.

Pap. Poor gentleman!

O. Wild. Why, I never heard this of him.

Y. Wild. That may be: but can there be a stronger proof of his practice than the flam he has been telling you, of fireworks, and the Lord knows what. And I dare swear, Sir, he was very fluent and florid in his description.

O. Wild. Extremely.

Y. Wild. Yes, that is just his way; and not a syllable of truth from the beginning to the ending, Marquis?

Pap. Oh, dat is all a fiction, upon mine honour.

Y. Wild. You see, Sir.

O. Wild. Clearly. I really can't help pitying the poor man. I have heard of people, who, by long habit, become a kind of constitutional liars.

Y. Wild. Your observation is just; that is exactly his case.

Pap. I'm sure it is yours.

O. Wild. Well, Sir, I suppose we shall see you this evening.

Y. Wild. The Marquis has an appointment with some of his countrymen, which I have promised to attend; besides, Sir, as he is an entire stranger in town, he may want my little services.

O. Wild. Where can I see you in about an hour? I have a short visit to make, in which you are deeply concern'd.

Y. Wild. I shall attend your demands; but where?

O. Wild. Why, here. Marquis, I am your obedient servant.

Pap. Votre serviteur tres humble. [*Exit* Old Wilding.

Y. Wild. So, Papillion, that difficulty is dispatch'd. I think I am even with Sir James for his tattling.

Pap. Most ingeniously manag'd: but are not you afraid of the consequence?

Y. Wild. I do not comprehend you.

Pap. A future explanation between the parties.

Y. Wild.

THE LYAR.

Y. Wild. That may embarrass: but the day is distant. I warrant I will bring myself off.

Pap. It is in vain for me to advise.

Y. Wild. Why, to say truth, I do begin to find my system attended with danger; give me your hand, Papillion —I will reform.

Pap. Ah, Sir!

Y. Wild. I positively will: why, this practice may in time destroy my credit.

Pap. That is pretty well done already. [*Aside.*] Ay, think of that, Sir.

Y. Wild. Well, if I don't turn out the meerest dull matter of fact fellow—but, Papillion, I must scribble a billet to my new flame. I think her name is——

Pap. Godfrey; her father an Indian governor, shut up in the strong room at Calcutta, left her all his wealth: she lives near Miss Grantam, by Grosvenor-square.

Y. Wild. A governor!—oh ho!—bushels of rupees, and pecks of pagodas, I reckon. Well, I long to be rummaging. But the old gentleman will soon return: I will hasten to finish my letter. But, Papillion, what could my father mean by a visit in which I am deeply concern'd?

Pap. I can't guess.

Y. Wild. I shall know presently. To Miss Godfrey, formerly of Calcutta, now residing in Grosvenor-square. Papillion, I won't tell her a word of a lie.

Pap. You won't, Sir?

Y. Wild. No; it would be ungenerous to deceive a Lady. No; I will be open, candid, and sincere.

Pap. And if you are, it will be the first time. [*Exeunt.*

Enter Miss Grantam *and* Miss Godfrey.

M. God. And you really like this gallant spark?

M. Gr. Prodigiously. Oh, I'm quite in love with his assurance! I wonder who he is: he can't have been long in town: a young fellow of his easy impudence must have soon made his way to the best of company.

M. God. By way of amusement he may prove no disagreeable acquaintance; but you can't, surely, have any serious designs upon him.

M. Gr. Indeed but I have.

M. God. And poor Sir James Elliot is to be discarded at once?

M. Gr.

M. Gr. Oh, no.

M. God. What is your intention in regard to him?

M. Gr. Hey?—I can't tell you. Perhaps, if I don't like this new man better, I may marry him.

M. God. Thou art a strange giddy girl.

M. Gr. Quite the reverse; a perfect pattern of prudence: why, would you have me less careful of my person than my purse?

M. God. My dear!

M. Gr. Why I say, child, my fortune being in money, I have some in Indian-bonds, some in the bank, some on this loan, some on the other; so that if one fund fails, I have a sure resource in the rest.

M. God. Very true.

M. Gr. Well, my dear, just so I manage my love-affairs: if I should not like this man—if he should not like me—if we should quarrel—if, if—or in short, if any of the ills should happen, which you know break engagements every day, why by this means I shall never be at a loss.

M. God. Quite provident. Well, and pray on how many different securities have you at present plac'd out your love?

M. Gr. Three: the sober Sir James Elliot, the new American-man, and this morning I expected a formal proposal from an old friend of my father.

M. God. Mr Wilding.

M. Gr. Yes; but I don't reckon much upon him: for you know, my dear, what can I do with an awkward, raw, college cub? though, upon second thoughts, that may'nt be too bad neither; for as I must have the fashioning of him, he may be easily moulded to one's mind.

Enter a Servant.

Serv. Mr Wilding, Madam.

M. Gr. Shew him in. [*Exit Servant.*] You need not go, my dear; we have no particular business.

M. God. I wonder now what she calls particular business.

Enter Old Wilding.

O. Wild. Ladies, your servant. I wait upon you, Madam, with a request from my son, that he may be permitted the honour of kissing your hand.

M. Gr.

M. Gr. Your son is in town then?

O. Wild. He came last night, Ma'am; and though but just from the university, I think I may venture to affirm, with as little the air of a pedant as——

M. Gr. I don't, Mr Wilding, question the accomplishments of your son; and shall own too, that his being descended from the old friend of my father, is to me the strongest recommendation.

O. Wild. You honour me, Madam.

M. Gr. But, Sir, I have something to say——

O. Wild. Pray, Madam, speak out; it is impossible to be too explicit on these important occasions.

M. Gr. Why, then, Sir, to a man of your wisdom and experience I need not observe, that the loss of a parent to counsel and direct at this solemn crisis, has made a greater degree of personal prudence necessary in me.

O. Wild. Perfectly right, Ma'am.

M. Gr. We live, Sir, in a very censorious world; a young woman can't be too much upon her guard; nor should I chuse to admit any man in the quality of a lover, if there was not at least a strong probability——

O. Wild. Of a more intimate connection. I hope, Madam, you have heard nothing to the disadvantage of my son.

M. Gr. Not a syllable: but you know, Sir, there are such things in nature as unaccountable antipathies, aversions, that we take at first sight: I should be glad there could be no danger of that.

O. Wild. I understand you, Madam; you shall have all the satisfaction imaginable: Jack is to meet me immediately: I will conduct him under your window; and if his figure has the misfortune to displease, I will take care his address shall never offend you. Your most obedient servant. [*Exit.*

M. Gr. Now there is a polite, sensible, old father for you.

M. God. Yes; and a very different, prudent daughter he is likely to have. Oh, you are a great hypocrite, Kitty.

Enter a Servant.

Serv. A letter to you, Madam. [*To Miss Godfrey.*]

Sir James Elliot to wait on your ladyship. [*To Miss Gran-*
tam.]   [*Exit.*
    M. Gr. Lord, I hope he won't stay long here. He
comes and seems entirely wrapt up in the dismals: what
can be the matter now?

                Enter Sir James Elliot.

    Sir Ja. In passing by your door, I took the liberty,
Ma'am, of enquiring after your health.
    M. Gr. Very obliging. I hope, Sir, you receiv'd a
favourable account.
    Sir Ja. I did not know but you might have caught cold
last night.
    M. Gr. Cold! why, Sir, I hope I did not sleep with my
bed-chamber window open.
    Sir Ja. Ma'am!
    M. Gr. Sir!
    Sir Ja. No, Ma'am; but it was rather hazardous to
stay so late upon the water.
    M. Gr. Upon the water!
    Sir Ja. Not but the variety of amusements, it must be
own'd, were a sufficient temptation.
    M. Gr. What can he be driving at now!
    Sir Ja. And pray, Madam, what think you of Young
Wilding? is not he a gay, agreeable, sprightly—
    M. Gr. I never give my opinion of people I don't
know.
    Sir Ja. You don't know him!
    M. Gr. No.
    Sir Ja. And his father I did not meet at your door!
    M. Gr. Most likely you did.
    Sir Ja. I am glad you own that, however: but, for
the son, you never——
    M. Gr. Sat eyes upon him.
    Sir Ja. Really?
    M. Gr. Really.
    Sir Ja. Finely supported. Now, Madam, do you know
that one of us is just going to make a very ridiculous
figure?
    M. Gr. Sir, I never had the least doubt of your talents
for excelling in that way.
    Sir Ja. Ma'am, you do me honour: but it does not
happen to fall to my lot upon this occasion, however.
                                                            M. Gr.

M. Gr. And that is a wonder!—What, then I am to be the fool of the comedy, I suppose.

Sir Ja. Admirably rally'd! but I shall dash the spirit of that triumphant laugh.

M. Gr. I dare the attack. Come on, Sir.

Sir Ja. Know then, and blush, if you are not as lost to shame as dead to decency, that I am no stranger to all last night's transactions.

M. Gr. Indeed!

Sir Ja. From your first entering the barge at Somerset-house, to your last landing at Whitehall.

M. Gr. Surprizing!

Sir Ja. Cupids, collations, feasts, fireworks, all have reach'd me.

M. Gr. Why, you deal in magic.

Sir Ja. My intelligence is as natural as it is infallible.

M. Gr. May I be indulg'd with the name of your informer.

Sir Ja. Freely, Madam. Only the very individual spark to whose folly you were indebted for this gallant profusion.

M. Gr. But his name?

Sir Ja. Young Wilding.

M. Gr. You had this story from him?

Sir Ja. I had.

M. Gr. From Wilding!—That is amazing.

Sir Ja. Oh ho! what, you are confounded at last; and no evasion, no subterfuge, no——

M. Gr. Lookye, Sir James; what you can mean by this strange story, and very extraordinary behaviour, it is impossible for me to conceive; but if it is meant as an artifice to palliate your infidelity to me, less pains would have answer'd your purpose.

Sir Ja. Oh, Madam, I know you are provided.

M. Gr. Matchless insolence! as you can't expect that I should be prodigiously pleas'd with the subject of this visit, you won't be surpriſed at my wishing it as short as possible.

Sir Ja. I don't wonder you feel pain at my presence: but you may rest secure you will have no interruption for me; and I really think it would be pity to part two people so exactly formed for each other. Your ladyship's servant. [*Going.*] But, Madam, though your sex secures you from any further resentment, yet the present object of your favour may have something to fear. [*Exit.*

M. Gr. Very well. Now, my dear, I hope you will acknowledge the prudence of my plan. To what a pretty condition I must have been reduc'd if my hopes had rested upon one lover alone.

M. God. But are you sure that your method to multiply, may not be the means to reduce the number of your slaves?

M. Gr. Impossible!—why, can't you discern that this flam of Sir James Elliot's is a mere fetch to favour his retreat.

M. God. And you never saw Wilding?

M. Gr. Never.

M. God. There is some mystery in this. I have too here in my hand another mortification that you must endure.

M. Gr. Of what kind?

M. God. A little ally'd to the last: it is from the military spark that you met this morning.

M. Gr. What are the contents?

M. God. Only a formal declaration of love.

M. Gr. Why, you did not see him.

M. God. But it seems he did me.

M. Gr. Might I peruse it?—" Battles—no wounds so fatal—cannon-balls—Cupid—spring a mine—cruelty—die on a counterscarp—eyes—artillery—death the stranger." It is address'd to you.

M. God. I told you so.

M. Gr. You will pardon me, my dear; but I really can't compliment you upon the supposition of a conquest at my expence.

M. God. That would be enough to make me vain: But why do you think it was so impossible?

M. Gr. And do you positively want a reason?

M. God. Positively.

M. Gr. Why, then, I shall refer you for an answer to a faithful counsellor and most accomplish'd critic.

M. God. Who may that be?

M. Gr. The mirror upon your toilette.

M. God. Perhaps you may differ in judgment.

M. Gr. Why, can glasses flatter?

M. God. I can't say I think that necessary.

M. Gr. Saucy enough!—But come, child, don't let us quarrel

quarrel upon so whimsical an occasion; time will explain the whole. You will favour me with your opinion of Young Wilding, at my window.

M. God. I attend you.

M. Gr. You will forgive me, my dear, the little hint I dropt; it was meant merely to serve you: for indeed, child, there is no quality so insufferable in a young woman as self-conceit and vanity.

M. God. You are most prodigiously obliging.

M. Gr. I'll follow you, Miss. [*Exit* Miss Godfrey.] Pert thing!—She grows immoderately ugly. I always thought her aukward, but she is now an absolute fright.

M. God. [*within.*] Miss, Miss Grantam, your hero's at hand.

M. Gr. I come.

M. God. As I live, the very individual stranger.

M. Gr. No, sure!—Oh Lord, let me have a peep.

M. God. It is he, it is he, it is he.

Enter Old Wilding, Young Wilding, *and* Papillion.

O. Wild. There, Marquis, you must pardon me; for though Paris be more compact, yet surely London covers a much greater quantity—Oh, Jack, look at that corner house: how d'ye like it?

Y. Wild. Very well, but I don't see any thing extraordinary.

O. Wild. I wish though you were the master of what it contains.

Y. Wild. What may that be, Sir?

O. Wild. The mistress, you rogue, you; a fine girl, and an immense fortune; aye, and a prudent sensible wench into the bargain.

Y. Wild. Time enough yet, Sir.

O. Wild. I don't see that: You are, lad, the last of our race, and I should be glad to see some probability of its continuance.

Y. Wild. Suppose, Sir, you were to repeat your endeavours, you have cordially my consent.

O. Wild. No; rather too late in life for that experiment.

Y. Wild. Why, Sir, would you recommend a condition to me, that you disapprove of yourself.

O. Wild. Why, Sirrah, I have done my duty to the public

blic and my family, by producing you: now, Sir, it is incumbent on you to discharge your debt.

Y. Wild. In the college cant, I shall beg leave to tick a little longer.

O. Wild. Why then, to be serious, son, this is the very business I wanted to talk with you about. In a word, I wish you married; and by providing the lady of that mansion for the purpose, I have proved myself both a father and a friend.

Y. Wild. Far be it from me to question your care; yet some preparation for so important a change——

O. Wild. Oh, I will allow you a week.

Y. Wild. A little more knowledge of the world.

O. Wild. That you may study at leisure.

Y. Wild. Now all Europe is in arms, my design was to serve my country abroad.

O. Wild. You will be full as useful to it by recruiting her subjects at home.

Y. Wild. You are then resolv'd.

O. Wild. Fix'd.

Y. Wild. Positively?

O. Wild. Peremptorily.

Y. Wild. No prayers——

O. Wild. Can move me.

Y. Wild. How the deuce shall I get out of this toil, [*Aside.*] But suppose, Sir, there should be an unsurmountable objection?

O. Wild. Oh, leave the reconciling that to me; I am an excellent casuist.

Y. Wild. But, I say, Sir, if it should be impossible to obey your commands?

O. Wild. Impossible!—I don't understand you.

Y. Wild. Oh, Sir!—But on my knees, first let me crave your pardon.

O. Wild. Pardon! for what?

Y. Wild. I fear I have lost all title to your future favour.

O. Wild. Which way?

Y. Wild. I have done a deed——

O. Wild. Let us hear it.

Y. Wild. At Abington, in the county of Berks——

O. Wild. Well?

Y. Wild. I am——

O. Wild.

O. Wild. What?
Y. Wild. Already married.
O. Wild. Married?
Pap. Married!
Y. Wild. Married.
O. Wild. And without my consent?
Y. Wild. Compell'd; fatally forc'd. Oh, Sir, did you but know all the circumstances of my sad, sad story, your rage would soon convert itself to pity.
O. Wild. What an unlucky event!—But rise, and let me hear it all.
Y. Wild. The shame and confusion I now feel renders that task at present impossible: I therefore rely for the relation on the good offices of this faithful friend.
Pap. Me, Sir, I never heard one word of the matter.
O. Wild. Come, Marquis, favour me with the particulars.
Pap. Upon my vard, Sire, dis affair has so shock me, that I am almost as incapable to tell de tale as your son. [*To Young Wilding.*] Dry o your tears. What can I say, Sir?
Y. Wild. Any thing.—Oh! (*Seems to weep*).
Pap. You see, Sire.
O. Wild. Your kind concern at the misfortunes of my family calls for the most grateful acknowledgement.
Pap. Dis is great misfortunes, sans doute.
O. Wild. But if you, a stranger, are thus affected, what must a father feel?
Pap. Oh, beaucoup great deal more.
O. Wild. But since the evil is without a remedy, let us know the worst at once. Well, Sir, at Abington.
Pap. Yes, at Abington.
O. Wild. In the county of Berks.
Pap. Dat is right, in de county of Berks.
Y. Wild. Oh, ho!
O. Wild. Ah, Jack, Jack, are all my hopes then—— Though I dread to ask, yet it must be known; who is the girl, pray Sir?
Pap. De girl, Sir—[*Aside to Young Wilding.*] Who shall I say?
Y. Wild. Any body.
Pap. For de girl, I can't say upon my vard.
O. Wild. Her condition?

Pap.

Pap. Pas grande condition; dat is to be sure. But here is no help.—[*Aside to* Young Wilding.] Sir, I am quite aground.

O. Wild. Yes; I read my shame in his reserve: some artful hussy?

Pap. Dat may be. Vat you call huffy?

O. Wild. Or perhaps some common creature! But I am prepar'd to hear the worst.

Pap. Have you no mercy?

Y. Wild. I'll stop to your relief, Sir.

Pap. O Lord! a happy deliverance.

Y. Wild. Though it is almost death for me to speak, yet it would be infamous to let the reputation of that lady suffer by my silence: she is, Sir, of an ancient house and unblemish'd character.

O. Wild. That is something.

Y. Wild. And though her fortune may not be equal to the warm wishes of a fond father, yet——

O. Wild. Her name?

Y. Wild. Miss Lydia Sybthorp.

O. Wild. Sybthorp.——I never heard of that name.—— But proceed.

Y. Wild. The latter end of last long vacation, I went with Sir James Elliot to pass a few days at a new purchase of his near Abington. There, at an assembly, it was my chance to meet and dance with this lady.

O. Wild. Is she handsome?

Y. Wild. Oh, Sir, more beautiful——

O. Wild. Nay, no raptures; but go on.

Y. Wild. But to her beauty she adds politeness, affability, and discretion; unless she forfeited that character by fixing her affection on me.

O. Wild. Modestly observed.

Y. Wild. I was deterr'd from a public declaration of my passion, dreading the scantiness of her fortune would prove an objection to you. Some private interviews she permitted.

O. Wild. Was that so decent?—But love and prudence, madness and reason.

Y. Wild. One fatal evening, the twentieth of September, if I mistake not, we were in a retir'd room, innocently exchanging mutual vows, when her father, whom we expected

expected to sup abroad, came suddenly upon us. I had just time to conceal myself in a closet.

O. Wild. What, unobserved by him?

Y. Wild. Entirely. But, as my ill stars would have it, a cat of whom my wife is vastly fond, had a few days before lodged a litter of kittens in the same place: I unhappily trod upon one of the brood, which so provok'd the implacable mother, that she flew at me with the fury of a tiger.

O. Wild. I have observed those creatures very fierce in defence of their young.

Pap. I shall hate a cat as long as I live.

Y. Wild. The noise rous'd the old gentleman's attention; he opened the door, and there discover'd your son.

Pap. Unlucky.

Y. Wild. I rush'd to the door; but fatally my foot slipt at the top of the stairs, and down I came tumbling to the bottom; the pistol in my hand went off by accident: this alarm'd her three brothers in the parlour, who, with all their servants, rush'd with united force upon me.

O. Wild. And so surpriz'd you?

Y. Wild. No, Sir; with my sword I for some time made a gallant defence, and should have inevitably escap'd, but a raw-bon'd, over-grown, clumsy cook-wench, struck at my sword with a kitchen poker, broke it in two, and compell'd me to surrender at discretion; the consequence of which is obvious enough.

O. Wild. Natural. The lady's reputation, your condition, her beauty, your love, all combin'd to make marriage an unavoidable measure.

Y. Wild. May I hope then you rather think me unfortunate than culpable?

O. Wild. Why your situation is a sufficient excuse: all I blame you for is your keeping it a secret from me. With Miss Grantam I shall make an aukward figure: but the best apology is the truth: I'll hasten and explain to her all——Oh, Jack, Jack, this is a mortifying business.

Y. Wild. Most melancholy. [*Exit* Old Wilding.

Pap. I am amaz'd, Sir, that you have so carefully conceal'd this transaction from me.

Y. Wild. Heyday! what, do you believe it too?

Pap. Believe it! why, is not the story of the marriage true?

Vol. I.   Q q   *Y. Wild,*

Y. Wild. Not a syllable.

Pap. And the cat, and the pistol, and the poker.

Y. Wild. All invention. And were you really taken in?

Pap. Lord, Sir, how was it possible to avoid it? Mercy on us! what a collection of circumstances have you crowded together!

Y. Wild. Genius; the mere effects of genius, Papillion. But to deceive you, who so thoroughly know me!

Pap. But to prevent that for the future, could you not just give your humble servant a hint, when you are bent upon bouncing. Besides, Sir, if you recollect your fix'd resolution to reform——

Y. Wild. Ay as to matter of fancy, the mere sport and frolic of invention: but in case of necessity—why, Miss Godfrey was at stake, and I was forc'd to use all my finesse.

Enter a Servant.

Serv. Two letters, Sir. [*Exit.*

Pap. There are two things in my conscience my master will never want: a prompt lie and a ready excuse for telling of it.

Y. Wild. Hum! business begins to thicken upon us: a challenge from Sir James Elliot, and a rendezvous from the pretty Miss Godfrey. They shall both be observ'd, but in their order: therefore the body first. Let me see—I have not been twenty hours in town, and I have already got a challenge, a mistress, and a wife; now if I can but get engag'd in a Chancery suit, I shall have my hands pretty full of employment. Come, Papillion, we have no time to be idle. [*Exeunt.*

ACT III.

Miss Grantam and Miss Godfrey.

M. God. UPON my word, Miss Grantam, this is but an idle piece of curiosity: you know the man is already dispos'd of, and therefore——

M. Gr. That is true, my dear; but there is in this affair some mystery that I must and will have explain'd.

M. God.

M. God. Come, Come, I know the grievance. You can't brook that this spark, though even a married man, should throw off his allegiance to you, and enter a volunteer in my service.

M. Gr. And so you take this fact for granted?

M. God. Have I not his letter?

M. Gr. Conceited creature!—I fancy, Miss, by your vast affection for this letter, it is the first of the kind you ever receiv'd.

M. God. Nay, my dear, why should you be piqu'd at me? the fault is none of mine: I dropt no handkerchief; I threw out no lure: the bird came willing to hand, you know.

M. Gr. Metaphorical too! what, you are setting up for a wit as well as a belle? why really, Madam, to do you justice, you have full as fine pretensions to the one as the other.

M. God. I fancy, Madam, the world will not form their judgment of either from the report of a disappointed rival.

M. Gr. Rival! admirably rally'd!—But, let me tell you, Madam, this sort of behaviour, Madam, at your own house, whatever may be your beauty, is no great proof of your breeding, Madam.

M. God. As to that, Ma'am, I hope I shall always shew a proper resentment to any insult that is offer'd me, let it be in whose house it will. The assignation, Ma'am, both time and place, was of your own contriving.

M. Gr. Mighty well, Ma'am!

M. God. But if, dreading a mortification, you think proper to alter your plan, your chair, I believe, is in waiting.

M. Gr. It is, Madam! then let it wait—Oh, what that was your scheme! but it won't take, Miss: the contrivance is a little too shallow.

M. God. I don't understand you.

M. Gr. Cunning creature! So all this insolence was concerted, it seems; a plot to drive me out of the house, that you might have the fellow all to yourself; but I have a regard for your character, though you neglect it. Fie, Miss! a passion for a married man! I really blush for you.

M. God. And I most sincerely pity you. But curb your choler a little: the enquiry you are about to make requires rather a cooler disposition of mind; and by this time the hero is at hand.

M. Gr. Mighty well; I am prepar'd. But, Miss Godfrey, if you really wish to be acquitted of all artificial underhand

derhand dealings, in this affair, suffer me in your name to manage the interview.

M. God. Most willingly. But he will recollect your voice.

M. Gr. Oh, that is easily alter'd. [*Enter a Maid, who whispers Miss Grantam and exit.*] It is he, but hide yourself, Miss, if you please.

M. God. Your hood a little forwarder, Miss: you may be known, and then we shall have the language of politeness inflam'd to proofs of a violent passion.

M. Gr. You are prodigiously cautious.

Enter Young Wilding.

Y. Wild. This rendezvous is something in the Spanish taste, imported, I suppose, with the guittar. At present, I presume, the custom is confin'd to the great; but it will descend, and in a couple of months I shall not be surpriz'd to hear an attorney's hackney clerk rouling at midnight, a milliner's 'prentice, with an Ally, Ally Croker." But that, if I mistake not, is the temple: and see my goddess herself. Miss Godfrey!

M. Gr. Hush.

Y. Wild. Am I right, Miss?

M. Gr. Softly. You receiv'd my letter, I see, Sir.

Y. Wild. And flew to the appointment with more—

M. Gr. No raptures, I beg. But you must not suppose this meeting meant to encourage your hopes.

Y. Wild. How, Madam!

M. Gr. Oh, by no means, Sir; for though I own your figure is pleasing, and your conversation—

M. God. Hold, Miss; when did I ever converse with him?

M. Gr. Why, did not you see him in the Park?

M. God. True, Madam: but the conversation was with you.

M. Gr. Bless me! you are very difficult—I say, Sir, though your person may be unexceptionable, yet your character—

Y. Wild. My character!

M. Gr. Come, come, you are better known than you imagine.

Y. Wild. I hope not.

M. Gr. Your name is Wilding.

Y. Wild.

Y. Wild. How the dence came she by that! True, Madam.

M. Gr. Pray have you never heard of Miss Grantam?

Y. Wild. Frequently.

M. Gr. You have. And had you never any favourable thoughts of that lady? Never mind, Miss.

Y. Wild. If you mean as a lover, never. The lady did me the honour to have a small design upon me.

M. God. I hear every word, Miss.

M. Gr. But you need not bear so heavy upon me; he speaks loud enough to be heard.——I have been told, Sir, that——

Y. Wild. Yes, Ma'am, and very likely by the lady herself.

M. Gr. Sir!

Y. Wild. Oh, Madam, I have another obligation in my pocket to Miss Grantam, which must be discharg'd in the morning.

M. Gr. Of what kind?

Y. Wild. Why the lady, finding an old humble servant of her's a little lethargic, has thought fit to administer me in a jealous draught, in order to quicken his passion.

M. Gr. Sir, let me tell you——

M. God. Have a care; you will betray yourself.

Y. Wild. Oh, the whole story will afford you infinite diversion: such a farrago of sighs and feasts. But, upon my honour, the girl has a fertile invention.

M. God. So! what that story was yours, was it?

Y. Wild. Pray, Madam, don't I hear another voice?

M. Gr. A distant relation of mine.——Every syllable false.——But, Sir, we have another charge against you. Do you know any thing of a lady at Abington?

Y. Wild. Miss Grantam again. Yes, Madam, I have some knowledge of that lady.

M. Gr. You have! Well, Sir, and that being the case, how could you have the assurance——

Y. Wild. A moment's patience, Ma'am. That lady, that Berkshire lady, will, I can assure you, prove no bar to my hopes.

M. Gr. How, Sir, no bar?

Y. Wild. Not in the least, Ma'am; for that lady exists in idea only.

M. Gr. No such person!

Y. Wild.

Y. Wild. A meer creature of the imagination.

M. Gr. Indeed?

Y. Wild. The attacks of Miss Grantam were so powerfully enforc'd too by paternal authority, that I had no method of avoiding the blow, but by sheltering myself under the conjugal shield.

M. Gr. You are not married then?—But what credit can I give to the professions of a man, who, in an article of such importance, and to a person of such respect—

Y. Wild. Nay, Madam, surely Miss Godfrey should not accuse me of a crime her own charms have occasion'd. Could any other motive but the fear of losing her prevail on me to trifle with a father, or compel me to infringe those laws which I have hitherto so invariably observ'd?

M. Gr. What laws, Sir?

Y. Wild. The sacred laws of truth, Ma'am.

M. Gr. There, indeed, you did yourself an infinite violence. But when the whole of the affair is discover'd, will it be so easy to get rid of Miss Grantam? the violence of her passion, and the old gentleman's obstinacy—

Y. Wild. Are nothing to a mind resolv'd.

M. Gr. Poor Miss Grantam!

Y. Wild. Do you know her, Madam?

M. Gr. I have heard of her: but you, Sir, I suppose, have been long on an intimate footing?

Y. Wild. Bred up together from children.

M. Gr. Brave!—Is she handsome?

Y. Wild. Her paint comes from Paris, and her *femme de chambre* is an excellent artist.

M. Gr. Very well—Her shape?

Y. Wild. Pray, Madam, is not Curzon esteemed the best staymaker for people inclin'd to be crooked?

M. Gr. But as to the qualities of her mind: for instance her understanding.

Y. Wild. Uncultivated.

M. Gr. Her wit?

Y. Wild. Borrow'd.

M. Gr. Her taste?

Y. Wild. Trifling.

M. Gr. And her temper?

Y. Wild. Intolerable.

M. Gr. A finish'd picture. But come, these are not your

your real thoughts; this is a sacrifice you think due to the vanity of our sex.

Y. Wild. My honest sentiments: and to convince you how thoroughly indifferent I am to that lady, I would, upon my veracity, as soon take a wife from the Grand Signior's seraglio. Now, Ma'am, I hope you are satisfy'd.

M. Gr. And you would not scruple to acknowledge this before the lady's face?

Y. Wild. The first opportunity.

M. Gr. That I will take care to provide you. Dare you meet me at her house?

Y. Wild. When?

M. Gr. In half an hour.

Y. Wild. But won't a declaration of this sort appear odd at——

M. Gr. Come, no evasion; your conduct and character seem to me a little equivocal, and I must insist on this proof, at least of——

Y. Wild. You shall have it.

M. Gr. In half an hour.

Y. Wild. This instant.

M. Gr. Be punctual.

Y. Wild. Or may I forfeit your favour.

M. Gr. Very well: till then, Sir, adieu.—Now I think I have my spark in the toil; and if the fellow has any feeling, if I don't make him smart for every article—Come, my dear, I shall stand in need of your aid. [*Exeunt.*

Y. Wild. So! I am now, I think, arriv'd at a critical period. If I can but weather this point—But why should I doubt it? it is in the day of distress only that a great man displays his abilities. But I shall want Papillion: where can the puppy be?

Enter Papillion.

Y. Wild. So, Sir; where have you been rambling?

Pap. I did not suppose you would want—

Y. Wild. Want!—you are always out of the way: Here have I been forc'd to tell forty lies upon my own credit, and not a single soul to vouch for the truth of them.

Pap. Lord, Sir, you know—

Y. Wild. Don't plague me with your apologies, but it is lucky for you that I want your assistance. Come with me to Miss Grantam's.

Pap.

Pap. On what occasion?

Y. Wild. An important one: but I'll prepare you as we walk.

Pap. Sir, I am really——I could wish you would be so good as to——

Y. Wild. What! desert your friend in the heat of battle! oh, you poltroon!

Pap. Sir, I would do any thing, but you know I have not talents.

Y. Wild. I do, and for my own sake shall not talk them too high.

Pap. Now I suppose the hour is come when we shall pay for all.

Y. Wild. Why, what a dastardly, hen-hearted——But come, Papillion, this shall be your last campaign. Don't droop, man; confide in your leader, and remember, *Sub auspice Teucro nil desperandum.* [*Exeunt.*

SCENE a Room.

Enter a Servant, conducting in Old Wilding.

Serv. My lady, Sir, will be at home immediately. Sir James Elliot is in the next room waiting her return.

O. Wild. Pray, honest friend, will you tell Sir James that I beg the favour of a word with him. [*Exit Servant.*] This unthinking boy! Half the purpose of my life has been to plan this scheme for his happiness, and in one heedless hour has he mangled all.

Enter Sir James Elliot.

Sir, I ask your pardon: but upon so interesting a subject, I know you will excuse my intrusion. Pray, Sir, of what credit is the family of the Sybthorps in Berkshire?

Sir Ja. Sir!

O. Wild. I don't mean as to property; that I am not so solicitous about; but as to their character: do they live in reputation? Are they respected in the neighbourhood?

Sir Ja. The family of the Sybtharps!

O. Wild. Of the Sybthorps.

Sir Ja. Really I don't know, Sir.

O. Wild. Not know!

Sir Ja.

Sir Ja. No; it is the very first time I ever heard of the name.

O. Wild. How steadily he denies it! Well done, baronet! I find Jack's account was a just one. [*Aside.*] Pray, Sir James, recollect yourself.

Sir Ja. It will be to no purpose.

O. Wild. Come, Sir, your motive for this affected ignorance is a generous, but unnecessary proof of your friendship for my son: but I know the whole affair.

Sir Ja. What affair?

O. Wild. Jack's marriage.

Sir Ja. What Jack?

O. Wild. My son Jack.

Sir Ja. Is he marry'd?

O. Wild. Is he marry'd! why, you know he is.

Sir Ja. Not I, upon my honour.

O. Wild. Nay, that is going a little too far: but to remove all your scruples at once, he has own'd it himself.

Sir Ja. He has.

O. Wild. Ay, ay, to me. Every circumstance; going to your new purchase at Abington—meeting Lydia Sybthorp at the assembly—their private interviews—surpriz'd by the father—pistol—poker—and marriage; in short, every particular.

Sir Ja. And this account you had from your son?

O. Wild. From Jack; not two hours ago.

Sir Ja. I wish you joy, Sir.

O. Wild. Not much of that, I believe.

Sir Ja. Why, Sir, does the marriage displease you?

O. Wild. Doubtless.

Sir Ja. Then I fancy you may make yourself easy.

O. Wild. Why so?

Sir Ja. You have got, Sir, the most prudent daughter-in-law in the British dominions.

O. Wild. I am happy to hear it.

Sir Ja. For though she mayn't have brought you much, I'm sure she will not cost you a farthing.

O. Wild. Ay; exactly Jack's account.

Sir Ja. She'll be easily jointur'd.

O. Wild. Justice shall be done her.

Sir Ja. No provision necessary for younger children.

O. Wild. No, Sir! why not?—I can tell you, if she answers your account, not the daughter of a duke—

Sir Ja.

Sir Ja. Ha, ha, ha, ha.

O. Wild. You are very merry, Sir.

Sir Ja. What an unaccountable fellow!

O. Wild. Sir!

Sir Ja. I beg your pardon, Sir. But with regard to this marriage—

O. Wild. Well, Sir.

Sir Ja. I take the whole history to be neither more nor less than absolute fable.

O. Wild. How, Sir!

Sir Ja. Even so.

O. Wild. Why, Sir, do you think my son would dare to impose upon me?

Sir Ja. Sir, he would dare to impose upon any body. Don't I know him?

O. Wild. What do you know?

Sir Ja. I know, Sir, that his narratives gain him more applause than credit; and that, whether from constitution or habit, there is no believing a syllable he says.

O. Wild. Oh, mighty well, Sir!—He wants to turn the tables upon Jack. But it won't do; you are forestall'd; your novels won't pass upon me.

Sir Ja. Sir!

O. Wild. Nor is the character of my son to be blasted with the breath of a bouncer.

Sir Ja. What is this?

O. Wild. No, no, Mr Mandeville, it won't do; you are as well known here as in your own county of Hereford.

Sir Ja. Mr Wilding, but that I am sure this extravagant behaviour owes its rise to some impudent impositions of your son, your age would scarce prove your protection.

O. Wild. Nor, Sir, but that I know my boy equal to the defence of his own honour, should he want a protector in this arm, wither'd and impotent as you may think it,

Enter Miss Grantam.

M. Gr. Bless me, gentlemen, what is the meaning of this?

Sir Ja. No more, at present, Sir: I have another demand upon your son; we'll settle the whole together.

O. Wild. I am sure he will do you justice.

M. Gr. How, Sir James Elliot, I flatter'd myself that you had finish'd your visits here, Sir. Must I be the eternal

eternal object of your outrage? not only insulted in my own person, but in that of my friends! Pray, Sir, what right——

O. Wild. Madam, I ask your pardon; a disagreeable occasion brought me here: I come, Madam, to renounce all hopes of being nearer ally'd to you, my son unfortunately being married already.

M. Gr. Married!

Sir Ja. Yes, Madam, to a lady in the clouds: and because I have refus'd to acknowledge her family, this old gentleman has behav'd in a manner very inconsistent with his usual politeness.

O. Wild. Sir, I thought this affair was to be reserv'd for another occasion; but you, it seems——

M. Gr. Oh, is that the business?—Why, I begin to be afraid we are here a little in the wrong, Mr Wilding.

O. Wild. Madam.

M. Gr. Your son has just confirm'd Sir James Elliot's opinion, at a conference under Miss Godfrey's window.

O. Wild. Is it possible?

M. Gr. Most true; and assign'd two most whimsical motives for the unaccountable tale.

O. Wild. What can they be!

M. Gr. An aversion for me, whom he has seen but once, and an affection for Miss Godfrey, whom I am almost sure he never saw in his life.

O. Wild. You amaze me.

M. Gr. Indeed, Mr Wilding, your son is a most extraordinary youth; he has finally perplex'd us all. I think, Sir James, you have a small obligation to him.

Sir Ja. Which I shall take care to acknowledge the first opportunity.

O. Wild. You have my consent. An abandoned profligate! was his father a proper subject for his—but I discard him.

M. Gr. Nay, now; gentlemen, you are rather too warm: I can't think Mr Wilding bad-hearted at the bottom. This is a levity——

O. Wild. How, Madam! a levity!

M. Gr. Take my word for it, no more; enslav'd into habit by the approbation of his juvenile friends. Will you submit his punishment to me? I think I have the means

in

in my hands, both to satisfy your resentments, and accomplish his cure into the bargain.

Sir Ja. I have no quarrel to him, but for the ill offices he has done me with you.

M. Gr. D'ye hear, Mr Wilding? I am afraid my opinion with Sir James must cement the general peace.

O. Wild. Madam, I submit to any—

Enter a Servant.

Serv. Mr Wilding to wait upon you, Madam. [*Exit.*
M. Gr. He is punctual, I find. Come, good folks, you all act under my direction. You, Sir, will get from your son, by what means you think fit, the real truth of the Abington business. You must likewise seemingly consent to his marriage with Miss Godfrey, who I shrewdly suspect he has by some odd accident mistaken for me: the lady herself shall appear at your call. Come, Sir James, you will withdraw. I intend to produce another performer, who will want a little instruction. Kitty.

Enter Kitty.

Let John shew Mr Wilding in to his father; then come to my dressing room: I have a short scene to give you in study. [*Exit Kitty.*] The girl is lively, and I warrant will do her character justice. Come, Sir James. Nay, no ceremony: we must be as busy as bees. [*Exeunt.*

O. Wild. This strange boy!—but I must command my temper.

T. Wild. [*Speaking as he enters.*] People to speak with me! see what they want, Papillion. My father here! that's unlucky enough.

O. Wild. Ha, Jack! what brings you here?

T. Wild. Why, I thought it my duty to wait upon Miss Grantam, in order to make her some apology for the late unfortunate——

O. Wild. Well now, that is prudently, as well as politely done.

T. Wild. I am happy to meet, Sir, with your approbation.

O. Wild. I have been thinking, Jack, about my daughter-in-law: as the affair is public, it is not decent to let her continue longer at her father's.

T. Wild. Sir!

O. Wild.

O. Wild. Would it be right to send for her home?

Y. Wild. Doubtless, Sir.

O. Wild. I think so. Why then to-morrow my chariot shall fetch her.

Y. Wild. The devil it shall! [*Aside.*] Not quite so soon, if you please, Sir.

O. Wild. No! why not?

Y. Wild. The journey may be dangerous in her present condition.

O. Wild. What's the matter with her?

Y. Wild. She is big with child, Sir.

O. Wild. An audacious—big with child! that is fortunate. But, however, an easy carriage, and short stages can't hurt her.

Y. Wild. Pardon me, Sir, I dare not trust her: she is six months gone.

O. Wild. Nay, then, there may be danger indeed. But should I write to her father, just to let him know that you have discovered the secret.

Y. Wild. By all means, Sir, it will make him extremely happy.

O. Wild. Why then I will instantly about it, pray how do you direct to him?

Y. Wild. Abington, Berkshire.

O. Wild. True; but his address?

Y. Wild. You need not trouble yourself, Sir: I shall write by this post to my wife, and will send your letter inclos'd.

O. Wild. Ay, ay, that will do. [*Going.*

Y. Wild. So, I have parry'd that thrust.

O. Wild. Though, upon second thoughts, Jack, that will rather look too familiar for an introductory letter.

Y. Wild. Sir!

O. Wild. And these country gentlemen are full of punctilios—No, I'll send him a letter apart; so give me his direction.

Y. Wild. You have it, Sir.

O. Wild. Ay, but his name: I have been so hurry'd that I have entirely forgot it.

Y. Wild. I am sure so have I. [*Aside.*] His name—his name, Sir—Hopkins.

O. Wild. Hopkins!

Y. Wild. Yes, Sir.

O. Wild.

O. Wild. That is not the same name that you gave me before: that, if I recollect, was either Sypthorpe, or Sybthorpe.

Y. Wild. You are right, Sir: that is his paternal appellation; but the name of Hopkins he took for an estate of his mother's; so he is indiscriminately called Hopkins or Sybthorpe; and now I recollect I have his letter in my pocket—he signs himself Sybthorpe Hopkins.

O. Wild. There is no end of this: I must stop him at once. Harkye, Sir, I think you are call'd my son.

Y. Wild. I hope, Sir, you have no reason to doubt it.

O. Wild. And look upon yourself as a gentleman?

Y. Wild. In having the honour of descending from you.

O. Wild. And that you think a sufficient pretension?

Y. Wild. Sir—pray, Sir—

O. Wild. And by what means do you imagine your ancestors obtain'd that distinguishing title? By their pre-eminence in virtue, I suppose.

Y. Wild. Doubtless, Sir.

O. Wild. And has it never occurr'd to you, that what was gain'd by honour might be lost by infamy?

Y. Wild. Perfectly, Sir.

O. Wild. Are you to learn what redress even the imputation of a lie demands, and that nothing less than the life of the adversary can extinguish the affront.

Y. Wild. Doubtless, Sir.

O. Wild. Then how dare you call yourself a gentleman? you, whose whole life has been one continued scene of fraud and falsity! and would nothing content you but making me a partner in your infamy? not satisfied with violating the great band of society; mutual confidence, the most sacred rights of nature must be invaded, and your father made the innocent instrument to circulate your abominable impositions.

Y. Wild. But, Sir!

O. Wild. Within this hour my life was near sacrific'd in defence of your fame; but perhaps that was your intention, and the story of your marriage merely calculated to send me out of the world, as a grateful return for my bringing you into it.

Y. Wild. For heaven's sake, Sir.

O. Wild. What other motive?

Y. Wild. Hear me, I intreat you, Sir.

O. Wild.

O. Wild. To be again impos'd on! No, Jack, my eyes are open'd at laſt.

Y. Wild. By all that's ſacred, Sir—

O. Wild. I am now deaf to your deluſions.

Y. Wild. But hear me, Sir, I own the Abington buſineſs—

O. Wild. An abſolute fiction?

Y. Wild. I do.

O. Wild. And how dare you—

Y. Wild. I crave but a moment's audience.

O. Wild. Go on.

Y. Wild. Previous to the communication of your intention for me, I accidentally met with a lady whoſe charms—

O. Wild. So! what, here is another marriage trumped up: but that is a ſtale device. And pray, Sir, what place does this lady inhabit? Come, come, go on; you have a fertile invention, and this is a fine opportunity. Well, Sir, and this charming lady, reſiding, I ſuppoſe, in Nubibus—

Y. Wild. No, Sir; in London.

O. Wild. Indeed!

Y. Wild. Nay, more, and at this inſtant in this houſe.

O. Wild. And her name—

Y. Wild. Godfrey.

O. Wild. The friend of Miſs Graemm?

Y. Wild. The very ſame, Sir.

O. Wild. Have you ſpoke to her?

Y. Wild. Parted from her not ten minutes ago; nay, am here by her appointment.

O. Wild. Has ſhe favour'd your addreſs?

Y. Wild. Time, Sir, and your approbation, will, I hope.

O. Wild. Lookye, Sir; as there is ſome little probability in this ſtory, I ſhall think it worth farther enquiry. To be plain with you, I know Miſs Godfrey; am intimate with her family; and though you deſerve but little from me, I will endeavour to aid your intention. But if in the progreſs of this affair you practiſe any of your uſual arts; if I diſcover the leaſt falſehood, the leaſt duplicity, remember you have loſt a father.

Y. Wild. I ſhall ſubmit without a murmur.

[*Exit Old Wilding.*

Enter

Enter Papillion.

Y. Wild. Well, Papillion.

Pap. Sir, here has been the devil to pay within.

Y. Wild. What's the matter?

Pap. A whole legion of cooks, confectioners, musicians, waiters, and watermen.

Y. Wild. What do they want?

Pap. You, Sir.

Y. Wild. Me!

Pap. Yes, Sir; they have brought in their bills.

Y. Wild. Bills! for what?

Pap. For the entertainment you gave last night upon the water.

Y. Wild. That I gave!

Pap. Yes, Sir; you remember the bill of fare: I am sure the very mention of it makes my mouth water.

Y. Wild. Prithee are you mad? There must be some mistake; you know that I—

Pap. They have been vastly puzzled to find out your lodgings: but Mr Robinson meeting by accident with Sir James Elliot, he was kind enough to tell him where you liv'd. Here are the bills: Almack's, twelve dozen of claret, ditto Champagne, Frontiniac, sweetmeats, pine-apples: the whole amount is 372 l. 9 s. besides music and fireworks.

Y. Wild. Come, Sir, this is no time for trifling.

Pap. Nay, Sir, they say they have gone full as low as they can afford; and they were in hopes, from the great satisfaction you express'd to Sir James Elliot, that you would throw them in an additional compliment.

Y. Wild. Harkye, Mr Papillion, if you don't cease your impertinence, I shall pay you a compliment that you would gladly excuse.

Pap. Upon my faith, I relate but the mere matter of fact. You know, Sir, I am but bad at invention; though this incident I can't help thinking is the natural fruit of your happy one.

Y. Wild. But are you serious? is this possible?

Pap. Most certain. It was with difficulty I restrain'd their impatience; but however I have dispatch'd them to your lodgings, with a promise that you shall immediately meet them.

Y. Wild.

Y. Wild. Oh, there we shall soon rid our hands of the croop. Now, Papillion, I have news for you. My father has got to the bottom of the whole Abington business.
Pap. The deuce!
Y. Wild. We parted this moment. Such a scene!
Pap. And what was the issue?
Y. Wild. Happy beyond my hopes. Not only an act of oblivion, but a promise to plead my cause with the fair.
Pap. With Miss Godfrey?
Y. Wild. Who else? He is now with her in another room.
Pap. And there is no—you understand me—in all this?
Y. Wild. No, no; that is all over now—my reformation is fix'd.
Pap. As a weather-cock.
Y. Wild. Here comes my father.

Enter Old Wilding.

O. Wild. Well, Sir, I find in this last article you have condescended to tell me the truth; the young lady is not averse to your union; but in order to fix so mutable a mind, I have drawn up a slight contract, which you are both to sign.
Y. Wild. With transport.
O. Wild. I will introduce Miss Godfrey. [*Exit.*
Y. Wild. Did not I tell you, Papillion?
Pap. This is amazing, indeed.
Y. Wild. Am not I a happy fortunate?—But they come.

Enter Old Wilding, and Miss Godfrey.

O. Wild. If, Madam, he has not the highest sense of the great honour you do him, I shall cease to regard him.—There, Sir, make your own acknowledgments to that lady.
Y. Wild. Sir!
O. Wild. This is more than you merit; but let your future behaviour testify your gratitude.
Y. Wild. Papillion! Madam! Sir!
O. Wild. What, is the puppy petrified? why don't you go up to the lady?
Y. Wild. Up to the lady?—that lady!
O. Wild. That lady!—to be sure. What other lady? to Miss Godfrey!
Y. Wild. That lady Miss Godfrey!
O. Wild. What is all this?—Harkye, Sir: I see what you

are at: but no trifling; I'll be no more the dupe of your double detestable—recollect my last resolution; this instant your hand to the contract, or tremble at the consequence.

Y. Wild. Sir, that I hope is—might not I—to be sure—

O. Wild. No further evasions! there, Sir.

Y. Wild. Heigh ho. [*Signs it.*

O. Wild. Very well. Now, Madam, your name if you please.

Y. Wild. Papillion, do you know who she is?

Pap. That's a question indeed! don't you, Sir?

Y. Wild. Not I, as I hope to be sav'd.

Enter a Servant.

Serv. A young lady begs to speak with Mr Wilding.

Y. Wild. With me!

M. God. A young lady with Mr Wilding!

Serv. Seems distress'd, Madam, and extremely pressing for admittance.

M. God. Indeed! there may be something in this! you must permit me, Sir, to pause a little: who knows but a prior claim may prevent—

O. Wild. How, Sir, who is this lady?

Y. Wild. It is impossible for me to divine, Sir.

O. Wild. You know nothing of her?

Y. Wild. How should I?

O. Wild. You hear, Madam.

M. God. I presume your son can have no objection to the lady's appearance.

Y. Wild. Not in the least, Madam.

M. God. Shew her in, John. [*Exit.*

O. Wild. No, Madam, I don't think there is the least room for suspecting him: he can't be so abandon'd as to—but she is here. Upon my word a sightly woman.

Enter Kitty as Miss Sybthorpe.

Kitty. Where is he?—Oh let me throw my arms—my life—my——

Y. Wild. Heyday!

Kitty. And could you leave me? and for so long a space? think how the tedious time has lagg'd along.

Y. Wild. Madam!

Kitty. But we are met at last, and now we will part no more.

Y. Wild. The deuce we won't!

Kitty.

THE LYAR.

Kitty. What, not one kind look, no tender word to hail our second meeting!

Y. Wild. What the devil is all this?

Kitty. Are all your oaths, your proteſtations, come to this? have I deſerv'd ſuch treatment? Quitted my father's houſe, left all my friends, and wander'd here alone in ſearch of thee, thou firſt, laſt, only object of my love.

O. Wild. To what can all this tend? Harkye, Sir, un-riddle this myſtery.

Y. Wild. Davus, non Œdipus ſum. It is beyond me, I confeſs. Some lunatic eſcap'd from her keeper, I ſuppoſe.

Kitty. Am I diſown'd then, contemn'd, ſlighted?

O. Wild. Hold; let me enquire into this matter a little. Pray, Madam—you ſeem to be pretty familiar here—do you know this gentleman?

Kitty. Too well.

O. Wild. His name?

Kitty. Wilding.

O. Wild. So far ſhe is right. Now yours, if you pleaſe.

Kitty. Wilding.

Omnes. Wilding!

O. Wild. And how came you by that name pray?

Kitty. Moſt lawfully, Sir: by the ſacred band, the holy tie that made us one.

O. Wild. What, married to him!

Kitty. Moſt true.

Omnes. How!

Y. Wild. Sir, may I never—

O. Wild. Peace, monſter!—one queſtion more: your maiden name?

Kitty. Sybthorpe.

O. Wild. Lydia, from Abington, in the county of Berks?

Kitty. The ſame.

O. Wild. As I ſuſpected. So then the whole ſtory is true, and the monſter is married at laſt.

Y. Wild. Me, Sir! by all that's—

O. Wild. Eternal dumbneſs ſeize thee, meaſureleſs liar!

Y. Wild. If not me, hear this gentleman—Marquis—

Pap. Not I; I'll be drawn into none of your ſcrapes, it is a pit of your own digging, and ſo get out as well as you can. Mean time I'll ſhift for myſelf. [*Exit.*

O. Wild. What evaſion now, monſter?

M. God. Deceiver!

O. Wild.

O. Wild. Liar!
M. God. Impoſtor!
Y. Wild. Why, this is a general combination to diſtruſt me; but I will be heard. Sir, you are groſsly impoſ'd upon: the low contriver of this woman's ſhallow artifice I ſhall ſoon find means to diſcover: and as to you, Madam, with whom I have been ſuddenly ſurpriz'd into a contract, I moſt ſolemnly declare this is the firſt time I ever ſat eyes on you.
O. Wild. Amazing confidence! did not I bring her at your requeſt?
Y. Wild. No.
M. God. Is not this your own letter?
Y. Wild. No.
Kitty. Am not I your wife?
Y. Wild. No.
O. Wild. Did not you own it to me?
Y. Wild. Yes—that is—No, no.
Kitty. Hear me.
Y. Wild. No.
M. God. Anſwer me.
Y. Wild. No.
O. Wild. Have not I—
Y. Wild. No, no, no. Zounds you are all mad, and if I ſtay I ſhall catch the infection.   [*Exit.*

Enter Sir James Elliot and Miſs Grantam.

Grant. Ha! ha! ha!
M. Gr. Finely perform'd.
O. Wild. You have kept your promiſe, and I thank you, Madam.
M. Gr. My medicine was ſomewhat rough, Sir; but in deſperate caſes, you know—
O. Wild. If his cure is compleated, he will gracefully acknowledge the cauſe; if not, the puniſhment comes far ſhort of his crimes. It is needleſs to pay you any compliments, Sir James; with that lady you can't fail to be happy. I ſhan't venture to hint a ſcheme I have greatly at heart, till we have undeniable proofs of the ſucceſs of our operations. To the ladies, indeed, no character is ſo dangerous as that of a liar.

They in the faireſt fames can fix a flaw,
And vanquiſh females whom they never ſaw.

THE

THE
PATRON;
A COMEDY,
IN
THREE ACTS.

TO THE RIGHT HONOURABLE
GRANVILLE LEVESON GOWER,
EARL GOWER,
LORD CHAMBERLAIN OF HIS MAJESTY'S HOUSEHOLD.

My Lord,

THE following little comedy, founded on a story of M. Marmontelle's, and calculated to expose the frivolity and ignorance of the pretenders to learning, with the insolence and vanity of their superficial, illiberal protectors, can be addressed to no nobleman with more propriety than to Lord Gower; whose judgment, though elegant, is void of affectation; and whose patronage, though powerful, is destitute of all fastidious parade. It is with pleasure, my Lord, that the public see your Lordship placed at the head of that department which is to decide, without appeal, on the most popular domain in the whole republic of letters; a spot that has always been distinguished with affection, and cultivated with care, by every ruler the least attentive to either chastising the morals, polishing the manners, or, what is of equal importance, rationally amusing the leisure of the people.

The Patron, my Lord, who now begs your protection, has had the good fortune to be well received by the public; and, indeed, of all the pieces that I have had the honour to offer them, this seems to me to have the fairest claim to their favour.

But the play, stripp'd of those theatrical ornaments for which it is indebted to your Lordship's indulgence, must now plead its own cause; nor will I, my Lord, with an affected humility, echo the trite, coarse, though classical compliment, of *Optimus patronus, pessimus poeta*: for if this be really true of the last, the first can have but small pretensions to praise; patronizing bad poets being, in my poor opinion, full as pernicious to the progress of letters, as neglecting the good.

In humble hopes, then, my Lord, of not being thought the meanest in the Muses train, I have taken the liberty to prefix your name to this dedication, and publicly to acknowledge my obligations to your Lordship; which, let me boast too, I have had the happiness to receive, untainted by the insolence of domestics, the delays of office, or the chilling superiority of rank; mortifications which have been too often experienced by much greater writers than myself, from much less men than your Lordship.

My Lord, I have the honour to be, with the greatest respect and gratitude,

Your Lordship's most obliged,
and most devoted humble servant,

North-End, June 20. 1764.

SAMUEL FOOTE.

DRAMATIS PERSONÆ.

Sir Thomas Lofty, } Mr Foote.
Sir Peter Peppperpot, }
Dick Dever, — — Mr Death.
Frank Younger, — Mr Davis.
Sir Roger Dowlas, — Mr Palmer.
Mr Rust, — Mr Weston.
Mr Dactyl, — — Mr Granger.
Mr Puff, — Mr Martin.
Mr Surface, — Mr Brown.
Robin, — Mr Parsons.
John, — — Mr Lewis.
Two Blacks.
Miss Jolie, — Mrs Garrick.

ACT

ACT I.

SCENE, *The Street.*

Enter Bever *and* Younger.

Young. NO, Dick, you must pardon me.
Bev. Nay, but to satisfy your curiosity.
Young. I tell you, I have not a jot.
Bev. Why then to gratify me.
Young. At rather too great an expence.
Bev. To a fellow of your observation and turn, I should think now such a scene a most delicate treat.
Young. Delicate! palling, nauseous, to a dreadful degree. To a lover, indeed, the charms of the niece may palliate the uncle's fulsome formality.
Bev. The uncle! ay, but then you know he is only one of the group.
Young. That's true; but the figures are all finish'd alike:—a sameness, a tiresome sameness throughout.
Bev. There you will excuse me; I am sure there is no want of variety.
Young. No! then let us have a detail. Come, Dick, give us a bill of the play.
Bev. First, you know, there's Juliet's uncle.
Young. What, Sir Thomas Lofty! the modern Midas, or rather (as fifty dedications will tell you) the Pollio, the Atticus, the patron of genius, the protector of arts, the paragon of poets, decider on merit, chief justice of taste, and sworn appraiser to Apollo and the tuneful Nine. Ha, ha. Oh, the tedious, insipid, insufferable coxcomb!
Bev. Nay, now, Frank, you are too extravagant. He is universally allowed to have taste; sharp-judging Adriel, the muse's friend, himself a muse.
Young. Taste! by who? undarling bards, that he feeds; and broken booksellers, that he bribes. Look ye, Dick, what raptures you plead when Miss Lofty is your theme; but expect no quarter for the rest of the family. I tell thee once for all, Lofty is a rank impostor, the buso of an illiberal, mercenary tribe; he has neither genius to create, judgment to distinguish, or generosity to reward; his

VOL. I.   T t   wealth

wealth has gain'd him flattery from the indigent, and the haughty infolence of his pretence, admiration from the ignorant. *Voilà le portrait de votre oncle.* Now on, to the next.

Bev. The ingenious and erudite Mr Ruſt.

Young. What, old Martin, the medal-monger?

Bev. The fame, and my rival in Juliet.

Young. Rival! what, Ruſt? why ſhe's too modern for him by a couple of centuries. Martin! why he likes no heads but upon coins. Married! the mummy! why 'tis not above a fortnight ago that I ſaw him making love to the figure without a noſe in Somerſet-Gardens: I caught him ſtroaking the marble plaits of her gown, and aſked him if he was not aſhamed to take ſuch liberties with adies in public.

Bev. What an inconſtant old ſcoundrel it is!

Young. Oh, a Dorimant. But how came this about? what could occaſion the change? Was it in the power of fleſh and blood to ſeduce this adorer of virtu from his marble and porphyry?

Bev. Juliet has done it; and, what will furprize you, his rafte was a bawd to the bufineſs.

Young. Prythee explain.

Bev. Juliet met him laſt week at her uncle's: he was a little pleaſed with the Greek of her profile; but, on a cloſer enquiry, he found the turn-up of her noſe to exactly reſemble the buſt of the Princeſs Popæa.

Young. The chafte moiety of the amiable Nero.

Bev. The fame.

Young. Oh, the deuce! then your bufineſs was done in an inſtant.

Bev. Immediately. In favour of the tip, he offered *carte blanche* for the reſt of the figure, which (as you may fuppoſe) was inſtantly caught at.

Young. Doubtleſs. But who have we here?

Bev. This is one of Lofty's companions, a Weſt-Indian of an over-grown fortune. He ſaves me the trouble of a portrait. This is Sir Peter Pepperpot.

Enter Sir Peter Pepperpot *and two blacks.*

Sir Pet. Careleſs ſcoundrels! harkee, raſcals! I'll baniſh you home, you dogs! you ſhall back, and broil in the fun. Mr Bever, your humble; Sir, I am your entirely devoted.

Bev.

THE PATRON.

Bev. You seem mov'd; what has been the matter, Sir Peter?

Sir Pet. Matter! why I am invited to dinner on a barbicu, and the villains have forgot my bottle of Chian.

Young. Unpardonable.

Sir Pet. Ay, this country has spoil'd them; this same christening will ruin the colonies. Well, dear Bever, rare news, boy; our fleet is arrived from the West.

Bev. It is?

Sir Pet. Ay, lad; and a glorious cargo of turtle. It was lucky I went to Brighthelmstone; I nick'd the time to a hair; thin as a lath, and a stomach as sharp as a shark's: never was in finer condition for feeding.

Bev. Have you a large importation, Sir Peter?

Sir Pet. Nine; but seven in excellent order: the captain assures me they greatly gain'd ground on the voyage.

Bev. How do you dispose of them?

Sir Pet. Four to Cornhill, three to Almack's, and the two sickly ones I shall send to my borough in Yorkshire.

Young. Ay! what, have the provincials a relish for turtle?

Sir Pet. Sir, it is amazing how this country improves in turtle and turnpikes; to which (give me leave to say) we, from our part of the world, have not a little contributed. Why, formerly, Sir, a brace of bucks on the mayor's annual day was thought a pretty moderate blessing. But we, Sir, have polish'd their palates. Why, Sir, not the meanest member of my corporation but can distinguish the path from the pee.

Young. Indeed!

Sir Pet. Ay, and sever the green from the fuell with the skill of the ablest anatomist.

Young. And they are fond of it?

Sir Pet. Oh, that the consumption will tell you. The stated allowance is six pounds to an alderman, and five to each of their wives.

Bev. A plentiful provision.

Sir Pet. But there was never known any waste; the mayor, recorder, and rector, are permitted to eat as much as they please.

Young. The entertainment is pretty expensive.

Sir Pet. Land-carriage and all. But I contrived to smuggle the last that I sent them.

Bev.

Bev. Snuggle! I don't understand you.

Sir Pet. Why, Sir, the rascally coachman had always charged me five pounds for the carriage. Damn'd dear! Now my cook going at the same time into the country, I made him clap a capuchin upon the turtle, and for thirty shillings put him an inside passenger in the Doncaster fly.

Young. A happy expedient.

Bev. Oh, Sir Peter has infinite humour.

Sir Pet. Yes, but the frolic had like to have prov'd fatal.

Young. How so?

Sir Pet. The maid at the Rummer at Hatfield popp'd her head into the coach to know if the company would have any breakfast: ecod, the turtle, Sir, laid hold of her nose, and flapp'd her face with his fins, till the poor devil fell into a fit. Ha, ha, ha.

Young. Oh, an absolute Rabelais.

Bev. What, I reckon, Sir Peter, you are going to the Squire?

Sir Pet. Yes; I extremely admire Sir Thomas. You know this is his day of assembly; I suppose you will be there: I can tell you, you are a wonderful favourite.

Bev. Am I?

Sir Pet. He says, your natural genius is fine; and, when polish'd by his cultivation, will surprize and astonish the world.

Bev. I hope, Sir, I shall have your voice with the public.

Sir Pet. Mine! O fye, Mr Bever.

Bev. Come, come, you are no inconsiderable patron.

Sir Pet. He, he, he. Can't say but I love to encourage the arts.

Bev. And have contributed largely yourself.

Young. What, is Sir Peter an author?

Sir Pet. O fye! what, me? a mere dabbler; have blotted my fingers, 'tis true:—some sonnets, that have not been thought wanting in salt.

Bev. And your epigrams.

Sir Pet. Not entirely without point.

Bev. But come, Sir Peter, the love of the arts is not the sole cause of your visits to the house you are going to.

Sir Pet. I don't understand you.

Bev. Miss Juliet, the niece.

Sir Pet.

THE PATRON.

Sir Pet. O fye! what chance have I there? Indeed, if Lady Pepperpot should happen to pop off—

Bev. I don't know that. You are, Sir Peter, a dangerous man; and, were I a father, or uncle, I should not be a little shy of your visits.

Sir Pet. Pilm! dear Bever, you banter.

Bev. And (unless I am extremely out in my guess) that lady—

Sir Pet. Hey! what, whot, dear Bever?

Bev. But if you should betray me—

Sir Pet. May I never eat a bit of green fat, if I do!

Bev. Hints have been dropp'd.

Sir Pet. The devil? come a little this way.

Bev. Well made; not robust and gigantic, 'tis true, but extremely genteel.

Sir Pet. Indeed!

Bev. Features, not entirely regular; but marking, with an air now, superior; greatly above the—you understand me?

Sir Pet. Perfectly. Something noble; expressive of—fashion.

Bev. Right.

Sir Pet. Yes, I have been frequently told so.

Bev. Not an absolute wit; but something infinitely better: an *enjouement*, a spirit, a—

Sir Pet. Gaiety. I was ever so, from a child.

Bev. In short, your dress, address, with a thousand other particulars that at present I can't recollect.

Sir Pet. Why, dear Bever, to tell thee the truth, I have always admir'd Miss Juliet, and a delicate creature she is: sweet as a sugar-cane, straight as a bamboo, and her teeth as white as a negro's.

Bev. Poetic, but true. Now only conceive, Sir Peter, such a plantation of perfections to be devoured by that caterpillar Rust.

Sir Pet. A liquorish grub! are pine-apples for such muckworms as he? I'll send him a jar of citrons and ginger, and poison the pipkin.

Bev. No, no.

Sir Pet. Or invite him to dinner, and mix rat's-bane along with his curry.

Bev. Not so precipitate; I think we may defeat him without any danger.

Sir Pet.

THE PATRON.

Sir Pet. How, how?

Bev. I have a thought—but we muſt ſettle the plan with the lady. Could not you give her the hint, that I ſhould be glad to ſee her a moment.

Sir Pet. I'll do it directly.

Bev. But don't let Sir Thomas perceive you.

Sir Pet. Never fear. You'll follow?

Bev. The inſtant I have ſettled matters with her; but ſo the old fellow ſo that ſhe may not be miſs'd.

Sir Pet. I'll nail him, I warrant; I have his opinion to beg on this manuſcript.

Bev. Your own?

Sir Pet. No.

Bev. Oh ho! what, ſomething new from the Doctor, your chaplain?

Sir Pet. He! no, no. O Lord, he's elop'd.

Bev. How!

Sir Pet. Gone. You know he was to dedicate his volume of fables to me: ſo I gave him thirty pounds to get my arms engrav'd, to prefix (by way of print) to the frontiſpiece; and, O grief of griefs! the Doctor has mov'd off with the money. I'll ſend you Miſs Juliet. [*Exit.*

Bev. Theſe is now a ſpecial protector! the arts, I think, can't but flouriſh under ſuch a Mecænas.

Young. Heaven viſits with a taſte the wealthy fool.

Bev. True; but then, to juſtify the diſpenſation,

From hence the poor are cloath'd, the hungry fed,
Fortunes to bookſellers, to authors bread.

Young. The diſtribution is, I own, a little unequal: and here comes a moſt melancholy inſtance; poor Dick Dactyl, and his publiſher Puff.

Enter Dactyl *and* Puff.

Puff. Why, then, Mr Dactyl, carry them to ſomebody elſe; there are people enough in the trade: but I wonder you would meddle with poetry; you know it rarely pays for the paper.

Dact. And how can one help it, Mr Puff? genius impels, and when a man is once lifted in the ſervice of the Muſes—

Puff. Why, let him give them warning as ſoon as he can. A pretty ſort of ſervice, indeed! where there are neither

neither wages nor vails. The Muses! and what, I suppose this is the livery they give. Gadzooks, I had rather be a waiter at Ranelagh.

Bev. The poet and publisher at variance! What is the matter, Mr Dactyl?

Dact. As God shall judge me, Mr Bever, as pretty a poem, and so polite; not a mortal can take any offence; all full of panegyric and praise.

Puff. A fine character he gives of his works. No offence! the greatest in the world, Mr Dactyl. Panegyric and praise! and what will that do with the public! Why, who the devil will give money to be told that Mr Such-a-one is a wiser or better man than himself? No, no; 'tis quite and clean out of nature. A good sousing satire now, well powder'd with personal pepper, and seasoned with the spirit of party; that demolishes a conspicuous character, and sinks him below our own level; there, there, we are pleas'd; there we chuckle, and grin, and toss the half-crowns on the counter.

Dact. Yes, and so get cropp'd for a libel.

Puff. Cropp'd! ay, and the luckiest thing that can happen to you. Why, I would not give two-pence for an author that is afraid of his ears. Writing, writing is (as I may say), Mr Dactyl, a sort of a warfare, where none can be victor that is the least afraid of a scar. Why, zooks, Sir, I never got salt to my porridge till I mounted at the Royal Exchange.

Bev. Indeed!

Puff. No, no; that was the making of me. Then my name made a noise in the world. Talk of forked hills, and of Helicon! romantic and fabulous stuff. The true Castalian stream is a shower of eggs, and a pillory the poet's Parnassus.

Dact. Ay, to you indeed it may answer; but what do we get for our pains?

Puff. Why, what the deuce would you get? food, fire, and fame. Why you would not grow fat! a corpulent poet is a monster, a prodigy! No, no; spare diet is a spur to the fancy; high feeding would but founder your Pegasus.

Dact. Why, you impudent, illiterate rascal! who is it you dare treat in this manner?

Puff. Heyday! what is the matter now?

Dact. And is this the return for all the obligations you owe

owe me! but no matter; the world, the world shall know what you are, and how you have us'd me.

Puff. Do your worst; I despise you.

Dact. They shall be told from what a dunghill you sprang. Gentlemen, if there be faith in a sinner, that fellow owes every shilling to me.

Puff. To thee!

Dact. Ay, Sirrah, to me. In what kind of way did I find you? then where and what was your state? Gentlemen, his shop was a shed in Moorfields; his kitchen, a broken pipkin of charcoal; and his bed-chamber under the counter.

Puff. I never was fond of expence; I ever minded my trade.

Dact. Your trade! and pray with what stock did you trade? I can give you the catalogue; I believe it won't overburden my memory. Two odd volumes of Swift; the Life of Moll Flanders, with cuts; the Five Senses, printed and coloured by Overton; a few classics, thumb'd and blotted by the boys of the Charterhouse; with the Trial of Dr Sacheverel.

Puff. Malice.

Dact. Then, Sirrah, I gave you my Canning: it was she first set you afloat.

Puff. A grub.

Dact. And it is not only my writings: you know, Sirrah, what you owe to my physic.

Bev. How! a physician?

Dact. Yes, Mr Bever; physic and poetry. Apollo is the patron of both: *apistrque per orbem dicor.*

Puff. His physic!

Dact. My physic! ay, my physic: why, dare you deny it, you rascal! What, have you forgot my powders for flatulent crudities?

Puff. No.

Dact. My cosmetic lozenge, and sugar-plumbs?

Puff. No.

Dact. My coral for cutting of teeth, my potions, my lotions, my pregnancy-drops, with my paste for superfluous hairs?

Puff. No, no; have you done?

Dact. No, no, no; but I believe this will suffice for the present.

Puff.

THE PATRON.

Puff. Now would not any mortal believe that I ow'd my all to this fellow.

Bev. Why, indeed, Mr Puff, the balance does seem in his favour.

Puff. In his favour! why, you don't give any credit to him: a reptile, a bug, that owes his very being to me.

Dact. I, I, I!

Puff. You, you! what, I suppose, you forget your garret in Wine-office-court, when you furnish'd paragraphs for the Farthing-post at twelve-pence a dozen.

Dact. Fiction.

Puff. Then, did not I get you made collector of casualties to the Whitehall and St James's? but that post your laziness lost you. Gentlemen, he never brought them a robbery till the highwayman was going to be hang'd; a birth till the christning was over; nor a death till the hatchment was up.

Dact. Mighty well!

Puff. And now, because the fellow has got a little in flesh, by being puff to the play-house this winter (to which, by the bye, I got him appointed), he is as proud and as vain as Voltaire. But I shall soon have him under; the vacation will come.

Dact. Let it.

Puff. Then I shall have him sneaking and cringing, hanging about me, and begging a bit of translation.

Dact. I beg, I, for translation!

Puff. No, no, not a line; not if you would do it for two-pence a sheet. No boil'd beef and carrot at mornings, no more cold pudding and porter. You may take your leave of my shop.

Dact. Your shop! then at parting I will leave you a legacy.

Bev. O fye, Mr Dactyl!

Puff. Let him alone.

Dact. Pray, gentlemen, let me do myself justice.

Bev. Younger, restrain the publisher's fire.

Young. Fye, gentlemen, such an illiberal combat—it is a scandal to the republic of letters.

Bev. Mr Dactyl, an old man, a mechanic, beneath—

Dact. Sir, I am calm; that thought has restor'd me.— To your insignificancy you are indebted for safety. But what my generosity has saved, my pen shall destroy!

Vol. I.   U u   *Puff.*

Puff. Then you must get somebody to mend it.
Daff. Adieu!
Puff. Farewell! [*Exeunt severally.*
Bev. Ha, ha, ha! come, let us along to the square.

Blockheads with reason wicked wits abhor,
But dunce with dunce is barb'rous civil war.

ACT II. SCENE continues.

Enter Bever and Younger.

Young. POOR Dactyl! and dwells such mighty rage in little men? I hope there is no danger of bloodshed.

Bev. Oh, not in the least: the *genus vatum*, the nation of poets, though an irritable, are yet a placable people. Their mutual interests will soon bring them together again.

Young. But shall not we be late? The critical senate is by this time assembled.

Bev. I warrant you, frequent and full; where

Stately Bufo, puff'd by every quill,
Sits, like Apollo, on his forked hill.

But you know I must wait for Miss Lofty; I am now totally directed by her. She gives me the key to all Sir Thomas's foibles, and prescribes the most proper method to feed them; but what good purpose that will produce—

Young. Is she clever, adroit?

Bev. Doubtless. I like your asking the question of me.

Young. Then pay an implicit obedience: the ladies, in these cases, generally know what they are about. The door opens.

Bev. It is Juliet, and with her old Rust. Enter, Frank; you know the knight, so no introduction is wanted. [*Exit Younger.*] I should be glad to hear this reverend piece of lumber make love; the courtship must certainly be curious. Good-manners, stand by; by your leave I will listen a little. [*Bever retires.*]

Enter Juliet *and* Rust.

Jul. And your collection is large?

Rust.

Ruft. Moſt curious and capital. When, Madam, will you give me leave to add your charms to my catalogue?

Jul. O dear! Mr Ruſt, I ſhall but diſgrace it. Beſides, Sir, when I marry, I am reſolv'd to have my huſband all to myſelf: now for the poſſeſſion of your heart I ſhall have too many competitors.

Ruft. How, Madam! were Prometheus alive, and would animate the Helen that ſtands in my hall, ſhe ſhould not coſt me a ſigh.

Jul. Ay, Sir, there lies my greateſt misfortune. Had I only choſe who are alive to contend with, by aſſiduity, affection, cares, and careſſes, I might ſecure my conqueſt: though that would be difficult; for I am convinc'd, were you, Mr Ruſt, put up by Preſtage to auction, the Apollo Belvidere would not draw a greater number of bidders.

Ruft. Would that were the caſe, Madam, ſo I might be thought a proper companion to the Venus de Medicis.

Jul. The flower of rhetorie, and pink of politeneſs.— But my fears are not confined to the living; for every nation and age, even painters and ſtatuaries, conſpire againſt me. Nay, when the Pantheon itſelf, the very goddeſſes riſe up as my rivals, what chance has a mortal like me.— I ſhall certainly laugh in his face. [*Aſide*.]

Ruft. She is a delicate ſubject. Goddeſſes, Madam! zooks, had you been on Mount Ida when Paris decided the conteſt, the Cyprian queen had pleaded for the pippin in vain.

Jul. Extravagant gallantry.

Ruft. In you, Madam, are concentrated all the beauties of the heathen mythology: the open front of Diana, the luſtre of Pallas's eyes,—

Jul. Oh, Sir!

Ruft. The chromatic muſic of Clio, the blooming graces of Hebe, the imperial port of queen Juno, with the delicate dimples of Venus.

Jul. I ſee, Sir, antiquity has not engroſs'd all your attention: you are no novice in the nature of woman. Incenſe, I own, is gratefal to moſt of my ſex; but there are times when adoration may be diſpens'd with.

Ruft. Ma'am!

Jul. I ſay, Sir, when we women willingly wave our rank in the ſkies, and wiſh to be treated as mortals.

Ruft. Doubtleſs, Madam: and are you wanting in materials

terials for that? no, Madam; as in dignity you surpass the heathen divinities, so in the charms of attraction you beggar the queens of the earth. The whole world, at different periods, has contributed its several beauties to form you.

Jul. The deuce it has! [*Aside.*]

Ruff. See there the ripe Asiatic perfection, joined to the delicate softness of Europe! In you, Madam, I burn to possess Cleopatra's alluring glances, the Greek profile of queen Clytemnestra, the Roman nose of the empress Popæa—

Jul. With the majestic march of queen Bess. Mercy on me, what a wonderful creature am I!

Ruff. In short, Madam, not a feature you have, but recalls to my mind some trait in a medal or bust.

Jul. Indeed! why, by your account, I must be an absolute olio, a perfect salamongundy of charms.

Ruff. Oh, Madam, how can you demean, as I may say, undervalue—

Jul. Value! there is the thing; and to tell you the truth, Mr Ruff, in that word value lies my greatest objection.

Ruff. I don't understand you.

Jul. Why then I will explain myself. It has been said, and I believe with some shadow of truth, that no man is a hero to his *valet de chambre*: now I am afraid, when you and I grow a little more intimate, which I suppose must be the case if you proceed on your plan, you will be horribly disappointed in your high expectations, and soon discover this Juno, this Cleopatra, and princess Popæa, to be as arrant a mortal as Madam your mother.

Ruff. Madam, I, I, I—

Jul. Your patience a moment. Being therefore desirous to preserve your devotion, I beg for the future you would please adore at a distance.

Ruff. To Endymion, Madam, Luna once listened.

Jul. Ay, but he was another kind of a mortal: you may do very well as a votary; but for a husband—mercy on me!

Ruff. Madam, you are not in earnest, not serious!

Jul. Not serious! Why, have you the impudence to think of marrying a goddess?

Ruff. I should hope—

Jul.

Jul. And what should you hope? I find your devotion resembles that of the world: when the power of sinning is over, and the sprightly first-runnings of life are rack'd off, you offer the vapid dregs to your deity. No, no; you may, if you please, turn monk in my service. One vow, I believe, you will observe better than most of them, chastity.

Ruff. Permit me—

Jul. Or, if you must marry, take your Julia, your Portia, or Flora, your Fum-fum from China, or your Egyptian Osiris. You have long paid your addresses to them.

Ruff. Marry! what, marble?

Jul. The properest wives in the world! you can't chuse amiss; they will supply you with all that you want.

Ruff. Your uncle has, Madam, confented.

Jul. That is more than ever his niece will. Confented! and to what? to be swath'd to a mould'ring mummy; or be lock'd up, like your medals, to canker and rust in a cabinet! No, no; I was made for the world, and the world shall not be robb'd of its right.

Bro. Bravo, Juliet! Gad, she's a fine-spirited girl.

Jul. My profile, indeed! no, Sir, when I marry, I must have a man that will meet my full face.

Ruff. Might I be heard for a moment?

Jul. To what end? you say, you have Sir Thomas Lofty's consent; I tell you, you can never have mine.— You may screen me from, or expose me to my uncle's resentment; the choice is your own: if you lay the fault at my door, you will, doubtless, greatly distress me; but take the blame on yourself, and I shall own myself extremely oblig'd to you.

Ruff. How! confess myself in the fault?

Jul. Ay, for the best thing a man can do, when he finds he can't be belov'd, is to take care he is not heartily hated. There is no other alternative.

Ruff. Madam, I shan't break my word with Sir Thomas.

Jul. Nor I with myself. So there's an end of our conference. Sir, your very obedient.

Ruff. Madam, I, I, don't—that is, let me—but no matter. Your servant. [*Exit.*

Jul. Ha, ha, ha!

Enter

Enter Beaver from behind.

Bev. Ha, ha, ha! Incomparable Juliet! How the old dotard trembled and totter'd; he could not have been more indamn'd, had he been robb'd of his Otho.

Jul. Ay; was ever goddess so familiarly us'd? in my conscience, I began to be afraid that he would treat me as the Indians do their dirty divinities; whenever they are deaf to their prayers, they beat and abuse them.

Bev. But, after all, we are in an aukward situation.

Jul. How so?

Bev. I have my fears.

Jul. So have not I.

Bev. Your uncle has resolv'd that you should be married to Rust.

Jul. Ay, he may decree; but it is I that must execute.

Bev. But suppose he has given his word.

Jul. Why then let him recal it again.

Bev. But are you sure you shall have courage enough—

Jul. To say No? that requires much resolution indeed.

Bev. Then I am at the height of my hopes.

Jul. Your hopes! your hopes and your fears are ill-founded alike.

Bev. Why, you are determined not to be his.

Jul. Well, and what then?

Bev. What then! why then you will be mine.

Jul. Indeed! and is that the natural consequence?—whoever won't be his, must be yours. Is that the logic of Oxford?

Bev. Madam, I did flatter myself—

Jul. Then you did very wrong, indeed, Mr Bever: you should ever guard against flattering yourself; for of all dangerous parasites, self is the worst.

Bev. I am astonish'd!

Jul. Astonish'd! you are mad, I believe! why, I have not known you a month. It is true, my uncle says your father is his friend; your fortune, in time, will be easy; your figure is not remarkably faulty, and as to your understanding, passable enough for a young fellow who has not seen much of the world: but when one talks of a husband—Lord, it's quite another sort of a—ha, ha, ha! poor Bever, how he stares! he stands like a statue!

Bev. Statue indeed, Madam; I am very near petrified.

Jul.

THE PATRON.   343

Jul. Even then you will make as good a husband as Ruft. But go, run, and join the affembly within; be attentive to every word, motion, and look of my uncle's: be dumb when he fpeaks, admire all he fays, laugh when he fmirks, bow when he fneezes; in fhort, fawn, flatter, and cringe; don't be afraid of over-loading his ftomach, for the knight has a noble digeftion, and you will find fome there who will keep you in countenance.

Bev. I fly. So then, Juliet, your intention was only to try—

Jul. Don't plague me with impertinent queftions: march! obey my directions. We muft leave the iffue to chance; a greater friend to mankind than they are willing to own. Oh, if any thing new fhould occur, you may come into the drawing-room for further inftructions.
[*Exeunt feverally.*

SCENE, *a Room in Sir Thomas Lofty's Houfe.*

Sir Thomas, Ruft, Puff, Dactyl, *and others, difcovered fitting.*

Sir Tho. Nothing new to-day from Paraffins?
Dact. Not that I hear.
Sir Tho. Nothing critical, philofophical, or political?
Puff. Nothing.
Sir Tho. Then in this difette, this dearth of invention, give me leave, gentlemen, to diftribute my ftores. I have here in my hand a little, fmart, fatyrical epigram; new, and prettily pointed: in fhort, a production that Martial himfelf would not have blufh'd to acknowledge.
Ruft. Your own, Sir Thomas?
Sir Tho. O fye! no; fent me this morning, anonymous.
Dact. Pray, Sir Thomas, let us have it.
All. By all means; by all means.
Sir Tho. *To Phillis.* Think'ft thou, fond Phillis, Strephon told thee true,
Angels are painted fair to look like you:
Another ftory all the town will tell;
Phillis paints fair—to look like an angel.
All. Fine! fine! very fine!
Dact. Such an eafe and fimplicity.
Puff. The turn fo unexpected and quick.
Ruft. The fatire fo poignant.

Sir Tho,

344 THE PATRON.

Sir Tho. Yes; I think it possesses, in an eminent degree, the three great epigrammatical requisites; brevity, familiarity, and severity.

Phillis paints fair—to look like an angel.

Dact. Happy! Is the Phillis, the subject, a secret?

Sir Tho. Oh, dear me! nothing personal; no; an impromptu; a mere *jeu d'esprit*.

Puff. Then, Sir Thomas, the secret is out; it is your own.

Dact. That was obvious enough.

Puff. Who is there else could have wrote it?

P.A. True, true.

Sir Tho. The name of the author is needless. So it is in vifition to the republic of letters, any gentleman may the merit that will.

Puff. What a noble contempt!

Dact. What greatness of mind!

P.A. Scipio and Lælius were the Roman Loftys. Why, I dare believe Sir Thomas has been the making of half the authors in town: he is, as I may say, the great manufacturer; the other poets are but pedlars, that live by retailing his wares.

All. Ha, ha, ha! well observ'd, Mr Ruft.

Sir Tho. Ha, ha, ha! *Mulle atque suavem*. Why, to pursue the metaphor, if Sir Thomas Lofty was to call in his poetical debts, I believe there would be a good many bankrupts in the Muses' Gazette.

All. Ha, ha, ha!

Sir Tho. But, *à propos*, gentlemen; with regard to the eclipse; you found my calculation exact?

Dact. To a digit.

Sir Tho. Total darkness, indeed! and birds going to roost! those philomaths, those almanack-makers, are the most ignorant rascals—

Puff. It is amazing where Sir Thomas Lofty stores all his knowledge.

Dact. It is wonderful how the mind of man can contain it.

Sir Tho. Why, to tell you the truth, that circumstance has a good deal engag'd my attention; and I believe you will admit my method of solving the phænomenon philosophical and ingenious enough.

Puff. Without question.

All. Doubtless.

Sir Tho.

Sir Tho. I suppose, gentlemen, my memory, or mind, to be a chest of drawers, a kind of bureau, where, in separate cellules, my different knowledge on different subjects is stor'd.

Ruff. A prodigious discovery!

All. Amazing!

Sir Tho. To this cabinet volition, or will, has a key; so, when an arduous subject occurs, I unlock my bureau, pull out the particular drawer, and am supply'd with what I want in an instant.

Dact. A Melbranch!

Puff. A Boyle!

All. A Locke!

Enter Servant.

Serv. Mr Bever. [*Exit.*

Sir Tho. A young gentleman from Oxford, recommended to my care by his father. The university has given him a good solid Doric foundation; and when he has receiv'd from you a few Tuscan touches, the Ionic and Corinthian graces, I make no doubt but he will prove a composite pillar to the republic of letters. [*Enter Bever.*] This, Sir, is the school from whence so many capital masters have issued; the river that enriches the regions of science.

Dact. Of which river, Sir Thomas, you are the source: *here we quaff; et purpureo bibimus ore nectar.*

Sir Tho. Purpureo! Delicate indeed! Mr Dactyl. Do you hear, Mr Bever? *Bibimus ore nectar.* You, young gentleman, must be instructed to quote; nothing gives a period more spirit than a happy Latin quotation, nor has indeed a finer effect at the head of an essay. Poor Dick Steel; I have obliged him with many a motto for his fugitive pieces.

Puff. Ay, and with the contents too; or Sir Richard is foully bely'd.

Enter Servant.

Serv. Sir Roger Dowlas.

Sir Tho. Pray desire him to enter. [*Exit Servant.*]— Sir Roger, gentlemen, is a considerable East-India proprietor; and seems desirous of collecting from this learned assembly some rhetorical flowers, which he hopes to strew,

Vol. I. X x with

with honour to himself, and advantage to the company, at Merchant-Taylors-Hall. [*Enter* Sir Roger Dowlas.]— Sir Roger, be seated. This gentleman has, in common with the greatest orator the world ever saw, a small natural infirmity; he stutters a little: but I have prescrib'd the same remedy that Demosthenes us'd, and don't despair of a radical cure. Well, Sir, have you digested those general rules?

Sir Rog. Pe—ett—y well, I am obli—g'd to you, Sir Thomas.

Sir Tho. Have you been regular in taking your tincture of sage, to give you confidence for speaking in public?

Sir Rog. Y—es, Sir Thomas.

Sir Tho. Did you ope at the last general court?

Sir Rog. I attem—p—ted fo—ur or fi—ve times.

Sir Tho. What hinder'd your progress?

Sir Rog. The pe—b—bles.

Sir Tho. Oh, the pebbles in his mouth. But they are only put in to practise in private; you should take them out when you are addressing the public.

Sir Rog. Yes; I will for the fu—ture.

Sir Tho. Well, Mr Rust, you had a *tête-à-tête* with my niece. A propos, Mr Bever, here offers a fine occasion for you; we shall take the liberty to trouble your Muse on their nuptials. O Love! O Hymen! here prune thy purple wings; trim thy bright torch. Hey, Mr Bever?

Bev. My talents are at Sir Thomas Lofty's direction; though I must despair of producing any performance worthy the attention of so complete a judge of the elegant arts.

Sir Tho. Too modest, good Mr Bever. Well, Mr Rust, any new acquisition, since our last meeting, to your matchless collection?

Rust. Why, Sir Thomas, I have both lost and gain'd since I saw you.

Sir Tho. Lost! I am sorry for that.

Rust. The curious sarcophagus, that was sent me from Naples by Signior Belloni—

Sir Tho. You mean the urn that was suppos'd to contain the dust of Agrippa!

Rust. Suppos'd! no doubt but it did.

Sir Tho. I hope no sinister accident to that inestimable relic of Rome.

Rust.

Ruſt. It's gone.

Sir Tho. Gone! oh, illiberal! What, ſtolen, I ſuppoſe, by ſome connoiſſeur?

Ruſt. Worſe, worſe! a prey, a martyr to ignorance: a houſemaid, that I hir'd laſt week, miſtook it for a broken green chamber-pot, and ſent it away in the duſt-cart.

Sir Tho. She merits impaling. Oh, the Hun!

Daſh. The Vandal!

All. The Viſigoth!

Ruſt. But I have this day acquir'd a treaſure that will in ſome meaſure make me amends.

Sir Tho. Indeed! what can that be?

Puff. That muſt be ſomething curious, indeed.

Ruſt. It has coſt me infinite trouble to get it.

Daſh. Great rarities are not had without pains.

Ruſt. It is three months ago ſince I got the firſt ſcent of it, and I have been ever ſince on the hunt; but all to no purpoſe.

Sir Tho. I am quite upon thorns till I ſee it.

Ruſt. And yeſterday, when I had given it over, when all my hopes were grown deſperate, it fell into my hands, by the moſt unexpected and wonderful accident.

*Sir Tho. Quod optanti divum promittere nemo
Auderet, volvenda dies en attulit ultro.*

Mr Bever, you remark my quotation?

Bev. Moſt happy. Oh, Sir, nothing you ſay can be loſt.

Ruſt. I have brought it here in my pocket; I am no churl; I love to pleaſure my friends.

Sir Tho. You are, Mr Ruſt, extremely obliging.

All. Very kind, very obliging indeed.

Ruſt. It was not much hurt by the fire.

Sir Tho. Very fortunate.

Ruſt. The edges are foil'd by the link; but many of the letters are exceedingly legible.

Sir Rog. A li--ttle roo--m, if you p--leaſe.

Ruſt. Here it is; the precious remains of the very North-Briton that was burnt at the Royal-Exchange.

Sir Tho. Number forty-five?

Ruſt. The ſame.

Bev. You are a lucky man, Mr Ruſt.

Ruſt. I think ſo. But, gentlemen, I hope I need not give you a caution: huſh—ſilence—no words on this matter.

Daſh.

Dad. You may depend upon us.

Ruft. For as the paper has not suffer'd the law, I don't know whether they may not seize it again.

Sir Tho. With us you are safe, Mr Ruft. Well, young gentleman, you see me cultivate all branches of science.

Bev. Amazing, indeed! but when we confider you, Sir Thomas, as the directing, the ruling planet, our wonder fubfides in an inftant. Science firft faw the day with Socrates in the Attic portico; her early years were spent with Tully in the Tufculan fhade; but her ripe, maturer hours, she enjoys with Sir Thomas Lofty, near Cavendish-Square.

Sir Tho. The moft claffical compliment I ever receiv'd. Gentlemen, a philofophical repaft attends your acceptance within. Sir Roger you'll lead the way. [*Exeunt all but Sir Thomas and Bever.*] Mr Bever, may I beg your ear for a moment? Mr Bever, the friendship I have for your father fecur'd you at firft a gracious reception from me; but what I then paid to an old obligation, is now, Sir, due to your own particular merit.

Bev. I am happy, Sir Thomas, if—

Sir Tho. Your patience. There is in you, Mr Bever, a fire of imagination, a quicknefs of apprehenfion, a folidity of judgment, join'd to a depth of difcretion, that I never yet met with in any fubject at your time of life.

Bev. I hope I shall never forfeit—

Sir Tho. I am fure you never will; and to give you a convincing proof that I think fo, I am now going to truft you with the moft important fecret of my whole life.

Bev. Your confidence does me great honour.

Sir Tho. But this muft be on a certain condition.

Bev. Name it.

Sir Tho. That you give me your folemn promife to comply with one requeft I shall make you.

Bev. There is nothing Sir Thomas Lofty can ask, that I shall not cheerfully grant.

Sir Tho. Nay, in fact, it will be ferving yourfelf.

Bev. I want no fuch inducement.

Sir Tho. Enough. But we can't be too private. [*Shuts the door.*] Sit you down. Your Chriftian name, I think, is—

Bev. Richard.

Sir Tho. True; the fame as your father's. Come let us

THE PATRON.

as be familiar. It is, I think, dear Dick, acknowledg'd, that the English have reached the highest pitch of perfection in every department of writing but one—the dramatic.

Bev. Why, the French critics are a little severe.

Sir Tho. And with reason. Now, to rescue our credit, and at the same time give my country a model, [*Shews a manuscript.*] see here.

Bev. A play?

Sir Tho. A chef d'œuvre.

Bev. Your own?

Sir Tho. Speak lower. I am the author.

Bev. Nay, then there can be no doubt of its merit.

Sir Tho. I think not. You will be charm'd with the subject.

Bev. What is it, Sir Thomas?

Sir Tho. I shall surprize you. The story of Robin Crusoe. Are not you struck?

Bev. Most prodigiously.

Sir Tho. Yes; I knew the very title would hit you.—You will find the whole fable is freely conducted, and the character of Friday, *qualis ab incepto*, nobly supported throughout.

Bev. A pretty difficult task.

Sir Tho. True; that was not a bow for a boy. The piece has long been in rehearsal at Drury-lane playhouse, and this night is to make its appearance.

Bev. To-night?

Sir Tho. This night.

Bev. I will attend, and engage all my friends to support it.

Sir Tho. That is not my purpose; the piece will want no such assistance.

Bev. I beg pardon.

Sir Tho. The manager of that house (who you know is a writer himself), finding all the anonymous things he produc'd (indeed some of them wretched enough, and very unworthy of him) placed to his account by the public, is determined to exhibit no more without knowing the name of the author.

Bev. A reasonable caution.

Sir Tho. Now, upon my promise (for I appear to patronize the play) to announce the author before the curtain draws up, Robinson Crusoe is advertis'd for this evening.

Bev.

Bev. Oh, then, you will acknowledge the piece to be your's!

Sir Tho. No.

Bev. How then?

Sir Tho. My design is to give it to you.

Bev. To me!

Sir Tho. To you.

Bev. What, me the author of Robinson Crusoe!

Sir Tho. Ay.

Bev. Lord, Sir Thomas, it will never gain credit: so complete a production the work of a stripling! Besides, Sir, as the merit is your's, why rob yourself of the glory.

Sir Tho. I am entirely indifferent to that.

Bev. Then why take the trouble?

Sir Tho. My fondness for letters, and love of my country. Besides, dear Dick, though the *pauci & felicti*, the chosen few, know the full value of a performance like this, yet the ignorant, the profane (by much the majority), will be apt to think it an occupation ill suited to my time of life.

Bev. Their censure is praise.

Sir Tho. Doubtless. But indeed my principal motive is my friendship for you. You are now a candidate for literary honours, and I am determin'd to fix your fame on an immoveable basis.

Bev. You are most excessively kind; but there is something so disingenuous in stealing reputation from another man—

Sir Tho. Idle punctilio!

Bev. It puts me so in mind of the daw in the fable—

Sir Tho. Come, come, dear Dick, I won't suffer your modesty to murder your fame. But the company will suspect something; we will join them and proclaim you the author. There, keep the copy; to you I consign it for ever; it shall be a secret to latest posterity. You will be smother'd with praise by our friends; they shall all in their bark to the playhouse, and there

Attendant fail,
Pursue the triumph, and partake the gale. [*Exeunt.*

ACT

ACT III. Scene continues.

Enter Bever, reading.

SO ends the first act. Come, now for the second. "Act the second, shewing"—the coxcomb has preface'd every act with an argument too, in humble imitation, I warrant, of Monſ. Diderot—" shewing the fatal effects of disobedience to parents ;" with, I suppose, the diverting scene of a gibbet; an entertaining subject for comedy. And the blockhead is as prolix—every scene as long as a homily. Let's see; how does this end? "Exit Crusoe, and enter some savages, dancing a saraband." There's no bearing this abominable trash. [*Enter Juliet.*] So, Madam; thanks to your advice and direction, I am got into a fine situation.

Jul. What is the matter now, Mr Bever?

Bev. The Robinson Crusoe.

Jul. Oh, the play that is to be acted to-night. How secret you were! Who in the world would have guess'd you was the author?

Bev. Me, Madam!

Jul. Your title is odd; but to a genius every subject is good.

Bev. You are inclin'd to be pleasant.

Jul. Within they have been all prodigious loud in the praise of your piece; but I think my uncle rather more eager than any.

Bev. He has reason; for fatherly fondness goes far.

Jul. I don't understand you.

Bev. You don't!

Jul. No.

Bev. Nay, Juliet, this is too much; you know it is none of my play.

Jul. Whose then?

Bev. Your uncle's.

Jul. My uncle's! then how, in the name of wonder, came you to adopt it?

Bev. At his earnest request. I may be a fool; but remember, Madam, you are the cauſe.

Jul. This is strange; but I can't conceive what his motive could be.

Bev.

Bev. His motive is obvious enough; to screen himself from the infamy of being the author.

Jul. What, is it bad, then?

Bev. Bad! most infernal!

Jul. And you have consented to own it?

Bev. Why, what could I do? he in a manner compell'd me.

Jul. I am extremely glad of it.

Bev. Glad of it! why, I tell you 'tis the most dull, tedious, melancholy—

Jul. So much the better.

Bev. The most flat piece of frippery that ever Grubstreet produc'd.

Jul. So much the better.

Bev. It will be damn'd before the third act.

Jul. So much the better.

Bev. And I shall be hooted and pointed at wherever I go.

Jul. So much the better.

Bev. So much the better! zounds! so, I suppose, you would say if I was going to be hang'd. Do you call this a mark of your friendship?

Jul. Ah, Bever, Bever! you are a miserable politician. Do you know, now, that this is the luckiest incident that ever occurr'd?

Bev. Indeed!

Jul. It could not have been better laid had we plann'd it ourselves.

Bev. You will pardon my want of conception: but these are riddles—

Jul. That at present I have not time to explain. But what makes you loit'ring here? Past six o'clock, as I live! why, your play is begun; run, run to the house. Was ever author so little anxious for the fate of his piece?

Bev. My piece!

Jul. Sir Thomas! I know by his walk. Fly, and pray all the way for the fall of your play. And, do you hear, if you find the audience too indulgent, inclined to be milky, rather than fail, squeeze in a little acid yourself. Oh, Mr Bover, at your return let me see you, before you go to my uncle; that is, if you have the good luck to be damn'd.

Bev. You need not doubt that. [*Exit.*

Enter

THE PATRON.

Enter Sir Thomas Lofty.

Sir Tho. So, Juliet; was not that Mr Bever?

Jul. Yes, Sir.

Sir Tho. He is rather tardy; by this time his cause is come on. And how is the young gentleman affected? for this is a trying occasion.

Jul. He seems pretty certain, Sir.

Sir Tho. Indeed I think he has very little reason for fear: I confess I admire the piece; and feel as much for its fate as if the work was my own.

Jul. That I most sincerely believe. I wonder, Sir, you did not chuse to be present.

Sir Tho. Better not. My affections are strong, Juliet, and my nerves but tenderly strung; however, intelligent people are planted, who will bring me every act a faithful account of the process.

Jul. That will answer your purpose as well.

Sir Tho. Indeed, I am passionately fond of the arts, and therefore can't help—did not somebody knock? no. My good girl, will you step, and take care that when any body comes the servants may not be out of the way. [*Exit Juliet.*] Five and thirty minutes past six; by this time the first act must be over: John will be presently here. I think it can't fail; yet there is so much whim and caprice in the public opinion, that—This young man is unknown; they'll give him no credit. I had better have own'd it myself: reputation goes a great way in these matters: people are afraid to find fault; they are cautious in censuring the works of a man who—hush! that's he; no; 'tis only the shutters. After all, I think I have chose the best way: for, if it succeeds to the degree I expect, it will be easy to circulate the real name of the author; if it fails, I am concealed, my fame suffers no—there he is. [*Loud knocking.*] I can't conceive what kept him so long. [*Enter John.*]—So, John; well; and—but you have been a monstrous while.

John. Sir, I was wedged so close in the pit, that I could scarcely get out.

Sir Tho. The house was full then?

John. As an egg, Sir.

Sir Tho. That's right. Well, John, and did matters go swimmingly? hey?

Vol. I. Y y *John.*

John. Exceedingly well, Sir.
Sir Tho. Exceedingly well. I don't doubt it. What, vast clapping and roars of applause, I suppose.
John. Very well, Sir.
Sir Tho. Very well, Sir? You are damn'd costive, I think. But did not the pit and boxes thunder again?
John. I can't say there was over-much thunder.
Sir Tho. No! Oh, attentive, I reckon. Ay, attention! that is the true, solid, substantial applause. All else may be purchased; hands move as they are bid: but when the audience is hush'd still, afraid of losing a word, then—
John. Yes, they were very quiet indeed, Sir.
Sir Tho. I like them the better, John; a strong mark of their great sensibility. Did you see Robin?
John. Yes, Sir; he'll be here in a trice; I left him list'ning at the back of the boxes, and charg'd him to make all the haste home that he could.
Sir Tho. That's right, John; very well; your account pleases me much, honest John. [*Exit John.*] No, I did not expect the first act would produce any prodigious effect. And, after all, the first act is but a mere introduction; just opens the business, the plot, and gives a little insight into the characters: so that if you but engage and interest the house, it is as much as the best writer can stir.—[*knocking without.*] Godso! what, Robin already! why the fellow has the feet of a Mercury. [*Enter Robin.*] Well, Robin, and what news do you bring?

Rob. Sir, I, I, I,——
Sir Tho. Stop, Robin, and recover your breath. Now, Robin.
Rob. There has been a woundy uproar below.
Sir Tho. An uproar! what, at the playhouse?
Rob. Ay.
Sir Tho. At what?
Rob. I don't know: belike at the words the playfolk were talking.
Sir Tho. At the players! how can that be? Oh, now I begin to conceive. Poor fellow, he knows but little of plays. What, Robin, I suppose, hallowing, and clapping, and knocking of sticks?
Rob. Hallowing! ay, and hooting too.
Sir Tho. And hooting!
Rob. Ay, and hissing to boot.

Sir Tho.

Sir Tho. Hissing! you must be mistaken.

Rob. By the mass, but I am not.

Sir Tho. Impossible! Oh, most likely some drunken, disorderly fellows, that were disturbing the house and interrupting the play; too common a case; the people were right: they deserv'd a rebuke. Did not you hear them cry Out, out, out?

Rob. No; that was not the cry; 'twas Off, off, off!

Sir Tho. That was a whimsical noise. Zounds! that must be the players. Did you observe nothing else?

Rob. Belike the quarrel first began between the gentry and a black-a-moor man.

Sir Tho. With Friday! The public taste is debauched; honest nature is too plain and simple for their vitiated palates! [*Enter* Juliet.] Juliet, Robin brings me the strangest account; some little disturbance; but I suppose it was soon settled again. Oh, but here comes Mr Staytape, my taylor; he is a rational being; we shall be able to make something of him. [*Enter* Staytape.] So, Staytape; what, is the third act over already?

Stay. Over, Sir! no; nor never will be.

Sir Tho. What do you mean?

Stay. Cut short.

Sir Tho. I don't comprehend you.

Stay. Why, Sir, the poet has made a mistake in measuring the taste of the town; the goods, it seems, did not fit; so they returned them upon the gentleman's hands.

Sir Tho. Rot your affectation and quaintness, you puppy! speak plain.

Stay. Why then, Sir, Robinson Crusoe is dead.

Sir Tho. Dead!

Stay. Ay, and what is worse, will never rise any more. You will soon have all the particulars; for there were four or five of your friends close at my heels.

Sir Tho. Staytape, Juliet, run and stop them; say I am gone out; I am sick; I am engaged; but, whatever you do, be sure you don't let sever come in. Secure of the victory, I invited them to the celebr——

Stay. Sir, they are here.

Sir Tho. Confound——

Enter Puff, Dactyl, *and* Ruff.

Ruff. Ay, truly, Mr Puff, this is but a bitter beginning;

ning; then the young man must turn himself to some other trade.

Puff. Servant, Sir Thomas; I suppose you have heard the news of—

Sir Tho. Yes, yes; I have been told it before.

Dact. I confess I did not suspect it; but there is no knowing what effect those things will have till they come on the stage.

Ruff. For my part, I don't know much of these matters; but a couple of gentlemen near me, who seem'd sagacious enough too, declar'd that it was the vilest stuff they ever had heard, and wonder'd the players would act it.

Dact. Yes; I don't remember to have seen a more general dislike.

Puff. I was thinking to ask you, Sir Thomas, for your interest with Mr Bever about buying the copy: but now no mortal would read it. Lord, Sir, it would not pay for paper and printing.

Ruff. I remember Kennet, in his Roman Antiquities, mentions a play of Terence's, Mr Dactyl, that was terribly treated; but that he attributes to the people's fondness for certain funambuli, or rope-dancers; but I have not lately heard of any famous tumblers in town: Sir Thomas, have you?

Sir Tho. How should I? do you suppose I trouble my head about tumblers?

Ruff. Nay, I did not—

Bev. speaking without. Not to be spoke with! Don't tell me, Sir; he must, he shall.

Sir Tho. Mr Bever's voice. If he is admitted in his present disposition, the whole secret will certainly out. Gentlemen, some affairs of a most interesting nature make it impossible for me to have the honour of your company tonight; therefore I beg you would be so good as to—

Ruff. Affairs! no bad news? I hope Miss Juliet is well.

Sir Tho. Very well; but I am most exceedingly—

Ruff. I shall only just stay to see Mr Bever. Poor lad! he will be most horribly down in the mouth: a little comfort won't come amiss.

Sir Tho. Mr Bever, Sir! you won't see him here.

Ruff. Not here! why I thought I heard his voice but just now.

Sir Tho. You are mistaken, Mr Ruff; but—

Ruff.

Rufs. May be so; then we will go. Sir Thomas, my compliments of condolence, if you please, to the poet.

Sir Tho. Ay, ay.

Dadl. And mine; for I suppose we shan't see him soon.

Puff. Poor gentleman! I warrant he won't shew his head for these six months.

Rufs. Ay, ay: indeed I am very sorry for him; so tell him, Sir.

Dadl. and Puff. So are we.

Rufs. Sir Thomas, your servant. Come, gentlemen. By all this confusion in Sir Thomas, there must be something more in the wind than I know; but I will watch, I am resolved. [*Exeunt.*

Bev. without. Rascals, stand by! I must, I will see him.

Enter Bever.

Bev. So, Sir; this is delicate treatment, after all I have suffer'd.

Sir Tho. Mr Bever, I hope you don't—that is—

Bev. Well, Sir Thomas Lofty, what think you now of your Robinson Crusoe? a pretty performance!

Sir Tho. Think, Mr Bever! I think the public are blockheads; a tasteless, stupid, ignorant tribe; and a man of genius deserves to be damn'd who writes any thing for them. But courage, dear Dick! the principals will give you what the people refuse; the closet will do you that justice the stage has deny'd: print your play.

Bev. My play! zounds, Sir, 'tis your own.

Sir Tho. Speak lower, dear Dick; be moderate, my good, dear lad!

Bev. Oh, Sir Thomas, you may be easy enough? you are safe and secure, remov'd far from that precipice that has dash'd me to pieces.

Sir Tho. Dear Dick, don't believe it will hurt you. The critics, the real judges, will discover in that piece such excellent talents—

Bev. No, Sir Thomas, no. I shall neither flatter you nor myself; I have acquired a right to speak what I think. Your play, Sir, is a wretched performance; and in this opinion all mankind are united.

Sir Tho. May be not.

Bev. If your piece had been greatly receiv'd, I would have declared Sir Thomas Lofty the author; if coldly, I would

would have owned it myself; but such disgraceful, such contemptible treatment! I own the burden is too heavy for me; so, Sir, you must bear it yourself.

Sir Tho. Me, dear Dick! what to become ridiculous in the decline of my life; to destroy in one hour the fame that forty years has been building! that was the prop, the support of my age! can you be cruel enough to desire it?

Bev. Zounds! Sir, and why must I be your crutch? Would you have me become a voluntary victim; no, Sir, this cause does not merit a martyrdom.

Sir Tho. I own myself greatly oblig'd; but persevere, dear Dick, persevere; you have time to recover your fame: I beg it with tears in my eyes. Another play will—

Bev. No, Sir Thomas; I have done with the stage: the Muses and I meet no more.

Sir Tho. Nay, there are various roads open in life.

Bev. Not one, where your piece won't pursue me. If I go to the bar, the ghost of this curs'd comedy will follow, and haunt me in Westminster-hall: nay, when I die, it will stick to my memory, and I shall be handed down to posterity with the author of Love in a Hollow Tree.

Sir Tho. Then marry: you are a pretty smart figure; and your poetical talents—

Bev. And what fair would admit of my suit, or family will to receive me? Make the case your own, Sir Thomas; would you?

Sir Tho. With infinite pleasure.

Bev. Then give me your niece; her hand shall seal up my lips.

Sir Tho. What, Juliet? willingly. But are you serious, do you really admire the girl?

Bev. Beyond what words can express. It was by her advice that I consented to father your play.

Sir Tho. What, is Juliet appriz'd? Here, Robin, John, run and call my niece hither this moment. That giddy baggage will blab all in an instant.

Bev. You are mistaken; she is wiser than you are aware of.

Enter Juliet.

Sir Tho. Oh, Juliet! you know what has happen'd.

Jul. I do, Sir.

Sir Tho. Have you reveal'd this unfortunate secret?

Jul.

Jul. To no mortal, Sir Thomas.

Sir Tho. Come, give me your hand. Mr Bever, child, for my sake, has renounc'd the stage, and the whole republic of letters; in return, I owe him your hand.

Jul. My hand! what, to a poet hooted, hiss'd, and exploded! You must pardon me, Sir.

Sir Tho. Juliet, a trifle: the most they can say of him is, that he is a little wanting in wit; and he has so many brother writers to keep him in countenance, that now-a-days that is no reflection at all.

Jul. Then, Sir, your engagement to Mr Rust.

Sir Tho. I have found out the rascal: he has been more impertinently severe on my play than all the rest put together; so that I am determined he shall be none of the man.

Enter Rust.

Rust. Are you so, Sir? what, then I am to be sacrific'd, in order to preserve the secret that you are a blockhead. But you are out in your politics: before night it shall be known in all the coffee-houses in town.

Sir Tho. For Heaven's sake, Mr Rust!

Rust. And to-morrow I will paragraph you in every newspaper; you shall no longer impose on the world; I will unmask you; the lion's skin shall hide you no longer.

Sir Tho. Juliet! Mr Bever! what can I do?

Bev. Sir Thomas, let me manage this matter. Harkee, old gentleman, a word in your ear: you remember what you have in your pocket?

Rust. Hey! how! what?

Bev. The curiosity that has cost you so much pains.

Rust. What, my Æneas! my precious relict of Troy!

Bev. You must give up that, or the lady.

Jul. How, Mr Bever!

Bev. Never fear; I am sure of my man.

Rust. Let me consider—as to the girl, girls are plenty enough; I can marry whenever I will: but my paper, my phenix, that springs fresh from the flames, that can never be match'd.—Take her.

Bev. And, as you love your own secret, be careful of ours.

Rust. I am dumb.

Sir Tho. Now, Juliet.

Jul.

www.ingramcontent.com/pod-product-compliance
Lightning Source LLC
Chambersburg PA
CBHW030252240426
43673CB00040B/950